The Reinvention
of Atlantic Slavery

The Reinvention of Atlantic Slavery

*Technology, Labor, Race,
and Capitalism
in the Greater Caribbean*

DANIEL B. ROOD

OXFORD
UNIVERSITY PRESS

Oxford University Press is a department of the University of Oxford. It furthers
the University's objective of excellence in research, scholarship, and education
by publishing worldwide. Oxford is a registered trade mark of Oxford University
Press in the UK and certain other countries.

Published in the United States of America by Oxford University Press
198 Madison Avenue, New York, NY 10016, United States of America.

Library of Congress Cataloging-in-Publication Data
Names: Rood, Daniel.
Title: The reinvention of Atlantic slavery : technology, labor, race, and
capitalism in the greater Caribbean / Daniel B. Rood.
Description: New York, NY : Oxford University Press, [2017] |
Includes bibliographical references and index.
Identifiers: LCCN 2016053523 (print) | LCCN 2016056878 (ebook) |
ISBN 9780190655266 (hardcover) | ISBN 9780197528426 (paperback) |
| ISBN 9780190655273 (Updf) | ISBN 9780190655280 (Epub)
Subjects: LCSH: Slavery—Economic aspects—Caribbean Area—History. |
Slavery—Economic aspects—United States—History. | Plantations—Economic
aspects—Caribbean Area—History. | Plantations—Economic
aspects—United States—History. | Technology—Economic aspects—Caribbean
Area—History. | Technology—Economic aspects—United States—History. |
Slavery—Caribbean Area—History—19th century. |
Slavery—United States—History—19th century.
Classification: LCC HT1071 .R66 2017 (print) | LCC HT1071 (ebook) |
DDC 306.3/6209729—dc23
LC record available at https://lccn.loc.gov/2016053523

This book is dedicated to the memory of Stewart Rood, the first academic I knew and a man who drew profound joy from both his work and his children.

Contents

Acknowledgments

THIS JOURNEY BEGAN in the English Department at the University of Pittsburgh in 1997, where I had the good fortune to stumble upon three truly great educators. Steve Carr, South Oakland's own Tristram Shandy, agreed to guide me on a directed reading in Critical Theory. Since reading "What is an Author?," I've never been the same. Susan Harris Smith and Phil Smith took me under their wing immediately. Without their love and encouragement I might never have gone to graduate school at all. When I was an exceedingly green master's student in the American Studies Program at NYU in 2000, Njoroge Njoroge, Ted Sammons, Betsy Esch, Forrest Hylton, Peter Hudson, and Walter Johnson first raised the questions and recommended the books with which I wrestle to this day.

I was fortunate to undertake my doctorate at one of the best remaining public institutions in the world: the University of California. Alice Fahs, Ken Pomeranz, Laura Mitchell, Heidi Tinsman, Sharon Block, Bill Maurer, and Rachel O'Toole made Irvine a special place and taught me well. Erin Trapp, Tricia Goldsworthy, Brock Cutler, Jessica Ostrower, Joey Carnie, and Ernesto Bassi provided comradeship, hilarity, and good company. With the help of Ranger, Colette Speer and Lynh Tran showed me the hidden beauty and deliciousness of Orange County. In Columbia, Missouri, Marc McKee and Camellia Cosgray laid a pallet on their floor for me at a difficult time. In Cuba, one could not have asked for a better group of archive buddies than Camillia Cowling, Matthew Casey, Jorge Giovanetti, Victor Goldgel-Carballo, Andrés Pletch, and Barbarita Danzie López. Julito López, along with the rest of the staff at the National Archives in Cuba, were incredibly kind and competent. Ernesto Alvarez Aramis Blanco, historian of the city of Cárdenas, was my generous host in *la Ciudad de las Primicias*. This project would not exist were it not for Adrián Lopez Denis, who seems to know everything about everything in Cuban history. Leida Fernández Prieto, José Guadalupe

Ortega, and Jane Landers have also taught me a great deal about late colonial Cuba. In Richmond, Gregg Kimball and Brent Tarter of the Library of Virginia shared their vast knowledge of the city's history, as well as key primary sources, that have both found their way into the book. Frances Pollard, Nelson Lankford, and David Ruggles guided my research and made me feel welcome as a Mellon Summer Fellow at the Virginia Historical Society. The archivists at both Richmond institutions were friendly, dedicated, and helpful. Local teacher Alysse Cullinan let me sleep in her attic in the summer of 2006, when I carried out the lion's share of my Richmond research.

A postdoc year at the superb American Antiquarian Society in Massachusetts provided the time and resources to become (I hope) a better agricultural historian. Kyle Volk, Sean Harvey, Lisa Wilson, Paul Erickson, Glenda Goodman, and Cate Rosenthal were points of light in the otherwise dim hallways outside the fellows' cubbies. At AAS and elsewhere, Elizabeth Dillon has been a model of humility, generosity, and flat-out brilliance. When I needed distraction from research and life in Boston, I could count on the good company and world-embracing curiosity of Rebecca Haw. I also turned to my billiard squad, the Flat Rats (especially Damien Fish and Al Roesch).

My one-year postdoctoral stint at the University of Pittsburgh was too short. As director of the renowned World History Center, Pat Manning patiently showed me how to navigate academic bureaucracies and networks. Marcus Rediker and Alejandro de la Fuente were generous with their time, while Vincent Leung, Elizabeth Campbell, and Matt Casey retreated with me to various North Oakland bars to nurse our wounds and toast our successes. Matt sets a disturbingly high standard for archival research, and also sings the hell out of "Stuck inside of Mobile." At the University of Georgia, in the wonderful town of Athens, I have benefited from the counsel and company of Steve Berry, Stephen Mihm, Reinaldo Román, Claudio Saunt, Shane Hamilton, Jamie Kreiner, and Casie Legette. I must also thank some UGA students who asked probing questions and forced me to re-examine some easily won insights: Rachel Bunker, Aleck Stephens, Laura Briscoe, Tim Johnson, Tore Olsson, Caroline Jackson, and Alex Faulkner (who have all since moved on to bigger and more exciting things). The support of new friends in Athens has also been crucial. Chris Shannon has never failed to lend his ear, his lumberman's expertise, or his truck. Casie Legette, Brett Szymik, Lauren Gregg, and Shil Patel make Athens a better place to live, especially when they disguise a surprise welcome-back party as yet another D&D night. "Just pray for me, baby."

About Brazil: one of the challenges to doing transnational history is doing transnational history well. I did not have the opportunity to do research in Brazil, but Rio and its surrounding coffee plantations were just too central to the reinvention of Atlantic slavery to ignore, so I simply did my best to avoid egregious errors and leaned heavily on other scholars. I also benefitted from digitized primary sources made available by the Center for Research Libraries Brazil project and the Biblioteca Nacional Digital Brasil. If any insights of value appear in this book's sections on Brazil, they are to the credit of Camillia Cowling, Rafael Marquese, Dale Tomich, Daryle Williams, Silvana Jeha, Ana Nadalini Mendes, Bryan McCann, and the large number of both U.S. and Brazilian scholars in the endnotes (especially Alan dos Santos Ribeiro and Juliana Texeira da Souza). Any errors of fact and interpretation are my own.

For generously reading chapters without remuneration I thank Rachel Bunker, Camillia Cowling, Brock Cutler, Matthew Casey, Steve Berry, Jamie Kreiner, Daryle Williams, and especially David Singerman, who not only let me take his vintage saccharimeter for a spin, but is perhaps the only living soul other than my advisor to have read the entire dissertation. And who has more fun talking about nineteenth-century millstone designs than Scott Nelson and Dan Rood? I must thank him as well. I finished this book during a blessed year at the Kluge Center at the Library of Congress. The Center provided generous funding and daily access to one of the world's largest collections of published materials, which allowed a thorough reconceptualization of the project at a fairly late stage. In DC I had the pleasure of discussing the ideas in this book with David Sartorius, Julie Green, Andrew Zimmerman, Danille Christensen, and Dara Orenstein. Other Kluge Fellows made the load feel lighter, especially the Kluge Krewe: Iván Chaar-López, Anna Brown Ribeiro, Katherine Luongo, and honorary member Will Slauter.

The library and reproduction staffs at AAS, UGA, the Virginia Historical Society, the Library of Virginia, the National Library and National Archives in Cuba, the Wisconsin Historical Society, the American Geographical Society at the University of Wisconsin-Milwaukee, and the Library of Congress were unfailingly generous with their time. I also received crucial monetary support from UGA's Willson Center for Humanities and Arts, the Department of History at UGA, the University of Pittsburgh and its World History Center, and the Hench Post-Dissertation Fellowship at the American Antiquarian Society. I would like particularly to thank public institutions like the Library of Virginia, the Library of Congress, and UGA for maintaining costly subscriptions to America's Historical Newspapers, JSTOR, and other databases that were important for my research.

I got valuable responses when I shared pieces of this work at meetings of the World History Association, the American Studies Association, the Latin American Studies Association, the Agricultural History Society, the Organization of American Historians, the Southern Historical Association, the "Beyond Sweetness" conference at Brown University, and the "Slavery's Capitalism" conference, also at Brown. At a variety of these meetings I received adroit criticisms as well as indispensable encouragement from Ada Ferrer, John Majewski, John Bezis-Selfa, Amy Dru Stanley, Ronald Bailey, Gavin Wright, Scott Nelson, Matt Karp, Ed Baptist, Claudia Dale Golden, Laird Bergad, and many others. An eloquent invitation from James Scott took me to Yale's workshop in Agrarian Studies, where I presented a version of chapter 1 and got particularly useful feedback from Ed Rugemer, Kalyanakrishnan Sivaramakrishnan, and Henry Cowles. I am grateful to Adam Rothman, Chandra Manning, and especially their deeply engaged graduate students in the Georgetown C19 Seminar, for reading a draft of what became chapters 5 and 6 and asking questions I could not answer at the time. Ana Lucia Araújo kindly invited me to share an earlier version of Chapter 7 at Howard University's "Slavery, Memory, and African Diasporas" seminar, where I got useful suggestions from Ana Lucia, and especially from Joe Reidy. Dale Tomich, Seth Rockman, and Frank Towers have followed my development and encouraged me since early in graduate school. It is hard to imagine a more generous colleague and friend than Jamie Kreiner. At the eleventh hour, she read my distended manuscript from cover to cover, offering incisive observations on each chapter. Everybody told me editors don't edit anymore, but Susan Ferber puts the lie to that idea. She marked every single page of my manuscript, questioning points of emphasis, pointing out redundancies, and demanding clarity. I was saved from many errors by the able copy-editing of Leslie Safford, while Jeremy Toynbee shepherded the manuscript through the final phases of production.

My family has been incredibly supportive and patient throughout. Du, Thanh, Annie, Julie, and Vivian Tran keep a place for me at the kitchen table even though Lynh and I can't sit there as often as we would like. Although they might shake their heads at such a notion, Bố and Mẹ taught me that a California Cab and *bánh cam* is the true meaning of Christmas. My Uncle Joe encouraged me by rooting for "another academic in the family," and my Uncle Elliot never failed to ask how the book was coming along. Beginning early in my life, my mother and my older sister, Toby Manke and Eden Burgess, instilled in me a love of reading that has sustained me through thousands of hours of research. Along with their partners Bill and Terry, they have offered love and reprieve at various points over the past decade. I narrowly missed the chance to thank my grandmother, Esther Rood, who passed away last winter at the age of a hundred. She made the old family house in Sheepshead Bay a landing pad for me when I started grad school in New York. My deepest thanks go to Lynh Tran, and not only for her mad editing skills. She meets life's challenges with wit, warmth, and honesty. She constantly pulls me back into the world.

The Reinvention
of Atlantic Slavery

Introduction

ATLANTIC INVERSIONS

SOMEWHERE WITHIN A roiling vat of cane juice on an 1842 Cuban plantation swam an elusive repository of value: sucrose, which would crystalize into "plantation white" sugar if processed correctly. Whiteness brought higher prices. Moreover, white sugar was nearly imperishable and thus allowed planters and merchants to hold out for better prices in export markets. In the early 1840s, sugar chemists hoping to maximize yields of plantation white discovered that high percentages of the sucrose produced by cane plants broke down quickly under the influence of excessive heat, exposure to air, and the action of microorganisms. This breakdown turned fresh cane juice into less valuable molasses and syrups. "Inverted" cane sugar, as it came to be called, was brown and wet, making it difficult to store, heavy for shipping, and prone to spoiling.

Rooted in new biological sciences, the mid-nineteenth-century notion of inversion—the idea that, particularly in the tropics, invisible creatures could suddenly turn upside down the color, taste, value, or even the essential identity of a substance—had multiple valences. The bloody results of slave rebels' inversion of the social order in Haiti had engendered an Atlantic-wide understanding of the precarity of plantation capitalism, worsened by another series of slave uprisings in Cuba in the early 1840s.[1] Sugar's inversion also threatened to convert the wealthiest class in Spain's most treasured colony into a mere supplier of cheap raw materials. Imagining themselves awash in a sea of brown molasses and black rebels, and stymied by Spanish laws, North American tariffs, and British abolitionism, planters anxiously pursuing whiteness in the sugar mill attempted to reinvent racial orders, production techniques, and Cuba's position in the Atlantic economy.

Across the New World slave societies of the nineteenth century, a new generation of elite slaveholders faced similar pressures. They responded by adapting European industrial technologies, combining planting with finance, taking control of modern transport infrastructures, and vanquishing small landowners to grab a larger share of the market. They also turned to "plantation experts" for assistance in reinventing the technologies of slavery. These experts circulated in a unified system that stretched across various empires and nation-states, reaching from Havana, New Orleans, and Rio de Janeiro to Baltimore, Richmond, and Paris. Some of them were US citizens, but others were subjects of the Spanish Empire, or of France, England, or Brazil. Many were trained as engineers, chemists, iron makers, or architects. Some merely thought of themselves as enlightened planters. Their travels, their translations, and their conscious reworking of racial ideologies in the plantation archipelago deepened the Atlantic economy's dependence on forced labor after a few revolutionary decades when it seemed as though the institution of slavery might be destroyed.

Plantation capitalists did not undertake these transformations lightly; with experts' assistance, they reinvented slavery in the context of converging crises in the 1830s and 1840s. From outside, they faced tariffs, imperialism, and British abolitionism. From within, they experienced rivalry among merchant groups. And from below, they grappled with slave resistance. This book traces the three main reinventions that underpinned the expansion of slaveholders' capitalism in the mid-nineteenth century. They forged a multi-centered Atlantic network of sellers and buyers to help them evade British and North American domination. New technologies of production and transport provided higher efficiencies, allowing them to keep parts of the manufacturing process at home. Finally, their adaptation of racial ideologies and associated racial divisions of labor facilitated the use of non-slave forms of labor, like indentured Chinese workers, in the Age of Abolition. Racial divisions of labor were reengineered in response to the incorporation of new machinery. Conversely, new technologies were shaped by notions of racially endowed aptitudes for different kinds of work.

Relocating the Second Slavery

In the wake of the Haitian Revolution, the Napoleonic Wars, the Industrial Revolution, and the gradual antislavery turn of the British Empire, slavery did not simply drift toward dissolution. Instead, it migrated to new places and incorporated new kinds of industrial technologies. Some scholars have come to call this resurgence the "Second Slavery."[2] With the old colonial circuits of exchange in tatters by 1815, the Second Slavery unfolded amid a fragmented world of nation-states engaged in increasingly competitive trade. Population growth, mass consumption, and unprecedented streams of European immigration to the Americas simultaneously transformed the contexts of commodity production.[3] Challenged by both increasing slave resistance and abolitionist politics, Cuban sugar planters, US cotton planters, and Brazilian coffee planters were not merely filling a hole in Atlantic markets left by British and French West Indian elites.[4] With the help of plantation experts immersed in the Industrial Revolution, they actively reinvented slavery in response to a different moment in the history of world capitalism.

Recent North Americanist scholars have singled out the Cotton South as the motor driving the British Industrial Revolution, whose mechanical technologies allowed a rapidly growing population in England to enjoy increasing per capita incomes. More than brilliant inventions or liberal institutions, an unprecedented supply of cheap raw cotton from the US South was the essential factor in Britain's economic modernization.[5] While works on the Cotton Kingdom have shed light on a crucial story in the history of global capitalism, their focus on antebellum imperialists has left important players in the shadows. In many ways, twenty-first-century historians have followed the selective geopolitical sight lines of antebellum imperialists. Prominent southern intellectuals like James Henry Hammond and J. D. B. DeBow wished for "direct trade" between the cotton South and Europe, industrialization within the cotton states, and the conquest of various Latin American nations for the sake of expanding cotton cultivation. Blinded by the glitter of the Deep South's "white gold," such men overlooked the fact that ties of expertise, commodities, and labor among the Upper South, Cuba, and Brazil created a densely entangled domain for slavery's capitalism that already boasted some of the features that "King Cotton" boosters could only dream of.

The antebellum silences may owe something to the realities of Upper South–Cuba–Brazil ties. As the travails of US-based plantation experts in Cuba and Brazil make clear, the United States did not have a dominant role in the Greater Caribbean before the US Civil War. The multi-centric system complicated comforting illusions of a slaveholder's Pan-American Empire governed from New Orleans, Richmond, or Charleston. Indeed, southern entrepreneurs were forced to acknowledge the economic might of "less white" slaveholders in Cuba and Brazil, a force that stood in tension with the southerners' racial ideas.[6]

In spite of the silences shared by pre–Civil War expansionists and recent scholars, an internally differentiated yet cohesive economic system was carved out of the social and economic upheavals of the Atlantic World after 1815. This book uses "the Greater Caribbean" as a geographic label to describe both the dense circuits of interaction among the Upper South, Cuba, and Brazil and the wider but less dense connections to Western Europe. This multi-centric Greater Caribbean was different from the unipolar "empire of cotton" linking the Deep South to Liverpool.[7] As the chapters in this book show, the interlocking dynamics of Cuba's sugar boom, Brazil's coffee expansion, and Virginia's wheat flour and ironworking industries quietly realized King Cotton's fantasy that diverse plantation regions could provision one another, mitigating dependence on northern US merchants. The Southwestern cotton states eagerly shipped an imperishable raw material to a single exterior place for industrial finishing. The commodities particular to the Greater Caribbean, on the other hand, required extensive on-site processing, inspiring merchants, planters, and experts to reengineer their place in nineteenth-century capitalism's global division of labor.

Largely unmoored from their old metropolitan centers, and straining at the neo-colonial links that tied other parts of the Atlantic economy to Liverpool or New York, the Upper South, Cuba, and Brazil forged an alternative set of links with one another.[8] In the process they wrought a new geographic hierarchy within Atlantic capitalism. Planters and merchants in all three places continually eluded the iron grip of the Yankee behemoth, maneuvering between European and North American markets as it suited their interests. In Brazil, planters responding to rebels' destruction of St. Domingue's coffee industry opened up a new "frontier of slavery" in the Paraíba Valley. Slave owners concentrated land holdings, plowed over subsistence crops, and displaced small farmers to make way for coffee. Enslaved workers made Brazil by far the world's largest coffee producer by the 1830s, pushing less efficient producers to the margins of an ever-expanding mass consumer market in Europe and the United States.[9]

Slaves in Virginia played an important role in southeastern Brazil's coffee boom.[10] North American coffee merchants, who purchased the majority of Brazil's coffee, desperately needed something to sell in Rio. Since Great Britain had cornered the market in cotton textiles, the only alternative to an ever-deepening trade deficit was wheat flour. Richmond flour came to be the commodity that exchanged at most favorable rates with Brazilian coffee. Rio's bakers, many of them African born and formerly enslaved, often discovered imported flour to be "sour," or rancid, by the time it arrived in port.

Richmond millers responded to the "fastidiousness" of Brazilian bread makers by transforming systems of wheat transport, flour milling, barrel production, and maritime shipping.

Using a combination of technical precision and enslaved labor, Richmond millers created a particularly white, fine, and clean product that ensured a more durable "sweetness," which they associated with the whitest grades of flour. Like sugar, Richmond white flour had been mechanically isolated from the colored parts of the grain more prone to spoiling. Industrially produced flour packed securely in mechanically made barrels was designed to preserve the product by excluding pests and suppressing the heat and moisture that hosted them. These technologies minimized the material fluctuations that the flour was to undergo as it traveled across climatic regions. Thus Richmond millers fought a bitter legal battle in the 1850s against state inspectors whose drill holes compromised the hygienic micro-environments inside barrels of flour. Other innovations, like the McCormick wheat-harvesting machine, emerged out of Virginia's entanglement with the Brazilian coffee industry. After 1840, Richmond's wheat-growing hinterland was deindustrialized largely because small, anonymous country mills could not compete in the Brazil-oriented export market, and local planters increasingly sent wheat by rail to be milled in Richmond. McCormick's invention served Piedmont planters increasingly dedicated to providing grain to export-oriented mills. With the nation's fifth-largest wheat harvest and largest flour mills in the country, Virginia was home to more enslaved people than was any other state in 1860, working in multiple industries.[11] Its links to southeastern Brazil go a long way in explaining this condition.

Similarly seeking to capture markets no longer supplied by the slaves of St. Domingue, Cuban planters in the late 1830s built the first railroad network in Latin America, an innovation that revolutionized the ways sugar was transported and in turn helped them secure dominance of an expanding world mass market in sugar consumption.[12] Since protective US tariffs penalized Cuba's "plantation white," a new generation of merchant-planters seeking to hold on to the value-added phases of sugar making pivoted to Great Britain, whose tariffs after 1849 were particularly forgiving. But this idea of market pivoting can be misleading. The renovation of commercial linkages to England required profound interventions into the social, economic, and technical landscape of Cuba.

On large sugar plantations, chemical experiments were aimed at yielding pure sucrose. This dry, fine, molasses-free inorganic product was manufactured in a new vacuum-sealed Derosne system (see Chapter 1, "A Creole

Industrial Revolution in the Cuban Sugar Mill"). Purchasers of this expensive machinery believed it could insulate the commodity from the degenerative effects of brute labor and tropical air. Paradoxically, the deathlike chemical environment of "plantation white" extended the life of sugar, maximizing opportunities for price arbitrage. The Derosne system was primarily a preservative technology, intended to keep the refining phases of production at home in the colony. Cuba's rapid adoption of modern transport technologies reflected the preservative priorities of the Derosne system: instead of storing boxes of sugar in their houses throughout Havana, the merchants shipped white sugar via railroad to new dockside warehouse complexes made of iron and glass. Iron construction allowed for uninterrupted indoor expanses that promoted airflow around the sugar, while glass eliminated excessive use of gas lighting; thus, by extending the shelf-life of exports, the warehouses provided marketing advantages not generally available to smaller planters.[13] New railroad-wharf-warehouse systems were designed to facilitate the flow of whiter grades of sugar to Europe; small planters unable to afford new technologies continued sending brown grades to the United States.

Like owners of the high-overhead Richmond mills and expanding Brazilian coffee plantations, Cuban slaveholders who engineered these new technologies had to find a way to push aside small competitors. While this interconnected web of preservative technologies reflected an internal struggle among different ethno-national and class groups of sugar planters, it abetted other social conflicts waged by the merchant-planters. Until the 1830s, middling merchants and free Afro-Cuban dockworkers exerted considerable control over a mercantile "infrastructure of fees" that had emerged with the first sugar boom after 1790. The new railroad lines purposely skirted the government docks controlled by Afro-Cuban dockworkers and avoided the old merchants' houses scattered throughout the city. At the same time, planters' massive backlash against the Escalera rebellions of 1840–1844 crushed free black worker power on the wharves. Rich planters thus deployed a combination of violence and technical development against their rivals to create new opportunities for themselves in the Greater Caribbean.

In the 1850s, a new generation of Spanish-born merchant-planters together with Upper South railroad engineers and iron makers took over Cuba's original railroad network and repurposed it to serve the needs of plantation-white sugar. Virginia railroad engineers, who had not been particularly prominent in the first spurt of Cuban railway construction in the 1840s, played an important role in this repurposing. In 1858, for example, Isaac Ridgeway Trimble applied his experience coercing slaves and driving machinery on Virginia railroads to his job as chief engineer of the Havana Railroad Company. Cuban railroad entrepreneurs recruited Trimble to develop technologies custom made for the plantation world. His "tropical" bona fides as a Greater Caribbean expert placed him above established English railway engineers, and secured him and many of his Virginian colleagues lucrative positions with Cuba's most well-known railroad firms. Success on the Cuban railroads quickly led this group of Virginia engineers to the other emerging "tropical" railroad market of Brazil, whose transport entrepreneurs likewise sought men with expertise in the "management of Negroes."[14] Trimble's travels shed light on the interdependence of slave iron production in Virginia and slave sugar production in Cuba, as well as the rapid transfer of tropical railroad knowledge from the northern hemisphere to Brazil.

Plantation experts like Trimble possessed the experience as industrial consultants and racial managers to serve the reinvention of Atlantic slavery. Following them from Virginia's Blue Ridge Mountains to the tidal inlets of Matanzas, Cuba, and from there to the coffee-planted hillsides of Brazil's Paraiba Valley, shows how the dynamic zones of the Second Slavery formed a single economic-technological bloc within the wider Atlantic world.

For Greater Caribbean capitalists, preservative technical revolutions were the preconditions for operating in a world economy under the auspices of British industrial capital. New mechanisms, along with new forms of control over labor and infrastructure, enabled semiperipheral producers to navigate and manipulate a nominally "free trade" world in reality dominated by a small number of Euro-American nation-states.[15] In Cuba, Brazil, and the Upper South, elites pursued an ideal white commodity that could exist in a state of suspended animation in barrels and boxes as products awaited sale. White commodities, and the infrastructures that supported them, allowed relatively disadvantaged postcolonial sellers to break through traditionally exploitative mercantile arrangements at the local level, and to maneuver effectively amid the price shifts of an increasingly unified world market. The merchant-planters, experts, and managers of the Greater Caribbean succeeded in staving off the role of colonial raw materials producer for a crucial half-century, a period that saw the entrenchment of new forms of capitalism that revised the racial divisions of labor originating in the early modern plantation complex.

The Multiple Creolizations of Capitalism and Modernity

Long before the US cotton boom, early modern Caribbean commodities like sugar and tobacco stirred a larger Atlantic system into being. Export-oriented West Indian plantations spurred the actions of grain producers in the mid-Atlantic colonies, shipbuilders in New England, providers of credit and manufactures in Western Europe, and slave-selling merchants in West Africa.[16] Building on the insights of scholars tracing back to Eric Williams, Dale Tomich concludes that "the world market and the plantation are necessarily interrelated, interdependent, and mutually constitutive. Neither exists without the other."[17] This is not to say that Caribbean plantations looked "just like" British factories, or that slavery-based economies operated "just like" wage-labor economies. On the contrary, the plantation complex generated for the first time a worldwide division of labor drawn together by the exchange of commodities among the heterogeneous nodes of an interdependent system ordered by the unending pursuit of profit.

C. L. R. James and Sidney Mintz suggest that the plantation complex, far from a peculiar atavism, was the site of modernity's first emergence.[18] Diasporic African people forced to assist in the settlement of the Americas were torn violently from kinship networks and linguistic groups. Creating new cultural forms and collectivities in response to this uprooting, slaves embodied the characteristics of "the modern individual" prior to the European bourgeois to whom the label has typically been applied. Furthermore, as Paul Gilroy explains, their liminal position *vis à vis* Western culture enabled critical insights on the modern condition not available to those more comfortably ensconced within Europe's intellectual tradition. The concept of "creolization" has been applied to enslaved people's improvisational reworking of various African, indigenous, and European cultural, linguistic, and agricultural practices. Such reinvention from below created new Afro-diasporic strategies necessary to withstand the plantation, while deeply influencing European settler cultures.[19]

Throughout the history of the Greater Caribbean, white creoles also calculated and improvised.[20] After European weapons and diseases had largely extirpated indigenous populations in the sixteenth century, the Caribbean became the site of unprecedented projects of social engineering.[21] Replicating the uniform vistas of cane fields across the landscape and fabricating an abstract category of laborer ("the Negro"), settler colonists created the sugar plantation, with its strict time discipline, managerial surveillance, repetitive tasks, and large-scale commodity production by gang labor, as well as a dependence on the market for everyday subsistence needs.[22]

Contending with European writers' idea that tropical climates doomed inhabitants to degeneration, white colonial intellectuals valorized their locale. Among other things, they used it to rationalize black slavery: the laziness encouraged by natural bounty could be counteracted with coercion, but only tropical races were able to withstand that coercion. In the tropics, white bodies required sanitary cordons, as well as European foods, to maintain their status as white and civilized.[23] White Creoles also insisted that knowledge of the New World be rooted in everyday intimacy with its fecund, degenerative, and dangerous nature—a new approach to scientific knowledge that augmented settlers' authority in relation to faraway European writers, but by extension enhanced the power of non-white, non-elite knowers of American flora, fauna, and geography.[24]

The plantation experts who figure prominently in this book consciously deployed discourses of tropical authenticity and creole expertise in the sugar factories, railroads, and flour mills of the Second Slavery. Experts across this transnational region theorized a shared tropical climate that made preservative technologies a key strategy of postcolonial economic strivings. They challenged the universalist presumptions of European industrial science while borrowing many of its tools. The original models of the industrial materials of sugar mills, iron factories, and railroads often came from Europe, but underwent considerable transformations in the plantation complex. To avoid various kinds of subjugation (to British and US abolitionists, to North Atlantic merchants and financiers, and to slaves themselves), experts claiming to possess unique expertise about the laboring potential and internal desires of black workers also engineered new racial divisions of labor. Greater Caribbean experts were thereby able to imagine themselves in control of an unstable yet immensely profitable system.

Creolization from Below

The presumption that these men made about "knowing negroes" pivoted uncomfortably on the question of negro knowledge. Reinventing Greater Caribbean capitalism required facing anew the issue that had most vexed masters since the inception of the plantation system: what should black people know? Colonial elites had long recognized that knowledge was necessary for all kinds of profitable work.[25] At the same time, too much knowledge in the hands of bondspeople would both unveil the speciousness of the racist ideology underpinning slavery and give slaves the capacity to knock it out. As their masters were painfully aware, skilled, literate, and networked slaves had played prominent roles in the Greater Caribbean's most notorious slave uprisings.

The problem of enslaved people's knowledge took on increasing urgency in the wake of the Haitian Revolution and the Industrial Revolution. On the one hand, heightened security concerns following the rebellion in Haiti, as well as many other less successful slave uprisings, brought African knowledges under suspicion.[26] The first half of the nineteenth century saw a hardening of "scientifically" backed racial categories. New theories of biological essential-ism consigned Africans and their descendants to a caste apart while positing that blacks lacked the cognitive ability to distinguish truth from falsehood. Resulting imperatives to exclude people of color from networks of "use-ful knowledge" stood in tension with the technical reinvention of Greater Caribbean commodity production, which made profits more dependent on workers' unique skills and knowledge than ever before. This paradoxical set of developments informed an internally contradictory racial division of labor.

In the nineteenth-century Greater Caribbean, the industrial processing of perishable commodities created the necessity for rapid technical change, making experimentation a daily feature of business. Quotidian plantation experiments could momentarily invert a racial order otherwise militantly maintained. At such moments, enslaved people could exert control over their daily lives, while shaping the trajectory of technological reinvention in nodes of Greater Caribbean capitalism. These individuals were still slaves in every sense of the word, but because their skill was in short supply, as well as stra-tegically important, they temporarily achieved an un-slavelike authority.[27] At Richmond's Tredegar Ironworks, for example, skilled slaves participated in the sorts of technological creolization required for success in the Cuban railroad market, at the same time insisting that their role as industrial work-ers brought with it tangible social power in a white-dominated world. Slaves were central to slavery's reinvention. Whether their craft skills continued to be sources of power after 1844 depended on where they were located in sprawling commodity chains.[28]

While the connection to the Brazilian and Cuban railroad markets opened up spaces for the assertion of black politics in the expanding industrial mills of Richmond, and in the experimental rural smithies of the Shenandoah Valley, the deindustrialization of Central Virginia's wheat-growing hinter-land trapped enslaved men in plantation spaces, or inspired them to escape northward. The contradictory and uneven geography of nineteenth-century racial capitalism shaped enslaved people's agency in unpredictable ways. Sometimes they were key technological contributors; other times they thwarted masters' designs; often they were a target for disempowerment so that reinventions could be carried out. In any of these cases, black workers throughout the Greater Caribbean, especially those with craft skills, recognized that the reinvention of Atlantic slavery innately involved them. For their part, planters and experts remained aware that slaves and free black workers simultaneously secured and endangered the success of grand capitalist ventures. In response, the planters and experts reconfigured long-held ideas of racial difference in the context of rapid economic and technological change.

A New Chapter in the History of "the Negro"

One of the first inventions to come out of the Greater Caribbean, "the Negro" was a fabrication whose supposed biological exceptionalism was turned into very real profit in the early modern world.[29] In the mid-eighteenth century, the French Jesuit Pierre-François-Xavier de Charlevoix claimed in a learned treatise on the human races that Africans required little or no food to survive.[30] This physiological peculiarity was unquestioningly assumed by generations of Greater Caribbean slaveholders and even shaped ideas of biological race beyond their circles.[31] A piece in a Civil War–era abolitionist newspaper saluted hard-working field slaves who were "nine-tenths production and only one-tenth consumption."[32] Reshaped by nineteenth-century discourses of political economy, physics, and engineering, the "construct of Negro" had come to embody a fantasy of black surplus that drew from ideas of Africans' tropical fitness for hard labor. As the seminal enabling fiction of racial capitalism, "the Negro" overproduced and underconsumed; labored for capital while being excluded from a privileged zone of waged work; and was simultaneously insulated from commodification and the ultimate commodity. Racial divisions of labor, stamped into capitalism from the early decades of the Caribbean's sugar industry, set the pattern for an enduring set of capitalist cost-cutting strategies.[33]

The imperative to push labor or nature to the very "horizon of extinction" without destroying its value started aboard the slave ship, as captives were packed into holds so tightly that they could barely move. High mortality rates in the Atlantic slave trade were so much a part of entrepreneurs' planning that early insurance policies were invented to turn the "collateral damage" of mass death on slave ships into profit for slave traders.[34] This biological brinksmanship continued into the "seasoning process" as well as the "working out" of sugar island slaves. Throughout the nineteenth century, working conditions, malnutrition, and disease contributed to an overall life expectancy of as little as seven years from the time of a captive's arrival in Cuba.[35] The pushing system of cotton or sugar harvesting, in which overseers may have terrorized slaves into producing ever-higher picking and cutting totals, aimed to maximize the yield on captives' life energy. By growing one crop, planters likewise forced the land to the edge of its ability to sustain life.[36]

With the discovery of inversion in tropical sugar production, rising prices for slaves, global competition in a free trade world, and the fallout from a massively successful and violent slave revolt in Haiti, came a new awareness of fragile balances in the Greater Caribbean. Under novel conditions, realizing the fantasy of black surplus required augmented levels of control. Sugar experts' religious parsing of profitable and unprofitable forms of very basic biological activity was imposed simultaneously on the daily lives of the enslaved, who were increasingly under the sway of capital's imperative for perfectly directed, value-enhancing, pliant labor.[37] Nineteenth-century slaveholders were also compelled by a growing antislavery movement to embrace new racial categories. Neither blindly loyal to the institution of slavery nor incipient abolitionists, they retooled a racially stratified workforce to labor on different parts of the new machinery of production. Most importantly, in response to abolitionist pressure on the African slave trade, around 200,000 Chinese men were brought in to the sugar industry on indenture contracts. Cuban planters and their hired experts concentrated different races, variously categorized as *cúlies chinos*, *bozales*, *ladinos*, *pardos*, *morenos*, *canáries*, and *yucatecos*, across the spaces and tasks of the estate. In the United States and Brazil, an internal slave trade, flexible systems of hiring, and indenture contracts were added on to the older system of chattel slavery.

Although distinctions must be made between racial ideology in Cuba, Brazil, and the United States, they had important commonalities, since all three varieties of anti-black racism emerged from a common root in the Atlantic slave trade.[38] Latin Americans' belief that both individuals and populations could "whiten" themselves through miscegenation was not shared in a United States governed by the "one drop rule," but they did share a general belief in the reality of white and black "blood," creating analogous anxieties about porousness and pollution. Even in the notoriously stringent racial politics of the United States, the very frailty of whiteness occasioned strong responses. While "black blood" was deemed ineradicable in even the tiniest measure, whiteness could be ruined by the slightest impurity. Voicing opposition to the expansion of slavery, for example, rendered members of Lincoln's party "Black Republicans," and picking up a shovel for a public works project could reduce poor white men to the status of "negroes." In Cuba and Brazil, a faith in the malleability of racial identity could just as easily amplify whites' determination to block any place where blackness might enter.

For all members of the Greater Caribbean's "pan-American master class," to whiten was to be respected, as Cuban Creole reformer Jóse Antonio Saco put it. To prevent economic subjugation at the hands of the wealthiest nations and to access European consumption habits necessitated expanding slavery, which at the same time endangered white rule.[39] Ideas of dangerous racial transformation and the bio-economic specificity of black labor clearly informed how people thought about commodities, energies, and values in the Greater Caribbean. The physical properties of fineness, dryness, whiteness, and frictionless motion created an environment inhospitable to the riotous life of microorganisms. The industrial preservative technologies that maintained this system promised to defer multifaceted inversions.

In spite of masters' and experts' best efforts to marshal state power, racial ideology, and technological precision to secure a stable whiteness in the Greater Caribbean, the dreaded inversions indeed recurred in the 1860s. In concert with the outbreak of war in the United States, Cuba, and Brazil, Afro-diasporic people succeeded in putting an end to chattel slavery. However, the worldwide racial division of labor that emerged from the plantation complex has proved far more durable.[40]

I

A Creole Industrial Revolution in the Cuban Sugar Mill

BEGINNING IN THE sixteenth century, European settlers transformed a series of Caribbean islands into "socio-economic sugar complexes" to feed Europe's ever-growing hunger for sweetness.[1] Each colony saw a similar sequence of events. First, indigenous residents were dispossessed or killed off through warfare, enslavement, and disease. With local sources of labor exterminated, colonists turned to the African slave trade. Small European farmers were then pushed aside and old-growth forests burned to make room for the sugar mill. Finally, ambitious planters brought in the extensive machinery needed to transform sugar-cane plants into a commodity for sale on European markets. Not until rebellious slaves destroyed francophone planters' estates in St. Domingue (Haiti) at the end of the eighteenth century did white planters in Cuba begin to turn their attention fully to making sugar.

The Haitian Revolution opened a gaping hole in Atlantic sugar markets that Cuban planters were poised to fill. This time, however, sugar's conquest of a colonial island's terrain was different. It unfolded not within a preindustrial Atlantic economy, but in the midst of Europe's Industrial Revolution, which was also transforming life in the United States. Far from colonizing an "empty" island, Cuban sugar planters also had to undo long-existing social arrangements and patterns of land use.

Prior to the 1820s, most slaves in Cuba were employed in urban, maritime, or domestic occupations. Slaves were swiftly re-concentrated in the sugar-plantation sector in the ensuing two decades. The percentage of captives working in the sugar industry rose from 25 percent to 50 percent—a massive reapportionment of resources to focus on the export of a single product.[2] Slaves became a capital-intensive element of a capital-intensive operation.

The labor and capital demands of the sugar industry robbed other sectors of investment, thus creating a vicious circle that favored further transfer of resources toward sugar.[3] As sugar planters in Western Cuba took over lands from small tobacco and coffee farms, and railroads opened up new parts of the countryside to potential cultivation in the 1840s, US, Spanish, and Cuban merchants expanded the illegal slave trade to meet sugar planters' burgeoning demand for labor (see Figure 1-1). In 1827 the island held 270,000 enslaved people. This population rose to 370,000 by 1862.[4]

In the context of increasing sugar production in a competitive Atlantic economy, enslaved people lost their modicum of self-determination. Eagle-eyed planters moved captive communities from dispersed cabins to closely packed huts. The increased regulation of slaves' dwellings accompanied a decline in their garden plots. Traditionally, bondspeople independently sold some of what they grew. Slaves often used the cash from these sales to purchase their own freedom through the Iberian institution of *coartación*.[5] With changes in transportation, as well as in sugar processing technologies in the mill, more acres of cane could be planted, thus shrinking the amount of marginal land that planters were willing to reserve for enslaved families' use. Spare plantation acreage was reduced further still by the need for pasture to feed the large livestock populations required for the operations of major sugar estates.[6] Finally, after the 1830s, the spread of railroads made it more cost effective for slaveholders to bring in staples like rice, flour, beans, and salt cod, liberating all available resources for sugar-cane planting. Thus, as more and more of Cuba's enslaved population was concentrated on sugar plantations, more and more of their waking hours were dedicated to sugar-related work. With planters focused single-mindedly on the amount of sugar their slaves produced, the "science" of labor management also changed. Any vestiges of paternalist obligation were replaced by an "instrumental concern with establishing the optimal social conditions for exacting the greatest amount of labor from the slave population and increasing the productivity of the plantation enterprise."[7] But sugar's colonization of Cuban society was not accepted quietly.

Between 1825 and 1844, enslaved Africans and Afro-Cubans raised a series of rebellions. The uprisings were concentrated in the provinces of Matanzas and Cárdenas, which held a disproportionate number of enslaved workers as well as the most modern machinery of sugar production. In one of the 1843 Cárdenas uprisings, which began in Ingenio Alcancía (the Alcancía sugar mill), 465 Afro-Cubans marched off plantations toward the village of Bemba, gathering recruits as they went.[8] While attracting numerous adherents, the insurgency was summarily put down by Spanish infantry and cavalry brigades, which shot 132 rebels on sight. The brigades proceeded to execute captured leaders, mutilating their bodies and displaying severed heads at the plantations where they had formerly been held. Less prominent participants were subjected to extended beatings before being put back to work.[9] During their uprising, rebels seemed to concentrate on the plantations of notable creole planters Domingo Aldama and Gonzalo Alfonso, the big shareholders in the Havana-Matanzas Railroad Company. These planters pleaded for military protection and an end to new slave imports after the revolt.[10]

A few months later, another uprising began in Matanzas, this time organized by captives on Ingenio Triunvirato, owned by another prominent creole, Julián Alfonso. After burning down Alfonso's home, and much of the mill and canefields, his slaves drove to neighboring plantations to recruit more followers and take weapons from overseers. When Spanish troops caught up with the rebels at the Ingenio San Rafael, a battle ensued in which fifty-six Africans and Afro-Cubans were killed, seventeen were wounded, and seventy taken prisoner. Eight survivors were condemned to death. Among them was a woman named Fermina Lucumí, famed for leading a local Maroon community (that is, hidden encampments of escaped slaves or their descendants).[11]

Contrary to authorities' expectations, these brutal reprisals redoubled the determination of many bondspeople to destroy slaveholders' world. Early in 1844, slaves in Cárdenas and Matanzas were linked to a conspiracy of free people of color, as well as wider movements for black freedom. Preempting this latest and most ambitious plan to emancipate all slaves and end white rule, Captain-General Gerónimo Valdés set in motion a counterinsurgency of unprecedented severity.[12] In all, writes the Cuban historian Gloria García, "more than 3,000 people, among them 96 whites, suffered prison or were condemned to the firing squad as a result of inquisitorial investigations."[13] The year 1844 was dubbed "*La Escalera*," or "The Ladder," after a common method of interrogating individuals suspected of insurrectionary activity, in which they were stretched along the length of a ladder laid upon the ground, face down, and whipped. The planters' backlash overwhelmed black people's resistance to a plantation revolution that had only recently come to the island.

While attempting to reorganize an unwilling workforce, Cuban planters faced economic and political conditions that stalled the first phase of the post-1790s sugar boom. Cuban creoles had long been the most favored colonists within the Spanish Empire, especially after demonstrating their loyalty during the wars of independence in Spanish America. Between 1790 and 1830, the first sugar boom had been facilitated by liberal trade and land-holding legislation for Cuba's planters, the opening of markets for African slaves, the duty-free import of plantation machinery, and permission to clear-cut forests that the Spanish navy had previously reserved for its own use. While these vital concessions were never reversed, the political climate changed in the 1830s. Spanish policymakers feared an invasion from British abolitionists or *yanqui* expansionists and also depended increasingly on the fiscal contributions of one of their last remaining colonies. Authorities in Madrid demanded more tax revenue from planters and ejected them from powerful political posts.

Moreover, competition from the European beet-sugar industry, as well as new cane-sugar plantations in India, the Pacific islands, and East Africa, concerned planters. Increased commodity exchange across imperial boundaries also intensified competition among makers of sugar. The Panic of 1837, which set off a decade-long recession throughout the Atlantic world, brought together these overlapping trends, and created a time of financial difficulties for Cuba's sugar elite. Great Britain suffered a crisis of its own in 1844–1847 that reduced the nation's purchases of sugar. While the rate of imports soon recovered, prices remained low. This crisis period coincided with two major hurricane years in Cuba, which suddenly ended a period in which cheap credit, open land, plentiful slave imports, and simple machinery were enough to secure many planters' fortunes.[14]

Between 1837 and 1848, a new generation of Spanish-born merchant-planters responded to the ongoing crisis through widespread experimentation with new sugar-making technologies like the Derosne system, which in turn required the reinvention of racialized labor management. These elites effectively reclaimed Cuba's preeminence in world sugar production, safeguarding the final phases of refining for themselves, and rejecting the role of colonial raw materials producer. Albeit only partial and temporary, their achievement was particularly notable because their conquest of the world sugar economy took place in an industrializing and globalized marketplace fundamentally different from that in which their predecessors in Barbados, Jamaica, and St. Domingue operated.

Although often lumped together as one long sugar boom lasting from the 1790s to the 1860s, Cuba's sugar-based economic expansion was characterized by three phases, each with an overarching technology of sugar processing. The first section of this chapter, "the single effect," tells the story of Cuba's emergence between 1790 and 1830 as a major sugar producer, which depended on a system of manufacture called "the Jamaica train." The second section analyzes the initial attempts to incorporate European beet-sugar technologies into Cuban colonial production—efforts that were undertaken in the context of economic recession and massive slave resistance. In spite of early excitement, machines emerging from Europe's beet-sugar industry like Charles Derosne's initial "double effect" design proved problematic when subjected to the stresses of a cane-sugar harvest in the Caribbean. The third section, covering 1848–1861, addresses the introduction of Rillieux's vacuum pan. A free man of color from New Orleans, Norbert Rillieux invented a "triple effect" design that added another cycle of waste heat reusage to the Derosne system. His system also protected sugar from the tropical elements more thoroughly. A product combining the ingenuity of European craftsmen with the expertise and local knowledge of an African-American engineer and the ambitions of capitalistic slaveholders, this invention ushered Cuba's top tier of sugar makers into a new age of expansion when general economic conditions improved in the 1850s.

FIGURE 1-1 Between 1830 and 1860, the landscape of the western and central parts of Cuba was rapidly transformed by the construction of new railroads, plantation districts, and warehouse complexes.

From Mapa de la Isla de Cuba a mediados del siglo XIX. Editores: Rubio, Grilo y Vitturi. B. Litografía de B. Criaranta (1868), reproduced in Justo Germán Cantero, *Los ingenios: Colección de vistas de los principales ingenios de azúcar de la Isla de Cuba* (Havana, Cuba: 1857), Luis Miguel García Mora and Antonio Santamaría García, eds. (Madrid: Editorial CSIC, 2005).

The Single Effect: Processing Sugar with the Jamaica Train

By all accounts, cane cutting was grueling work. Since fresh soil was frequently needed for planting, and timber required for boiling house fuel, slaves chopped down old growth forest to "open" the land. Then field gangs dug hundreds of acres of trenches and laid cane cuttings in them. New shoots grew from the nodes of the old cuttings. Several months of weeding around the growing canes ensued, and the fields were set aflame to remove weeds just before the harvest began in January, initiating five months of unremitting toil for workers.

During the harvest, enslaved men and women worked up to sixteen hours a day, stripping six-foot-tall canes of razor-sharp leaves, then stooping low to swing machetes to fell the three-inch-thick stalks. Behind the cutters, others picked up canes and loaded them into ox-drawn wagons to take rapidly to the mill. Immediately after workers extracted the juice by passing the canes through a roller mill (turned by oxen or, increasingly, by steam engines), workers transported the cane juice to the boiling house. This building held the Jamaica train. Originally cane juice was evaporated in a row of open-lid cauldrons each heated by an independent furnace. The rapidly deforesting countryside of western Cuba, however, as well as the lack of local sources of coal on the island , encouraged the use of one tunnel-shaped reverberatory furnace that conducted the heat from a single fire to all the cauldrons. Nameless inventors of the Jamaica train ultimately welded a succession of individual processing units into a single clumsy but fuel-efficient machine.[15]

Each batch of cane juice passed through the cauldrons of the Jamaica train in succession. First, the juice went to the clarifying pan where it was heated and mixed with quicklime which bonded with undesired byproducts and floated to the top. Slaves standing over open-lid boiling pans endlessly skimmed the surface of the juice. They then used large ladles to transfer the thousands of gallons of clarified juice through two evaporating pans to reduce its water content. Finally, slaves scooped the condensed substance into the "strike" pan, where the cane juice transformed into granulated sugar. Since the levels of sucrose present in sugar cane decline quickly after cutting, continuous flow of production was a necessity, not merely an economic goal. Work was so unceasing that some slaves simply collapsed in a corner to sleep when they were relieved by the next shift. Long hours led to industrial accidents: so many slaves lost fingers, hands, and arms in the iron wheels of the cane-crushing mill that some estates kept an axe on hand to hack workers free of the machine.[16]

After cooling and initial air drying, the moist, yellowish-brown, partially granulated sugar (*mascabádo*) was packed into cone-shaped receptacles with a hole at the apex and hung on racks to drain off the "liquor." After two to three weeks of drainage, the artisan sugar master broke open the mold and carefully sliced the loaf into three grades: white at the top; yellow, or *quebrado*, in the middle; and wet brown stuff called *cucurucho* at the bottom. Each grade was then broken up, packed according to quality, and shipped. The two lower grades were further refined in the receiving country, while the white might be sold directly to consumers as "unrefined white" sugar.[17] Finally, molasses (otherwise known as *mieles finales*, or "syrups") that had drained out of the cones was sold abroad, typically to make rum.

In the minds of plantation reformers pushed into action by the 1840s crisis, the Jamaica train presented serious shortcomings. Although its purpose was to economize on firewood, cooking in open-air pans could take up to five hours per batch, still requiring a lot of fuel. In the steam-heated versions of the open-pan Jamaica train, a given amount of water heated into steam and piped under the pans could evaporate out only an equal amount of water from the cane juice. The vapor abstracted from the simmering cane juice, although full of heat energy, simply escaped into the air. Thus it was understood to be a "single-effect" device.

Jamaica train pans also damaged the sugar. While critics did not yet speak exactly in modern molecular terms, they were in the process of figuring out just how much of the sucrose in freshly milled cane juice was inadvertently converted into molasses by the slow pace and temperature imprecision of the Jamaica train process. Among many others, Hispanic chemist José Luis Casaseca had begun performing laboratory analyses in the 1840s to measure the quantities of crystallizable sugar lost to the imperfections of the colonial process of making sugar. The long cooking times of Jamaica trains squandered resources while "destroying the grain, burning the sugar, and converting it into syrups," as sugar industry observer Ramón de la Sagra put it.[18] If the heat was lowered, and the processing times shortened, Sagra promised, less invert sugar would be produced. And, Casaseca observed, "the better will be the color and quality of the sugar obtained."[19] Planter and author Justo Germán Cantero got to the point: "Sugar-mills were established primarily with the goal of manufacturing purged white sugar" that would not need further refining in consuming countries. However, due to "the difficulty of obtaining in our Jamaica trains white sugar that can compete with those using European refining procedures," many mills had fallen back to making the lower-value brown byproducts.[20] Of each cone of sugar made by Jamaica train technology, only about five percent was high-value "plantation white."[21] Sugar inversion was a serious economic problem, another planter concluded, because "molasses rarely sells for more than one third of the price of sugar per pound" as purged sugar (fully drained white or *quebrado*).[22]

For sugar experts like Louisiana planter Judah Benjamin, white sugar was "natural." Molasses, on the other hand, "far from being naturally an element of the juice, is in reality manufactured by our imperfect process."[23] Industrial food processing peeled off excess layers and liberated the true essence of the sugar cane. If carried out prudently, the manufacturing process left a batch of dry, white sugar, denuded of other nutritional elements. The judicious application of technology promised to emancipate white crystals from the "colored" byproducts clinging to them. When it came to sugar making, then, whiteness was two things at once: an enlightened escape from Nature through science, and the embodiment of Nature itself.

Reformers' criticism of the Jamaica train was probably fueled by the "Africanization scare" that followed La Escalera. Many policymakers of the 1840s came to fear the demographic takeover of Cuban society by blacks and people of color. "The sudden minority status of the white population became a source of concern to colonial authorities," historian Louis Perez explains, leading to "systematic policies designed to encourage white immigration to the island." Creole planters even sought external protection: the elite-run *Club de la Habana* conspired with US citizens to annex Cuba to the more robust pro-slavery republic in the 1840s.[24] Encouraging white colonization from Europe and even looking forward ambivalently to the end of the slave trade for demographic reasons, proponents of racial "balance" feared a loss of political control within plantations that could leak outward to the island as a whole. They subtly raised the specter of colonial inversion, finding common ground with experts anxiously pursuing whiteness in the sugar mill.

For many observers, then, the Jamaica train embodied broader anxieties of colonial sugar production particular to the Caribbean setting. This fear led a large group of elite planters to import the latest technologies developed in Europe's beet-sugar refineries. Through a lengthy process of plantation experimentation, however, they discovered that the island's exceptional conditions made the haphazard, wholesale importation of European technology untenable. The Industrial Revolution in European sugar refining therefore needed to be creolized. A mere thirty years after the Jamaica train had become popular across the island, the process of making it obsolete was well advanced.

Making an Ecological Machine

The Derosne system, which was first introduced in 1842 and began to replace Jamaica trains on elite Cuban estates, allowed for cutting more acres of cane on more sprawling estates. Since it used steam to heat the juice as well as drive the engines, the new vacuum-sealed Derosne devices were prodigious consumers of water. The expansion of acreage on individual plantations, meanwhile, required larger holdings of draft animals to move cane from field to mill, as well as expanded workforces of slaves to cultivate and harvest the crop.

The precise temperature control of the new system of sugar processing had made water supplies essential. Unlike the furnaces used in the Jamaica train, the Derosne devices heated the sugar indirectly. Steam boilers located at a safe remove from the sugar funneled heat through pipes either underneath or within the body of the juice. The fire (maintained by slave firemen) that created the steam in the boilers ran continuously through the grinding season and consumed as much as 200,000 gallons of water per day on some *ingenios*.[25] Some of the estates with Derosne systems had eight boilers or more, necessitating large supplies of water. The reservoir of Ingenio Santa Susana of Cienfuegos, for example, which drew water from several brooks and creeks, stretched for two miles.[26]

Slaves built and maintained complicated systems of water supply on the major plantations. In Trinidad, slaves of the Ingenio Güinia dammed a pond and installed pipes leading up into the boiling house. This set-up supplied "water needed by the machinery, the draining house, and other dependencies."[27] Situated along a river that powered "a great number of rice and corn mills," the property of well-known Güines planter Joaquin de Ayestarán had one of the island's few water-powered sugar mills. It was fed by a long aqueduct made of stone.[28] Ingenio Santa Rosa, belonging to planter and railroad magnate Domingo de Aldama, also had a large dam, which was connected to the boilers by an aqueduct about 600 feet long. On the Ingenio Trinidad in Matanzas, meanwhile, an aqueduct brought "potable water from a spring . . . to a principal reservoir located at the highest point of the property, and from there . . . distributed in various branches that supply all of the workshops and establishments of the farm with water."[29]

Grinding mills also went through a rapid technological transformation in the 1840s and 1850s. Although they had been vertically aligned for centuries, the grinding cylinders of the mills were turned sideways to link more simply with the motion of a horizontal steam engine's piston. The arrangement of the cylinders allowed for the canes to be crushed twice, yielding as much as 25 percent more juice from the plants. Steam engines, unlike draft animals, applied consistent torque to the cylinders, an innovation that also improved yields. The slowness of the mill's turn allowed the juice to drip down before being pressed back into the canes from which it had just been squeezed. Because they were relatively cheap and easily repaired by British or US machinists resident on the island, the steam engines were far more widely adopted than the Derosne systems. Whereas in 1846, only 18 percent of grinding mills were steam driven, in 1860 the percentage was 69.5 percent.[30]

Primarily designed to turn the heavy iron cylinders waiting at the end of the conveyor belt to crush the cane, the sugar-mill engine was in many cases tasked with moving water as well. For example, the Fawcett-Preston steam engine, common on larger estates, drove a water pump that sucked up a local reservoir to supply the steam boilers, as well as the rest of the farm, with the water it needed.[31] On Julián de Zulueta's *ingenio*, one of the "best and biggest" masonry dams on the island held a large stock of water that could also be pumped to various parts of his estate by the power of the mill's steam engine.[32] Since the steam engine bringing water to the boilers was itself powered by that water, the steam engine consumed coal to keep itself supplied with water, a double-effect cycle that was adopted in the Greater Caribbean to save scarce resources.

The water was pumped from the reservoirs into the steam boilers, which in the Derosne system were typically located outside the sugar-boiling house. Fire tubes inside the boiler quickly heated the hundreds of gallons of water and created high-pressure steam. Then a network of pipes and valves eased the pressurized steam into the mill engines as well as the vacuum pans.[33]

Plantation experts were rarely awestruck by the operations of individual machines and instead concerned themselves with how the heterogeneous elements of a multistage process might be fused into what Casaseca reverently called a "*sistema completo*."[34] He was most taken by "the wisely combined linkages among all parts of the apparatus." Even though the most basic approaches to sugar processing appeared to have an assembly line quality, the "immense ductwork that crossed the space in all directions," as Sagra admiringly put it, presented a very different appearance from what had come before.[35] Casaseca declared himself a proponent of Derosne over competing vacuum pan inventors because Derosne's "entire system functions as if it were a single and unique apparatus, that receives sugarcane and puts out sugar at the point of crystallization, without nuisance, without uncertainty, and without anxiety." With timing always of importance, the completeness of the system would also "ensure punctuality in execution, exclude all fear of delay, and avoid all accident."[36] In particular, new connecting mechanisms between different phases of the production line led to new efficiencies.

Instead of the juice dripping into the first pan by the force of gravity, or being scooped by slaves using large ladles, each Derosne system was equipped with a "*sube-guarapo*," or automated juice lifter, also dependent upon the steam issuing from the boilers. An operative opened a valve that admitted pressurized steam into the cane-juice receptacle underneath the grinding cylinders and forced the juice upward to the clarifying pans. With high-pressure steam driving the mill engine and pushing the juice from point to point, and low-pressure air in the vacuum pans accelerating the condensation of the juice, the Derosne train operated through the manipulation and channeling of opposing pressures.

The Derosne system embodied contemporaneous transformations in European science. By the 1830s and 1840s, the steam engine—explosive, consumptive, and entropic—had become a master metaphor for how nature, society, and economics functioned, replacing the Enlightenment-era metaphor of a "cosmic balance."[37] Perhaps no thinker better illustrated this shift than the French engineer Sadi Carnot. Like breezes blowing from ocean to land to power coastal windmills, Carnot reflected, "only the existence of a difference of temperatures allows the production of 'moving power.'"[38] For Enlightenment thinkers, "natural" meant stable and balanced. For mid-nineteenth-century thinkers like Carnot, equilibrium was the enemy, since a system in balance was powerless. Recognition of disequilibrium as a constant in nature and as a necessity in production led to "a much more general concern with progression, with directionality and development in time, with the 'universal law of decay.'"[39] Disequilibrium was recast as simultaneously productive and destructive, because every moment of work performed was also a moment of energy consumed and forever unrecoverable. The European version of the Derosne system was part of the engineering world that gave rise to these new philosophical reflections. The Greater Caribbean setting defined by racial difference, tropicality, island resource limitations, and a semiperipheral economic position intensified the new concerns, and pushed the Derosne design in new directions.

After a steam-heated quicklime clarification, the juice was released down to the top of a hulking row of cylindrical iron tanks. At least six feet tall by five feet in diameter, but sometimes much taller, the Dumont filters subjected the juice to a further stage of cleaning for making white sugar. Although not made by Derosne, the filters were conceived of as integral parts of a "*tren completo*" in the Derosne system. Each was filled with roughly a ton of "bone char" made from pulverized and roasted animal bones. When the clarified cane juice flowed slowly through the bone matter, sugar's "coloring matter" was left behind. The filters also absorbed any excess quicklime, a substance that imparted undesirable color to the final product.[40] Judah Benjamin claimed that the invention of the filters was more important in the history of sugar making than vacuum-pan technology.[41] "Bone char filters are the soul of good fabrication," Casaseca agreed.[42]

While some planters clearly saw large-scale filtration as indispensable to the project of competing with metropolitan-refined sugar, supplies of the bone char, a byproduct of the foreign meat-packing industry, were not easily obtained in the Caribbean. In Europe, Dumont filtration was cheap, simple, and effective, but some observers noted that tropical plantations often obtained inferior bone char from Europe or simply kept reusing a single batch to avoid the expense of importing more. With four large filters, for example, Wenceslao de Villa Urrutia's *ingenio* required almost 9,000 pounds of bone char per day. Since he imported his bone char from France, Villa Urrutia calculated that he would spend 3,398 pesos on this auxiliary substance alone to make 5,000 boxes of sugar in a season.[43] Thus some recommended replacing bone char "with something more appropriate to our needs and our local conditions."[44]

Benjamin and others claimed that high-tech filtration could be made affordable in the plantation context by recycling the bone char through a new process called revivification. In preparation for reuse, the filtering medium was first heated in large ovens, then power washed with diluted acid to remove the sticky brown molasses. Some large estates used Cail's patented "screw washer," which squeezed the particles of coal against the sides of a tub while washing them with water and acid. This process re-pulverized the coal, separated the molasses from it, and filtered out the two materials.[45] The acids also burned new pores in the carbon, which had become clogged during the filtration process. To further economize on resources, planter Juan Poey's carbon washers were hitched to the Derosne condensers, using the hot water that had evaporated out of the cane juice to wash the char and linking the machines together in ways their original inventors may not have envisioned. Poey reported that, of the many filters in his boiling house, two had to be cleaned out and refilled every day. Keeping enough filters in rotation required three revitalization ovens and 5,000 pounds of bone char.[46]

Recycling bone char was such a labor-and energy-intensive process that it sometimes occupied the majority of workers in the boiling house. While tending the fires, slaves heaved several tons of bone char in and out of the ovens, into wagons, and up to the top of the filters, often aided only by shovels and handcarts.[47] With the largest operations utilizing as much as 400,000 pounds of bone char per season, however, some of the recycling operations had begun to be automated as well.[48] In the Ingenio San Martín, which had eight bone char ovens and four washers, a vertical conveyor belt (buckets attached to a loop of chain), most likely driven by one of the mill's steam engines, automatically refilled the filters "without manual labor."[49] On the Ingenio Santa Susana in Cienfuegos the revivifying system also had chain buckets to lift the bone char to the top of the filters. With a long line of thirty Dumont filters, and twenty-four centrifuge bowls, this *ingenio* was designed for the mass production and rapid flow of unrefined white sugar.[50]

In the process of filtration and revivification, combined manual and machine labor moved the bone char from the filters to the ovens, to the washers, into the receptacles, and back into the filters. In the moment of filtration, the carbon's loop intersected with the interdependent and intertwining circuit of sugar; in the moment of revivification it interacted with the steam (see Figure 1-2). The automated loops of water, sugar, steam, and fuel, while adopting much from European engineering firms, took on new urgency when

FIGURE 1-2 Working the carbon loop. In order to maintain thorough filtration, slaves moved the spent bone black from the filters (center), to the ovens (right), into receptacles (foreground), and back up to the tops of the filters. This sugar mill also used Rillieux's horizontal tube, triple-effect vacuum pans, which can be seen at top center.

Justo Germán Cantero, "Casa de Calderas del Ingenio Asuncion," in *Los ingenios: Colección de vistas de los principales ingenios de azúcar de la Isla de Cuba* (Havana, Cuba: 1857), Luis Miguel García Mora and Antonio Santamaría García, eds. (Madrid: Editorial CSIC, 2005).

natural resources were finite, and shortages internal to the firm. Hence evolved the imperative not to waste "even an atom of steam," as Cantero wrote.[51] The prodigious consumption and disposal of raw materials was one key characteristic of Europe's Industrial Revolution that could not be exported to the colonial setting. Instead, plantation experts engineered a double-effect system geared around reuse.[52] Railroad companies appear to have adopted a similar pneumatic logic as the industrializing sugar mill whose product they carried. Cuba's Western Railroad Company wanted to expand their lines so that "not a single atom of the production of the region escapes. . . ."[53]

Although broken down into discrete stages of production, the sugar-making system must be conceived ultimately as a single entity. Ratios of pace and scale required harmonizing. On the Ingenio Santa Rosa, Domingo de Aldama had twelve clarifiers of 400-gallon capacity, which could purify 4,800 gallons of juice simultaneously. To keep pace with the considerable flow of juice moving through the mill and the clarifying pans, Aldama installed sixteen filters that each contained 10,000 pounds of bone black, as well as twelve Derosne condensers, two vacuum pans, and six English centrifuges, which power dried the granulated sugar. Gas illumination enabled twenty-four-hour a day operation, which meant unceasing toil for the 300 slaves, thirty Chinese men, and twelve white operatives who handled the harvest season.[54]

The Double Effect: Sugar Processing in French

After thorough filtration, the cleansed cane juice passed to a fully sealed vacuum pan. The concept was simple: boiling occurs when there is enough energy in the body of a liquid for the molecules to overcome the atmospheric pressure that holds them in place. The lower the atmospheric pressure around the fluid, the less energy is required for the molecules to escape into the air. First coming into wide use in the 1830s, steam-powered vacuum pumps designed for the beet-sugar industry in Europe drew the air out of a sealed chamber, allowing cane juice to reach boiling point at as low as 130°F, whereas in open air the juice had to be raised to 235 or 240°. Under a vacuum, the watery constituents of cane juice departed the mixture rapidly.[55]

While European sugar-beet refiners used vacuum technology because it allowed for more precise control of cooking temperatures to minimize inversion, it was even more useful in Cuba. Tropical heat, humidity, and the nature of the cane plant itself (cane juice, it was said, was denser than beet-sugar juice at the same temperatures and therefore required more energy to boil) made inversion all the more likely. Wealthy Cuban planters' investments in vacuum-pan technology were also driven by the savings in fuel and water. Since the chemical and environmental pressures on planters were thought to be so different in the sugar islands from those in European beet refineries, the imported machines required significant tweaks. As Casaseca concluded, regarding one of Derosne's competitors, "if we are speaking of a European refinery in a locality blessed with abundant water, the preference goes to the improved Roth apparatus."[56] The water usage, however, made Roth's machine a bad fit for Cuba. Derosne competed with other European manufacturers to supply the cane-sugar archipelago with new technologies, and he prevailed because his travels made him more familiar with plantation experts' conception of their own tropical requirements.

The future head of Havana's Instituto de Investigaciones Químicas, Jose Luis Casaseca, thought he was inaugurating attempts to replace the Jamaica train when he toured European refineries in 1842 in hopes of bringing back the best technologies. In his zeal to redeem those he viewed as backward Caribbean sugar planters, however, he overlooked experimental efforts already being conducted on the island. Cárdenas landowner Wenceslao Villa Urrutia found it "difficult to explain" how Casaseca was unaware of the fact that he had already used the Derosne apparatus for two successive seasons and that Derosne himself had even been a guest on Villa Urrutia's plantation, "personally directing the experimental first run of his system." Showcasing his own far-reaching connections, Villa Urrutia also pointed out that "Mr. Derosne who three months before was here in Havana" overlapped with Casaseca in Paris, though the chemist had "failed to confer" with the well-known French manufacturer. Villa Urrutia called for Casaseca to return to the island in order to "study on the land the real inconveniences or difficulties that the adoption of the Derosne trains may present."[57] Demanding immersion in the racial-mechanical system of the Cuban plantation, Villa Urrutia implied that witnessing a machine's operation in a Parisian refinery, as Casaseca had recently done, missed the point.

Villa Urrutia protested too much, however. How would he have learned of the Derosne apparatus without first looking abroad? Investigatory trips abroad were no less necessary than sustained experimentation at home. Planters and experts had been traveling throughout the Atlantic World to compile reports on the state of the art in sugar refining since the 1790s.[58] They imbibed new ideas from abroad, and refined them in a "thousand experiments" in Cuba's mid-century sugar mills, as Sagra put it.[59] Although the rhetoric of creole elites like Villa Urrutia was inflated, it was for a particular reason. They sought to use engineering and chemical expertise to forestall becoming peripheral in the world economy. At first trying to make white sugar cheaply and efficiently within the overarching Jamaica train system, they ended up remaking that system between 1840 and 1860.

Many planters in the early 1840s, increasingly aware of the limitations of their Jamaica trains, first chose to upgrade piecemeal instead of leaping fully into an unknown technological regime of steam and pneumatics. They imported beet-sugar vacuum pans that replaced the strike pan and continued to carry out the rest of the process in the Jamaican style. But hybrid systems were a waste of money, critics like Casaseca pointed out, because the damage was already done to the sugar by the time it reached the protective cover of the vacuum pan.[60] As many European men of science were grappling with the irreversibility of energy use in the natural and mechanical worlds, in the world of sugar it became clear that no technology was wondrous enough to synthesize broken-down sucrose molecules. Major Cuban boiling houses required, it turned out, a more cohesive, systematic approach to sugar processing—an innovative creolization of technology that kept a valuable product protected from the tropical elements.

As he transitioned from his post as a chemist in the French beet-sugar industry to fabricating machines especially for cane sugar, Charles Derosne worked in Cuba, Guadalupe, Martinique, and the east African island of Borbón, gradually gaining familiarity with a "global archipelago of sugar knowledge."[61] He and his partner Jean-François Cail altered their designs in response to data culled from tropical plantation experiments. Unlike machines made specifically for European sugar beets, Casaseca affirmed, the Derosne system is "applicable to our *ingenios*," both because of the completeness of the system, and its simplicity of operation—the latter a response to planters' concerns about the fitness of their labor force to deal with complex machinery.[62]

Derosne and Cail's brochure assured planters that their modernized, mechanized boiling train only "seems complicated at first." In fact, the French manufacturers pointed out, their design "facilitates operations, making them independent of the carelessness of the operatives; such that today the operative is subjected to the apparatus itself, which will keep him from the kind of errors that in the old system highlighted his incapacities." The Derosne train promised to reinforce slaves' subordination to the master with their subjection to the machine.[63] Wealthy planters, of course, had their own ideas about racial divisions of labor and skill. Just as Derosne apparatuses began to be incorporated into boiling-house designs in the early 1840s, elite planters who had made fortunes in the illegal slave trade began importing tens of thousands of Chinese laborers who many felt were better suited to high-technology machine operation. Like pure sugar or a perfect vacuum, a spatially segregated and racially orchestrated workforce was more of an ideal than a reality. Chinese workers were attainable only for wealthier planters, and in this time of slave trade suppression, planters cobbled together a workforce by whatever means necessary. However spurious and partial it was, though, racial knowledge comforted planters investing in costly and unfamiliar devices.

Sagra paid homage to the "free Asiatic laborer, intelligent, dexterous, active, and above all not prone to routinism, but on the contrary, to innovation."[64] Praising a particularly Chinese flexibility of mind, Sagra simultaneously likened their mental attitude to "the constant regularity of industrial operations submitted to the incessant strike of the piston, or the pressure of steam, or to the fixed grade of the thermometer." At one of Cuba's large boiling houses, Sagra watched "a double file of Chinese, rapid in their movements like a driving belt, carrying out the filling of the molds, with the mathematical regularity of the pendulum." [65] Perceived as machine-like themselves, Chinese workers were ideally suited to serve Derosne's machine.

These idealized "coolies," marching in lockstep to the thrum of the machines, existed primarily in Sagra's imagination. Attempting to shape their own working lives, indentured Asian laborers in Cuba lodged hundreds of formal complaints against planters and mobilized the support of a proactive Chinese Embassy in Havana.[66] Thus often viewed with ambivalence, they were also to be excluded from direct contact with the sugar by the complete Derosne system. In one 1857 engraving of a Derosne apparatus in operation, a pigtailed operative stands on tiptoe to peer through a glass eyepiece into the interior of the vacuum pan to read its internal instruments[67] (Figure 1-3). An obligatory flourish in sterotyped portrayals of Chinese men, the hairstyle suggests the worker was a "coolie." Protected by thick layers of copper, iron, and glass as it coursed through the mechanism, the viscous sugar was buffered both from black and Asian workers in the boiling house. Vacuum-pan designs thus promised a sanitized space of pure, transparent whiteness at the center of the "colored" world of the tropical plantation.[68]

The idea of cutting off operatives from direct interaction with fragile sucrose intruded into other aspects of contemporary production as well. Casaseca emphasized how the new technology led to "the suppression of all hand transport."[69] Derosne processing began with slaves dumping the cane from oxen-pulled wagons onto a conveyor belt, a first step that made it quicker for the cane loaders to drag their empty wagons back into the fields.

FIGURE 1-3 Stereotyped portrayal of a "coolie" in intimate association with the machine, peering into the eyepiece to read the instruments inside the vacuum pan.

Detail, Justo Germán Cantero, "Casa de Caldera del Ingenio Sta. Rosa," in *Los ingenios: colección de vistas de los principales ingenios de azúcar de la Isla de Cuba* (Havana: 1857), Luis Miguel García Mora and Antonio Santamaría García, eds. (Madrid: Editorial CSIC, 2005).

At the Ingenio San Martin in Cárdenas, for example, the conveyor belt bringing the cane into the grinding mill was eighty feet long.[70] The long feeding mechanism also vibrated the individual canes into flat, even rows, as opposed to their entering the grinding wheels stacked one upon the other.[71] Creolizing experts homed in on continuous, regular, and proportioned distribution of materials through the system, as well as a neat disaggregation of slave and machine (Figure 1-4).

While lengthy conveyor belts prevented limbs being drawn into the mill and crushed, black workers were still driven to exhaustion through longer hours and intensified physical labor in the canefields. For sugar-mill improvers like Sagra, "*los negros*" belonged in the fields.[72] As he put it, although improvers have already initiated "reforms that require perfected instruments, machines, and above all care and reasoning on the part of workers, it was not possible to hope for these qualities from workers brutalized by a system

FIGURE 1-4 The conveyor belts in the background spatially separated field from factory, distancing slaves from the machinery of the boiling house.

Detail from Justo Germán Cantero, "Casa de Calderas del Ingenio San Martin," in *Los ingenios: Colección de vistas de los principales ingenios de azúcar de la Isla de Cuba* (Havana, Cuba: 1857), Luis Miguel García Mora and Antonio Santamaría García, eds. (Madrid: Editorial CSIC, 2005).

that completely eliminated the intelligence of the operative, so that muscular power predominated exclusively in them."[73] In other words, mechanization demanded precisely the skills of care and reasoning that slaveholders had eliminated.[74] The conveyor belt marked the boundary between the canefields (extensive spaces of force, violence, and consumption), and the boiling house (an intensive space of dexterity, continuousness, and efficiency), facilitating the arrangement of a racially segmented workforce around these spaces. The conveyor belt hitched the gentleness and subtlety of the Derosne system to the terror of the canefields; the creative reuse of materials with the prodigious consumption of people. These were the twin faces of a single process of production, each enabling and urging the other to refine the subtlety of its machinations, and its technologies of enclosure and flow (Figure 1-5).

FIGURE 1-5 Enslaved workers swimming in cane. The endless rows of clarifiers, filters, and vacuum pans were necessary to process the cane rapidly losing its sucrose content. The image merely hints at the coercion in the fields that brought mountains of cane to the doorstep of the boiling house, revealing how violence is often abstracted, but not reduced, by technical innovation.

Detail from "Ingenio Flor de Cuba," in Justo Germán Cantero, *Los ingenios: Colección de vistas de los principales ingenios de azúcar de la Isla de Cuba* (Havana, Cuba: 1857), Luis Miguel García Mora and Antonio Santamaría García, eds. (Madrid: Editorial CSIC, 2005).

Classical economists like Adam Smith and David Ricardo had understood that machines facilitated a division of labor that "led to increases in productivity due to increases in dexterity, saving of time, and stimulation of invention." Their idea of a machine-led division of labor, however, remained rather general. As machinery became an increasingly common element in European production in the 1830s, writers like the Englishman Charles Babbage began to argue that machinery "separates skill from brute force in order that the manufacturer does not have to pay for both simultaneously. And it picks out for increased specialization those tasks which require higher skill and smaller time, so as to optimize the ratio of a few highly paid workers and managers to the many lower paid ones." His razor-thin accounting of different levels of labor "applies to the entire hierarchy, to machines as to human laborers and mental as to physical labor, requiring that the numbers and kinds of all sources be allocated so as to minimize cost of production."[75] Plantation experts likewise redesigned the Derosne system with clear if spurious racial ideas of skill level and cost allocation in mind.

The Derosne system necessitated a new spatial organization oriented along the lines of a novel racial division of labor in Cuba. Each level of a carefully segmented racial hierarchy of labor was connected to a given sector of 9000-acre sugar plantations: Anglo machinists, white creole overseers and sugar masters, Chinese skilled laborers, and an internally divided population of enslaved workers, with Cuban-born operatives often placed in skilled positions, and African-born *bozales* left to cut the cane. Continued dependence on skilled slaves shows the internal contradictions within the sugar mill's overarching racial order. Nevertheless, planters, chemists, and engineers took the differential endowments of the races seriously.

Sometimes this racial division of labor was quite finely tuned: Judah Benjamin said that only "white persons" should be trusted to work the latest machinery. But he went on to say that "the Negroes too, who are employed in the sugar-house, require some instructions in the different processes of defecation, filtration, revivification of the bone black, etc."[76] Slaves were removed from the heart of the system, but put to work around its fringes. The experts who engineered Cuba's second sugar boom thus fixed a civilizational ladder to the *ingenio*'s different parts. Racial hierarchies infused supposedly technocratic innovations, as planter-industrialists, chemists, and engineers refined biologically ordered divisions of labor inherited from the Atlantic slave trade amid Europe's global age of empire.[77]

Sugar Processing in Caribbean Creole: The Triple Effect

The final phase in evaporating the sugar took place in Derosne's "serpentine condenser." The cane juice left the Dumont filters, and was carried by another pump to the top of this device. Pressure pushed the juice through a pipe with a multitude of perforations, which sprayed the juice in small particles down onto parallel rows of copper pipes. Just before this process commenced, an operative opened another valve, sending the water vapor drawn out of the previous batch of juice into the serpentine tubes.[78] The juice, spread in small particles over the surface of the steam-heated tubes, quickly evaporated. The further-condensed juice dripped down to a receptacle, one step closer to complete processing. The steam inside the pipes, after passing its own heat to the cane juice, condensed into liquid water. A water pump powered by the mill engine then carried the water back to the boilers for reuse in producing steam for the engine (see Figure 1-6, center-right, middleground).

The serpentine design used the cane juice's water content to evaporate remaining water content, thereby halving the fuel needed to create granulated sugar. The Derosne serpentine apparatus was called a condenser because of how the steam served the juice, and the mutual impact of the steam on the sugar and the sugar on the steam was known as the "double effect." Sugar was thus both the medium and the outcome of the production process, a concept which embodied developments in post-Enlightenment physics.

Among his other well-known discoveries, the French engineer Sadi Carnot did away with the eighteenth-century idea that a special substance known as "caloric" was being consumed as power was generated inside a steam engine. Instead, he insisted that the motive force of the piston "depends solely upon the temperature differential between source and sink, and not upon the nature of the working substance heated and cooled."[79] Analogous to an emergent concept of the circulation of value in a capitalist economy, work (in Carnot's metaphorical steam engine) was not the special property of a unique substance. It was simply energy moving through a system and manifesting itself in different forms. This is precisely the logic of the Derosne system, designed so that steam or precious sugar could be the "working substance," as long as a dry, crystalline sweetness was the end result of the process. This turned out to be the main problem with the original serpentine condenser.[80]

The continual process of experimentation in Cuba's plantation laboratories had given rise to doubts about the appropriateness of Derosne's serpentine design for the Caribbean context. Sagra complained in 1860 that the serpentine condensers, while promising greater enclosure, still exposed sugar to open air, as well as overheating the juice—the two main factors experts thought responsible for the breakdown of sucrose. The owners of the particular *ingenio* that inspired these critical observations promised that they would soon be phasing out the serpentine condensers.[81] Benjamin held similar misgivings. The Derosne system, he wrote, caused liquid sugar to be "exposed to the open air in a state of minute subdivision as it falls in a cascade over the frame of pipes which form the condenser."[82] European designs failed sufficiently to account for the effects of tropical heat. Also, the horizontal rows of steam pipes were likely to be knocked out of square at some point, and this misalignment was very hard to fix. If the pipes were not level, the juice tended to collect in the corners and invert by being exposed to the heating surface for too long. Once its unceasing and carefully calibrated flow had been interrupted, cane juice turned bitter. Most importantly, the Derosne double effect still lost all of the steam evaporating out of the juice while it dripped down the surface of the serpentine tubes. Cuban plantation experts, hoping to avoid the climatically induced breakdown of whiteness into less valuable brownness, condemned a system that both wasted water and put the frail substance of sugar at risk.

The search for alternatives to the original serpentine condenser had begun as early as 1847, when José Maria de la Torre, a professor at the University of Havana, traveled abroad to learn about global advances in agricultural, industrial, and commercial techniques.[83] Torre was particularly interested in collecting information on the Rillieux vacuum pan in Louisiana.[84] As a Paris-educated engineer who came of age in Louisiana sugar country, free man of color Norbert Rillieux possessed knowledge both of the subtropical particularities of cane sugar and the latest developments in French beet-sugar technology. Instead of keeping the vacuum pans and serpentine condenser separate as in the Derosne system, Rillieux combined the two by enclosing the serpentine tubes inside a vacuum-sealed vessel. While Derosne's serpentine condenser released the water vapor from the juice into the air, Rillieux's model conserved the steam and pumped it into the tubes of the next pan to further condense the juice. By reharnessing the waste steam a third time, Rillieux's system produced a "triple effect." With the improvements made by the New Orleans engineer, Cantero effused, "the system does not lose even an atom of steam."[85] The Rillieux system also more securely enclosed the sugar. The juice is "evaporated in a close pan, and is excluded from atmospheric action," Benjamin explained.[86]

Unlike the Derosne machines, first invented for the European beet industry and exported by their French manufacturers, Rillieux's apparatus originated in the Greater Caribbean cane-sugar world and found its way back to Europe by surreptitious means. A German employee of the Philadelphia manufacturers Merrick & Towne copied Rillieux's drawings and smuggled them to Magdeburg, Germany. After Derosne died in 1846, his partner Jean-François Cail got hold of the papers. On his many trips to the Caribbean, Cail also witnessed the advantages of Rillieux's approach and adapted them into his own model. A year after he received the purloined sketches, Cail was granted a patent in France with drawings that looked suspiciously like those in Rillieux's second patent.[87] By 1852, Cail had built a triple-effect evaporator in Europe for the first time, where it had to be readapted back to function with beet sugar.[88] Thus the technology had to be reverse-creolized to function in the peculiarities of the European climate.[89] The two men must have resolved their differences, because Cail eventually partnered with Rillieux, installing Rillieux triple-effect vacuum pans on a variety of plantations in Cuba and Louisiana.[90]

Elites possessed the wealth and collateral to hedge their bets by installing multiple models. As of 1857, slave merchant and coolie trader Julián de Zulueta had three generations of steam condensers in his boiling house at the same time. While Zulueta still had fourteen Derosne serpentine condensers, he had also purchased an updated vertical tube condenser and finally a brand-new set of three fully enclosed steam-tube triple-effect pans[91] (Figure 1-6). The newest was the latest "Derosne" model, manufactured by Cail, incorporating Rillieux's latest improvements, and fully hybridized for the Cuban setting.

Instead of Derosne's old lineup of one or two vacuum pans followed by a serpentine condenser, the new "Derosne" apparatus used a three-vessel vertical tube system that borrowed heavily from Rillieux's concept of total enclosure while also improving on it. The condensation process was divided into multiple pans to keep the juice flowing from the mill into protected, airless spaces, as opposed to fermenting in an open-air tank. Juice was admitted into the first tank until it had entirely submerged the set of tubes, while waste steam from the mill engine was admitted into the tubes themselves. After the juice had been quickly brought to a boil in this low-pressure environment, the evaporated steam from the juice passed out the top of the first vessel, through a pipe, and into the upright tubes of vessel number two. The juice, now slightly condensed, passed out the bottom of the first vessel and into the second vessel, bubbling up until it submerged the steam-filled tubes. The

FIGURE 1-6 A sense of scale and spatial organization. Following the sugar from beginning to end of the manufacturing process, from left to right: the piles of unground cane, as well as the upper parts of the steam-powered grinding mill; the rows of clarifying pans on the highest deck; the Dumont filters; the row of Derosne serpentine condensers, linked up to spherical vacuum "strike pans," which are being drained of crystallized raw sugar; the drainage racks and the centrifuges, which completed the separation of molasses from the sucrose crystals and yielded "plantation white" sugar. In the far background, ground level, are the furnaces that provided heat to the boilers, which themselves gave heat energy to the whole complex. Above and behind the serpentine condensers are Cail's new fully enclosed vertical-tube triple-effect condensers.

"Casa de Calderas del Ingenio Alava," from Justo Germán Cantero, *Los ingenios: Colección de vistas de los principales ingenios de azúcar de la Isla de Cuba* (Havana: 1857), Luis Miguel García Mora and Antonio Santamaría García, eds. (Madrid: Editorial CSIC, 2005).

tubes in the second vessel had two functions. While reheating the juice, they acted as condensing surfaces for the vapor that had evaporated out of vessel number one. The condensation of this vapor inside the tubes helped create the vacuum in the first vessel, obviating the need for a vacuum pump there. The vacuum pump acted directly only on the third vessel. The increasing strength of the vacuum from pans one, to two, to three suctioned the cane juice through its tubes. As the water vapor condensed, it passed its latent heat to the juice in the second vessel, bringing it to a boil.

The dynamic between the second and third pans was much the same as between the first and second; the only difference was that the vacuum was strongest in the third vessel and brought the sugary mass to the point of crystallization. Before passing to the final vessel, the condensed juice was removed from vessel number two and run through the Dumont filters a second time.[92]

After further condensation in the third vessel, granulated sugar, still in need of some draining and centrifugal action, was suctioned out an auxiliary pump often powered by the main vacuum pump.

The multiple effects of steam upon sugar and sugar upon steam were quite different in the "antique" serpentine model and the Derosne triple-effect of the late 1850s. Not only did the process remain insulated from the inversionary impacts of tropical air, but another loop in the cycle was also added. The basic sugar-making concept of the "triple-effect," rooted in Rillieux's insights and gradually improved upon by a collaborative network of plantation experts, became the state of the art in sugar mills until the early twentieth century.

This technology, not solely a French, English, or Cuban invention, underwent continuous editing in the global archipelago of sugar knowledge. While the earliest efforts to utilize any new technology amounted to transplanting European technologies to the Caribbean setting, experimenters quickly found that a uniqueness of climate, chemistry, labor system, and global economic position required adapting the machinery to its new environment. By the 1850s, plantation improvers had reinvented the apparatuses and found places for them in the upper tiers of Cuba's socioeconomic complex of sugar. In 1857, Cantero took stock of the improvements that had been made since the first experiments with the vacuum system. He disparaged the early condensers as "*los antiguos serpentines de* Derosne" a mere fifteen years after their introduction on the island.[93] With each rapidly emerging iteration, sugar technology became more deeply creolized.

An Industry Transformed?

In response to a multifaceted crisis that hobbled the first phase of Cuba's sugar boom in the late 1830s, planters, chemists, engineers, and the state invested large amounts of capital and time in the experimentalization of the Cuban sugar industry. The investments paid off for some. The advanced creolization of vacuum-based sugar-processing systems readied Cuba's top tier of sugar makers for boom years in the Atlantic economy of the 1850s. While in 1827 Cuban mills produced 74,380 tons of sugar, by 1861 they boxed 477,660 tons. The productivity per mill also jumped from an average of 74.4 tons per year to 328.8 annual tons.[94] Cuban plantations outpaced competitors in the eastern Caribbean, Brazil, South Asia, and the Pacific islands. While in 1820, Cuba accounted for 13.64 percent of the total world production of 402,425 metric tons of sugar, by 1850, Cuban planters, merchants, and officials could claim over one-quarter of a total world production that had itself more than doubled in the thirty intervening years.[95] The 1850s saw a more rapid expansion of export figures, which was premised partly on technological transformation, and partly on a profound reshaping of Cuba's workforce.

How important a role did the new technologies play in the expansion? Some planters, confident that their creole science had yielded a knowable sugar estate with reliable machines, constant harvesters, and careful managers, conducted experiments to test the contribution technology made. In 1843, in one of the first quantified runs of the new system, Villa Urrutia's enslaved workforce got 1.7 million pounds of cane to the mill, yielding 75 percent white sugar and 25 percent *quebrado*. It yielded 70 percent more total sugar (white, *quebrado,* and *cucurucho*) than in Villa Urrutia's best pre-Derosne harvest of 1835. This increase showed elite planters with access to large amounts of capital how much yield and quality potential lay in the new system, even before its creolization. By Villa Urrutia's calculations, an average *ingenio* with a Jamaica train would produce 3,500 boxes, while a modern mill equipped with vacuum pans would yield 5,000 boxes from the same quantity of cane by reducing the proportion of low-value muscovado and syrups. This change in proportions increased gross income from 54,727 pesos fuertes to 81,900. Including all of the additional expenses of installing, maintaining, and running the modern train, Villa Urrutia calculated that the modernizing planter would end the harvest with 15,676 pesos fuertes of additional capital each year.[96] But this option was within reach only of wealthy planters with mercantile or banking connections and sufficient collateral to purchase the heavy machinery. Moreover, Villa Urrutia very likely underestimated the costs of maintenance and breakdown of machines. How many planters bought into Villa Urrutia's optimistic accounting in the heady days of 1843, when planters were made dizzy both by the threat of another Haiti and the promise of Europe's Industrial Revolution transplanted to Cuba?

Jamaica trains still predominated in Cuba's total production in 1860. Sagra counted only fifty-one "complete modern trains" out of 1365 *ingenios* on the island (or 4 percent of the total). Islandwide statistics, however, conceal the technological situation in the most productive provinces. In Matanzas, 13 percent of *ingenios* used Derosne or Rillieux trains. In newer Colón, where the largest share of the island's sugar was produced in 1860, 25 percent of *ingenios* used the most advanced vacuum methods.[97] This top 4 percent of Cuba's total *ingenios* made 11.5 percent of total sugar; the other 88.5 percent was made in Jamaica trains. However, since the purged sugar made in Jamaica trains was only around 5 percent white, while modern trains yielded as much as 75 percent white sugar, I estimate that the Derosne and later models accounted for nearly two-thirds of Cuba's white sugar exports in 1860. And by value, it seems, white sugar brought in roughly half of Cuba's purged sugar earnings.[98] Derosne systems of some sort probably manufactured around two-thirds of that. The technological creolization that yielded these quantities of plantation white helped a new merchant-planter elite to penetrate mostly British markets for finished goods. More importantly, given that the higher profits were monopolized by elite merchant-planters with maritime, financial, transport, and agricultural connections, the large-scale production of European-quality white sugar opened up by the Derosne system encouraged the broader transformation of Cuba's infrastructure and labor allocation.

When it came to sugar technology, Cuban sugar chemist Carlos Moissant concluded in 1861, "there is not a single European method that can be used here just as it was where it was invented."[99] Moissant grounded his axiom on two decades of experience in Cuba's plantation laboratories, where the creolization of Europe's Industrial Revolution was advancing rapidly, if only at strategic spots. The creolized sugar-mill models of nineteenth-century Cuba were microcosms and local expressions of a global reconceptualization of political economy taking its cue from the machine. From the bubbling tubes of Rillieux's throughput mechanisms, the imperative of enclosure and grading moved out to the level of the plantation, to Cuba's transport system, and the economic geography of the Atlantic World as a whole. At each of these spatial scales, race, climate, and counterinsurgency guided plantation experts' vision of reform.

El Principio Sacarino

PURITY, EQUILIBRIUM, AND WHITENESS
IN THE SUGAR MILL

SUGAR MANUFACTURING WAS in many ways different from other forms of nineteenth-century food processing. In coffee culture and winemaking, producers essentially tried to build up a variety of molecules to create a layered smell and taste. Sugar, by contrast, is one-dimensional and breaks down quickly. The brain experiences this breakdown as "sweet." Thus the urgent tempo of sugar production carried through to a sugar crystal's fleeting moment on the tongue of a factory hand in London or a midwife in Massachusetts.

The ease and quickness with which sucrose broke down, while constituting its sweetness, also made the product difficult to preserve. Makers of sugar sought to isolate one kind of simple molecule, removing the water content, plant material, and trace minerals from the cane juice before inversion began. But the very act of cutting down, juicing, and boiling the cane exposed the vulnerable sucrose to destruction. Greater Caribbean plantation experiments were aimed at figuring out what exactly caused this destruction and how to isolate the sucrose without the agents of destruction having their way.

This chapter looks at how the 1830s discovery of "ferments" (soon to be renamed enzymes) in organic chemistry transformed sugar experts' understanding of inversion. The concept of ferments compelled sugar experts to reimagine the tropical plantation boiling pan as teeming with microorganismic life, some of it threatening, some of it useful. The imperative to channel useful forms of organic energy, while suppressing threatening ones, led to a new way of understanding sugar production and labor control in the plantation environment.[1]

The more they studied cane sugar's behavior with new instruments of analysis, the more sugar chemists came to grips with its vulnerability to rapid change. Lacking an established molecular vocabulary, mid-nineteenth-century experimenters struggled for words that could capture sugar's puzzling vulnerability. North American chemist Richard Sears McCulloh, for example, described cane sugar as a curious compound "whose elements seem to be held together by chemical forces of very feeble intensity, so that very slight causes are sufficient to alter its nature and change it into entirely different bodies."[2] Contending with the volatility of the cane plant's sweet essence made clarifying cane sugar more difficult than isolating iron from ore, for example, and even distinguished it from the closely related European industry of sugar-beet refining. Hence, tropical sugar chemists spoke of *el principio sacarino*, the saccharine principle, a phrase meant to indicate the exceptional climatic, chemical, and racial nature of the Caribbean sugar mill.

In response to emerging microbial awareness, deeper studies of inversion, and the resource limitations of plantation production, Greater Caribbean sugar experts developed a new preoccupation with quantifying and targeting waste. As one observer remarked of open-pan manufacturing, "the loss to the planter exceeds belief" and, while a Jamaica train yielded only 5 percent white crystals, "the sugarcane treated with care in the laboratory of the chemist yields 18 percent of its weight in pure sugar."[3] John Scoffern similarly wondered at the losses. He wrote, "if the reader were to be told of the existence of a manufacture" in which the removal of impurities destroyed 66 percent of the desired product, "his credulity would be largely drawn upon."[4] Experts' programs for saving the sugar complex demanded that every crystal of sucrose, every atom of steam, and every minute of work be captured, utilized, recaptured, and used again. Reformers feeling short on resources and labor rigorously suppressed any expenditures of energy not directly related to the production of sugar, especially after the Escalera backlash of 1844 (see Chapter 1, "A Creole Industrial Revolution in the Cuban Sugar Mill").

Adopting but inverting the concepts of a nineteenth-century vitalist chemistry that posited an ineffable "life-force" driving all organic phenomena, sugar experts cultivated an attitude of what I call "plantation vitalism." Fermentation, which broke down sucrose, was conceptualized as the poorly governed motion of disobedient life, while sucrose was defined as salutary chemical immobility. Sucrose was also found to be pH-neutral, inorganic, and in static equilibrium. In the midst of the animal-human-plant complex on the plantation, then, lay a stable and lifeless core of whiteness whose surgical extraction was the only purpose of the system.

Precisely because the chemical complexity of sugar processing felt new, and because vocabularies of organic chemistry were still in flux, sugar experts adopted a ready-made set of concepts from the Greater Caribbean. Racial blackness and its biological particularities came to be used as the overarching model for mid-nineteenth-century sugar chemistry's understanding of microscopic life in the boiling pan.[5] Twin concerns about the preservation of white sugar and the perpetuation of white racial security generated new notions of a frail but primordial whiteness indelibly linked to a derivative but inevitable blackness. This new *principio sacarino* linked racial-spatial order and sugar chemistry, redefining both in the process.

In their new microscopic preoccupation with singling out the causes of inversion, sugar experts also cultivated a new definition of sugar itself. They overthrew the long-standing mercantilist concept of sugars as a loose clump of qualitatively distinct substances. They sought to replace the "unscientific" customary notions of sugar, molasses, sirop, *jarabe*, and *muscovado* as qualitatively unique essences with a "scientific" notion: they were all sucrose mixed in different proportions with water, minerals, and invert sugar. In spite of having different political ends, two groups of experts arrived at the notion of a unitary *principio sacarino* by the 1850s.

On one side stood experts like José Luis Casaseca concerned with Cuba making plentiful white sugar and keeping manufacturing profits on the island, rather than losing them to refiners in the United States and England. On the other side stood US Customs officials like McCulloh, who sought to prevent smugglers from sneaking foreign refined sugar into the country without paying tariffs. Port investigators were aided by a new optical instrument called the saccharimeter, which could detect the chemical differences between different varieties of liquid sugar that appeared identical to the unaided eye. While allegedly more precise, the saccharimeter also enabled investigators to examine the cane juice without upsetting its delicate balance, to quantify without disturbing its "natural" crystalline whiteness. Treasury Department technocrats like McCulloh sought to use the new optical techniques to extend state power into the microscopic realm of molasses barrels, and outward, into the macroscopic realm of empire.

This fractured collective of sugar experts shared a typically mid-nineteenth-century approach with cutting-edge scientific thinkers in Europe. They assumed that discovery lay in isolating a single, often hidden, entity that passed through a variety of physical states, but remained self-identical.[6] New notions of irreversibility and entropy in natural processes also resonated with plantation experts reckoning at the microscopic level with the delicacy of sugar, the irrevocability of sucrose inversion, and the voracious fuel consumption of the steam engine.[7]

While the dialectical emergence of white sugar and the "negro" slave has a genealogy going back to the sixteenth century, a new sense of the unique character and frail constitution of sucrose interacted with a racial fracturing of labor organization to redefine the sugar complex and its discourses of color in the 1840s and 1850s. The slave revolts of the early 1840s, together with the introduction of indentured Chinese workers, African-born *emancipados*, and tens of thousands of "white" immigrants from Spain and the Canary Islands, instigated a reinvention of racial ideology. Presumed indispensable to sugar production for over three centuries, black workers were recast as necessary but ultimately threatening to a fleeting and lifeless white purity that called for preservation.[8]

While some experts expounded on the mismatch between "brute" black labor and sophisticated machines, they often found themselves incapable of imagining a meticulously segregated plantation factory. Technological creolization still leaned on the unquestioned presence of enslaved workers, as well as their alleged amenability to management. Ironically, it was antislavery modernizers who most powerfully naturalized the mechanization of black labor; even as chattel slavery continued to be challenged across the Atlantic world, these experts embedded notions of racialized disposability in designs for industrial work. At this broader moment of crisis in Atlantic slavery, notions of racial fixity merged with ideas of plantation vitalism, making racial divisions of labor and draconian oversight inescapable—even in the absence of outright bondage.

Unusual Suspects: Invisible Perpetrators in the Clarifying Pan

Heat, exposure to open air, and excessive time in the pans of the Jamaica train destroyed what experts saw as the true nature of sugar cane. However, experimenters who saw the salvation of Cuba's sugar industry in the Derosne system soon discovered that undesirable chemical processes were already under way as the juice rushed from the mill into the clarifying pan. Since Derosne systems only mitigated these losses, Cuban chemist Carlos Moissant insisted on "the preservation of the syrup at the moment of its separation" from the cane.[9]

Louisiana sugar planter Judah Benjamin explained the problem in vivid terms. "The juice, as it runs from the mill," he wrote, "is impregnated with feculencies." Such pollutants included "the dust and earth which have adhered to the cane when cut," as well as "the coloring matter of the rind" and the "fragments of the fibrous matter," splintered into the cane juice by the crushing action of the mill.[10] Many planters filtered the juice through a wire mesh to get rid of the grossest impurities even before it passed into the clarifying pans, but for planters on the hunt for white sugar, this step was not sufficient.[11] Smaller particles, like trace minerals and proteins, remained in the juice, staining the ultimate product and affecting the flavor. Since the eighteenth century, it had been customary to pour quicklime into the cane juice to coagulate these byproducts. Other substances like bullock's blood had been tried, but lime, either imported from abroad or mined from local limestone quarries and cooked in kilns, had been the clarifier of choice for sugar manufacturers, as it was for those engaged in soap boiling, glass making, iron smelting, and lead smelting across Europe and the Americas.[12]

Experiments beginning in the early 1840s suggested that quicklime created problems of its own within the unforgiving chemical world of cane-sugar processing. While the agency of heat was sufficient to invert fragile sucrose, quicklime, as an alkaline material that tipped pH-neutral cane juice out of balance, broke it down even faster.[13] Quicklime's resource-intensive character brought it under further criticism. In an age of rapid concentration of slave workforces on sugar estates, most planters considered any time spent on tasks not directly related to sugar production wasted. The 1840s cycle of uprisings, coupled with hikes in the prices for captives, had elevated the psychological and financial costs of maintaining large slave populations. Moreover, the steady advance of the sugar-plantation frontier encouraged planters and experts to think of forests mostly as barriers in the way of sugar-cane fields or as standing fuel reserves for boiling houses.

More disturbing discoveries awaited. Through lengthy, on-the-spot plantation experiments, sugar chemists discovered that albumin, a gelatinous protein typically associated with egg whites, also exists in large amounts in sugar cane.[14] Just like the white of an egg, the albuminous parts of sugar cane coagulate when cooked, getting very clingy, meaning that drainage became very difficult and led to greater losses of crystallizable sugar.[15] Worse yet, albumin contains enzymes that break down sugars when they are oxidized or heated. In the tropics, where room temperatures in the boiling house could be well over a hundred degrees, and boiling was done in open-air pans, inversion could happen with disturbing rapidity. Quicklime clarification apparently worked too slowly to impede albumin's destructive effects. "Under the action of immediate contact with atmospheric air," Moissant explained, "and due to the instantaneous and energetic influence of that air, the albuminous material oxidizes and becomes an active ferment, thereby transforming all the other albuminous particles into ferments, turning the crystallizable sugar into glucose, and finally turning some of that glucose into alcohol, lactic acid, acetic acid, etc."[16]

This wave of unwanted chemical reactions reflected a deeper desire in the global archipelago of sugar knowledge to eradicate invisible forms of noncompliant life. "The brown sugars in general use," wrote a London food inspector in 1856, "are actually in a state of slow fermentation," due to the presence of leftover albumin in the barrels.[17] The inspector implied that undesirable elements stowed themselves away among tropical imports that appeared inert (Figure 2-1). Echoing the London inspector's microorganismic xenophobia, Scoffern called the molasses created by inversion "a foreign impurity."[18] For profits to be generated in the industry, sucrose had to be kept in constant motion: canes were brought rapidly to the mill, juice flowed steadily through the evaporation process, and boxes or hogsheads were rushed to the docks. The manufacturing process, while drawing on the life energy of people, animals, and plants, was a synthetic movement designed to suppress biological activity like fermentation.

Plantation experts' preoccupation with "ferments" and oxidation reflected then-recent developments in the field of organic chemistry. In the early nineteenth century, chemists began to apply the laboratory and descriptive methods of their field to the microscopic world of living things. They discovered that a certain amount of "activation energy" was required to make biochemical reactions happen. This requisite amount of heat forced open the bonds of a molecule to make room for a new molecule to join in. Enzymes, which are large molecules these researchers called "ferments," can shortcut this energy requirement by grabbing a small molecule and holding it in the right position to bond with another. In the context of sugar factories, ferments were particularly troublesome because they could do the work of inversion even in the absence of heat. These new ways of thinking about life emerged in part from the sugar-refining industry.[19] In 1833 Anselme Payen, a sugar chemist with experience in French refineries, isolated one of the first known enzymes while working in a brewery. Louis Pasteur picked up on his work and advanced it in the laboratory, while Payen stayed close to the point of production. Payen was frequently quoted by Cuban sugar chemists. While McCulloh assessed his suggestions for enhancing cane juice yields, Casaseca translated his *Essay on the Structure and Chemical Composition of Sugar-Cane* for the widely read *Memorias of the Sociedad Económica* in 1854.[20]

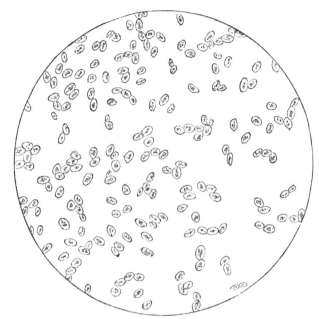

Sporules of the FUNGUS found in brown sugar.   Drawn with the Camera
Lucida, and magnified 420 diameters.

FIGURE 2.1 Invisible and unwanted life in the sugar barrel. Arthur Hassall, a food inspector and medical scientist in London, used chemical and microscopic methods to investigate various pollutants and adulterants in the food trade. A new sense of microorganisms' ubiquity and destructive power changed ideas of what constituted sugar, as well as exchange value, in the Atlantic economy.

From Arthur Hill Hassall, "Sporules of the fungus found in brown sugar," in *Food and Its Adulterations; Comprising the Reports of the Analytical Sanitary Commission of "The Lancet" for the Years 1851 to 1854 Inclusive, Revised and Extended: Being Records of the Results of Some Thousands of Original Microscopical and Chemical Analyses of the Solids and Fluids Consumed by All Classes of the Public* (London: Longman, Brown, Green, and Longmans, 1855), 20.

Sugar experts creolized nineteenth-century chemistry's explorations of life at the microcosmic level. Their thinking about organic movement and the frailty/desirability of whiteness implied an analogy between the machinery of the boiling house and new understandings of the digestive processes of the animal gut. Much animal life is sustained by breaking down carbohydrate chains (i.e., sugars,) into digestible chunks. *Ingenio* operations mimicked parts of animal digestion by adding heat and oxygen, and by physically breaking down the food, but reserved the final moment of digestion for the consumer of sucrose. Stripped of its organic surroundings by the manufacturing process, sugar was theoretically transformed into a pure and unchanging repository of exchange value. Boxes of white sugar held stores of vital energy in suspended animation as they traveled across the Atlantic.

Because of quicklime's apparent shortcomings in abetting this suspended animation, experts began seeking new clarifiers in the 1840s. José Luis Casaseca hoped that plantations would be able to use synthetic substitutes imported from abroad. During the harvest of 1852, at the Ingenio San Francisco in Guanajay, Casaseca met with a German merchant who was promoting a new product called "Dr. Stolle's Arcanum." A German industrial chemist, Stolle claimed his invention was superior to quicklime. Eager to test his claims, a committee of Cuban merchants, planters, and chemists submitted it to real-time experiment at a functioning mill during the harvest.[21]

As the clarifying pans full of freshly ground juice were heated, Casaseca poured in the recommended quantity of "Arcanum," along with the proportion of quicklime prescribed by Stolle, and peered over the rim of the cauldron to observe what would happen next. One can sense Casaseca's panic as the irreversible boiling process went forward: "it was noted that, being completely neutral at first, the mixture began to turn acid as it started to boil."[22]

At that moment, the plantation's sugar master stepped forward and poured an extra dose of quicklime into the pan, using the same amount "habitually employed on this plantation during this harvest season."[23] The use of "arcanum," Casaseca later conceded, "would have undoubtedly given a fatal result," because acidification of cane juice rapidly breaks down the sucrose.[24] Had the sugar master not intervened, an expensive batch of sugar would have been ruined.[25] As Casaseca's failed experiment demonstrated, newly synthesized chemicals that robbed ferments of oxygen also caused other unwanted reactions in the juice. What Stolle mysteriously branded "Arcanum" was actually the highly acidic aluminum sulfate, which Casaseca could not have known because the ingredients were kept secret.[26]

While "Dr. Stolle's Arcanum" might have performed well in the beet-sugar refineries of Germany, the inventor had "not foreseen" its inapplicability in Cuba's average boiling house.[27] Stolle's method depended on exact temperature control of the individual pans, since the juice would have to have been cold in order for the aluminum sulfate to coagulate the contaminants without inverting the sugar. After full skimming, the juice would then have to be reheated. However, in the colonial Jamaica train, with its single heat source running under the line of pans, "to reduce the heat in the last cauldron, the entire boiling process would have to have been suspended."[28] Since the levels of sucrose present in sugar cane decline quickly after grinding, as the readers of his report would have known, such a delay would have ruined the cane juice boiling in the other cauldrons.

The chemist thus chastised his European colleagues for failing to take into account not only how most Cuban planters actually made sugar, but also for ignoring the Caribbean climate in which they worked and how that might affect chemical processes carried out in open-air cauldrons. "I strongly believe that European chemists should renounce the use of all sulfides," Casaseca intoned, "which they only recommend because of their ignorance of the frightful rapidity with which cane juice transforms under the influence of the tropical climate. . . ."[29] Far from attempting to elide his tropical roots, Casaseca mobilized his creole authenticity to establish authority in the Paris-centered world of applied industrial chemistry.[30] Driven by interest in a German product, and preparing for a career-defining visit to the French Academy of Sciences, Casaseca employed locally based knowledge to legitimate his rejection of the new clarifying procedure.

White colonials in the Atlantic World's early modern scientific community had long insisted on the value of fieldwork, thereby reserving a privileged place for themselves as firsthand observers of New World nature.[31] Caribbean sugar experts went a step further than their eighteenth-century creole predecessors, arguing that the unique character of their creole knowledge was also rooted in cane sugar's chemical specificities. While they acknowledged having learned much from European innovators, they insisted that because many European chemists worked on "grape sugar," they did not have to reckon with "*el principio sacarino*."[32] As Judah Benjamin said, because French experimenters focused on the sugar beet, "the light shed by science on the composition of the cane is still so defective, you may think published works on the subject are calculated in some instances to mislead."[33]

Plantation experimenters uniquely acquainted with the fickle nature of sucrose lobbed vague accusations of charlatanism from their sugar mill. These same accusations, however, could also be turned on the least suspecting. In early 1842, planter and rum distiller Miguel Arango y Quesada needled Casaseca for puttering in a Havana laboratory during his rum researches. The planter wrote that, to assure accuracy, one must work at the plantation distillery itself on "improvements of known utility to which certain stills are subject."[34] Arango y Quesada thus dismissed Casaseca for lacking the same local, practical knowledge that the chemist prided himself on possessing.

Casaseca's former chemistry pupils piled on in 1861, noting that his "repeated and varied experiments" were conducted "in complete ignorance of both the general laws of science and the special conditions of the locale in which they were carried out."[35] Collectively, they faulted the illustrious professor for failing to apprehend the depth of the technological transformation unfolding in the upper echelons of Cuba's plantation complex. While he wrote approvingly of Derosne and Rillieux trains, Casaseca assumed the Jamaica train to be the norm of sugar making in the tropics for the foreseeable future.

Born and raised in Spain, Casaseca had a peninsular identity that may have exacerbated tensions with creole planters and researchers.[36] Joaquin Aenlle, Cuban born and twenty-five years Casaseca's junior, wrote about clarification procedures with the then-modern systems in mind. The Derosne system was to open up uses for synthetic sulfides that failed with the Jamaica train whose ubiquity Casaseca assumed. Under the sustained and excessive heat applied by the old technology, Aenlle noted, the salutary combinations that sulfurous acid formed with both molasses and albumin were undone: the sulfurous acid began to react with oxygen, turning into dangerous sulfuric acid, while the coloring and albuminous materials "remain in the liquid, the former recuperating the properties they had when they entered into combination with the sulfur, and the latter going back to their congealed state suspended in the liquid."[37] Aenlle thus blamed "the ancient Jamaica trains," not sulfides, for inversion.[38]

While Aenlle was most concerned with lengthy exposure to atmospheric air, Scoffern held that the "full defecating agency of lime" could safely be unleashed as long as cooking temperatures were precisely controlled. If the juice was allowed to boil during clarification, the "supernatant crust becomes broken into fragments, and mechanically incorporated with the fluid so intimately, that it can no longer be removed by skimming."[39] Such precise temperature control was very difficult to maintain in directly fire-heated Jamaica trains, but the liquid could be held carefully just below boiling point in steam-heated, valve-operated Derosne clarifying pans. It could also be quickly heated and cooled in different pans along the line. In such favorable conditions, the top layer of scum separated cleanly, forming a neat "*sombrerete*," or cap, atop the liquid that could simply be left there while the juice was emptied out the drain at the bottom of the pan. The scum followed it down and was channeled into an alternate depository, where it was recycled for use as animal feed, fertilizer, or, if high in sugar content, mash with which to make rum.[40] So it was really the Jamaica train that was at fault, not sulfides themselves.

Thus Casaseca worked on one side, while his clamorous students worked and thought on the other side of a broad technical gulley in the early 1860s, when synthetics could be used effectively.

They found the creole answer to inversion in a combination of vacuum enclosure with calcium bisulfite (a solution of sulfurous acid, water, and traditional quicklime). Poured into the cane juice as soon as possible after grinding, it froze the unwanted chemical processes taking place and bonded with the coloring and albuminous materials that coagulated with the lime and floated to the top.[41] By 1860, while use of calcium bisulfite was not yet widespread, chemical manufacturers in Havana had begun to master several different methods for creating this synthetic clarifier in the laboratory.

When calcium bisulfite was finally settled upon to solve the problem of clarification, chemists like Moissant used the language of early organic chemistry, still infused with vitalist concepts, to explain it. Influential vitalist chemists of the late eighteenth and early nineteenth centuries like Joseph Black and Joseph Priestley posited that every living thing in nature was animated by in an ineffable core of vital energy.[42] Plantation experts turned vitalist understandings of nature inside out: at the center of sugar cane lay not a humming engine of life, but a silent and immobile, snow-white world that required protection.[43] Moissant, for example, understood calcium bisulfite to preserve white sugar in two related ways. In the first, "the combination of sulfurous acid with coloring materials" produced "a white body, that is to say: the combination, the condensation, the neutralization of luminous rays of THE COLOR WHITE, EQUILIBRIUM OF COLORING FORCES." In the second instance, "the combination of sulfurous acid with albuminoid materials" produced "a stable body, that is to say: the combination, the condensation, the neutralization of molecular movements. STABILITY, EQUILIBRIUM OF THE FORCES OF AFFINITY."[44] For experts, whiteness embodied an inhospitality to life that was fundamentally important for the sustained profitability of the product on its long journey to the world's markets.

Late-eighteenth and nineteenth-century racist science provided the vocabulary and the scale of values undergirding "scientific" understandings of sucrose: whiteness was natural and essential, valuable but vulnerable; blackness was derivative and faulty, but impervious and irreversible.[45] It is no coincidence that the idea of "the Negro" as a unique biological entity and a salable commodity emerged in tandem with the idea of "sugar" as a unique biological entity notable most of all for the lifelessness that technological refinement

could bring to it. Mid-nineteenth-century plantation experts' chemical imaginary, however, augured something new in the relationship between "sugar"
and "the negro." In this period, the delicate balances of *el principio sacarino*,
experts' preoccupation with atoms wasted or reused, and the "scarcity of
hands" together intensified the logic of social death always present within
slavery.[46]

Moreover, the 1840s crisis for sugar producers, low demand for sugar,
increasing timber shortages, and global competition in a free-trade world
ratcheted up desires for perfectly directed, value-enhancing pliant labor.[47]
The *barracón* (essentially a large prison in which workers were given rations,
received limited medical care, and were locked overnight) supported this
effort by containing and isolating workers according to race and gender, and
closing off access to both old provision grounds and neighboring estates.
Within a system of plantation vitalism defined by fears of irretrievable waste,
uncommodifiable expenditures of enslaved energy were unforgivable. As in
the clarifying pan, signs of life not harnessed to the immediate production of
profit were brutally stamped out. The sugar experts actually pushed the logic
of social death emanating from nineteenth-century racial capitalism into the
deep chemical structure of organic fluids.

Sugar in Disguise: The Science of Optics, the Collection of Tariffs, and the Redefinition of Sugar

While Casaseca, Villa-Urrutia, Scoffern, and Benjamin worked out their
racially infused definition of sugar from within the sugar mill, a very different group in the Greater Caribbean cultivated a similar understanding of the
nature of sweetness. Like the experts working in Cuba, North Americans
worked to reshape territorial divisions of labor within the global sugar economy. By policing sugar smugglers, they sought to reinforce the position of
Cuba as a quasi-colonial provider of raw materials to US industry. In the
investigations of US customs agents, *el principio sacarino* was also featured
as the natural, valuable, fragile, constitutive essence of commodified sweetness—cane juice's secret identity.

In the early 1840s, the US Treasury Department had been informed that
merchants in the Cuba trade were sneaking partially condensed cane juice
into East Coast ports by passing it off as molasses. Under both US and
Spanish regulations, cane juice was charged a higher duty than molasses,
since the former could be turned into higher-priced white sugar by domestic

refiners. Because the two fluids could be similar in appearance, however, importers were able to disguise their cane juice (which they called "sirop") as molasses. One New Orleans–based refiner went so far as to build a factory in Cuba with the express purpose of dissolving sugar in water and importing his "sugar in disguise" as molasses.[48] After successful smuggling, certain US refineries purified and evaporated the cane juice into table sugar. Merchants thus evaded the tariff enacted to protect Louisiana sugar planters and northeastern refiners.

Since huge government expenses like the invasion of Mexico came largely from tariffs, smuggling was taken quite seriously. Many experts and officials were involved in the Treasury investigations, creating a network of correspondents who could not seem to agree on anything, least of all if molasses was an actual thing. As a customs officer in New Bedford, Massachusetts reported, "Dealers here generally agree the varieties of molasses are so infinite, that . . . *in some cases* it would be difficult to decide whether a lot ought to be classed as sirup or molasses, or whether any lot entered as molasses contain any unlawful portion of sugar."[49] McCulloh agreed. "Much vagueness of opinion has heretofore existed as to what is the chemical nature of molasses," he wrote.[50] Treasury Secretary Robert J. Walker also noticed the "close likeness of sirop de batterie to molasses of a good quality."[51]

The methods used to identify different sweet liquids also varied widely. Some employed traditional chemical analysis, breaking down samples with sulfuric acid, heating it, and weighing the constituent solids. Others diligently used the hydrometers issued them by the Treasury Department. Most, however, merely asked reputable merchants what they thought the fluid was: sirop or molasses? In spite of the obvious ambiguity, the "dealers" insisted "that *in most cases* the true character of the article may be ascertained by any competent inspector, without any chemical analysis, by merely sounding the cask with a stick."[52]

The Treasury Department undertook a broad set of investigations at various East Coast customs houses with the aim of reforming these loose practices of inspection, as well as to ascertain the frequency of fraud.[53] By hiring professional chemists to lead the analysis, the New York City Customs House was clearly moving from tacit acceptance of mercantile definitions to an emerging saccharine principle. The consulting chemists excoriated Treasury for lacking "any *fixed standard*" that might help in "directing their action and defining the per centage of crystallizable sugar" in either sirop or molasses.[54] Even though they conceded that sugar smuggling was indeed a problem, the chemists used a sucrose-centered logic to prove it: sirop was only quantitatively distinct from molasses. They placed the two fluids at different points on the same continuum, weakening any qualitative, conceptual distinction between them.

McCulloh, as well as the chemists hired by the customs houses, used the saccharimeter to show that the difference between the two liquids was one of degree and not kind. Nineteenth-century models resembled a small telescope, with the main tube containing a pair of prisms that polarized a beam of light. The polarized light was passed through a sample of liquid sugar to produce optical evidence of the percentage of dissolved sucrose in a sample. It worked according to the following optical principle: crystals dissolved in a liquid refract polarized light. Dissolved sucrose rotates polarized light in the opposite direction from that of fructose and glucose; thus the two substances came to be called invert sugars. McCulloh, or other inspectors trained in its use, could use the instrument to determine the relative quantities of sucrose and fructose/glucose in a sample and therefore if a product being passed off as low-value, low-tariff molasses was actually cane juice.[55]

But this neat bifurcation of the two substances was an ideal. In practice, most fluids characterized as either molasses or cane juice had some combination of sucrose, glucose, fructose, and other byproducts of the plant, as well as "impurities" introduced during processing (like excess quicklime). The saccharimeter, an object that both drew from and provided daily evidence of *principio sacarino*, put molasses and cane juice on a single scale, with law or convention fixing the boundary between them. Since the inverted byproduct of sugar-beet refining was not usable (its different trace minerals apparently imparted a noxious flavor), the optical technique of saccharimetry was meant to zero in on the inimitable chemical signature of tropical sucrose.

The volatile nature of sugar gave the saccharimeter another advantage over other modes of analysis. Cane sugar's susceptibility to the elements, McCulloh pointed out, posed challenges to "the chemist [who] has found his trouble" in developing knowledge of cane sugar, since it is hard to find methods of investigation that do not "destroy the substance experimented upon." The user of the saccharimeter was able to identify "a characteristic property of cane sugar without first subjecting it to the action of heat or chemical reagents." As McCulloh admiringly put it, "there is something apparently so abstract, so totally different from the usual methods of evaporation, precipitation, weighing &c., in the employment of a ray of light to determine quantities of gross matter in solution, that it seems almost too fanciful to be real."[56]

The saccharimeter's capacity to harvest knowledge from sucrose without breaking it down it was also a key feature in the Derosne system. Closed off from operatives, the vacuum pan required what Cuban experts called the *clar-avoya*, a peephole through which the evaporation process could be observed and controlled without damaging the expensive product. Casaseca described "an air register," or a barometer to gauge air pressure inside the pan, that had its indicator on the external face of the dome. The pan also boasted "a very ingenious scoop to take the test without letting any air in." This scoop might have been a mechanical replacement of the finger and thumb test, used by the sugar master to see how stringy the juice was, to gauge when the batch was ready. Finally, Casaseca described a hydrometer mechanism attached to the Derosne vacuum pan, which an operative could use at any moment to get the precise density of fluid most conducive to complete crystallization.[57] The nineteenth-century trend of mechanical enclosure, intensified within the Greater Caribbean, required non-physical forms of penetration, so that observers could understand the process without impinging. Thus the truths hidden behind the facades of commodities were laid bare by new analytical methods, at the very moment that those same products were thought to need protection from the harsh elements of nature as well as the clumsy hands of artisans and inspectors. The new visual instruments provided enclosed spaces where the irrevocable sequence of physical and chemical reactions could unfold at a site close to, but insulated from, laboring bodies. Sugar chemists also discovered that fragile sucrose demanded data gathering in the tropical plantation context.

In December 1846, McCulloh himself set sail for the world's most productive sugar island. Like Casaseca, he fabricated a creole scientific identity for himself. In challenging a Parisian chemist with regard to the emergence of sucrose within the maturing cane plant, for example, McCulloh showcased his newfound familiarity with planters in Cuba: "Messieur Hervy of France" was led into error because he conducted his experiments in a hothouse in Europe. Hervy's mistake further proved that making usable knowledge about sugar required one's presence at tropical plantations. When limited to laboratory work in the United States, McCulloh had agreed with Hervy, but as one observer explained in 1847, McCulloh "has since been engaged himself in analyses of the cane in the island of Cuba," studies that had changed the mind of "the able chemist."[58] While increasingly enamored with scientific instruments, McCulloh only trusted them in combination with the practical, experience-based knowledge of the planters residing in Cuba.

While Casaseca seemed unable to avoid conflicts with elite creole planters, McCulloh received a relatively warm welcome from the North American
planters whose estates he used as testing grounds. Upon his arrival, he went
to Matanzas, visiting the plantations of prominent men associated with a
wealthy merchant-planter family, the Drakes. McCulloh circulated mostly
in these Anglo-centric networks, with his letters of introduction from a
Mr. Brinkerhoff, a partner in the mercantile branch of the Drake family's
operations.[59] The thread of connections led back to the elite merchants of
New York City, since Brinkerhoff was an associate of Moses Taylor, a well-
known muscovado trader.[60]

The administrator of Drake's estate sent an employee with a team of pack
mules to fetch McCulloh's bulky chemistry equipment, which was then set
up in a room of the plantation's main house. McCulloh was quite pleased
with his accommodations. "At any moment," he effused in his report to the
Treasury Department, "I could obtain the cane juice perfectly fresh, and at all
stages of the process of manufacture, as well as the canes themselves, and every
other interesting product . . . I found myself in the possession of every facility,
and of a laboratory as well furnished and convenient for analytical research
as any chemist could desire."[61] A few weeks after McCulloh's arrival in Cuba,
a full-fledged plantation laboratory was in operation. He had finally arrived
at the origin point, he thought, with unmediated access to hidden chemical
phenomena.

Through his work at these sites, McCulloh found that some planters *thought* they were committing fraud by relabeling sirop as molasses. He
wrote, "I also learned in Cuba, upon good authority, that much of the highly
esteemed 'Nuevitas molasses' is *sirop de batterie*."[62] The difference between
these two, in the minds of planters, was that molasses was cane juice that had
already been through the evaporation process, while *sirop de batterie* was taken
out of the first pan (the *batterie*) and barreled. While his informants let him in
on the local secret that one entity was being disguised as another, McCulloh
drew a different conclusion from their admissions: "And if it be asked, what
then is the chemical difference between molasses and *sirop de batterie*? I would
reply, none."[63] They were simply two fluids with different relative percentages of sucrose and invert sugars. He thus declared that the whole discourse
about sugar smuggling was based on the faulty idea of a qualitative distinction between the two. Even merchants and planters who thought they were
committing fraud had it wrong. McCulloh asserted that the circumstances
of production did not constitute the nature of the product, only its chemical

makeup and the way it refracted light. The sucrose principle provided a sweetness without a past.[64] With the right instruments wielded at the right location, the truth of a unitary commodity began to emerge through the cloudiness of traditional notions. Even if instrumental analysis replaced the subjective judgments of merchants, however, the temporal decay to which sugar was subject required the investigator's presence at the plantation.

Treasury Secretary Robert J. Walker latched onto McCulloh's sucrose principle. He pointed out that while some cane juice "may have been passed for" molasses, his famous Walker Tariff of 1846, "by placing sirups and molasses under the same rate of duty, will, it is conceived, effectually remove any incentive to attempts at fraud."[65] A split tariff between molasses and sirop (say, two and six cents) would produce less revenue than a uniform four-cent tariff because the old tariff incentivized merchants to smuggle sirop. The theory was that under the new policy, merchants would not find smuggling worth the effort, and government revenues would increase because the black market would disappear.

Whether it worked in practice or not, the idea impacted the larger political economy of an expansionist, slaveholding republic. After several southwestern states repudiated their bond debts in the wake of the Panic of 1837, British investors, who had until then underwritten the US national debt, as well as many private North American railroads and southern cotton plantations, swore never to trust American borrowers again. The 1846 promise of enhanced revenue collection via the Walker Tariff showed British bankers that the federal government was serious about fiscal health and encouraged them to place trust back in US bonds. This invitation brought a renewed flood of British capital, which among other things paid for Walker's pet cause: the invasion of Mexico.[66]

As well as being Secretary of the Treasury under President Polk, Walker was a prominent planter, slaveholder, and Democrat from Mississippi. He was also an ardent expansionist whose efforts helped bring northern Democrats in line with southern designs on Texas by stoking white racial paranoia: without fresh territory on which the plantation system could expand, Walker argued, a surplus population of unusable black people would emerge within the Old South. Lacking the beneficial restraints of masters, he reasoned, free African-Americans would become indolent and criminal. Dreading anything short of full employment for the enslaved, Walker boasted that 90 percent of slaves in sugar districts worked directly in sugar production.[67] He also sought to use the expansion of the plantation complex and its system of slavery to maintain an equilibrium of political representation between slave and free states in Congress. Balances, countervailing forces, and equilibria structured Walker's racial political economy, just as it did his political, economic, and chemical conceptualization of liquid sugar.[68] His vision of an empire of whiteness ranged from the micro-scale of the molasses barrel to the macro-scale of hemispheric racial demography. Walker could comfortably have chanted along with Cuban chemist Carlos Moissant, "the color white. Equilibrium of coloring forces."[69]

Post-Escalera Cuba, with its white colonization programs and the "coolie" trade in the 1840s and 1850s, of course, also reflected such anxieties. In the early 1850s, Captain-General Pezeula introduced reforms to the slave system. His officials began investigating the treatment of slaves on the sugar estates, and began to enforce slave trade laws. These piecemeal measures to rein in the spread of slavery and the impunity of masters gave rise to a panic among some in the United States, who feared "another Haiti" so close to home. Pro-slavery writers predicted that, because of the demographic predominance of black Cubans, a racial apocalypse would follow Pezuela's ill-advised tinkering with a volatile system, leaving the whole island eventually "Africanized," or blackened, like a carelessly boiled batch of sugar.[70] Southern designs on Cuba were central to the *principio sacarino* story. Tariffs were just one aspect of the United States' broader goal of controlling a Greater Caribbean division of labor, through which it could preempt the possibility of "another Haiti," internationalize North Americans' own approach to racial capitalism, and ensure that North American industry developed on the backs of "tropical" producers of cheap raw materials.

Within Cuba itself, the understanding that racial identities were changeable heightened anxieties about demographic imbalance, since it was thought possible for government activism to "darken" or "whiten" the nation as a whole through programs of population control.[71] Intellectuals and government officials voiced their own concerns about a black majority on the island and initiated government programs of white colonization wherein European immigrants were encouraged to settle in Cuba as parts of a general program of "whitening."[72] Spanish loyalists reined in burgeoning independence movements among white creoles by threatening to unleash "social revolution" among the enslaved and promising that Cuba would be "either Spanish or African." As historian David Sartorius points out, white colonization was advocated to increase the "loyal" population.[73] Greater Caribbean elites' sense of pure whiteness as delicate, hidden, but ultimately attainable began with plantation chemists' experimental analysis of the boiling-house process.

From Grades of Sugar to Shades of Man: Allocating Races around the Machine

As in the *principio sacarino*, emerging anthropological ideas of the nineteenth century united "the races of man on a common path of progress and a single scale of development."[74] New iterations of racist concepts claimed to disqualify black workers from the occupations around the Derosne system. While creole scientists surely continued to depend on enslaved informants for reliable information on tropical plants, animals, and diseases, the laboratory-like space of the industrial boiling house mobilized a more strict racial division of labor.[75] The modern sugar mill was not a space of nature, or even an artisanal space, but an industrial one, thought to function at the apex of technological precision in pursuit of isolated whiteness. Yet a strong counter-trend characterized the plantation experiments themselves. Taking inspiration from saccharimeter analysis, experts sought to transform the *ingenio* itself into a precision instrument. For planters to know with certainty what truly constituted sugar, the operations of the plantation had to unfold unimpeded. It would yield truth only in its undisturbed ecology, so to speak. And who was a more "natural" element of the boiling house than bondspeople themselves? Slaves thus formed a constant element in the truth-yielding ecosystem of the modern sugar mill.

While some planters, chemists, and engineers at times decried the inefficiency of "negro labor," they nevertheless assumed slaves to be a permanent and functional aspect of the productive apparatus.[76] To isolate the variable at issue in his experiments with his "Tren Modelo," for example, Juan Ramos made a point of using "the same quantity of cane juice, the same pieces of cane . . . And the hands that are normally employed."[77] Striving for a mechanical reproduction of the conditions of the Jamaica train in order to be sure that it was his improved train that made the difference, Ramos showed that mechanization would necessitate no change in the labor force—the workers were literally one of the "constants" in the experiment.[78] Ramos's experimental practice thus naturalized the presence of slaves on the mill floor.

Likewise, in his influential *Cuba en 1860*, Sagra bracketed his antislavery politics. He continually employed terms like "*los negros*," "*la dotación*," and "*los brazos*" (collective labels referring to undifferentiated masses of racialized labor power) to discuss estate workers. Through Sagra's use of conventional slaveholders' labels, slaves continued to be an assumed element in the unit of production.[79] He further undermined his hopes for a future without chattel slavery whenever he slipped into calculating efficiency in units of "average production per Negro."[80] Even *emancipados* liberated from slave smugglers were construed as allocatable labor. Those people freed from slave smugglers became central to plans for a government school of agriculture organized around a "model sugar mill." "It would cost the government very little to develop a farm of this kind," argued another agricultural reformer, "having, as we suppose it does, lands to choose from, and the necessary number of emancipated blacks."[81] The technocratic language of plantation experts imparted to racialized workforces an aura of availability or disposability. What is the actual promise of a free labor future, one might have asked, when this kind of thinking penetrated the language even of those who claimed to loathe slavery?

While McCulloh had no sympathy with antislavery movements, he engaged in similar kinds of contradictory thinking. Discussing in the abstract why cane growers did not often refine their own sugar, McCulloh noted that the planter had "to contend with the disadvantages of climate [and] with the ignorance and stupidity of negro workmen."[82] Later in the text, however, the "stupid negro workmen" were slipped without comment into the machinery itself, becoming a natural, even a blameless, cog. Watching how the unsynchronized pacing of sugar-mill activity in Cuba created dead times in the flow of production, McCulloh observed "the negroes . . . frequently having stowed themselves about the sugar-house in snug corners, and fallen soundly asleep, heedless of noise or care."[83] McCulloh's description both called attention to a foolish squandering of labor power and normalized the sugar mill as slaves' natural habitat, painting exhausted women and men as carefree catnappers.

Many planters instructed their slaves to grind the cane as fast as possible, an order that left the juice sitting in open reservoirs while the cooking was carried out, during which time the grinding ceased completely. Instead, McCulloh recommended slowing the grinding down so as to maintain all operations (including the workers) in calibrated motion. Slow, continuous, and thorough grinding would ensure total production increases without necessitating "a larger force of negroes, or more work of those employed." Blurring the boundary between black workers and the machine, McCulloh linked "the number of negroes" with the "velocity of the rollers" of the mill. He suggested dividing the larger mill gang into shifts, which would make possible "short intervals of rest to the negroes," without stopping the process. Calibrated continuity of motion would avoid exposing cane juice to "the danger of fermentation by long standing in the reservoirs."[84] While inversion was often due to management's unwise allocation of workers, "the poor negro" was typically blamed.[85]

At most points in their writings, mid-century sugar experts' self-proclaimed dedication to "science" encouraged a preoccupation with the chemistry and machinery of sugar production, along with a reluctance to write at length about labor.[86] On the level of principle they disdained non-white labor. But when entering into detailed technological analysis, experts slipped into speaking of abstract and collective "negroes" as a natural auxiliary to the machinery, disciplined by the inexorable power of the mechanism's operation[87] (Figure 2-2). Insisting vaguely that labor would somehow have to get "smarter," they nevertheless acknowledged that a specific kind of intelligence was needed, one that mirrored the chugging pistons and frictionless spins of centrifuge bowls and magnified commodity values without distorting the image of a perfect whiteness now positioned at the center of the plantation system.

PACKING SUGAR.

FIGURE 2-2 In this view of undifferentiated but racialized labor, slaves are portrayed as working like machines, standing in serrated rows, packing sugar with a piston-like motion of the arms. Yet, even in this idealized image, some refused the role. The man at left foreground is using only one arm; his other is held in front of his stomach, perhaps from a digestive illness or injury. The man to his left appears to be looking back at the artist.

From Samuel Hazard, *Cuba with Pen and Pencil* (Hartford, CT: Hartford Publishing Company, 1871), 370.

False Equivalents

With a saccharimeter in hand in the late 1840s, McCulloh returned to the truth-yielding *ingenio*, inspired by queries about the boundaries between commodity and person, between life and not-life, between value and motion. No matter how deeply McCulloh penetrated the syrupy depths of the sugar mill, no matter how tightly he zoomed in on molecules' activity, no matter how rigorously he quantified biology and value, he still got it hopelessly wrong.

A chemistry professor at Columbia University, McCulloh defected from the Union during the US Civil War. Throwing in his lot with slaveholders by absconding to Richmond in 1863, he spent the remainder of the war at the Confederate Ordnance Laboratory trying to create an incendiary device that could be used to burn down northern cities.[88] By siding with the Confederacy, McCulloh gambled that enslaved women and men could not become political actors—that they would slumber happily through their own history. This was a lifelessness he thought he saw reflected in the sheer white stillness of sucrose's microscopic world at the center of the Cuban sugar mill. But one was not in reality the mirror image of the other. In the two years after his defection, McCulloh witnessed half a million enslaved African-Americans take their fate into their own hands by leaping the chasm between the master's world and another, yet to be determined, world in the making. Within five years of his flight, many Afro-Cubans had joined an anticolonial rebellion against Spain and destroyed the foundations of their own enslavement. McCulloh's sloppy analogical thinking cost him seven months in a Federal prison—it could have cost him much more. Before the 1860s, however, this future was far from apparent. In fact, creole techno-scientific transformations of the 1840s were laying the groundwork for a fateful expansion of the Second Slavery in the 1850s. The reinvention of sugar, which began in the invisible realms of the plantation clarifying pan, was quickly funneling out to demand a reinvention of the larger Cuban transport system that moved these sugars into the world market.

From an Infrastructure of Fees to an Infrastructure of Flows

THE WAREHOUSE REVOLUTION IN HAVANA HARBOR

ONE AFTERNOON LATE in the fall of 1844, members of the upper crust of Cuban society boarded ships in the old quarter of Havana and headed across the bay (Figure 3-1). They first steamed past the fortresses guarding the waterway's narrow mouth, which were adorned with a new, state-of-the-art Fresnel lighthouse, whose twice-a-minute flood of light shone twenty miles offshore. The small flotilla then moved on toward its ultimate destination: the *Almacenes de Regla*, a new sugar storage complex holding its grand opening festivities that day.[1]

The wharf/warehouse complex was organized as a joint stock company that promised to revolutionize the transport and marketing of the island's sugar by providing a centralized, seaside location at which sugar-laden railway cars could meet the empty holds of northbound vessels. It sat upon man-made embankments that extended the town of Regla out into the bay.[2] Cuban sugar warehouses like this one, which included large wharves, multiple cranes, and internal railways, were to rank as the largest cast-iron structures in the world by 1860, with their components prefabricated at a foundry in New York and assembled on site in Cuba. Running its own railroad, and offering banking and insurance services to planters, the Regla Warehouse Company and others of its ilk were to anchor the infrastructural reinvention of the island's sugar-making economy. By 1855, a mere decade after their inauguration, the facilities held over 645,600 boxes of sugar, nearly half of Cuba's total.[3]

When the steamboats arrived at Regla that December afternoon, Captain-General Leopoldo O'Donnell, flanked by the island's political elites,

FIGURE 3-1 The Naval Shipyard and Spanish flags in the foreground highlight the complicated connection between imperial security and private, large-scale commercial infrastructure, like the Regla Warehouses (the white A-frame buildings across the bay).

From Justo Germán Cantero, *Los ingenios: Colección de vistas de los principales ingenios de azúcar de la Isla de Cuba* (Havana, Cuba: 1857), Luis Miguel García Mora and Antonio Santamaría García, eds. (Madrid: Editorial CSIC, 2005).

disembarked on the wharf. Revelers performed a "beautiful *paseo*" on the docks, followed by a polka.[4] The synchronized stamping of dancers' feet filled the eerie weekend quiet of a new sort of space. Until 1844, the docks of Old Havana had been key nodes of African and Afro-Cuban power. Free black work-gang leaders had recruited and organized their own groups of stevedores and longshoremen, also making arrangements with shipping companies. The grand opening marked the end of that system.[5] The panic surrounding the Escalera uprisings enabled anxious agents of imperial security to whiten Havana's wharves as they whitened their sugar. Exploiting slaves and indentured Chinese instead of free black workers, the warehouse companies relocated them to Regla, across the bay from the city proper.

The attack on Afro-Cuban communities and the revolutionizing of Cuba's infrastructure of sugar transport were intimately related. They represented decisive moves on the part of a new merchant-planter elite to take more control of shipping and boiling of high-quality grades of sugar. The violence was a necessary facet of Cuba's long transition to a plantation complex, which would not be complete until Afro-Cuban control of the littoral was broken.

Havana, a key Atlantic port with a 350-year history, was far from a blank slate for new projects. Entrenched interests, not just those of black-led stevedore organizations, would have to be co-opted or pushed aside. In the old system, Havana commission merchants had made fortunes from handling the sugar of planters. With hundreds of merchant houses scattered throughout the city, the sugar that came in to town by coasting schooner had first to be unloaded, then taken to these houses by the planters' mercantile agents, then sold to exporters, and brought back to the docks for export. The merchants in control of this process charged high prices for handling, storage, short-term loans, and marketing. This layout of Havana—with government-built wharves, wagon transport, and dispersed merchant houses—enabled the accumulation of *rentier* profits by Spanish merchants, making it an "infrastructure of fees."

The pre-1844 sugar boom, with its early railroads and *ingenio* expansion, was built within this system, but quickly outgrew it. As of 1827 only 4 percent of arable land was under cultivation in Cuba; the rest was too far out of reach of the island's limited network of water and overland transport. The rapid development of railroads brought plentiful new soils within reach for the first time, and slaves carved new centers of production out of swamp, plain, and forest. Making possible the cultivation of more acreage, the railroad revolution forced increasing labor requirements upon the enslaved, who worked longer hours at a faster pace to harvest sugar cane. The increase in sugar brought to Cuban ports soon overwhelmed the limited wharf space.

By transforming not only the handling of the world's sugar, but its financing as well, the merchant-planters who pushed through the revolutionary changes at the wharves sought to replace an infrastructure of fees predicated on a maze of shipping and handling charges, with a low-cost, rapid-movement "infrastructure of flows." The new complex at Regla ensured that boxes of sugar would no longer enter the city at all; instead they were carried by rail directly to the seaside warehouse complexes, where all business was conducted. A new generation of Spanish-born elite merchant-planters won marketing flexibility, low overhead, and speed of transport with this new logistical organization. Unlike middling commission merchants, these powerful traders did not profit primarily from storage fees and commissions, but from buying and selling sugar on the world market, financing illegal slaving voyages, and underwriting sugar-mill operations. The new joint-stock warehouse firms they established still made money on storage fees (even though they charged less per box) because the new infrastructure meant they spent less money handling each box, while gaining access to more sugar with less effort, at the same time allowing customers to compare prices and qualities.

These merchant-planters also succeeded in creating specialized economic roles for different cities. Havana, with its transnational financial connections, its deep-water harbor, its established imports business, and its proximity to the halls of political power, brought in big ships and white sugar.[6] Matanzas sent white sugar to Havana but directly exported muscovado through the traditional means of small merchants. Cárdenas, with a comparatively shallow harbor, but access to the most modern *ingenios* and best lands on the island, directly exported molasses on US schooners and shipped white sugar to the centralized warehouses surrounding Havana. While Matanzas and Cárdenas began to fall increasingly under the control of US interests, the merchant-planters producing and marketing white sugar through Regla strengthened Havana's ties to the United Kingdom, which had favorable tariffs on white sugar.

Just like in the Derosne system, warehouse spaces kept sugar in gentle but unceasing movement. These huge cast iron buildings allowed for broad, open spaces uninterrupted by load-bearing walls or bulky pillars. High ceilings and strategically placed openings ensured a constant flow of air around the boxes of purged sugar, lengthening shelf life. Spaces were rented to individual planters, and merchants were able to respond quickly to sudden price changes on Atlantic markets, making it possible to sell at the opportune moment. Liberating the movement of commodities while inhibiting the mobility of workers, these hulking new seaside structures enabled heightened levels of racial and imperial security and low-viscosity passageways for commodities and capital. For merchant-planters who had lived through the recession years and slave uprisings of the early 1840s, continued access to economic independence was enabled by the *principio sacarino*. An independent infrastructure specifically for white sugar magnified its ability to resist spoilage and opened up new opportunities for Cuba's elite entrepreneurs to maneuver around the creeping financial hegemony of British and North American capital.

Expansion within the Infrastructure of Fees: The Government Wharves of Old Havana

The Spanish Empire had long treasured Havana's capacious and well-sheltered deep-water harbor. Throughout the early modern period, it was used as a stopover point for the famous silver-laden *flotas* returning from South America and as the New World headquarters for Spain's formidable Navy.[7] After the British temporarily occupied the city during the Seven Years War, the Spanish Crown appointed military strategists to repair and expand waterfront structures. While they created a formidable new arsenal, presidios, walls, and defensive weaponry, wharf space for merchant ships remained minimal.

With the steady growth of Cuba's export economy after the Haitian Revolution, the total number of ships visiting Havana continually overwhelmed available wharf space on the western side of the bay.[8] Ships were increasing both in number and in size. The average annual number of ships in the port of Havana from 1826 to 1830 was 1,778. By 1861–1863, the annual number of ships had increased to 4,841,[9] and the mean capacity of these vessels had more than doubled.[10] Without an overhaul at the wharves, overcrowding would have slowed transactions to a crawl. Since Cuba provided as much as 40 percent of the world's sugar supply during this period, prices would then have risen, sending much of the business to other ambitious producers in the global sugar archipelago.

Piecemeal plans to improve operations on the wharf therefore began in the early 1820s, but boxes of sugar always seemed to pile up faster than the wharves could be expanded. In 1849, government engineer Francisco Albear was employed to come up with a remedy.[11] First he was sent to Europe to investigate how major ports solved the traffic issue. While global trade powerhouses like Liverpool possessed almost twenty times the wharf footage of Havana, Albear lamented upon his return, even second-tier European ports, whose commerce "cannot be compared with Havana in activity or in commercial importance," enjoyed much more ample space.[12] In the pre-Regla phase of the sugar boom, there were so many ships clamoring to tie up at the wharves that officials established a fine for ships taking longer than three days to complete their unloading and loading activities.[13]

"If their short length were their only defect," Albear continued, "the state of the wharves in Havana would be understandable; but observe their narrowness, their lack of space; observe the exertions of the multitudes that work on them under the insufferable summer sun; observe the packs of wagons, mules, Negroes, sailors, clerks, workers, and merchants, all enveloped in a sea of boxes, packages and dust; without broad lateral streets by which to comfortably move freight; without sufficient shelter to protect men and goods from sun and rain; . . . facilitating disorder, disgust, and disputes." While the wharves of Havana should be "an agreeable spectacle of orderly mercantile activity," Albear concluded, they more closely resembled "a small private hell where those having even the smallest relation to it suffer."[14] The congestion even spawned innovations like the *zorra giratoria* developed by Pedro Lopez in 1837. A sturdy wagon specially designed to carry "heavy weights" off ships, its free-floating wheels (like on a shopping cart) turned on a dime in cramped spaces.[15]

In response to the chaos, the government undertook a new set of projects to expand the public wharves. To increase the total number of feet available to visiting ships, Albear headed projects that expanded and unified the three neighboring wharves of San Francisco, Carpineti (which had been destroyed by an 1846 hurricane), and Piedra.[16] He planned to widen the existing surface space, creating an area generous enough for the construction of shelters to protect people and merchandise from sudden rains. Albear contracted the work out Pedro Lacoste, a noted merchant-planter and railroad entrepreneur who "possessed extensive reserves of lumber near the Embarcadero de Perros, as well as a good number of coasting schooners." Lacoste also had a construction crew of at least a dozen slaves who carried out the work quickly and economically. Alfred Cruger, a North American engineer who had first worked on the railroad in South Carolina before playing a central role in Cuba's railroad expansion, noted how Lacoste "moved them from task to task," as they built warehouses, wharves, and other waterfront structures.[17]

Lacoste's project was completed in five months, at a total cost of 20,000 pesos. It went quite smoothly except for the fact that the Piedra Wharf had over the years sunk into the sea floor by a foot and was thus at a different level from that of its neighboring San Francisco Wharf. Since no wagons could roll across its planks, it was still, in effect, discontinuous, unless Lacoste built a new wooden surface on top of the Piedra Wharf. The auxiliary surface would put all three wharves on one level—then, a single shelter could run the length of the newly unified structure. Lacoste would have had to spend 2,000 or 3,000 more pesos to do the adjustment, and he insisted on simply putting stairs in instead. His engineer's aesthetic offended, Albear sniffed that the stairs have merely "been concealed by a little ramp"[18] (Figure 3-2).

In the end, Albear's project proved quite limited, as did Lacoste's willingness to spend more resources perfecting it. While Albear recognized that wharf expansion had been made "more urgent both by the heavy traffic of the interior of the port as well as the growing number of warehouses distributed throughout the city," he simply sought through his improvement projects to serve those existing urban warehouses by making sure that "the entire littoral of the port be surrounded by wharves and warehouses, whose construction can be carried out commodiously and easily."[19] Government engineers like Albear took the length of available coastline as a frustrating but inexorable

FIGURE 3-2 An 1850 aerial view of Havana from the east. In the foreground are the Carpineti, Luz, and Piedra wharves, unified the year before by Francisco de Albear's single shelter and interrupted by Pedro Lacoste's "little ramp." Notice the extreme traffic congestion and the vessels docked prow first. Underneath the viewer would be the new Regla Warehouses.

From La Habana al mediar del siglo XIX. 1851. Reproduction from Levi Marrero, *Cuba: Economía y sociedad* (1977). Courtesy of the University of Miami Library, Cuban Heritage Collection. chc0468000086000100I.tif

constant and tried to pack in as much wharfage as they could. By focusing solely on the issue of wharf space, Albear ignored the root of the problem—the awkward and dated mercantile infrastructure within the city itself. He also failed to acknowledge an infrastructural revolution already under way in the private sector.

The Regla Warehouse Company and the Santa Catalina Warehouse Company literally changed the map of the Bay of Havana.[20] While the large warehouse workforces, together with plenty of animal labor, constructed temporary coffer dams to hold back the waves, tons of Cuban earth were carted to the shoreline and dumped into the temporarily exposed floor of the bay. Once this fill had been packed down and leveled, and the new chunk of land completed, steam-powered dredges removed earth from the new, manmade shoreline, to maintain a depth adequate for large ships. The first big warehouse projects entirely reshaped the eastern side of the bay in this manner. As Cuban geographer José Maria de la Torre recalled in 1857, prior to the extension of the port area, "the sanctuary of Regla was surrounded by the sea, waves lapping against its walls. Today a railroad passes by, traveling down a street formed by spacious warehouses built upon what was formerly sea." Torre stood in wonder before the iron structures built on parts of the bay that only "a few short years ago, were traversed by schooners."[21]

Domestic Architecture, Urban Planning, and Traffic Congestion

The deeper spatial problem that Albear ignored stemmed from the sugar boom beginning in the 1790s, which had transformed the city of Havana. To deal with the narrow colonial streets and their heavy wagon traffic, wealthy commercial families built three-story homes with the ground floor (known as the *solar*) used as a storehouse for commodities; the second story functioned as the counting house, and the third story was reserved for family use.[22] Because most sugar came to the city overland, from within the province of Havana, this dispersed system of storage worked. But as sugar production moved eastward, more hogsheads and boxes came to the capital in coasting schooners. Boxes of sugar were removed from ships' holds by crews of Afro-Cuban stevedores and loaded onto ox-drawn wagons that were guided by slaves or free black teamsters through the streets of Havana to the merchant *solar*. The goods were stored there until buyer and seller had reached an agreement. The exporters then shipped the boxes back to the docks to be loaded onto a ship.[23]

By the early 1830s, influential observers were noting how untenable this odd system was: "It cannot be obscured," wrote Juan de Lara, an officeholder of the Junta de Fomento, "that the wasteful system of receiving sugar and other produce on the wharf, transporting it in wagons to storehouses in diverse points of the city, and re-transporting it to the wharf [for final export], has the inevitable consequence of loading upon our produce an additional expense that could be avoided."[24] While perhaps easing congestion at the docks a bit, simply expanding wharfage according to Albear's approach would do nothing to cut out the excess stages of transportation peculiar to Havana's mercantile geography.

The Regla Warehouse Company, as well as competitors who soon followed suit, bypassed the crowded old quarter of the city and its dispersed *solares*. New railroads or packet lines brought sugar from the countryside straight to the warehouse, where merchants gathered to conduct business. Once the boxes had been sold, smaller vessels carried the shipments to oceangoing ships waiting offshore. As sugar became an increasingly dominant sector of the Cuban economy in the first half of the nineteenth century, the product itself, as well as the laborers who both produced it and moved it about, became a less visible part of urban society. White sugar never entered Havana at all.

One-stop shopping at the new warehouses was a boon for exporters, who formerly had to go from merchant's house to merchant's house in search of the best deals. Anchoring in the bay, as opposed to tying up on the docks, saved merchant ships further expense by reducing wharfage fees.[25] Planters storing sugar at the new warehouses also saved money, since their commission merchants (who transported and sold the products to exporters on behalf of the planters) charged them for all the extra handling associated with the merchant *solar*. Regla thus cost planters less than half as much per box as the old system.[26] The sheltered location where the Regla warehouses were built, together with the northeasterly prevailing winds in the harbor, also made "the cost of getting products from the warehouses to the ships . . . less than at any other point of the bay."[27]

The warehouse structures impressed observers by their scale alone. Two of the three buildings of the Regla Warehouse Company were 820 × 480 feet, and the third to be built was larger yet, at 820 × 600 feet. In 1850, because of growing business, yet another building was constructed, the largest yet, at 1,026 × 600 feet.[28] In these cavernous new structures, gas lamps and one hundred pane-glass skylights illuminated hundreds of iron columns extending uniformly along the length of the warehouse. Spacious and well ventilated, the buildings were designed to minimize moisture retention, which accelerated clumping and spoilage of sugar.[29] By 1860, among the largest cast-iron buildings in the world, the warehouses allowed workers, sugar, inspectors, and air to flow freely along their designated channels.

Along the front of each building stood seven loading bays (each forty-eight feet high and twenty-four feet wide) large enough for two-way traffic of loaded wagons. The back and sides of each building had doors of the same dimensions. Railways ran down each aisle, providing mobility for the wheeled cranes used to stack and lower the boxes of sugar, which weighed about 400 pounds each. After being lowered from a stack of boxes in an individual planter's section, the boxes were then placed on cars, often in high stacks, and glided along rails in and out of the warehouses.

The Santa Catalina Warehouses, built in 1859, had twenty-eight such internal railways. Overhead, small iron carriages ran in tracks bolted to the underside of the rafters. Workers could use falls and tackle hitched to those carriages to lift and move boxes if a railcar was not available.[30] The generous amount of vertical space, as well as the hardware slung overhead, allowed for rapid and gentle rearranging of the heavy boxes, and thus for several different transactions and cargo-loading operations to be carried on simultaneously. The San José Warehouses offered, in addition to three cranes for moving boxes of sugar and hogsheads of molasses on and off of ships, "a special large crane, available for the unloading of particularly large and heavy pieces of machinery."[31] This form of mechanically assisted cargo handling, the *Diario de la Marina* explained, protected valuable and vulnerable boxes of sugar from "the damage and extraordinary deterioration" to which they had been subject in the old transport system.[32]

In spite of the cranes and railways, the sheer number of boxes and the speed of transactions at the centralized warehouses required large workforces. The Regla Warehouse Company alone employed eighty-five slaves and 134 Chinese indentured workers, rivaling the workforce of a mid-sized sugar plantation[33] (Figure 3-3). The Planters' Warehouse Company built a *barracón*

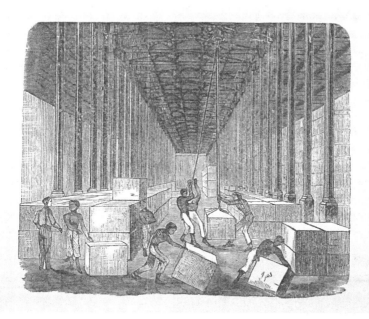

FIGURE 3-3 At the new warehouses, slaves and indentured workers still engaged in hard lifting labor, aided by mechanical solutions like the blocks and tackle slung on trucks from the rafters. Tall stacks of identical boxes are seen to the right, as well as spaces of flow up and down the aisles. No molasses hogsheads, but only purged sugar, appear.

From Samuel Hazard, *Cuba with Pen and Pencil* (Hartford, CT: Hartford Publishing Company, 1871), 268.

(see Chapter 2, *El Principio Sacarino*) for over 300 slaves and indentured Chinese in 1857.[34]

Because of the large number of captive laborers needed to make the new transportation infrastructure work, as well as to the counterinsurgent moment at which they were built, such structures featured prominently on the grounds of warehouse complexes. In 1858, when Spanish-born carpenter Felipe Matti began making preparations for the huge Santa Catalina warehouse construction project, he immediately sought permission to build *barracones* to house construction workers. Perhaps fearing that a sudden uprising would compromise the security of an armory located nearby, authorities stipulated that Matti's worker housing be temporary. The proposed *barracón's* proximity to a military fort may have led the authorities to garrison five guardsmen at the construction site. Putting mechanisms of worker containment in place first, Matti then traveled to New York City to contract "30–40 German and Irish hirelings" to round out his construction crew.[35]

Once the firms had begun operations, these motley workforces were treated as possessions of the company. When the Havana-Matanzas Railroad Company bought out the Bay of Havana Steamship Company in 1861, *emancipados* (nominally free Africans who had been confiscated from traders by the government and were often rented out in very exploitative conditions) were transferred to the railroad firm's control, along with "wharves, steamers, and other properties" belonging to the shippers.[36]

The new wharf infrastructure and its mass of captive workers enabled a single plantation to store up to 600 boxes of sugar (around 240,000 pounds, or 120 tons) at a time. The stacks were organized so that any of the different grades could be taken out and sampled at any time.[37] If the plantation's total production exceeded this quantity, additional space could be rented. With all of these resources, noted the *Diario de la Marina*, one planter "can have up to twelve stacks and different classes [of sugar] able to be delivered to eight purchasers at once."[38] In a time of decreasing sugar prices owing to new competitors on the global sugar market, noted the president of the Regla Warehouse Company, selling to eight purchasers simultaneously would have the happy effect of "increasing the number of speculators in times of oversupply," which helped "sustain prices."[39] The new warehouse-wharf system, he implied, was the infrastructural precondition for reestablishing a market equilibrium that commission merchants' schemes had knocked off kilter. Warehouse advocates insisted that their particular infrastructural transformation, more than just enabling increased supply, gave free rein to consumer demand that had previously been restrained by an urban space that had been outgrown by the sugar boom.

The transparency that the new system gave to sugar-related transactions was considered one of its chief attributes. As Havana's *Diario de la Marina* noted, the centralized warehouses "allow for knowledge of the available products, providing a guide to the merchant."[40] Government officials sponsoring the project echoed the paper's sentiment, emphasizing that the warehouse system would create a central meeting place for planters, merchants, and inspectors, "offering better knowledge of the market and greater ease and clarity in purchases and sales."[41] The spatial reorganization offered merchants, as well as colonial officials, a comprehensive, systemic view of regional production. The "small, private hell" of government wharves in Old Havana characterized by an infrastructure of fees was, in the eyes of some merchants and engineers, replaced by a transparent and apolitical infrastructure of flows, represented by the spacious, single-purpose warehouse complexes at Regla.

Commission merchants had long utilized the merchant *solar* infrastructure of fees to dampen the operation of market forces. They were especially notorious for charging astronomical interest rates on their long-term loans to planters. At their warehouses, the merchants also "collected liberal storage fees even higher than the 12 to 15 percent interest on the money advanced to finance the harvest." They were suspected of having pans under the floor to collect the molasses that dripped out of the barrels. Finally, the indebted and capital-hungry planter was subjected to hidden surcharges. With postproduction expenses sometimes consuming one-third of total sugar sales, merchants' dubious money-making stratagems vexed planters.[42] In the 1830s and 1840s, planters began increasingly to characterize merchants' infrastructure of fees as political in nature. That most merchants were Spanish-born and many planters Cuban-born made that argument more convincing. Warehouse reformers thus tried to paint their projects as free of the corrupt and inefficient colonial merchant's infrastructure. Claiming to let efficiency guide the structure of the physical economy, they were in fact forcing a transition to a differently politicized infrastructure of flows.

Head of the Regla Warehouse Company Eduardo Fesser touted a refined spatial division of labor when he reassured the government that their grand project would not "damage the commercial operations on the already existing wharves." Comforting those who feared the new warehouse complexes would hurt some entrepreneurs, Fesser diplomatically pointed out that overcrowding on those public wharves made life more difficult for everyone. He predicted that the removal of sugar-laden craft from the old city wharves "would give an increase of 150 feet for unloading" personal belongings of travelers. Furthermore, the heavy freights that damaged the government wharf surfaces and endangered the strolling public would no longer be an issue.[43] Thus his prose depoliticized what was in two major ways a political project: a rebalancing of merchant-planter relationships and the weakening of black workers' power on the docks.

It was clear to some businessmen that the new, centralized warehouses limited middling merchants' ability to gouge planters. Their wealthier counterparts reshaped Cuba's industrial system in ways that benefitted the top tier of planters and merchants, as well as international investors. Unlike middling commission merchants, these powerful traders did not profit primarily from storage fees and commissions, but from navigating the world sugar market and producing white sugar themselves. This Havana-based elite made up of well-known names like Fesser, Diago, Zulueta, Pedroso, and Torriente largely made their initial fortunes in the illegal African slave trade before shifting into licit trading.[44] They turned their commercial fortunes into huge plantations with hundreds of slaves, and began to make their presence known in the sugar industry. "This newer group of modernizing entrepreneurs," the historian Laird Bergad explains, "who often had business interests extending to New York, London, Barcelona, and Seville ... would control Cuban sugar production until the 1880s."[45] By partnering with old-line creole planters, who rarely engaged directly in commerce, they took over the trade in white and *quebrado* sugar. As they moved into planting, they began to forgo the old way of making profits through gouging sugar planters, figuring out they could make more consistent profits through an engineered infrastructure of flows for white sugar.[46]

Differing investments in plantation mechanization reflected and reinforced an ethno-national division of capitals: Catalán planter-merchant-banker-shippers, with financial links to Baring Brothers in London, invested in advanced filtration systems and complete vacuum systems to capture a newly opened English market in white sugar. *Criollo* and *Yanqui* planters, dependent on Moses Taylor and New York associates for financing and shipping, built railroads into local ports for all sugars because they sold mostly brown sugar to a US market whose refiners had effectively rigged the system with duties to keep Cuba's "plantation white" out of the market. So it made no sense for creole and *Yanqui* planters to invest in the full Derosne technology, nor to participate as fully in the bifurcation of the sugar transport system. They were also shut out of the slave trade. Because of frequent price fluctuations in sugar, elite merchant-planters diversified. While they dealt in some lower-grade byproducts, their surplus value came largely from plantation white. Even though this was not the majority per pound of Cuba's cane-derived exports, the particular demands of white sugar largely drove the reinvention of the transport system.

Compelling logistical issues reinforced entrepreneurial rivalries in encouraging spatial segregation by grades of sugar. Molasses and syrups had a limited shelf life, and they had to be marketed almost immediately after they were packed.[47] Filtered, centrifuged, and clayed sugar, having so little organic material or moisture, could be stored indefinitely because it would not go bad. Furthermore, the lower-quality *"mascabádos clásicos,"* which were basically a sweet, yellowish-brown mush taken straight from the strike pan and placed in giant hogsheads, were costly and difficult to maneuver. Sometimes the hogsheads were minimally purged by drilling a hole in the bottom. Oftentimes, they were not drained at all.[48] Constant leakage of hastily drained shipments meant that many hogsheads of muscovado arrived in Europe or North America weighing 20 percent less than they had at embarkation.[49] Moreover, hogsheads were bulky in relation to the value of the product they contained. Unlike boxes of sugar, they could not be stored in tall stacks in a warehouse, so warehousers therefore charged far higher rates for hogsheads of molasses than they did for muscovado or purged sugar.

Because storing hogsheads of perishable, low-grade sugar in warehouses was cost ineffective, its sellers had little freedom to arbitrate against the daily price shifts of the world sugar market.[50] The marketing agility made possible by imperishable white sugar, combined with the price spread between grades of sugar and merchant-planters' unique access to European markets, made it far more appealing to elite merchant-planters.[51] Also sitting on the boards of major railroads, these men made sure the new lines went right up to their plantations. Smaller planters lacked not only such convenient rail access, but also the technology for making larger proportions of white and yellow sugar. They may not have transported by rail and probably remained in the grasp of local Matanzas sugar dealers. Regla customers mostly were big planters, according to company head Eduardo Fesser.[52]

It was not the intention of Havana merchant-planters to monopolize the trade of all products deriving from sugar cane. Across the island, the spread of the steam-powered grinding mill in the 1830s and 1840s brought a lot more cane juice into plantation boiling pans, but without the Derosne system, ratios of purged sugar to muscovado and syrups remained fixed, leading Cuba's total exports of syrup to grow from 3.2 million gallons in 1815 to 43.7 million gallons in 1868.[53] Cárdenas and Matanzas became globally significant sugar ports on the strength of this byproduct. The two towns exported 62.7 percent of all the molasses on the island, while the molasses export of Havana plummeted from a peak of 54 percent in 1830 to a paltry 4.7 percent in 1863–1864. On the other hand, Cárdenas exported only 2.6 percent of Cuba's boxed sugar in 1851, in spite of its surrounding plantations producing more boxed sugar than any other jurisdiction on the island. Over 50 percent of boxed sugar exports went out of Havana.[54] With the help of infrastructural transformation, Havana's merchant-planters abandoned the export of molasses and muscovado, while increasing their share of white and *quebrado*.

The destinations for these products also differed. With steep duties protecting US refiners, very little "white, clayed, or powdered" sugar from Cuba found its way to North American markets. The United States took only 196,485 boxes of Cuban sugar (about 28.5 percent of Cuba's total) while taking 100 percent of the island's molasses exports in 1852.[55] The tariff wall was not always disadvantageous to entrepreneurs in Cuba. Spain helped funnel cheap byproducts to the United States by lowering the duty on molasses exports, exempting US vessels dealing in that product from otherwise burdensome tonnage charges.[56] Incentivizing North American traders to concentrate on molasses, this colonial policy helped wealthy Spanish immigrants to the island exert continued control over the trans-Atlantic trade of white sugar to England.

After Parliament reopened England's market to slave-grown sugar on equal terms with "free labor" sugar in 1846, much of the expansion in Cuba's purged-sugar exports went to the British Isles.[57] Imports increased from a low of 197,460 hundredweight in 1845, to a high of 1.64 million hundredweight in 1859, although the figures varied widely from year to year.[58] In 1849, England received nearly four times as many boxes as the United States, and two times more than Spain.[59] The distinction between US and UK markets for different grades of sugar even overrode the control New York merchants exerted in Matanzas and Cárdenas. In 1861, for example, Matanzas shipped only 15 percent of its boxed sugar to the United States; 85 percent went to Europe. On the other hand, the United States was the destination for 81 percent of the muscovado hogsheads, and 55 percent of the molasses hogsheads that left Matanzas.[60] The centrifugal splitting of Cuban sugar complicates the usual story of increased US imperial influence over the island. While Matanzas and Cárdenas had indeed begun to look like US neocolonies, as a center of purged-sugar export Havana actually had closer links with Europe until the 1860s. The island's other major sugar ports augured the unappealing future of Cuba's sugar economy, but other avenues still appeared possible at the time.

On the Waterfront: Labor, Skill, and Strategic Location in the Warehouse Age

Small-scale, dispersed wharf construction around the harbor often drew the ire of government officials for clogging up ship traffic in the bay and abetting contraband activities. The new warehouse projects at Regla and Santa Catalina were uncontroversial in part because they facilitated state surveillance of foreign merchants as well as the collection of duties at a time of heightened colonial anxiety.[61] They also seemed to promote a liberal-capitalist view of the general good that was becoming increasingly common in elite Cuban circles. As Juan de Lara, a spokesman of the Junta, explained, "the purpose of [the Regla Warehouse Company] is not to monopolize branches of commerce or necessary articles, but to make their supply more plentiful."[62] He reminded his colleagues on the Junta that, as the "admirable doctrines of economic science" instructed, the general good must trump personal injury to a few. Any innovation that could enhance what Cuban elites often called "*la economía de brazos*" was not to be taken lightly. "In a country that has a surplus of work and a shortage of workers," Lara warned, "employing uselessly a considerable number of hands . . . wastes precious time, and sinks considerable capital into what? Into depreciating the value of our produce."[63]

Lara brushed aside accusations that the warehouse company operated "to the benefit of the rich class of planters and to the disadvantage of the poor, orphans, and widows." He insisted instead "that the fortunes of all classes of society depend on the fortunes of the planters" and concluded, "The diverse secondary industries prosper and decay as the price of our Island's most important product rises and falls." Even though he began by saying the warehouse project served the general good, he hedged when pushed: the "secondary industries" of Cuba "find themselves links in an unbreakable chain with the mother industry, the production of sugar." The infrastructure of flows, Lara unwittingly acknowledged, could also be an infrastructure of fetters.[64]

In spite of Lara's glib assurances about the widespread social benefits of the new system, the construction of massive *barracones* at the Regla warehouse complex augured poorly for Afro-Cubans. Until the reprisals of 1844 following the Escalera conspiracy, free people of color had dominated the artisanal trades of Cuba's cities and towns. Known as "*negros oficiales*," they held a variety of urban occupations, including in the fine arts such as music, sculpture, and painting.[65] The crowded public wharves had been a locus of power for free Afro-Cuban workers. "At the end of the Seven Years War," Robert Paquette explains, "the Spanish Crown permitted certain free colored militiamen to command the disposition of colored dockworkers in the cities. . . . This privilege carried considerable prestige within the Afro-Cuban community and higher-than-average payment from the commercial houses that engaged the labor."[66] By 1840 leaders of *cabildos* (legally approved religious brotherhoods organized by African ethnicity) like Jose Agustín Ceballos and Marcelino Gamarra controlled dockworker gangs.[67] They recruited crews, supervised work, and dealt with shippers and merchants.

Descriptions of the waterfront "disorder" bemoaned by law-and-order technocrats like Albear and Captain-General Miguel Tacón typically featured black dockworkers as part of the cacophony. One visiting memoirist wrote in 1844 that the quay was "covered with bales of merchandise, barrels and boxes of produce, heaps of not very fragrant dried beef, of cheese, garlic, hides, lard, etc., and was so crowded with negro laborers engaged in loading or unloading the vessels. . . ."[68] An English visitor, waving away clouds of cigar smoke blown in his face by "unemployed seamen," also disapprovingly noted groups of men organizing their own labor. "A multitude of semi-nude negroes yell and sing while loading and unloading ships," he wrote.[69] Associated with the general din, disorder, and filth of the waterfront, Afro-Cubans overseeing freight handling at the important interstitial node clearly made whites nervous.

Beyond the wharves, black teamsters, coachmen, and "innumerable negro porters with wheelbarrows, or carrying huge loads on their heads" dominated city streets. Before the opening of the Regla warehouses, one contemporary observed, "when the crops of sugar, molasses, and coffee are brought here for exportation, [the streets] are sometimes so blocked up by the laden carts, and the whole place becomes so filled with the accumulated produce, that it is not unusual for the Captain-General to grant permission to labor not only on the Sabbath, but during the whole of each night. . . ."[70] (Figure 3-4). High season thus threatened to make the streets a round-the-clock work space, like the boiling house. To some observers, though, the distribution of power seemed much different in the streets than it did in the sugar mill.

In the years before Escalera, Afro-Cuban transport workers and dockworkers thus drew the unwanted attention of authorities. Increasingly, free artisans of color in Havana were attacked for taking white immigrants' jobs. In 1837, Captain-General Tacón made it illegal for any foreign-born free person of color to enter the country. The excluded population included the many black sailors serving in the British Navy, who were forced to remain onboard during their vessel's stay in Havana.[71] The measure was passed at least partly in response to an 1835 shoreline brawl between a contingent of West India regiments (stationed in the harbor to process captured

FIGURE 3-4 The thoroughfares of Old Havana were notoriously narrow. At times it seemed there was not enough room for both goods and people to maneuver, spurring both public and private interests to find ways around the colonial quarter's traffic congestion. From Samuel Hazard, *Cuba with Pen and Pencil* (Hartford: Hartford Publishing Company, 1871), 164.

emancipados) and a group of white creoles who suspected them of fomenting rebellion among the enslaved.[72] The measure was just one aspect of Tacón's stepped-up policing of urban free blacks' daily lives along the waterfront in the 1830s.[73]

For many agents of colonial security, free dockworkers presented the urban face of the pre-Escalera rebellions. In 1839, the *Abakuá* secret society, a more radical Afro-Cuban organization that grew out of the *cabildos*, contributed to an uprising of workers in Havana's harbor. Led by a black militia officer named León Monzon, the uprising involved dockworkers, artisans, and enslaved people.[74] In the following years, several officers of the free colored militia "orchestrated uprisings in eastern Cuba composed of soldiers, slaves, dock workers, and artisans."[75] One stevedore named Margarito Blanco, a member of the Afro-Cuban *Carabalí* organization, was implicated in a possible Havana conspiracy in 1841 and exiled to Spain.[76]

Because leaders of color had joined with slaves to foment resistance at strategically important wharves, Escalera prosecutions focused heavily on black labor captains on the waterfront. In Matanzas, so many stevedores were arrested in 1844 that commerce came to a standstill. Teamsters in the employ of Matanzas warehouses were convicted of hatching a conspiracy to seize a military fort.[77] Agustín Ceballos, captain of the dockworkers in Havana, was also outed as "President of Havana, and Captain of the Blacks" in post-uprising confessions and imprisoned until he died.[78] When an official investigated "the slave gangs that worked the docks for the various sugar merchants," he became convinced "that hundreds were under the command of a slave named Domingo Lucumí."[79] Punishments duly ensued. Even those who escaped death by torture or execution lost their livelihoods while in jail or exile. Finally, as part of the 1844 reaction to the uprisings, all "foreign born free people of color" residing in Cuba were expelled. Counted among this number were other dockworkers like Diego Domingo, a transplant from Florida.[80]

The new warehouses, while not as directly violent, formed a key part of the mid-nineteenth-century assault on free Afro-Cuban autonomy and economic power. Generally, they employed enslaved men and indentured Chinese, a labor force more closely contained in *barracones*, politically disempowered, and internally divided. The enslaved and indentured also worked at a new location, remote from the locus of their pre-1844 power. Moreover, advances in transport efficiency made possible the transfer of enslaved women and men to sugar plantations in the countryside after La Escalera.

Regla itself was partly cleansed of disorderly elements for the infrastructure of flows to be set in place. The town reputedly had been a pirate hideout in the eighteenth century. A US travel guide reported that "the last act of piracy occurred in 1839, when the brig Halcione bound from Jamaica to Nova Scotia, was taken off Cape San Antonio and all of the crew were murdered except one man, who eluded discovery, swam ashore and gave information which led to the capture of the pirates, and all of them were garroted in Havana."[81] What followed in Regla was a far more orderly node in the plantation complex.

The complex at Regla also created open space in the city itself. By 1857, the new wharfside warehouses removed an estimated 700,000 wagon trips per year from the streets of Havana.[82] The relative quiet of the city's major thoroughfares must have soothed racial anxieties. Observers' sense of both sugar and black workers vanishing from the city was, at least in part, a delusion of the white-sugar sector. Muscovado and syrups continued to move largely along the same trajectories, as can be seen in Albear's 1849 complaints about wharf congestion. Whether entirely accurate or not, these reports of urban clearing strongly signaled the political nature of transportation reforms.

By the 1850s, transportation between Regla and Old Havana was dominated by several lines of North American-made steamships, which displaced hundreds of small ferrymen. Afro-Cuban craftsmen had historically been prominent in the building trades. Like their counterparts on the docks, these men, too, expected to exert some control over their labor. In 1841, around forty slaves engaged in the construction of the Palacio Aldama went on strike. Authorities ordered Spanish soldiers to open fire on the strikers; the attack killed six people and wounded ten more.[83]

The post-Escalera changes in the sugar industry brought European-educated architects and builders to displace native-born craftspeople, reinforcing physical violence with professional exclusion. The prefabricated architecture of the Regla warehouses helped de-skill construction work, minimizing opportunities for artisan builders. The prefabricated parts were "sometimes actually assembled into manageable subsections before they reached the construction site, needing only to be set in place and bolted down, which yielded economies in time, energy, and money," explain two architectural historians.[84] Designed by the American architect James Bogardus, an early inventor of prefabricated buildings, the iron and glass warehouses further weakened the position of individuals skilled in the lumber and brick-based building trades.[85]

Because he had only a small foundry, Bogardus outsourced the casting work to New York City establishments like West Point Foundry and Novelty Works, both of which had already sold sugar mills and other iron equipment to Cuban planters.[86] These firms likely obtained their raw iron and coke from nearby eastern Pennsylvania mines. After the precast parts were delivered to Bogardus's factory, about seventy employees used steam-powered mills to plane, clean, and trim the parts to ensure that the modules fit together snugly when the building was erected in Cuba (Figure 3-5).[87]

Partnering with the director of the Santa Catalina Warehouse Company, Bogardus was awarded a patent for his designs in Havana in 1859.[88] Soon after, Regla company director Eduardo Fesser used Bogardus's products to expand the original buildings, which had reached capacity by the end of the 1850s. The warehouses were far from the only prefabricated imports to

FIGURE 3-5 The Santa Catalina Warehouse, still under construction in 1860. Note the retaining wall built out on the water, and Bogardus's prefabricated iron structure being filled in with brick walls.

From "Scenes in Cuba: Vistas Cubanas. No. 84. View of the Large Iron Sugar Warehouse at Havana, with the Cabaña Hill in the Distance." Stereoscope slide in author's possession.

reshape the Cuban system. Cuba also looked to the United States for completed sugar boxes, hogsheads, and rum pipes, not to mention for steam engines and sawmills.[89] This turn toward imports helped complete Cuba's late transition to a plantation society.

With hundreds executed, hundreds more exiled, and the rest of the free colored population subject to draconian regulations, eking out an independent living by using craft skills like carpentry, baking, or brick laying became much more difficult for Afro-Cubans after 1844.[90] In a time of anxiety over labor scarcity, many of these residents were pushed out of the port city and joined a larger labor force on sugar plantations. The logistical changes, disadvantageous to free and collectively mobilized dockworkers and shippers as they were, would very likely have been resisted. But in the traumatized quiet of December 1844, the merchant-planter elite at the Regla warehouses prevailed.

Planters without Merchants

When the remarkable cast-iron structures first went up in Havana, they were a major attraction. Creole planters, who thought they might be able to erect their own majestic buildings to shelter themselves from the usurious grasp of merchants, particularly admired them. However, it turned out to be a more complicated process than simply snapping together some prefab walls and watching the money flow in. Begun with great optimism in 1856, the Marimelena Warehouse Company sought to reproduce the Regla model of cast-iron warehouses fronting deep-water wharves. However, as opposed to making the storage of boxed sugar cheaper, the planters who organized this venture sought egress for cheaper byproducts like aguardiente, muscovado, and syrups.[91]

Planter and company director Narciso de Foxá rallied investors by reciting time-honored producerist grievances against underhanded merchants. Most planters depended on advances from merchants in order to finance the year's purchase of slaves, equipment, and other supplies. In turn, they committed to delivering an agreed-upon number of boxes to the lending merchant. These ubiquitous deals restricted their freedom of action in the markets, a freedom further constricted by merchants' infrastructural control in the pre-Regla world. Foxá added that increased rum production at home and in the United States had lately made molasses "an object of grand speculation." While this change might have presented an opportunity for planters, "a number of speculators, distributed throughout the many productive centers of the island," robbed them of profits. These dishonorable individuals purchased syrups at the plantations themselves "far in advance" and paid "half the market value," because, "as they exclusively possess wharves, lighters, and other means of transport," they exercised control and skimmed many of the profits from cultivators. One can perceive echoes of the Regla rationale of "selling to eight purchasers simultaneously," a plan that must have sounded ideal to planters trapped in Foxá's situation. Marimelena was founded on the promise that planters could solve their problems by cutting out the middlemen, handling the storage of molasses on their own, and dealing directly with foreign markets.[92]

Enthused by the promise of emancipation from the merchants' infrastructure of fees, well over a hundred planters signed on in 1857. The firm quickly acquired coasting schooners needed to bring molasses to the city, as well as the lighters needed to deliver hogsheads to oceangoing ships after sale. Even deciding to handle some of the packing business, the company built a cooper's shop on site. Finally, it signed an accord with the Regla-Guanabacoa Railroad

Company to put the Marimelena warehouses in communication with new sugar districts in Matanzas.[93]

In spite of the optimism shown in the company's inaugural year, by 1862 it had yet to take flight. Many investors never paid up on their subscriptions. Even the Board of Directors, read one report, had "completely abandoned the company." The government inspector of corporations David de Arcos drolly described the board members as "determined not to meet." The board finally admitted in 1865 that "the small number of warehouses built, [and] the lack of elements facilitating our access to commerce, have reduced our operations to the deposit of a single article of trade."[94] It turned out that focusing on syrups alone would not get the investors where they needed to go financially. A well-placed syrups warehouse might have helped put-upon planters spend less on overhead, but as a joint stock enterprise that had shareholders to satisfy, planters without real roots in the transport system could not hope to fully extricate themselves from the morass of debt and logistics in which merchants held them. Nor would dealing in lower-cost byproducts alone be sufficient to accumulate the necessary capital to uproot the system without bankrupting the company.

When the directors finally held a meeting and issued a report to the shareholders and the government, they only did so in order to liquidate the corporation. They were taken to court repeatedly for unpaid debts in the early 1860s, and some of their buildings went up for auction. However, only one buyer was interested: the Regla Warehouse Company, an envied rival. To add to the insult, Regla managers indicated that they wanted to purchase the buildings in order to extract them from the site to feed their own expansion.[95]

The contrast between the Marimelena warehouses and those of Regla could not have been more stark in the late 1850s. As Regla sought to augment its capital, expand storage space for higher-quality purged sugar, and build a new *barracón* for its captive workforce, Marimelena failed to fill its byproduct warehouses, to collect promised funds from skittish investors, or even to hold the attention of its Board of Directors.[96] Marimelena struggled because indebted planters could not extricate themselves from advance contracts and continued to sell to middlemen who had their own established paths of egress and valorization, especially when it came to syrups.

A similar project also foundered. Established by a group of elite planters in 1857, the Compañía de Almacenes de los Hacendados (the Planters' Warehouse Company) invested hundreds of thousands of pesos in building twelve warehouses, spacious wharves, construction shops, and a railroad spur that would intersect with that of the Havana Railroad Company (HRC). They also established a planters' bank to obtain credit on better conditions than those offered by merchants. Designed to hold boxes of sugar as well as hogsheads of molasses, facilities were also constructed to house and control over 300 workers, a combination of slaves and indentured Chinese.[97]

The success of the project depended on a proposed connection to the lines of the HRC. In 1862, the warehouse company president nervously acknowledged the linkage as "a question of life or death" for the firm.[98] The Ferrocarril del Oeste (the Western Railroad Company, or WRC) already reached the warehouses, but it competed for freights with the HRC's western branch, and was losing out. In order to take business away from the HRC, the WRC had reduced fares to an unprofitable level in its first years of operation. Thus drawing from a shallow pool of capital in the following years, the WRC never succeeded in completing its projected lines.[99]

Starved of sugar by its struggling railroad partner, the Planters' Warehouse Company tried to build a spur connecting the two lines so that the HRC's much more plentiful freight could ride the WRC's line to their buildings on the shore. However, construction of this railroad spur was delayed by a conflict between the HRC and the WRC over rights of way. Once that issue had been cleared up at the end of 1860, the Planters' Warehouse Company got government approval for a new line and contracted the work out to the HRC for 75,000 pesos at 10 percent annual interest. Unfortunately for the warehousers, the HRC had just received permission from the government to relocate their own freight terminal to a long-coveted seaside location. As the HRC poured all available resources into its own project, its directors held off the increasingly desperate Planters' Warehouse Company with promises that they would begin working on the projected spur by the end of 1862.[100]

Because of the warehouses' continued lack of railroad connections, the only shipments they received between 1858 and 1862 were those deposited by the shareholders themselves. The company president bemoaned the insufficient freight and the loans coming due, and appeared to be losing faith. When the HRC's directors renewed their promise to complete the connection in 1863, he responded with skepticism. The one-kilometer spur connecting the two railroad lines was not actually built until 1867, so all that time the warehouse continued to depend on the trickle of "minor products," as well as some coffee, brought in by the floundering WRC.[101] Having hitched itself to this unlucky railroad firm, the Planters' Warehouse Company struggled.

Although it still appeared on maps in 1875, the company was of little importance in sugar transport.[102]

It was big merchant-planters like Fesser and Lacoste whose cooperation, expertise, and wealth were integral to the success of the Regla, Santa Catalina, and San José warehouse firms. Planter-led warehouses struggled because of lack of access to capital, lack of access to sugar, and their inability to reshape the transport system to their own advantage. By contrast, prototypical big merchants like the Andalucian capitalist Eduardo Fesser were able to carry off ambitious shoreline projects.[103] Calling him a "merchant" does not capture the complexity of his economic activity, because, like other elite sugar men such as Drake, Zulueta, or Torriente, Fesser doubled as a planter. He gained access to the established planter elite by marrying into the Diago family, and through these family ties had the ear of some of the region's most powerful political officials.[104]

Even the wealthiest planters and merchant houses on the island, however, had to deal with sugar importers in New York, Baltimore, Boston, or London whose profits and power were much greater their own.[105] For this reason, the biggest Hispanic merchant houses in Havana and Matanzas opened branch offices in the United States and Europe in order to sell directly to refiners or retailers and thus cut out the middlemen like Moses Taylor. Fesser took this step in Liverpool, as did Zulueta, Baró, and others. Adept financial maneuvering enabled merchant-planters to take control of warehousing and avoid subservience to British or US commercial forces.

Having private urban warehouses themselves, they were able to see clearly how much the infrastructure of fees cost them. Some of them, like Zulueta and Poey, built private warehouses outside city limits of Old Havana. Others formed joint-stock companies, built large warehouses, reshaped the railroad network and the bay itself, and, by the 1860s, commandeered most of the island's purged sugar.

Vast amounts of wealth were plowed into warehouse projects in the 1840s and 1850s because the new incorporated storage firms made money for their shareholders by cheapening and accelerating the shipment of sugar. Thus the firms organized by Catalán merchant-planters attracted investors as well as customers. By 1866, the warehouses of Regla could hold 3 million boxes of clayed sugar (sometimes plantation white)—almost the entire product of the island. The simplified pathway for made transport far cheaper: with several of the warehouse firms also running their own railroads, these new large-scale operations reduced storage costs from seven or eight *reales* per box per year to three, a reduction that allowed planters' agents to hold onto their sugar until marketing it at the opportune moment—that is, if their crop had not already been mortgaged to finance the mill's operations, as the harvests of small planters usually were.[106]

Thus the 1837–1844 crisis, with its deflated prices and costly uprisings, moved elite merchant-planters to overthrow the old system in favor of an infrastructure of flows exclusively designed for white sugar producers. Their vertical integration of the planting, processing, shipping, and selling aspects of the sugar business, as well as connections to European bankers, provided them with deep pools of capital that freed them up to reshape Cuba's infrastructure to their own advantage, and to separate themselves from peer planters through their investments in machinery and thus the quality of sugar they manufactured. They also distinguished themselves from the merchant community in how they made their money: not from service fees, storage, and a never-ending chain of small loans, but by cheapening the movement of sugar at every stage. From squeezing more and more work out of enslaved people in the fields and factories, to wresting control of one of the most important Atlantic ports from both small merchants and Afro-Cuban organizations, elite merchant-planters and the experts they employed engineered an infrastructural revolution in the 1840s that brought them huge profits in the global flush times of the 1850s.

The Ongoing Transformation of Industrial Cuba

While the Warehouse Revolution was motivated in part by new railroads that shuttled overwhelming quantities of sugar to the ports of western Cuba after 1836, the dynamic was mutually reinforcing. Railroads that had been built within the old merchant-*solar* geography were quickly compelled to reshape themselves in response to the gravitational pull of the new wharf-warehouse complexes on the bay. In the mid-1830s, for example, the creole patriciate of Cuba, led by the Intendant Conde de Villanueva, had fought an acrimonious public battle against its nemesis, the fiercely pro-peninsular Captain-General Miguel Tacón, to locate the colony's first railroad station in the geographic center of the city, along Tacón's beloved Paseo del Prado. While the grandiose building that was eventually erected at the site bore witness to Villanueva's steadfast defense of creole rights, its location many blocks from the waterfront made it an inconvenient clearing house for much of the island's sugar. In the early years of railroad operation, trains brought sugar into Villanueva station from Güines, south of Havana, and one of the most important sugar-producing jurisdictions in Cuba. Commission merchants handling planters' product then had the sugar unloaded and taken to their private warehouses throughout the city, waiting, if they could, for a good day to sell. From those dispersed points of sale, export firms bought the sugar and took it to the docks for loading. Extra steps added considerable expense to the shipping of every box of sugar. Associated surcharges, of course, fell on the planter.

The Regla Warehouse Company sought to take advantage of this inefficiency by building a railroad line between Güines (a major stop of the HRC) and its warehouses across the bay from Havana. Fesser explained, "bringing [the sugar] directly to the warehouses of Regla without entering the city would provide an obvious utility ... to the planters, who will not pay as high a price for the transport of their product as they did from Villanueva Station to their warehouses within the city." The merchants, "who would take the product from those warehouses to the wharf," where one of their customary shippers would take it on board, would also benefit if the system oriented around the central station no longer determined how sugar was moved around.[107] Planters who owned those Güines plantations had invested unprecedented amounts of capital in the railroad line ending at Villanueva station, but railroads, they eventually came to understand, worked no magic in and of themselves. Even a mechanized infrastructure that still depended on the merchant-*solar* geography added unnecessary costs—costs that became increasingly clear as *ingenios* were established in the provinces east of Havana and began shipping their goods to the Regla Warehouse Company. A monument to creole modernity in 1837, Villanueva Station looked more like a tombstone by 1852.

In order not to lose to the Regla Warehouse Company all of the sugar coming from Güines, the HRC submitted a proposal in 1852 to separate its freight handling from its passenger terminal and relocate the sugar warehouse to a waterfront site at the edge of Old Havana. HRC General Administrator José Antonio Echeverría proposed repurposing the old *Factoría de Tabacos* into a sugar warehouse.[108] Relic of a restrictive government tobacco monopoly that had been abolished in 1817, the Factoría was perhaps the most eloquent architectural icon of a mercantilist world of Cuban international commerce. It is possible that Echeverría was urged to consider the *Factoría* by government officials because the vast structure stood unused at the time. The dock of the *Factoría*, however, barely had enough room for coastwise sailing schooners, much less the oceangoing vessels that played an increasingly prominent role in Cuban shipping.[109] Echeverría coveted the high-ceilinged Regla warehouses, lamenting that the *Factoría*'s "interior distribution is inappropriate for warehouses, much of its roof being found in a poor state." Even worse for the new era of speed and economy were the slowdowns caused by "the hulks of old ships [that] scatter the floor of the bay," hampering harbor access.[110]

After the *Factoría* plan had been deemed unfeasible, the HRC offered an alternate plan to build grand warehouses on the waterfront and use embankments to extend the land further out into the bay so that ships of all sizes could dock there to load sugar. The proposed railroad-controlled warehouse project would, however, be quite costly. In order to raise the necessary capital the railroad would have to sell its parcels of land around Villanueva Station and the old *Jardín Botánico* (another creole point of pride), for which the railroad still owed mortgage payments to the state. The state's interest in the newly segregated infrastructure led it to forgive the debt, a gesture that enabled the railroad to sell the land once so valued for its central location and move closer to the shoreline.[111]

The 1852 proposal never bore fruit. In 1856, 1,200-lb. hogsheads of molasses that had come in to Villanueva Station were still being hauled out to the government wharves by mule wagon. Because of the weight, and the lack of suitable equipment, workers simply rolled the hogsheads off the carts and let them slam onto the wooden wharf, gradually depressing that section of the wharf, as well as occasionally damaging the iron columns that held up the shelter.[112] Another ambitious proposal for an HRC freight terminal was denied by Naval officials in 1858. Thwarted by the state, the HRC contented itself with the half-measure of building interior urban railways from Villanueva station to the nearby warehouses of San José.

Their real solution was more radical, but also more in keeping with what planter-led railroad firms had become accustomed to doing. In 1859, the HRC bought the Güines-Matanzas Railroad Company and expanded its lines, gaining direct access to new plantation districts, as well as a maritime outlet through the railroad terminal in the Bay of Matanzas.[113] The HRC continued to use the San José Warehouses for the sugar marketed out of Havana. The planter-dominated HRC, in other words, wisely decided to leave warehousing alone.

In the meantime, the Regla Warehouse Company abandoned plans to build their own branch out of Güines, and sank their capital into the Bay of Havana-Matanzas line, which gave them access to newer plantation districts and traveled between the two cities considerably faster than coastal schooners. The railway's western terminus did not even reach Havana. Its main purpose was to bring within the orbit of Havana merchants the rich, new sugar-producing areas of Matanzas, Coliseo, Colón, and Sagua la Grande, which lay to the east of Cuba's original sugar heartland and clearly represented the future of the colony's plantation complex.

In the same years the merchant-planter elite, together with the plantation experts they gathered around themselves, extended their infrastructural revolution out into the bay, erecting large dry docks to repair merchant ships and speed their voyages, while constructing more warehouses for white sugar (Figure 3-6). In combination with efficient railroad/wharf/warehouse facilities, whiteness of sugar gave sellers more flexibility in marketing, which provided a boost within a broader Atlantic world where concentrations of New York and

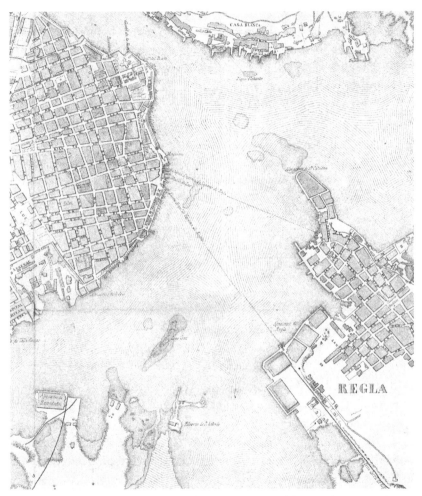

FIGURE 3-6 This 1875 map gives a useful "after" picture of the Warehouse Revolution. The old *Factoría de Tabacos* has been turned into the Hospital Militar, and the San José Warehouses, which replaced the Villanueva Station as the drop-off point for overland sugar shipments, are just to the east of the Arsenal. But the big story is on the eastern side of the bay. Contrast the scale of the Regla and Santa Catalina Warehouses to the planter-run Marimelena Warehouses (southeast of Santa Catalina).

From Esteban Pichardo, *Carta Geo-topográfica de la Isla de Cuba* (Habana, Cuba, 1875), plate 25. Archivo Nacional de Cuba. Sala de Mapas y Planos. Digital copy made available by Jorge Macle, Archivo Nacional de Cuba.

London capital were far larger than that of even the wealthiest of Cuba's elite. Beginning in the 1840s, the built landscape of Cuba's coastline was reshaped according to the temporal and environmental strictures imposed by *el principio sacarino*, but always in connection with the island's unstable position within capitalism's global geographic division of labor.

4

Wrought-Iron Politics

RACIAL KNOWLEDGE IN THE MAKING OF A GREATER
CARIBBEAN RAILROAD INDUSTRY

EIGHTEENTH-CENTURY MERCHANTS' LETTERS contained a litany of complaints about the difficulty of moving goods over roads and rivers that were passable only in given parts of the year. Railroads were the first all-season, all-weather mode of overland transportation, and their reliability was at least as important as their speed.[1] The strict time frames of the Derosne system and the new Havana warehouses would have been meaningless without the dependability of the railroads, which enabled the increased systemization of the sugar trade in Cuba.

The expert personnel who managed the new phase of Cuba's transportation system after 1844 represented a departure from the pioneering group of railroad builders. US engineers, in particular West Point–trained southerners with experience laying out tracks, bridges, and tunnels in "tropical climates," replaced many English engineers on new lines in Cuba. To win contracts, this North American cohort mobilized particular topographical and environmental knowledge, as well as self-proclaimed experience in racial management, gained on major Upper South railroad projects like the Baltimore and Ohio (B&O) and Virginia and Tennessee routes. The new generation of southern railroad experts in Cuba depended in part on hardware manufactured at the Tredegar Ironworks of Richmond, Virginia. For a key element of its expansion in the late antebellum years, Tredegar widened its customer base by exporting railway equipment, along with steam-powered sugar mills and steam-powered sawmills, to Cuba. Doing brisk business with the HRC, the Matanzas Railroad Company, and other firms, Tredegar sent numerous agents to the island and even stationed one permanently in New Orleans, in part to capitalize on Cuban sugar economy linkages there.[2] In 1857 the company gained access to what may have been the island's most important railroad undertaking since the completion of the first line: the Bay of Havana–Matanzas Railroad Company. By connecting the new remote warehouse districts of Havana and Matanzas to one another, the coastline route created a specialized circuit for white sugar.[3]

Because railroads were a relatively new line of business in the 1840s and 1850s, equipment had yet to be standardized to any significant degree. Iron makers fashioned custom goods to meet the discerning needs of a clientele that, in the case of Cuba, saw itself as uniquely tropical. To win their business, Tredegar invested in new machinery and production processes to manufacture a variety of creolized hardware specially tailored to the Caribbean climate. For example, since standard English spikes often popped out of moisture-softened wooden cross ties, Tredegar rigged their spike machines to add a trademark tapered point to allow for deeper fixing within the wood.

Making new products presupposed skilled workers who were not overwhelmingly attached to an entrenched way of doing things. In a 1840s experiment to "introduce slave labor generally" into a factory dominated by white ethnic artisans, Tredegar manager Joseph Reid Anderson was trying to cultivate just this kind of malleable workforce. Although Anderson neglected to say so, the reason the experiment could even be entertained was that enslaved, skilled ironworkers had long held a prominent place in Virginia manufacturing, working as plantation blacksmiths, rural smelters and colliers, and urban tradesmen of various kinds. Breaking white artisans' monopoly on iron-making expertise and redesigning racial divisions of labor on the shop floor, Anderson facilitated Tredegar's access to the emerging "tropical railroad market." However, his experiment with enslaved ironworkers violated the premise of racial stratification that suffused the culture of working-class whites in antebellum America. They responded by going out on strike in 1847.

Significantly, Anderson focused his managerial reforms in the parts of the factory where relatively new processes in wrought-iron manufacture gave the small number of white artisans who knew its trade secrets considerable power and where his ability to transform ways of working was weakest. In the foundry, where cast-iron goods were made, tasks were relatively simple, and intransigent workers could usually be replaced. In the wrought-iron world of puddling furnaces and rolling mills, on the other hand, skilled laborers worked with new machinery to tame a more temperamental raw material and produce a superior set of products. This chapter begins by showing how managers and workers at the Tredegar ironworks fought in the realm of "wrought-iron

politics," at the node of production most indispensable to the firm's expansion
into the Caribbean market, controlled by white ethnic workingmen whose
sense of privilege was rooted in clear racial divisions of labor. Since Tredegar's
workforce was only about 10 percent enslaved in 1860, Anderson's effort to
alter the prevailing arrangements of work, race, and power in the factory has
been seen as a failure. But if his main intent was to use the most vulnerable
southerners to exert new kinds of control over skilled artisans, his experiment
can be viewed as more successful.

Installing a flexible regime of production at Tredegar was necessary for
the firm's Caribbean ambitions, but proprietors of this ironworks still needed
to know precisely what new equipment Cuban railroad firms desired. They
required up-to-the-minute intelligence reported from the track beds across
the Cuban countryside. The chapter thus moves on to trace Tredegar's
knowledge of tropical railroads through an information-gathering network
that began with enslaved operatives working along the tracks in rural Cuba.
Slaves working as watchmen, brakemen, and switchmen for railroad firms had
unparalleled daily knowledge of worn rails, missing spikes, and loose crossties.
They had also played a prominent role in the 1840s uprisings, so were treated
with suspicion by government officials. Their trackside intelligence passed
through several intermediaries before reaching Richmond factory managers
who may never have suspected the origins of their insider information. The
technological creolization at the root of Tredegar's entry into the railroad
market of Cuba was a product of racialized vectors of knowledge circulation
across the Greater Caribbean.

While the Upper South engineering network used expertise in tropical
environments (including racial knowledge) to market their individual skills,
their success in Cuba was also rooted in robust North American institutions,
especially the US Army Corps of Topographical Engineers and the engineering staff of the B&O Railroad.[4] Furthermore, Southern engineers with
experience on early railroads in South Carolina and New Orleans had been
employed on Cuban railroads since 1833. In spite of Tredegar's institutional
ties to these early experts, its managers still had to embark on an aggressive
campaign to get into the Cuban market.

As Tredegar began supplying the Cuban railroad market in earnest in
the late 1850s, it had to undertake expensive innovations in machinery and
industrial processes in precisely those parts of the factory shaken by racialized worker-management conflicts. Thus wrought-iron politics reappeared
ten years after the 1847 strike. Workingmen in the racially integrated rolling
mill both pioneered innovations tailored for the Cuban market and refused

to follow other specifications demanded by southern engineers in charge of Cuban railroad improvements. Enslaved skilled workers, incentivized by overtime pay, were very likely involved in developing the innovations that enabled Tredegar to capture segments of the Cuban railroad market. Of the eighty slaves working at Tredegar in 1860, thirty were skilled operatives working in the blacksmith shop and, crucially, in the rolling mill.[5] They worked alongside some of the more widely traveled artisans in the country, many of whom hailed from Wales or northeastern cities. These craftsmen had the latest knowledge of puddling and rolling, and slaves apparently learned those skills thanks to the forceful interventions of Anderson and his managers.[6] The creole alterations that Tredegar directors ordered slaves to introduce on the shop floor in Richmond combined local knowledge of the Cuban landscape with networked ironworking knowledge from across the Atlantic World. Two streams of enslaved knowledge—in fact, two complicated webs of willfully hidden and partially extracted knowledge—became deeply entangled in the Greater Caribbean of the 1850s.

By the time Virginia's political leaders elected to secede, Tredegar had been supplying Cuban railroads for four years. The firm was in the process of building a wider network of direct links with Cuban engineers and railroad board members when the demands of war and the Union blockade put an end to their railroad contracts. During the Civil War, however, their business relationships in the Caribbean became more vital than ever. Junior managers recast the firm's relationship with Cuba by using Havana as a base for running war materiel through the blockade. Thus its ties to Cuba helped the firm underwrite the ambitions of a hemispheric plantation empire. Tredegar's enslaved workers, however, had their own plans for how to forge a new wrought-iron politics in a war for emancipation.

Wrought-Iron Politics: The Tredegar Strike of 1847

When Cuba's inaugural line was built in 1836, Tredegar was a small, struggling ironworks facing the problems of scarce skilled labor and competition from northern firms. By 1858, through capturing new markets and cutting costs, it had become one of the top iron manufacturers in the United States. The expansion of cotton and sugar plantations across the southwest sparked an explosion of railroad construction in the 1850s, resulting in unprecedented demand for iron rails, spikes, locomotives, and other equipment manufactured by Tredegar.[7] Tredegar had also become one of four national ironworks to have major contracts with the expanding US Navy and Army. The firm built large-bore cannons for the Navy throughout the 1840s, an iron steamer, and the engines and boilers for two navy frigates.[8]

Tredegar's plentiful government contracts helped it achieve initial financial success. In the antebellum republic, politicians seeking to protect slavery advocated military buildup to expand the horizons of the plantation complex and to resist alleged abolitionist aggressions from the British. Southern federal office holders like Jefferson Davis, Abel Upshur, and Robert M. T. Hunter did not so much oppose federal power as attempt to grasp it and turn it to the defense of slavery.[9] Tredegar supplied iron to a burgeoning New World empire and sold railroad equipment in the booming cotton zones of Louisiana, East Texas, and Mississippi.

Tredegar used its newfound national prominence to engineer unprecedented city-hinterland relationships in Virginia. The completion of the James River and Kanawha Canal, along with the Virginia Central and other railroads by the early 1850s, facilitated a new pattern in the commodity chains of the Virginia iron industry. Iron ore was still mined in western parts of the state and converted to "pig iron" by smelting the ore in local blast furnaces.[10] It was then shipped to Richmond, where it could be cast directly into products like cannon and muskets.[11] Because of its business with southern railroads, as well as with the Army and Navy, however, Tredegar outgrew the Valley furnaces, purchased several of them outright, and also brought in additional pig iron from Europe. By 1860, Tredegar alone consumed more pig iron than all sixteen of the state's blast furnaces produced.[12]

Given Tredegar's success in the North American plantation empire, it is not surprising that the firm attempted to gain access to other plantation centers of the Atlantic World like Cuba and Brazil. For ambitious southern elites, who ultimately sought to internationalize US slavery, Cuba was the key to the future. In the 1850s, Tredegar used profits and reputation built from its government ordnance contracts, local business in Virginia, and customers among the new railways of the cotton kingdom to expand its capitalist activities into the Caribbean, deepening longstanding ties between the Upper South and the slavery-based economies of Latin America.

Tredegar's first step, taken fifteen years prior to its expansion into Cuba, was an experiment. In the spring of 1842, the board of directors of Tredegar gathered to discuss problems besetting the recently established firm. Faced with an inadequate local supply of skilled labor, competition from northern iron makers, and generally unfavorable economic conditions, the company's directors requested a "curtailment of expenditures" from their ambitious young manager, West Point–educated engineer Joseph Anderson. He replaced "five white men employed there at $1.00 per day ... by negroes" hired from local slave owners for $180 per year.[13] Anderson found that work continued satisfactorily while labor costs were substantially reduced. The unspoken premise underlying Anderson's gambit was the existence of a population of slaves with skills in iron. Even if the slaves he proposed to employ did not already know how to puddle and roll, black ironworkers had plenty of expertise in other facets of metalworking. They would also have been eager to acquire new and valuable skills, which could give them added bargaining power and even eventual freedom.

On the basis of the success of the shop floor experiment, Anderson confidently recommended that the firm should introduce "slave labour generally in the several branches of Iron manufacture."[14] In his opinion, Tredegar should maintain only a small number of white men to train the slaves and oversee them. His cost projections led him to believe that such "reforms" would save the company $11,181 per year. Even more than cost savings, he proposed a racial redesign of the factory workforce so as to exert control over ironworking knowledge that was at the time the nearly exclusive province of white artisans.

The white craftsmen employed at Tredegar had, in exchange for five years of guaranteed employment, agreed to "instruct such persons, hired men, apprentices, or servants as may at any time be placed in the establishment."[15] They were making a considerable concession by agreeing to work alongside black employees and in allowing their underlings to be chosen for them at a time when skilled ironworkers selected and trained their own assistants.[16] While metals artisans of the antebellum era were not known for being particularly interested in sharing the secrets of their craft with anyone, working-class racial politics had thus far made the training of industrial slaves particularly difficult. Anderson complained that "certain operations, as Puddling, Heating, Rolling etc. are known only to foreigners and a few Americans who have been from interest opposed to imparting this knowledge to negroes."[17] Anticipating white artisans' reluctance, Anderson drew up employment contracts in 1842 that made explicit the company's right "to discharge any or all" of them for the grave offense of "not imparting information to others."[18]

Anderson's goal was never to convert entirely to slave labor, but to gain greater flexibility by bringing in new players: hired slaves, directly owned slaves, apprentices, convict laborers, wage workers, and inside-contracting craftsmen.[19] Anderson sought to mitigate the power of skilled white artisans in his factory, especially in the event of a labor conflict. His "reform"

strategically reallocated slaves in an explicit disavowal of iron puddlers'
entrenched authority in and around the furnaces.[20]

The skilled workmen responded to Tredegar's initiative by launching one
of the defining labor conflicts of the antebellum South in 1847. Unanimously
condemned by the Southern press, many of the white ironworkers were at
least temporarily dismissed after Anderson refused to meet their demands
that black workers be removed from the plant. Whether the strike failed or
succeeded, Anderson's language and the strikers' response make clear that the
Tredegar Strike was fundamentally a conflict over the racial and class politics
of industrial knowledge.[21]

During the strike, Anderson addressed an open letter "to my late workmen
at the Tredegar Iron Works," in which he insisted on the right to distribute
racialized units of labor across the factory as he saw fit. The white workmen were very specific about the politics of placement at particular tasks.
Anderson claimed they "would not work for me again until I had discharged
my negroes from the Squeezer and Puddle Rolls where they have been working several years and until the Armory Iron Company had discharged theirs
from the Puddling furnaces." Dismissing the ironworkers' accusation that he
had planned on replacing them entirely with slave labor, Anderson told the
strikers that he "had not designed to put Negroes to puddling at the Tredegar
Works, but that now I should be compelled by your quitting my employment
to do so."[22] Anderson claimed to have planned for slaves to occupy subordi-
nate positions, but the strike had "compelled" him to train and employ blacks
in puddling, one of the best-remunerated and highest-status jobs in a nineteenth-century iron mill.[23]

First developed in England in the 1780s, Henry Cort's puddling process
enabled the use of mineral coal for conversion of pig to wrought iron. Until
Cort's new furnace design, only charcoal could be used, because anthracite or bituminous fuel contaminated the iron with damaging byproducts
like sulfur. His long reverberatory furnace put the fuel at one end and the
iron at the other, preventing contamination (believing it to impart a special
character to their products, Tredegar continued to use charcoal in its puddling furnaces). After heating the furnace with coal for four or five hours,
the puddler and his assistant charged the opposite end of the furnace with
a load of pig iron and a small amount of heavily oxidized scrap metal left
over from other activities at the ironworks. A "draw" of air from the chim-
ney's open flue pulled the heat from the coal across the top of the iron, also
heating the brick lining of the furnace surrounding the iron.[24] The metal was

thus heated until it became semi-molten. The puddler then used his puddling bar to knead together the two metals until the oxygen from the scrap
reacted with the carbon and other byproducts in the pig, leaving the chim-
ney as gases (carbon monoxide foremost among these).

The refined wrought iron was then transferred to the rolling mill, where
it would be rolled and cut into "merchant bars" to be sold to other iron makers. Or it could be rolled into thin, ductile sheets, and rolled layer upon layer
into moldable but strong hardware like train rails. Before the emergence of
the rolling mill in the early nineteenth century, sheets of iron were painstak-
ingly produced under the forge hammer. The puddling process, combined
with new rolling mill technology, allowed for faster and more precise fining
of cast iron into wrought iron.[25] Both operations were crucial to the expansion of railroads, as they made it possible to produce sufficient amounts of
affordable high-quality rails.[26] After adding puddling furnaces and rolling
mills to the traditional charcoal methods still being used across much of
Continental Europe, Tredegar had the capacity to manufacture a wide variety of industrial hardware, as long as it could control the skilled puddlers
and rollers brought in from European or northern cities to carry out the new
wrought-iron processes.[27]

Aimed at offsetting high labor costs associated with skilled white ironworkers, Anderson's incorporation of slaves also sought to establish a sem-
blance of managerial control over them—desirable in the metalworking
industries, in which experimentation was an expected part of the business
because few specialized machine tools existed. The individual parts of complicated steam engines and textile machines were still made by craftsmen
using handheld tools.[28] This characteristic was even more pronounced in the
new railroad industry, where a decentralized firm structure prevailed. While
railroad hardware was particularly suited to standardization, specialized
machines capable of mass-producing heavy iron equipment were only slowly
coming into use in the 1840s.[29]

The lack of customary, well-known products drew managers, engineers
and ironworks owners into proximity with craftsmen, whom they would have
been more likely to leave in peace had the same old products been demanded
by customers. In the case of the shop floor experiment of 1842, the engineer,
the manager, and board of directors intervened decisively in the space of
production. When many of the white strikers were dismissed after the failed
labor action, the slaves with whom they had worked were to take an increasingly prominent role in the new puddling and rolling activities.

Enslaved Knowledge on the Cuban Railroad
Network

Between 1844 and 1860, Cuba's physical landscape underwent a broad and rapid transformation. Steamship lines, electromagnetic telegraphs, cast-iron warehouses, and a countryside dotted not only with industrialized sugar mills, but also with the workshops of machinists and watering stations for locomotives changed the face of the Spanish colony. Most discussed among these transformations has been the railroad industry, which put Cuba among the first few countries in the world to have a cohesive system of locomotive transportation.

The growth of railroad mileage accelerated in the last four years of the 1850s. In fact, the rate of construction between 1855 and 1860 was four times the rate of 1850–1854. By the close of the decade, twenty separate joint-stock railway companies operated hundreds of miles of line in Cuba.[30] Moreover, as local shareholders gradually became accustomed to the large capital outlays and delayed returns characteristic of the new business, and railroads proved themselves a permanent part of the sugar industry, the larger firms became willing to invest in the tailor-made, high-cost niche products in which Tredegar had begun to specialize. In the Caribbean railroad market, where consumers were prone to see their climatic, topographical, and political-economic conditions as unique, Tredegar could foreground the special regional character of its Virginia metal. Moreover, because of improvements in locomotive design, railroad companies began to tackle more challenging terrain. Steep, winding routes called for new kinds of topographical expertise, which was found among veteran managers of the Virginia Central and Virginia and Tennessee railroads.

This group of experts also boasted skills in racial management. Since the beginning of its construction in 1850, the Virginia and Tennessee Railroad rented hundreds of slaves from area slaveholders per year. Bondspeople, both women and men, were manual laborers, boilermakers, firemen, brakemen, sawyers, cooks, and shovel hands. Fragments of evidence even suggest the existence of enslaved engineers.[31] One northern visitor riding Virginia's City Point Railroad in 1846 noted that the "engineer, conductor, and sole manager" was "an old man who had no doubt been a slave for seventy years."[32] From the perspective of white managers, slaves, whatever their job, should be pushed to their physical limits. In most cases railroads preferred "hiring" bondspeople over outright purchase, because then the companies had to

worry only about short-term productivity, not the longevity of their workers. Masters at times resented this. One railroad contractor wanted to push
the hired slaves harder, but a local slaveowner "don't want [me] to Push the
hands nor even make them Doo what every Industrious man would make
them doo." The local master's interference was "a disadvantage to the Works
and spoils all the Negroes."[33] Hiring also ensured that the firm could quickly
unload slaves back onto their owners when not needed.[34] Finding that the
benefits of slave hiring outweighed the constraints, railroad experts would
bring these managerial practices to Cuba, as they designed racially diverse,
captive workforces to lay out a sprawling transportation system.

Far from exerting colonial dominance in any straightforward way,
Tredegar and its fellow engineering and iron-making firms from Virginia
and Maryland sought to join up with this dynamically expanding system.
To win contracts for the Cuban railroads' 1850s renovation, Tredegar
needed intelligence it could act on about what specific designs the company's engineers might want. Technical and commercial knowledge started
with railroad repairmen, watchmen, signalmen, and switchmen in western
Cuba. Repairmen walked up and down the lines after trains passed, looked
out for damage to the fixed way, and made rapid repairs. Watchmen kept an
eye out for livestock or possible vandalism along the lines, as well as equipment malfunction that could cause accidents. Switchmen stood alongside
track intersections and flipped a lever to send trains in one or the other
direction.[35] In each of these jobs, slaves were key information gatherers,
reporting problems along the line, and signaling pertinent news to train
conductors as they passed by. Slaves occupied strategic positions in the railroad network of Cuba.

While government inspector Juan Campuzano recommended that
the HRC replace these workers with white employees, company director
Gonzalo Alfonso insisted that slaves already trained for the job remain in
those positions.[36] A history of depending on enslaved knowledge in the
Greater Caribbean created the irony of railroad surveillance itself being
carried out by enslaved informants. While the very idea of black Cubans
acting as agents of surveillance presented a challenge to the racial status
quo, slaves had long been seen as possessing crucial local information
in plantation societies.[37] In a sense, railroad managers found themselves
tethered to the compromises in the racial hierarchy that they had uneasily
settled on during Cuba's rushed transformation into an unprecedentedly
large and modern sugar-plantation complex. When voicing his concerns

about slaves occupying strategic positions on the rail network, inspector Campuzano may have been recalling that enslaved railroad workers
had been primary participants in one of the Matanzas uprisings of 1843.
Clearly seen as potential insurgent leaders early in the revolt, these workers
had been imprisoned as a precautionary measure, but their fellow rebels
managed to break them out. Many then joined the uprising and fought to
the death against Spanish soldiers.[38]

In the pre-Escalera uprisings of the early 1840s, the most modern
nodes of the Cuban system (railroads, warehouses, cane fields, and large
ingenios) had been a focus of attacks because insurgents identified them
as strategic nodes of a system that oppressed them. Planters, merchants,
and the Spanish military apparatus designed counterinsurgent policies
to "cleanse" those spaces.[39] During the Escalera interrogations, scores
of state functionaries fanned out across the rural areas of Matanzas and
Cárdenas provinces, invading the sugar estates and investigating everything. Captain-General Pezuela undertook the same sort of plantation-
level inquiries in the early 1850s. Government inspection of the railroads
were an extension of these investigations and, in a similar manner, state
agents depended on enslaved people for their knowledge. The agents had
to acknowledge that their freedom of repressive action was limited by a
longer history of depending on black and mulatto labor and leadership,
making slaves' control of certain informational nodes unavoidable. Rulers
grudgingly accepted the reality that the people they trusted least possessed unique knowledge.

Some railroad company directors may have insisted on employing slaves
in particular strategic positions because of the failure of various nineteenth-
century schemes to "whiten" the island's laboring population by bringing in
"colonies" of Irish and Canarian railroad workers. The "Irish" were actually a
polyglot group of US immigrants brought to the tropics on contract. Their
death rate from disease was extremely high; those who survived fled to cities and towns in large numbers. The Canary Island "colonization" program
ended similarly. Finally, a troop of men imported from Galicia to build the
Trinidad Railroad rioted in the town until brought under control by a detach-
ment of Spanish infantry.[40]

After these whitening schemes failed, railroads mainly employed
slaves rented from local owners or directly purchased by themselves. Like
sugar planters, they also eagerly employed indentured Chinese, who
began to enter the country in 1847 and worked for very low wages.[41] Their

widespread employment aligns precisely with Cuba's renewal and renovation of lines, which provided the opportunity for Tredegar. By the time Tredegar spikes and rails began to be laid down on the new route to the warehouses of Regla in 1858, convicts, *emancipados*, slaves, coolies, and small contingents of free black and white day laborers were sharing much of the work sometimes holding positions of some authority (Figure 4-1).

Concerned by slave uprisings, as well as recent annexationist activities of creole railroad boosters, the Spanish state sought to reinsert its functionaries on the cutting edge of communications developments in Cuba, creating a new set of laws with respect to the railroads in the mid-1850s.[42] Until then, they had largely gone unregulated. As the saying went, "Spain has the laws and no railroads, while Cuba has the railroads but no laws." Government inspections were an important aspect of the new policies; military engineers like Campuzano performed mile-by-mile inspections every three months. Inspectors also ensured the proper maintenance of the graded roadbed, as well as the tunnels, bridges, and drainage works of every railroad in operation. The level and parallel position of the rails, how they were joined, and the condition of the cross-ties were also evaluated.[43]

FIGURE 4-1 Traveling sketch artist Samuel Hazard was struck by the "half Cubanized Chinois,'" commonly acting as conductors aboard trains in the 1860s.

From Samuel Hazard, *Cuba with Pen and Pencil* (Hartford: Hartford Publishing Company, 1871), 260.

Inspections were typically carried out on horseback, or in handcars, but inspectors were also encouraged to "move up and down the lines in trains of diverse speeds, in order to include kinds of movement and their effects."[44] The military engineers carrying out the inspections were instructed to communicate "the results of their investigations and observations not only to the authorities ... but also to the conductors, trains, stations, etc., sharing the latest developments."[45] The different inspectors were also ordered to gather information on one another. The railroad company's watchmen checked the work of the construction crews and the repairmen, while the repairmen responded to the watchmen, all of whom were beholden to the tri-monthly inspections of the government's engineers.

The language of data transmission was also important. The railroad workers were directed by the companies to deliver reports to the conductor through a set of hand and flag signals as the locomotive chugged from station to station. Conductors were instructed to "immediately obey all signals from the watchmen, repairers, switchmen or any other servants of the Company ... Any engineman neglecting to obey a signal, is liable to dismissal, and moreover the civil and criminal responsibility for his oversight."[46] The Cuban railroad network, thickly populated with observers and repairers, many of them enslaved, reverberated with up-to-the-minute technical reportage. When the network functioned right, it carried information from the periphery to the center of the railroad firms, as well as to an imperial railroad administration eager to assert control.

On the basis of such reports, Campuzano learned of "the damaged state of the great part of the rails." He blamed "the excessive service they have given to train traffic."[47] Several derailments had also given the HRC a bad reputation. Campuzano blamed not the rails themselves, but the small wooden keys wedged between the rail and the chair to keep the rails in place. He urged that the keys be made from "the correct wood," and that the wood be "pressed," so as to be less subject to warping and other humidity-induced changes in size and shape.[48] HRC president Gonzalo Alfonso echoed Campuzano's criticisms of the key design, complaining that "the task of replacing the sleepers and rails on all of the lines does not cease for a moment. . . ." Surely they had been apprised of the condition of the tracks by their own surveillance personnel. Alfonso's claim that the company's chief engineer had told him the renewal and repair were constant certainly put pressure on the engineers to act immediately to replace worn-out cross-ties, spikes, keys, and rails. However, climatic notions that the tropical air of Cuba caused keys to moisten, soften, and loosen in their seats led to discussions about purchasing equipment tailor made for the environment.

While the railroad company's engineers agreed with Campuzano about the problem with the keys, they proposed a more ambitious solution. As opposed to simply improving the make of the keys, the HRC's technical experts recommended investing the revenue of the successful firms in "the most advanced systems for the road-bed as well as for the super-construction, introducing to Cuba for the first time improvements that, while costly, have earned the approval of foreign countries for the benefits they bring to rail transport."[49] Not surprisingly, the most modern and costly equipment was that designed and patented by HRC's own chief engineer, New Yorker Miles Oliver Davidson. His patented design used iron spikes to fix the rails in the chairs, dispensing with the troublesome keys altogether.

The observations of enslaved switchmen and watchmen reporting on the large quantity of loosened or unaligned rails most likely encouraged Davidson to develop the new rail chairs. Upper-level HRC officials like General Administrator José Antonio Echeverría, creole engineer Manuel Bosque, Virginian railway engineer and HRC independent contractor Isaac Ridgeway Trimble, and Chief Engineer of the HRC Miles Oliver Davidson were sources of local, specific expertise—albeit one degree removed. These men had daily contact with the operatives who provided mile-by-mile knowledge of the conditions on HRC tracks. They were also the very engineers who were in contact with managers and partners of the Tredegar Ironworks like John Tanner and Joseph Reid Anderson during Cuba's railroad renovation of 1858–1861.

Company engineers translated slaves' local intelligence gathering along the railway lines in the Cuban countryside into specific hardware requests and thus shaped the course of industrial development in at least one Richmond factory. Even when it came to more standardized spikes, Tredegar foregrounded the special tropicality of its designs. Because of the difficulties of transporting old growth hardwoods over land, early Cuban railroads had imported white pine and oak from the United States. However, this "imported lumber showed low resistance to humidity and heat," a defect that probably contributed to the problem of spikes and keys popping out of place and eventually led inland railroads of the second generation to incorporate Cuban hardwoods. Tredegar was well aware that Cuban railroads had begun to use local lumber for their crossties and in the company catalogue touted their creolized spikes as particularly suited for hardwoods.[50] In

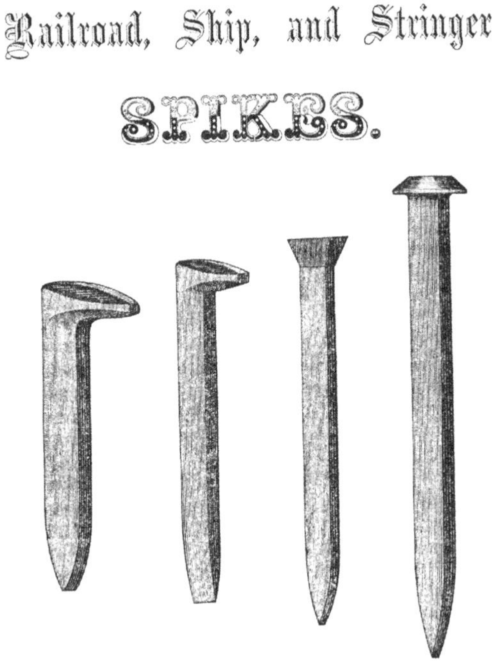

Railroad, Ship, and Stringer

SPIKES.

FIGURE 4-2 Tredegar marketed its machine-made spikes as specially tailored for tropical climates.

From *An Illustrated and Descriptive Catalogue of Manufactures of Tredegar Iron Works: Joseph
R. Anderson & Co., Richmond, Va., Edmond M. Ivens, General Agent* (Richmond, VA:1860), 16.

a letter to a Cuban company, the managers explained that Tredegar's spikes
"are made from charcoal iron and after a mode entirely unusual, making a
long sharp taper point" which made it possible to hammer them into place
(Figures 4-2 and 4-3).[51]

The Cuban economy exerted significant pressure on North American
companies to tailor their products to Cuban elites' perceptions of their
particular needs. Tredegar brought to the table experience working in hot,
humid climates, experience working with bridges and among mountains, and,
most of all, experience working with a captive, racialized workforce. In spite
of these advantages, Tredegar found that servicing the lucrative Cuban railroad market would require help from a broader community of West Point–
trained railroad engineers who had employed Tredegar for train-related work
in the 1840s.

TREDEGAR IRON WORKS

RAIL ROAD SPIKE MACHINE.

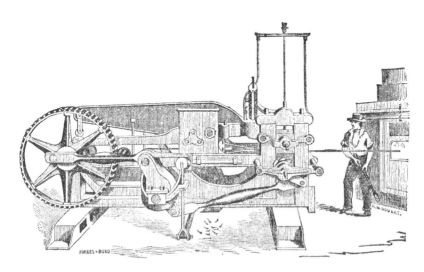

FIGURE 4-3 Tredegar's apparatus for mass-producing a set variety of spike designs. The heated iron rod passed out of the furnace directly in front of the workman, entered the mechanism, and was transformed rapidly into spikes, which were spat out under the belly of the machine.

From *An Illustrated and Descriptive Catalogue of Manufactures of Tredegar Iron Works: Joseph R. Anderson & Co., Richmond, Va., Edmond M. Ivens, General Agent* (Richmond, VA: 1860), 63.

Military and Engineering Networks in the Greater Caribbean

North Americans were widely employed as machinists on Cuba's large sugar estates, and as engineers on Cuban railroads in the first few decades of construction and operation. Planning for a first railroad in 1833, Spanish officials in New Orleans and New York contacted the few prominent engineers with railroad experience in both the United States and the United Kingdom, asking them to carry out initial studies for a railroad linking Havana and Güines. Alfred Cruger, who was well known for his work on the Erie Canal and for leading initial construction of the South Carolina Railroad, was hired first.[52] One of his important early projects, carried out in collaboration with a Spanish engineer, was the Coliseo railroad, which linked a rich new sugar-growing area to the nearby port of Matanzas.[53] For this project, Cruger hired Miles Oliver Davidson, a colleague from his Erie Canal days.

Before his first stint in Cuba, Davidson had worked almost exclusively in his native New York by participating in the construction of the Croton Aqueduct and the Erie Railway. Not until after his first stay in Cuba did he get involved in the US South, working for the B&O in particular.[54] Apparently, Davidson had to go to Cuba to get connected to inter-regional job opportunities back in the States, using Greater Caribbean networks established in Cuba to build a career in Tredegar's neck of the woods. When he returned to the island in 1857 to take up a higher post with the Havana Railroad Company, he brought his new Maryland and Virginia relationships with him. As chief engineer, Davidson was charged with recruiting suppliers and experienced engineers for the railroad. In spite of his Yankee upbringing, Davidson largely hired engineers and iron makers from the slave states of the South.

Tredegar was to become one of these suppliers, but winning the contract from Davidson was not easy. Davidson had subcontracted portions of the HRC's new construction to a Virginia engineer named Isaac Ridgeway Trimble, with whom he had worked on the B&O.[55] Trimble was employed as an independent contractor for the renewal of preexisting routes in Cuba; he laid down more durable and higher-quality road-bed and rails, and replaced wooden bridges with iron ones. While Tredegar first targeted Davidson, they also contacted Trimble directly, competing with Wilmington, Delaware ironmakers for Trimble's favor.[56] To earn Trimble's business, Tredegar owner Joseph Anderson could play on the fact that both men were Virginians who graduated from West Point, rather than Southern military academies.[57] Both men began military careers in hopes of social mobility, but found themselves either bored or thwarted by the routine.[58] Nevertheless, the Army taught them the skills they would later apply to the railroad business. Most importantly, Trimble knew of the quality of Tredegar's goods because it had supplied rail spikes to the B&O Railroad.

Anderson also made contacts with a third Havana-bound B&O colleague, the Baltimore ironworker Wendell Bollman, who accompanied Davidson to the island in search of clients.[59] Bollman had recently struck out on his own after spending a long career with the well-established B&O. He was eager to find a dependable base of consumers and was under the impression that the Cuban railroads were a strong candidate. Bollman presumably knew Anderson because Tredegar had supplied the B&O and they continued to do business together in the 1850s. Tredegar supplied Bollman's new private shop in Baltimore with high-quality charcoal iron bars used to make railroad bridges, engine boilers, and rails.[60]

In the early decades of rail transport, when there were few industry-wide hardware standards, each client, like the HRC, had unique needs it imagined could be fulfilled only by already established suppliers.[61] Once Cuban railroads committed themselves to a particular model of hardware, they settled into a technological pattern or style, guided by the small club of North American engineers who worked for many of them. Thus, for suppliers like Tredegar, it was vital to be an early entrant in developing markets, since business would very likely follow trusted suppliers of unique rail designs. Tredegar's management offered to "come out" to Cuba if necessary, asking Davidson "as early as practicable, [to] look into the matter for us and give us your news."[62]

Tredegar manager John F. Tanner assured Bollman "that we will be disposed to share liberally in the expense" of making sure that Davidson secured Cuban customers for Tredegar.[63] Tanner thus offered remuneration in return for helping forge business connections. In this way, local knowledge from the railway lines of the Cuban countryside was transformed into an income stream for Davidson. Because of the novelty of the railroad industry, it was not possible to forecast systematically, and since no supplier yet maintained inventories of any machinery or track hardware, the railways had to order equipment well ahead of time, on the basis of the best projections possible. In this context of personal relationships, and one-of-a-kind, non-transferable products, Tredegar's management was willing to pay Bollman "liberally" for plugging it into the stream of information relating to the changing needs of the company—what had made the chairs and rails fail in the past, what types of spikes were needed for the climatic particularities of the island, and so forth.

The essential role of personal connections made Tredegar's management wary of depending on intermediaries. Submitting to Davidson's paramountcy as a member of the HRC's board of directors, Tredegar's directors also found ways to let him know that they were in contact with other engineers involved with the company. Tredegar seemed eager to have its "own people" on the island, while not wanting to offend any of the associates on whom the company depended for navigating the industrial worlds of Cuba.

In the end, Tanner decided to travel to the island himself. His presence must have helped matters, because by January, 1859, Tredegar could write Davidson in Havana, thanking him for "the last order received for spikes

from Mr. Echeverría. . . ."[64] Relationships among Tredegar's upper management and Cuban railroad insiders like Trimble, Bollman, Davidson,
Echeverria, Bosque, and Alfonso were woven together by inspectors' reports,
patent licenses, gentlemen's agreements, and letters of introduction traveling
between Richmond, New York, Baltimore, and Havana. The social and economic networks slaveholding southern engineers forged with Cuban railroad
men were made possible by over a decade of market expansion and network
building in the US South. They also found their way into major infrastructural projects captained by elite merchant-planters like Fesser, Samá, and
Lacoste, who were engineering a system of warehouses, wharves, and international shipping that cohered with new railroad routes. Tredegar operated
in the same experimental mode as the Cuban planters whose mass-produced
sugar was to travel over Virginia-made iron rails.

Tredegar's managers were able to plug into a Greater Caribbean network
of engineers, iron makers, bridge builders, planters, and government inspectors so as to familiarize themselves with the particulars of industrializing
Cuba. Manufacturing commodities adapted to Cuba's geography and climate,
some of which had hitherto existed only as a set of sketches and instructions
from Davidson, raised a set of logistical difficulties that brought to the surface
long-simmering conflicts in the realm of racialized wrought-iron politics in
Richmond.

Creolizing Railway Technologies and
the Reappearance of Wrought-Iron
Politics at Tredegar

As opposed to the "southern dream" of aggressive pro-slavery expansion into a neocolonial Caribbean, it would be more accurate to say that
Tredegar was pulled into Cuba's orbit. Managers saw the future of the firm's
non-military business in the railroads, sugar mills, and sawmills required
by plantation frontiers in Cuba, Brazil, and Louisiana.[65] They were willing
to spend time and money in making contacts and experimenting with new
methods and products in order to serve promising emerging markets. In the
mid-1850s, Tredegar began customizing spikes and rails to fulfill the most
urgent needs of its prospective clients in Cuba. Their innovations were carried out by an interracial workforce whose white artisans had been forced
into working alongside black iron makers for over a decade. In spite of the
flexible innovation that Tredegar's manager-engineers sought to establish in

wrought-iron spaces through manipulation of racial politics, power dynamics remained complicated. While ironworkers did help invent new methods specifically for the Cuban market, they appear to have done so on their own terms.

On September 21, 1859, a year or more after it had made the first sales of its specialty spikes in Cuba, Tredegar won a major contract from the HRC for 500 tons of Davidson's patented rails and 2,400 chairs.[66] Davidson's "Bridge rail" was one of many rail designs prevalent at the time. Each rail was seated on bedplates (the "chairs") that had a lip to wrap over the top of the bottom outer edge of the bridge rails. Spikes fixing the chair to the cross-tie, and the rail slipping snugly under the lip of the chair, meant that no wooden or iron key was needed to hold the components in place[67] (Figure 4-4). While Trimble and Bollman were the big names in the venture, it was Davidson who had positioned himself to make money coming and going, all along the commodity chain. As chief engineer of the HRC, he probably earned a salary of between two and four thousand dollars.[68] In this capacity, he exerted considerable influence over what kind of equipment the company would use on its road, and he of course chose his own designs, contracted the work out to Tredegar, and charged Tredegar $92 per mile for the right to make and sell his rails back to him.[69]

Committed both to protecting his brand and minimizing complications once the rails had been shipped several hundred miles on the Atlantic, Davidson gave strict and detailed instructions to the puddlers, heaters, and rollers at Tredegar, including the following:

> the lower plate shall be made of strictly fibbrous iron, when placed in the pile to be not less than one inch thick . . . The head shall be of refined iron twice rolled and double heated, it shall be of hard chrystaline texture. A single plate shall be used in the pile to form the head, of a sufficient thickness to make not less than ¾ of an inch in the depth of vertical section of rail when completed . . . All iron to form the pile shall extend its entire length. The rails when finished shall be truly straightened the ends cut square to lengths of 18, 20, or 24 feet.[70]

Davidson thus laid out very detailed specifications. Quickly, however, the complexities of iron working overwhelmed the clarity of his written instructions.[71] In the contract, Davidson had stipulated that the "lower flange [be] neatly cut like model, oblong holes punched, trimmed to fit chair. . . ."

RAIL ROAD CHAIRS.

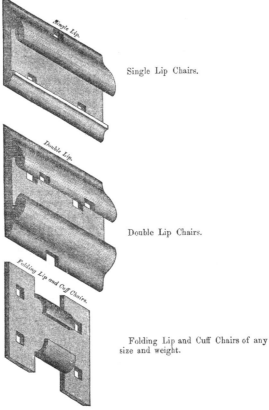

Single Lip Chairs.

Double Lip Chairs.

Folding Lip and Cuff Chairs of any
size and weight.

We also manufacture any required description of Chair not here
enumerated to order when required.

FIGURE 4-4 In Tredegar's new design, the bottom flanges of an I-shaped rail would
slide under the lips and be held securely in place with spikes.

From *An Illustrated and Descriptive Catalogue of Manufactures of Tredegar Iron Works: Joseph
R. Anderson & Co., Richmond, Va., Edmond M. Ivens, General Agent* (Richmond, VA: 1860), 18.

With lip chairs, the outer (flange) edges of the bottom section of the rail had
to be fairly precise in order to slip snugly under the lip of the chair. However,
in the opinions of Tredegar's owners and workmen, Davidson's command to
punch the holes would push out the edges of the flange, preventing them from
fitting in the lip chairs. Technically, they argued, the holes should have been
drilled, a slower and more painstaking process.[72] So far, they had chosen speed
of production over precision, punching the rails in accord with Davidson's
instructions in spite of their misgivings.

Tredegar had also experimented with new ways to produce Davidson's patented chairs—experiments that failed "at great expense." They then built a second set of machinery for a new attempt.[73] In order actually to make Davidson's products, Tredegar's engineers discovered, it would be necessary to create new machines and develop novel methods, which would be quite expensive in terms of man-hours and materials. This retooling of the firm's productive infrastructure suggests the importance Tredegar accorded the Cuba business.

Tredegar's managers justified the delays in delivering the rails and chairs to Davidson by appealing to a shared ethos of innovation. They pointed out that "this valuable improvement, like many others is at first hard to attain but we anticipate when the first difficulties are [resolved] all will go smoothly so we must ask you to bear with us a little longer and we trust all will be to satisfaction."[74] Two weeks later the firm had resolved most of the problems. Anderson happily reported, "we have succeeded after many trials in making a perfect chair for your beautiful Bridge Rail. . . It is obvious you will have the best rail & chair in Cuba. Indeed all the Rails and chairs on one side of Track will be equivalent to a continuous one." Once again, Anderson justified the delay by experiment and invention:

> it was an experiment to manufacture them, and one which has cost us both time and money. In fact we have only succeeded in making the chairs, by the <u>invention</u> of a method hitherto unknown; and we are now prepared to execute any order you may desire to give for the rail and fastenings, which we think you will find, on trial, to constitute one of the very best expedients yet invented.[75]

Anderson made it clear that the "rolling mill men" had invented the new method for making Davidson's rails and chairs.[76] Tredegar also emphasized in its 1859 catalogue that "the ingenious machinery for rolling and straightening [Davidson's patent splice] is entirely novel and the invention of one of our skilful workmen."[77] All of the iron components that constituted the fixed way of the railroad, including the rails, the chairs, the splices, and the spikes, were made by machines or processes growing out of experiments on the ironworks' shop floor. Moreover, the rollers and machinists themselves appear to have been the inventors of the new processes and machines that made Tredegar's entry into the Cuba market possible. This innovation would not have been uncommon in the nineteenth-century iron business.

Although we cannot know for sure, it is likely that skilled enslaved workers were involved in developing the innovations. While Anderson focused his

flexible labor experiments in the rolling mill, he also installed the most modern of equipment there and let other departments stagnate.[78] Of the eighty
slaves working at Tredegar in 1860, thirty were skilled operatives working in
the blacksmith shop and, crucially, in the rolling mill. Such operatives had
considerable motivation. Slaves who obtained useful skills were given opportunities to engage in "overwork" for cash. They also enjoyed greater autonomy than their fellow bondspeople.[79]

    While crediting, without naming, his workmen with creating useful
experimental methods, Anderson also emphasized that the company's fixed
capital had been altered, at considerable cost, in order to manufacture rails
and chairs to Davidson's specifications. Now that its machinery and methods
were suited to making designs for Cuban railroads, the company was prepared
to produce at scale. The delays with this relatively unprecedented undertaking
finally ended in the early summer of 1860.

    On June 23, Anderson addressed a letter to the HRC's second engineer
Manuel Bosque, letting him know that a shipping arrangement had been made
by New York merchant David Dodge to forward the 300 tons of rails that
were already in New York. He added as an afterthought that the rail dimensions "Correspond with the sketch you sent except that the bar is about one
quarter of an inch narrower than yours, but no others in market correspond so
closely and we think you will be well pleased."[80] Anderson demonstrated deep
knowledge of the Atlantic iron-making game, banking that Bosque would not
challenge Anderson's authoritative knowledge. At the same time, Anderson's
assumption that Davidson's specifications were negotiable suggests that the
quantitative, precise language of the engineering schematic had not assumed
the unquestionable and universally legible status it did later in the century.[81]
The wiggle room Anderson thought he saw in Davidson's drawings was not
shared by the designing engineer.

    In spite of the pressure he had put on the shippers to expedite matters,
Davidson ultimately decided to remain in Cuba until the shipment of rails
arrived. By August 5, 1860 the rails were there, almost a year after the order
had been placed, and Davidson was very upset. The shoddy workmanship,
Davidson wrote, "will necessarily cause many rails to be rejected. . . . This process of selecting and fitting also consumes much time, and enhances the cost
and trouble of tracklaying. . . . All it was necessary for the manufacturer to
do," Davidson fumed, "was to follow the model & specifications."[82] Perhaps
recalling the shortcomings of his own specifications, or simply tempering
his accusations, Davidson then softened his tone, first by offering a piece of
sage advice from a fellow civil engineer that gave Anderson a way to evade

responsibility: "It strikes me that it will be proper for you, if it is in your power so to do, to hold the Rolling Mill men who made the Rails responsible for any reclamations which the Company may make upon you on account of their defective workmanship."[83] Davidson related to Anderson as a colleague and invited him to participate in an authority they shared over nameless "rolling mill men." Nevertheless, the power of the rolling mill men is made clear in the fact that Davidson was not sure if Anderson had the power to reprimand them or dock their pay. Indeed, "if it is in your power to do so" seemed like an open question, as well as an implicit challenge to Anderson. Over a decade after the 1847 strike, wrought-iron politics acted as a brake on Anderson's disciplinary and technological freedom to alter production processes.

Davidson continued in a more conciliatory tone for the remainder of the letter, concluding that in spite of the unusable rails, "so far as the track has been laid, it promises to answer the expectations respecting its superior qualities." Davidson found the chairs "to be a perfect piece of workmanship, and if the rails had only been finished half as truly, it would have made a very complete and satisfactory job."[84] In spite of the difficulties, Tredegar had performed well enough to use HRC as a reference and went about expanding its customer base in different parts of Cuba and even Brazil.

Bridges of Industry: Tredegar Plants Independent Roots in Cuba

When Tredegar was first drawn into the Cuban railroad market in the 1850s, the enterprising railway engineer Miles Davidson had strategically ensconced himself at the intersection of a small series of bipolar, supplier-purchaser relationships linking Upper South iron makers with Cuban railroad firms. He occupied the crucial middleman position, controlling both ends of the circuit. Almost immediately, both Cuban railroad firms and North American manufacturers successfully challenged this arrangement. Each group attempted to dislodge Davidson from his strategic position in the flow of industrial transactions by building unmediated relationships with one another through visits and frequent correspondence.[85]

As Cuban managers, engineers, and machinists gained experience in railroad technology, they became less dependent upon the unquestioned expertise of foreigners. They established direct relationships with a variety of American suppliers, rather than taking the perhaps self-interested recommendations of *yanqui* engineers like Davidson.[86] Suppliers like Tredegar had to gain the approval of Cubans, not just fellow American engineers, in order to expand. In the winter of 1859, for example, Joseph Anderson, accompanied by his wife, Sally Ann, set off from Richmond to visit important nodes of southern commerce. They went to Nashville first, then to Charleston, Mobile, New Orleans, and Houston before boarding a steamer for Havana.[87] Manufacturers like Bollman and Anderson went to Cuba themselves either to forge personal connections or actually to assemble the products they manufactured in their US works.

Such direct contacts enabled Tredegar to have other Cuban companies vouch for their products. On August 1, 1860, for example, Anderson sent a letter of introduction to Sr. Dn. C Cadalzo of Havana that starts, "At the suggestion of our friends Msrs. Bollman Co. we address you with the purpose of saying that the price of our Spikes is as follows. . . ."[88] While still using Bollman's voucher as a marketing device, the company was no longer entirely dependent on the Baltimore bridge builder for its reputation in Cuba. It was also able to suggest that Cadalzo pay a visit to the HRC or to Eduardo Echarte of Remedios if he wanted to acquaint himself with Tredegar's products. Echarte had purchased a steam-powered sawmill from Tredegar and had had a chance to acquaint himself with Tredegar employees because the ironworks had sent their "faithful mechanic" Mr. Hagan to "superintend the erection" of the sawmill on Echarte's estate in Remedios[89] (Figure 4-5) In their 1859 catalogue, which they circulated to prospective customers, Tredegar listed

STRICTLY PORTABLE ENGINE.

FIGURE 4-5 Oxen typical of Cuba are led by a teamster as they drag one of Tredegar's portable steam engines into the woods. These engines often powered portable sawmills used to clear forests and collect fuel on Cuban and Louisianan sugar estates.

From *An Illustrated and Descriptive Catalogue of Manufactures of Tredegar Iron Works: Joseph R. Anderson & Co., Richmond, Va., Edmond M. Ivens, General Agent* (Richmond, VA: 1860), 45.

Bosque, Davidson, James Clarke, and Trimble as their references in Havana, but also suggested that interested parties contact Feris & Co. or C. E. Ponjaud & Co. in Matanzas, and Morales & Co. or Juan Ferin in Cárdenas.[90]

The fruit of Tredegar's broad-based approach to the Cuban railroad market and the intelligence apparatus they had plugged into encouraged them to predict future expansion. The exclusive deals that Tredegar agents Anderson and Tanner had arranged with the Baltimore bridge builder Wendell Bollman gained Tredegar access to what may have been the major railroad undertaking since the inaugural road of 1837: the Bay of Havana-Matanzas Railroad Company, begun in 1857, which fed sugar directly to the Regla Warehouse Company. The coastwise route planned out by the new company between Havana and Matanzas crossed one of the only areas of western Cuba with many steep grades and river crossings.[91] Tredegar's managers were wise to have remained close to Bollman after his departure from the B&O, for he arguably became the most important builder of iron bridges in Cuba.[92] Tredegar was a key part of this cutting-edge project, supplying Bollman with merchant bar iron and charcoal iron for the many custom bridges his firm forged in Baltimore, shipped to Cuba, and erected in the countryside. As late as April of 1861, Tredegar was marketing its services to a broader Cuban railroad market. To that end, Tredegar disseminated a general letter of introduction to the railway men of the island of Cuba and even established a sales agency in Havana.[93] The company had also begun to expand its sales of steam-powered sawmills and sugar mills to plantation owners in Cuba through a full-time commercial agent in New Orleans, the mechanical engineer Edmund Ivens.

By reaching out to the Greater Caribbean's world of sugar producers, Tredegar built on a long history of economic exchanges between the United States and the Latin America. The company capitalized on a sense, however contrived it was, that a shared tropical identity among American slave societies made Tredegar's products particularly well suited to Cuba's unique climate, topography, and economy. But its outreach was a gamble that paid off only because the Cuban economy was undergoing a rapid techno-scientific transition of which railroads were a crucial aspect.

When the state of Virginia seceded in 1861, Anderson joined in the celebrations, in spite of his family's venerable Whig background. Although he longed to defend the South on the battlefield, the Confederate government needed him and his large workforce to provide the military with weaponry and the states with railway equipment. Anderson and his subordinates penned letters of regret to Tredegar's Cuban customers, saying that they could not fulfill orders for the time being. In spite of the wartime cessation of hardware exportation, ties to Cuba remained important for the firm. Junior members used Havana as a base from which to run goods through the Union blockade until 1865.[94]

Tredegar's enslaved workers appear to have recast wrought-iron politics during the war for emancipation in a different way. In a scrapbook in the Tredegar archives an unidentified company official from the early twentieth century pasted an excerpt from *Four Years in Rebel Capitals*, a supposed first-hand account of the Civil War penned by the journalist T. C. DeLeon in 1892. DeLeon thought a particular tale gave a "general estimate of the importance of the Tredegar Works" during the brief but eventful life of the Confederate States. Late in the war, he recounted, "at a time when transportation was rare, a huge negro, blacker than the soot upon his face, sat placidly on the plat-form of the rear car" of a train passing over a bridge between Richmond and Petersburg. The officer in charge of the bridge demanded to know what the man was doing on the train and if he had paid his fare. The man in DeLeon's story replied that he didn't have to pay, as he "rides onner pass, I does!" The officer thus assumed he worked for the government. In response, how-ever, "Ebo rolled his eyes, with expression of deep disgust, as he responded, grandly: 'No-sah! Fur t'uther consarn!'" By "the other concern," he meant the Tredegar Ironworks.[95] Although the story was recalled in patronizing tones, it nonetheless reveals the ironworker's sense that his post at the Richmond factory granted him particular authority, as well as a position from which to challenge the racial and military hierarchies of the Confederacy. His confi-dence was rooted in the wrought-iron politics forged by slaves in the previous twenty years at the works. Amid the social upheavals of the late Civil War, a black Tredegar worker could assert these politics visibly on the militarized highways and byways of the Confederacy.

In spite of security anxieties, in the techno-centric environment of the Second Slavery the answer to the question "what should black people know?" could rarely be "nothing". Managers in the throes of technical reinvention began to ask, in their oblique way, "what can black people figure out for us?" Compromises continued to be hammered out in an atmosphere of violence and danger. Most experts never felt threatened enough to lose confidence in the continued expansion of racial capitalism.

5

Sweetness and Debasement

FLOUR AND COFFEE IN THE RICHMOND-RIO CIRCUIT

AFTER ESTABLISHING THEMSELVES in Cuba, Tredegar's owners then reached out to another plantation economy seeking to revolutionize its transport system. In the few years before the US Civil War, Tredegar sought contacts and sent samples of rail spikes to the Dom Pedro II Railroad Company, which was beginning construction on two major lines in the new coffee-growing regions of Brazil. Marketing its high-end spikes to different North American contractors working in the areas around Rio de Janeiro, Tredegar used its success in the Cuban market as promotional material in the former Portuguese colony.[1]

Tredegar's clients in Brazil resembled the group of engineers with whom they worked in Cuba. One of the contractors was another Richmond-based engineer, Robert Harvey. Harvey had formed a partnership with Philadelphians Milnor Roberts and Charles J. Harrah, as well as a Marylander named Jacob Humbird, to build a second trunk line of the *Dom Pedro II*. Harrah had already established a successful shipbuilding business in Rio Grande do Sul and Rio de Janeiro in the 1840s. He was then hired by the Brazilian government to gather expertise from abroad on railroad construction.[2] Harrah contracted with this group of engineers, and the resulting partnership (Roberts Harvey and Company) took charge of building "the mountainous portion" of the projected line, starting in 1858.[3]

Tredegar also pursued relations with a group of engineers headed by Andrew and William Ellison, brothers who had worked out of Lynchburg on the Virginia and Tennessee Railroad before going to Brazil.[4] As in the case of the Upper South engineers who predominated on Cuban railroads of the late 1850s, both the Ellison brothers and Roberts Harvey and Company were hired in part for the challenge of building a railroad up the steep escarpment that separated the port city from the Paraíba Valley. These two groups of Virginia-based engineers undertook in collaboration with Brazilians, Philadelphians, and others the leveling, grading, tunneling, and rail construction to climb from the coast over a small mountain range and into the coffee-growing lands beyond.

In 1858 Harvey placed an ad in the *Richmond Dispatch* in which he was quite explicit about the common qualifications required for railroad projects in Virginia and Brazil. "The contractors for the construction of the Dom Pedro Segundo railroad, in Brazil," it read, "wish to employ 50 YOUNG MEN, natives of the state of Virginia, or any of the Southern States, who may understand the management of Negroes on public works, to go to Brazil as Managers or Foremen." Even if they lacked in railroad experience, the company was willing to employ "young men who are now engaged on farms, or who are employed as overseers on farms." Clearly, Harvey found supposed skills in racial management as useful as those in railroad engineering. Harvey had long appreciated the cost savings associated with using unpaid labor. He had repeatedly tried to extricate himself from a contract with the Richmond and Danville Railroad in 1850 because the latter declined to give his firm extra money to pay for white labor.[5] Perhaps, like Joseph Anderson at Tredegar, he learned his lesson about white workers and saw an enslaved workforce as preferable.

Harvey's ad also foregrounded the topographical similarities between the Virginia Blue Ridge and the escarpment leading from the Brazilian coast up to the Paraíba Valley. Because "the line of the railroad to be constructed will pass on and through the Sierra de Nor, or North Mountain," Harvey desired employees who "understand thoroughly the construction of heavy rock work, including Tunneling etc."[6] Thus the predominance of these particular engineers on the railroads of southeastern Brazil can be explained in part by claims of unique expertise in racial management, and in part by a fundamental principle of railroad physics: reduced friction owing to the small point of contact between rail- and wheel-enabled steam locomotives to pull incredible masses of freight; this same low friction also meant that trains could not get good traction and handled ascents poorly as a result. Thus graded and excavated hills, in combination with bridges, tunnels, and rail switchbacks, were frequently needed in areas other than the flattest country. The uncooperative terrain northwest of Rio gave Upper South engineers, who had well-known experience scaling mountain ranges for the B&O, the Virginia Central, and the Virginia and Tennessee Railroads, and building iron bridges in Cuba, a distinct advantage. Nodding to issues of technological, topographical, racial, and climatic affinity between Virginia and southeastern Brazil, Harvey neatly articulated the mid-nineteenth-century forms of Greater Caribbean expertise that would count as prerequisites for managers.

About 130 men considered themselves qualified under Harvey's terms, and they departed for Rio in early 1859.[7] In managing the construction of the road, these engineers and overseers followed the survey lines conscientiously laid out by other Virginians who had preceded them in the South American country. In 1857 the railroad surveyor and engineer Richard Morton was hired by the Dom Pedro II Railroad Company to plan routes that would traverse the coffee-growing regions of the Paraíba Valley. Theodore Moreno, who hailed from Pensacola, Florida, and studied civil engineering at the University of Virginia, spent two-and-a-half years working with Morton for the Dom Pedro II before returning to work on the Virginia and Tennessee Railroad and then for the Confederacy.[8]

By the end of the 1850s, Brazil's new railroad lines had not only begun to ship out coffee at a predictable rate but they also carried barrels of Richmond wheat flour into the Paraíba Valley. Thus, whether they knew it or not, Virginia engineers working in and around Rio were smoothing the path for America's most important export to Brazil. In the decade preceding the secession of the southern states, Brazil had become a top export market for US wheat flour, just as it became North America's near-exclusive supplier of coffee.[9] With an exclusive focus on export crops and growing urban populations, the "sugar islands" had purchased more US flour than had any other region until the 1830s. With the eruption of a tariff war between the United States and Cuba, and the decline of British West Indian markets following the emancipation decree of 1834, US flour exports were redirected southward toward an emerging slave economy in southeastern Brazil.

While US flour merchants had longstanding ties with other parts of Latin America and the Caribbean, the relationship with Brazil arose rather suddenly. In 1837, Brazil imported 52,662 barrels of flour from the United States and 73,918 "from elsewhere." Fourteen years later the respective shares were 180,609 barrels from the United States and a mere 26,309 from everywhere else.[10] The boom in US flour exports to Brazil, those coming from Richmond and Baltimore in particular, were part of a broader effort by US merchants to get highly desired Brazilian coffee on slightly more advantageous terms of exchange. Quite rapidly after 1820 or so, African slaves working under the command of planters and merchants transformed the Paraíba Valley of southeastern Brazil. The pattern of monoculture and declines of local food production that had already occurred in sugar-producing zones of Cuba were repeated here, along with the contemporaneous expansion of urban population (especially bread-eating European immigrants) in Rio. At the same time, multinational merchant groups like Maxwell, Wright & Co. encouraged lawmakers to pass legislation favoring coffee production and discouraging domestic flour milling, because increased supplies of coffee would continue bringing wholesale prices down, and because they needed Brazilians to require some widely consumed good. Since for these merchants, flour was essentially a medium of exchange to buy coffee, quality mattered little. They hoped Brazilian bakers would gradually lose their "prejudice" for high-quality brands.

On the contrary, the local flour bakers and brokers who bought barrels from Maxwell and its ilk had found that traditional imported flours were often caked, musty, or rancid after the long trip across the equator. Richmond products seemed to hold "sweetness" better than any other brands. While their speculative behaviors at first glance seem detached from an interest in quality control, Rio brokers in fact depended on the permanency of Richmond flour to carry out market-manipulating maneuvers, like slowing down the arrival of new shipments so as to push up prices on current stocks. As their main customers repeatedly insisted, the flour still had to be "sweet" whenever they decided to bring it into the Rio market.

Rio bakers in the midst of transforming the tastes of urban Brazil, in part by recreating a taste of home for a large influx of Portuguese immigrants, demanded Richmond superfine brands. Their practices abetted the divergence of diets along racial and class lines. In an urban society brimming with recent immigrants and ex-slaves of precarious status, the consumption of professionally baked bread in the "French style," made from exotic imported flour, was an important marker of non-slave status, as well as a signifier of one's own whitening.[11] The mechanization of baking through the adoption of the French "Rolland system" (which consisted of a recently invented mechanical mixer/kneader and an "aerothermal oven") in the 1850s brought whitening cultural practices within reach of immigrants, ex-slaves, and the free poor.

Many of the skilled master bakers and ovenmen, as well as other laborers in Rio's bread industry, were enslaved or formerly enslaved Afro-Brazilians. Their insistence on preservable, white, superfine Richmond brands (an insistence international merchant firms patronizingly labeled as "fastidiousness" or "prejudice") reshaped the entangled technological system of the Greater Caribbean by pushing Upper South capitalists and merchant firms into several important reinventions.

The special relationship between the slave societies of Virginia and Brazil, dominated by their slave-produced commodities of wheat flour and coffee, suggests multiple, interlocking Atlantic worlds drawn together by constellations of commodities whose modes of production and paths of circulation shaped one another. This chapter shows how global shifts in the production and consumption of cotton, coffee, sugar, and wheat were tightly interrelated in the nineteenth century. The decline of coffee cultivation in Cuba was entangled with its expansion in southeastern Brazil, as well as with the take-off of sugar production in Cuba and, finally, with the shifting destination of US wheat flour exports.[12] This combination of factors reshaped the agricultural and urban landscapes, as well as the productive technologies, of each node of the Greater Caribbean.

The Atlantic System and the Growth of Capitalist Flour Milling

The growth of an export-focused wheat-growing and flour-milling economy in colonial and early national North America was largely dependent on demand from the Caribbean sugar islands. In 1790, for example, the West India sugar islands alone received half of US flour exports.[13] Between 1794 and 1822 Havana accounted for large proportions of the total trade of Philadelphia, a leading flour city.[14] Highly leveraged planters in the Caribbean dedicated available acres and labor power to a single export crop and bought from abroad what little food they gave to slaves.

Spanish policymakers made the connection between North American flour and the slave trade quite explicit: eighteenth-century laws required that every African slave brought to Cuba be imported along with a certain quantity of flour, to ensure that the newcomers had a proportional quantity of food to feed him or her. But the enslaved rarely ate the wheat flour. Merchants instead sold it to urban bakers, who worked it into loaves for moneyed residents of the cities.[15] The Cuba flour trade thus established a pattern that reappeared in southeastern Brazil: European immigration into urban outposts of growing plantation societies created a community of professional bakers who demanded particular kinds of flour.[16] Yet the more salient point here is that merchants wanting to bring slaves into Cuba had to obtain barrels of wheat flour. The flour itself was less important than its role in facilitating the more lucrative business of selling African captives.

If flour was to play this role of coinage in the Atlantic economy, its vexing debasability had to be taken into account. Even when colonial North

American flour was admitted into Cuba in the 1760s, for example, mercantilist policy required it to be taken to a European port like Cadiz first, then
examined and recorded in Havana. By the time it reached secondary Cuban
ports like Santiago, it had often turned rancid. When the flour-import-
ing monopoly demanded that bakers use rotten flour anyway, townspeo-
ple responded by throwing the barrels into the harbor. Flour issues were an
important factor pushing policy makers to concede "free trade" for Cuba in
1778.[17] Free Cuban farmers and millers were already meeting some domestic
demand for flour, but were, for a variety of reasons, put out of business with
the help of Upper South wheat flour imports. As Cuba's plantation revolution, as well as the upheavals of the Haitian Revolution and Napoleonic Wars,
increased the island's free population and discouraged food crop production,
consumption of imported flour increased. For a few crucial decades, it was
supplied by North Americans.[18]

    This connection to Caribbean consumers transformed flour milling in
early-nineteenth-century Baltimore and Philadelphia—the leading flour-
milling cities of the era. Rather than relying on local gristmills that ground
the grain of area farmers for a toll, merchant millers in the second half of
the eighteenth century began to purchase grain from cultivators and sell the
output of the mill on their own account. In need of more raw materials to
occupy larger sets of equipment, merchant millers purchased grain from faraway producers and sold flour to merchants who passed on the product to
distant customers.[19] Mid-Atlantic entrepreneurs pioneered the shift to this
early capitalist form of milling, largely with the goal of capturing Caribbean
markets.[20] Merchant millers found that international arbitrage in flour barrels could be lucrative. Baltimore's wide-traveling traders could buy a barrel of
flour for four Spanish dollars on the Baltimore docks and unload it for thirty-
six at Havana. High profit margins in the export business drew surrounding
country millers closer to the Maryland port. Local capital and a banking system grew to meet the needs of the new Cuba-oriented trade.[21]

    The technology of milling changed as well. With the increasing com-
mercialization of milling in the late 1700s, the flour had to be sifted, separated, and graded according to demanding and ever-changing standards.[22]
In response to these new labor- and time-intensive operations, as well as the
pressure of ever-increasing flows of wheat, a Delaware engineer named Oliver
Evans designed the world's first automated, large-scale wheat flour mills.[23] The
Evans mill turned a batch of wheat into a barrel of flour with minimal human
intervention. Evans's automatic mill utilized a combination of water power
and gravity to drive an interconnected series of elevators, conveyor belts, and

gears that took the raw material through the various operations (cleaning, grinding, bolting, cooling/drying, and finally packing into barrels). Discrete innovations in the individual stages of flour milling included the "hopper boy" (a mechanical rake rotated by a series of shafts and gears connected to the water wheel) that sped the drying process and prevented fermentation, as well as new mechanisms to clean and bolt wheat (Figure 5-1).[24] These mechanisms yielded more flour per input of unprocessed grain and extended the shelf life of flour, which was typically around three months at the time.[25] With the incorporation of these advances in the early national period, the

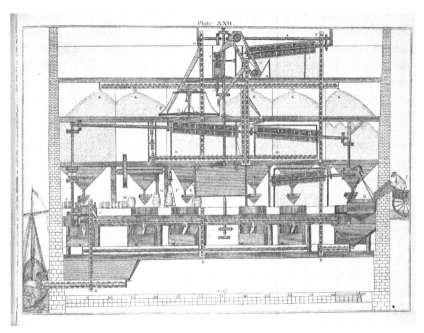

FIGURE 5-1 Evans's engraving of his "improved mill." While the major Richmond millers adopted many of Evans's automated mechanisms for moving the wheat through the different phases of production with little human intervention, note that in Evans's original, there are only six pairs of millstones, while the company of Warwick & Barksdale had over thirty. Note also the automated packing of barrels, the ability to move raw wheat from either land or water by mechanical means, the chains of small white buckets that moved the material through the various vertical processing locations, and the maze of gears to draw power from the waterwheel (not portrayed here), as well as to change the directionality and speed of motion started from the wheel.

From Oliver Evans, *The Young Mill-Wright and Miller's Guide: Illustrated by Twenty-Eight Descriptive Plates. By Oliver Evans; With Additions and Corrections, by Thomas P. Jones . . . With a Description of an Improved Merchant Flour-Mill, with Engravings. By C. & O. Evans, Engineers* (Philadelphia: Blanchard and Lea, 1853), plate xxii. Rare Book and Special Collections Division of the Library of Congress, Washington, DC.

mills of Baltimore, expanding largely on the strength of the Cuban and West Indian markets, increased their grinding capacity to 150,000 bushels of wheat per year (or about 30,000 barrels of flour). The mills owned by one Baltimore family, the Ellicotts, could put out ten times as much flour as the first generation of Evans factories.[26]

While the Cuban and West Indian markets drove the transformation of the early republic's grain and flour industries, they faded from prominence after Spanish Americans gained independence in the 1820s. In the wake of defeat, Spanish merchants redoubled their efforts to secure privileged access to remaining colonial flour buyers, with Cuba the most sought-after prize. By 1838 the government in Madrid had hiked duties on non-Spanish flour imports to the island and thus provoked a tariff war, dubbed *la Guerra de Harinas*. The United States responded by temporarily doubling the duty on Cuban sugar imports.[27] Things got worse for US flour exporters in the Cuban market with an 1853 tariff stipulating that foreign products carried by non-Spanish ships would be levied an *ad valorem* tax of 30 percent. "Not infrequently," one eminent scholar of US-Cuban relations concludes, "consumers in Cuba paid more than double the original market price for US imports."[28] At the same time, US sales in the British West Indian colonies stagnated amidst the destruction of plantation economies.[29]

Brazilian markets made up for the loss of the Caribbean. This shift was accompanied by important changes in the location of US wheat flour production, as well as in the class makeup of consumers. The flour sold in British West Indian markets for the feeding of slaves was a lower-priced article milled in small to medium-sized merchant mills in Philadelphia and Baltimore.[30] Cheaper, browner, and dirtier "western flour" continued to be exported to western Europe in large quantities. The world-renowned "city flour" of Richmond, baked by artisan bakers of Rio, was sold at higher prices to the growing urban free population of artisans, clerks, coffee factors, storekeepers, middle-income families, and merchants, as well as the elite of southeastern Brazil. The large quantities of bread being baked in Rio called for steady imports of high-quality Richmond wheat flour. By 1851, 87 percent of the imported flour that found its way to the tables of residents of Rio de Janeiro and the surrounding coffee estates was American, predominantly from Richmond and Baltimore millers.[31] In 1857, it was 95 percent, and around two-thirds of this quantity was from Richmond and Baltimore.[32] When the US flour industry turned to Brazil, the millers and planters of Virginia capitalized on notions of a shared tropical environment to capture a uniquely quality-conscious market.

While the Richmond-Rio flour trade was important, it emerged to facilitate a far larger business: the export of Brazilian coffee to the United States. Coffee first gained popularity among elite North American consumers in the 1760s, when it began to be framed as a patriotic, anticolonial drink consumed in place of English tea. Sweetened by cheap Cuban sugar, it soon spread to the middle and working classes. A post-1830 flood of non-English-speaking European immigrants like Germans and Scandinavians, already accustomed to drinking coffee, added to the numbers of Americans consuming it with frequency.[33] Coffee imports grew from under 200,000 sacks in 1820, to 1.8 million sacks by 1860.[34]

US consumers' new and unslakable thirst for what Sidney Mintz describes as a "soft-drug temperance beverage" drove North American merchants to Rio and transformed the trade relationship between the two countries.[35] During the days before the coffee boom, US traders ran a surplus in Brazil. Baltimore supercargoes visiting Brazilian port towns sold small amounts of flour and went elsewhere in South America for commodities to bring home. By the 1830s, US merchants eager for full shipments of coffee lacked something to sell in return. By 1850 the United States ran a considerable trade deficit with Brazil, due to the explosion of coffee production in the Paraíba Valley.[36]

The democratization of coffee drinking in North America was made possible by low production costs in Brazil. Global coffee prices fell between 1822 and 1849 because a new alliance of slaveholders, merchants, and the state mobilized over a million captive laborers to transform southeastern Brazil's plantation frontier.[37] In response to widespread slave revolts and political instability in the 1830s and 1840s, these export-oriented elites unified as a conservative bloc and shared state power with the emperor of Brazil, Dom Pedro II.[38] The "saquarema" reaction, as it was known, promoted coffee cultivation along with the illegal African slave trade and as a result deepened the country's connections with an Atlantic import-export economy rooted in slavery. The slave trade brought 580,000 captives into south-central Brazil alone between 1821 and 1851. So flour was not the only commodity pulled strongly into the vortex of the coffee export zone of the Paraíba Valley.[39] Added to this boon for the coffee economy was a series of legislative achievements. An 1850 Commercial Code and an 1850 Land Law "regularized and established commerce and landholding in favor of the merchant-planter interests." A state-sponsored expansion of port infrastructure was begun in 1851. The first concession for railroads was granted in 1852. In 1853, export taxes were reduced.[40] State facilitation by both US and Brazilian governments was central to the changing relationship. General trade agreements were signed in 1828, and in 1832 the

United States specifically lowered tariffs on coffee. When the US "tariff war" with Spain began two years later, making Cuban coffee more expensive in the US market, the door was opened wider for Brazilian imports, while simultaneously making Rio a much more attractive destination for wheat flour than Havana.[41]

Under such favorable conditions for merchants and planters, profits from the *arabica* bean proved irresistible. Brazilian slave owners concentrated land holdings, plowed over subsistence crops, and pushed out small farmers to make way for coffee trees. By 1830, Brazil was already the largest coffee producer in the world, well ahead of Cuba, Java, and other significant growers.[42] From a negligible quantity of production in 1820, it was producing about 175,000,000 tons of coffee in 1860.[43] Thus slaves in Brazil, many of them African born, were responsible for over half of total world coffee production by 1850.[44]

Liberalizing foreign trade while concentrating land, labor, and animal power in coffee production, the *saquaremas* also brought a flood of foreign flour into the country. In effect, wheat farmers and millers in southern Brazil were sacrificed for the coffee industry.[45] British and North American–dominated merchant groups like the Commercial Association of Rio de Janeiro counseled authorities to promote export-oriented growth in part by abandoning local food crop production.[46] This was not disinterested advice, as traders selling coffee in the United States desperately needed a product to bring on their return trips to Rio.

Fretting over the sizable US trade deficit with Brazil in 1858, Virginia Governor and former Minister to Brazil Henry Wise noted that, while the South American country was selling its coffee to the US, it bought its manufactures from England. Instead of paying for coffee with US-made goods, Wise grumbled, North American merchants were forced to shell out "bills of exchange on London" when they did business in Rio.[47] Brazilians then used those London bills to purchase English manufactures. Thus the English, who bought comparatively little from the South American country, enjoyed "all the advantages of the great increase of the coffee trade with the United States."[48] US merchants, meanwhile, brought ships "in ballast for coffee, paying for it cash at most exorbitant rates of exchange."[49] This created a large trade deficit (Table 5-1).

To continue trading profitably in coffee, Maxwell, Wright needed an export that did well in Rio—but as Wise pointed out, the British had already cornered the market in most important lines of business. Flour was the exception. Thus Maxwell, Wright, with unique access to quality flour

Table 5-1 US-Brazil Balance
of Trade, 1821 and 1857

Imports from Rio to US

1821: $605,126

1843: $5,948,814

1850: $9,324,429

1857: $21,460,733

Exports to Rio from US

1821: $1,388,760

1843: $2,601,502

1850: $3,197,114

1857: $5,545,207

"United States and Brazil," *Hunt's Merchant Magazine* 41 (1859), 553.

from Baltimore and nearby Richmond, began bringing full shipments of ground grain to Brazil, primarily to recover the profitability of its coffee business. Of the 389 Rio-bound voyages organized by the firm between 1827 and 1848, over 90 percent carried wheat flour as their principal cargo.[50] The firm's special access to flour had important aggregate effects, which Governor Wise noted in his article: between 1847 and 1857 the exports of US flour to Rio increased one hundred times, while the sales of coffee going in the other direction only grew 10 percent.[51] Thus, by the end of the decade, merchants with access to Richmond and Baltimore flour were able to trade profitably. At Rio's main customs warehouse, Maxwell, Wright sold the flour to local brokers for Brazilian *mil-réis* and used that currency to buy coffee, which they sold in Baltimore to westbound merchants in exchange for either US currency or more bills of exchange[52] (Figure 5-2). By 1858, the three chief exporters of Brazilian coffee (Maxwell, Wright, Phipps Brothers, and Roston Dutton & Co.) supplied 60 percent of Rio's wheat flour [53] (Table 5-2). Wheat flour, however, made for a strange medium of exchange, as it debased easily.

Maxwell, Wright sought to promote the overall consumption of imported flour in Rio, but it never intended to encourage loyalty to Richmond brands. The growing dominance of particular Richmond companies was caused by changes in the food culture of southeastern Brazil and its artisan bakers. Rio's internal flour trade was run by a small number of flour brokers/bakers (fewer than ten in the 1850s) who bought up the imported flour from firms

FIGURE 5-2 Bay of Rio de Janeiro. Flour brigs entered the bay from the south, where they were inspected by customs officials before discharging their cargo at Maxwell's Wharf on the east side of the city (near 3 on the map).

From Daniel Kidder, *Brazil and the Brazilians Portrayed in Historical and Descriptive Sketches* (Philadelphia, Childs & Peterson; New York, Sheldon, Blakeman & Co., 1857), after page 12.

Table 5-2 **Average Comparative Imports of Coffee, by Bags, and Percent
Increase, for Periods of (Calendar) Years**

Port	1841–45	1846–50	% change	1855–59	% change
Baltimore	120,072	164,076	37	213,922	30
Boston	37,069	37,651	2	6,860	−81
New Orleans	135,514	245,338	81	361,331	47
New York	150,086	195,867	31	340,410	74
Philadelphia	28,998	38,872	34	115,442	197
Other (Southern) ports	9,054	25,241	179	57,598	128
Total	480,793	707,045	47	1,095,563	55

Imports of Brazilian coffee into US ports. Table reproduced from Rutter, "South American Trade of Baltimore," 30. Richmond wheat flour appears largely responsible for Baltimore's ability to compete with New York and New Orleans in terms of coffee imports. The flour connection helped Maxwell, Wright get more coffee at more advantageous terms, which pulled back against the emergent New York–centric continental geography of US capitalism. "Other southern ports" shared equally in the trade: Richmond and Hampton Roads combined took 12,341 sacks of coffee in 1855, Charleston 16,000, and Mobile 10,000. *Hunt's Merchant Magazine and Commercial Review* 34 (1856): 608.

like Maxwell for use in their own establishments or to sell to retail bakers. American merchants found these individuals particularly "fastidious as to quality."[54] Hoping to sell as wide an assortment as possible, Maxwell took a dim view of Brazilian bakers' preferences, calling them "prejudices in favour of particular brands" that would be overcome in time.[55] However, bakers' tastes came not from prejudice but from careful examination, "as all flour is usually tried by the bakers, who bake a few barrels previously to purchasing to any extent."[56] Joseph Maxwell himself admitted that "flour from the United States sometimes arrives here caked, sour, or musty."[57] Surely, dissatisfied bakers had taught him that.

Elite Rio bakeries trumpeted the quality of their raw materials in advertisements. The Padaria dos Amantes, for example, claimed to use "the best flours that are imported into this market."[58] Proprietors of the Padaria Rio Comprido informed local residents that they had recently hired a master baker to make bread, *roscas*, and other wheaten goods. "Having bought a good assortment of the best flour that exists today," they added, "we will be able to work better than ever."[59] Finally, a new bakery on Rua Sabão da Cidade Nova bragged of being "quite superior in craft, as in the quality of the flours."[60]

Like a number of the larger bakeries, the establishment on Santa Rita combined the sale of bread products with the marketing of "superior, new Haxall flour, along with a variety of other flours appropriate for manufacture."[61] Far from overcoming their "prejudice," then, bakers in Rio were willing to pay higher prices for Richmond flour, and buying more of it in the late 1850s than ever before. Bakers' demand for these brands also became price inelastic. In 1851, for example, the average price of Gallego and Haxall flours was (in mil-réis) 14$670; Baltimore, 12$166; Philadelphia, 12$254; and New Orleans, 12$666 [62] (Table 5-3). Even though the price differential was even larger by the second half of the 1850s, Richmond brands continued to sell more readily than any other. In 1860, according to Carlos Valencia Villa's examination of Rio's main commercial newspaper, four Richmond mills alone accounted for 58 percent of total wheat flour in the port of Rio (Table 5-4).[63]

The bakers of Rio preferred Virginia flour partly because the wheat Richmond millers used contained more gluten and less water than Northern wheat, making it less vulnerable to rotting on the lengthy voyage. Shelf life was particularly important in the Richmond industry, in which export-oriented millers frequently held onto stocks of flour "with an expectation of higher prices."[64] Because of its lower water content, Virginia wheat yielded more bread per pound of flour, since it absorbed more water during baking.[65] When prices rose in Rio, bakers were frequently accused of selling undersized loaves of bread, making Virginia flour particularly desirable. The soft red winter wheat grown in warmer climes was easier to grind than harder

Table 5-3 Flour Prices in Rio de Janeiro, 1856–1857 (Mil-réis per barrel)

	Feb	Mar	Apr	Jul	Nov	Dec	Apr 57	Jun 57	Average
Haxall	NR	27	30	29$5	25$25	23$5	24	24	**26$17**
Gallego	27	29	31	NR	NR	23$5	27	24	**26$9**
Baltimore	20	21$5	23$5	NR	23$5	20	18$5	16	**20$42**
Philadel	21	22	NR	NR	NR	NR	20	18	**20$25**
Europe	30	30	NR	NR	NR	NR	NR	NR	**30**
N. Orleans	NR	NR	NR	NR	NR	NR	NR	NR	**21$5**

Prices reported for select months in 1856 and 1857 in *Diario do Rio de Janeiro*, February 13, 1856, March 15, 1856, April 14, 1856, July 31, 1856, November 6, 1856, December 3–4, 1856, April 21, 1857, and June 13, 1857. NR = Not Reported. It is significant, of course, that only Richmond brands were recorded by individual firm—all other suppliers were noted only by city. While European prices were high due to the transport costs, arrivals were rare, as they were from Philadelphia.

	1848	1849	1850	1851	1852	1853	1854	1856	1857	1858	1859	1860
Baltimore	90,414 (Rio)	83,056 (Rio)		85,714 (Rio)				158,052 (1856–60 avg)		169,868 (Brazil)		
Richmond	62,644 (Rio)	90,401 (Rio)		88,964 (Gallego and Haxall only)	59,000	80,000	79,000		156,295 (South America)	241,516 (Brazil)	231,067 (South America)	218,859 (South America)
Philadelphia				18,194						56,308 (Brazil)		
New Orleans										78,735 (Brazil)		
New York										42,334 (Brazil)		
Europe	5,640	8,377	26,309	27,770					15,846 (Brazil)			
Other				63,251								
Total Rio Imports				363,294					269,553 (Brazil)	350,251 (Brazil)		
Total Brazil Imports from US									518,788 (Brazil)	602,116 (Brazil)		

1848 and 1849 imports into Rio figures from "Trade and Commerce of Rio de Janeiro," *Hunt's Merchant Magazine and Commercial Review* 22 (1850): 666. The 1851 imports into Rio figures from "Commerce and Navigation of the Port of Rio de Janeiro in 1851," *Hunt's Merchant Magazine and Commercial Review* 26 (1852): 48–48). Richmond 1852–1854 flour exports to Brazil (not just Rio) from *Hunt's Merchant Magazine and Commercial Review* 31 (1854): 600. Baltimore's 1856–1860 average from Comp. "Grain and Flour," 167, 187, 189, and 1860 direct exports to South America (although I argue elsewhere that nearly all of this flour bound for "South America" went to Brazil. Rood, "Bogs of Death," 22n5) figures from "Virginia Flour Trade," *Hunt's Merchant Magazine and Commercial Review* 43 (1860): 231. Total Rio imports, 1851, from *Diário do Rio de Janeiro*, February 4, 1852, (Suplemento ao Diário do Rio de Janeiro). The 1857 and 1858 export figures, as well as total Rio imports and total Brazil imports from United States, from "Exports of Flour to South America," *Hunt's Merchant Magazine and Commercial Review* 40 (1859): 351. The 1850 imports from Europe from "Commerce of Rio Janeiro," *Hunt's Merchant Magazine and Commercial Review* 24 (1851): 621. The 1857 imports from Europe, "United States and Brazil," *Hunt's Merchant Magazine and Commercial Review* 41 (July–December 1859): 556.

varieties and meant that southern wheat came out of the mill looking especially white.[66] However, it was not simply flour made from southern wheat
for which Brazilian bakers clamored. Consistent quality became associated with the brands of particular Richmond mills, like Haxall-Crenshaw
or Gallego. Indeed, the power of flour brands like Haxall-Crenshaw was so
influential in the Brazilian market that merchants from other foreign ports
may have resorted to shady practices in order to capitalize on it. New York
traders allegedly bought up the coarse flour also made by the big Richmond
mills, scraped the inspector's stamps of "middlings" from the barrels, and
resold them in Brazil as fine flour with only the brand of the miller to identify the product.[67]

The export of coffee was so profitable, and the influence of merchants
so potent, that the government never restricted the entry of foreign flour
into Rio. As important as tariff reductions and North American merchants'
desire for coffee was, the coffee revolution had broader impact on domestic
food production in southeastern Brazil. The rapid diffusion of monocrop
coffee plantations meant that areas of the Paraíba Valley formerly dedicated
to providing the city with its primary food needs concentrated on coffee
export. Densely populated with enslaved workers, as well as overseers, managers, and bookkeepers, not to mention grain-hungry draft animals like
oxen, horses and mules, the farms of Rio's rural hinterland became "centers
of consumption."[68]

Rio's population, meanwhile, continued to grow; the capital had transitioned out of its role as a political seat to become the mercantile center of
a dynamic agricultural export sector.[69] Even Rio's outskirts were urbaniz-
ing, a transition that reduced land previously reserved for garden crop production and increased the numbers of people dependent on the market for
everyday dietary needs.[70] By 1830, authorities had begun to take note of a
substitution of primary foods traditionally produced in the province of Rio
by products brought in from other regions. Black beans from Rio Grande
do Sul supplanted local beans (*feijão*); manioc flour began to be shipped in
from Porto Alegre, and most importantly, "wheat flour that used to come
mostly from southern Brazil began to be supplemented almost exclusively
by the United States."[71] The material refinement of daily life for elite planters followed quickly on the heels of new coffee fortunes. Diets diverged
from the traditional *feijoada* and manioc or maize flour most Brazilians,
high class and low, had eaten in earlier times. French-style white bread was
the staple *du jour*, and bakeries were established in the villages of the plantation zones.[72]

In the overall import picture of Brazil, flour's importance also grew over time. Between 1850 and 1855 it was the fourth most valuable import, behind cotton cloth, gold/silver coin, and wool cloth. By 1855–1860, however, it had moved up to number two, trailing only cotton cloth from Great Britain.[73] The official statistics of the customs office (Alfândega) in Rio reported 318,954 barrels of flour imported "for consumption" in 12 months spanning 1857–1858.[74] With about 200,000 people in the capital city in 1850, that would have added up to 312 pounds of flour consumed per capita in that year[75] (Figure 5-3). Per capita figures for consumption, however, can be misleading. Who was suddenly eating all of this bread?

Changing Diets

Traveling through the Paraíba Valley in 1857, Virginia railway engineer Richard Morton noted that coffee planters raised "every thing in the world that they eat except flour & wines & they do not buy flour but the bread already baked . . . they all eat cold bread bought from the bakers who are established all through the country."[76] Had he visited the region thirty years earlier, he would have had a different experience, as the foodways had changed in southeastern Brazil. While the small population of elite planters did not represent the majority of white bread consumers, they led a broader shift in rural culture that associated "French style" white bread with economic success and political power. Any extensive rural consumption of imported wheat flour by the 1850s would have to be explained by middling coffee cultivators who aspired to elite status and often had connections to local planters who were consuming white bread.[77] Portuguese immigrants, many of whom found work as overseers on the new coffee estates, brought European bread-eating habits to the countryside.[78] Finally, the increasing involvement of local merchants in carrying coffee from the valley to the coast would have inserted them at the same time in wheat-flour-based commodity change, bringing more half-barrels into the villages of the valley.[79]

Overall, new urban consumers would have been a more significant driver of flour imports. Rio's population doubled in the 1840s to 205,903. While the population of ex-slaves and their descendants increased substantially, newcomers from Europe comprised the fastest-growing sector of the urban community.[80] Portuguese as well as Italian immigration accelerated in the 1850s. Agricultural changes in the countryside of northern Portugal, together with growing opportunities in southeastern Brazil, brought a flood of young people on indenture contracts.[81] Perhaps to increase the likelihood of finding

SLAVES WITH A TRUCK WAGON.

Two negroes passed me one day with a huge cask of oil suspended from a pole resting on their shoulders. The poor fellow in the rear stumbled and fell—I thought he had been killed. His companion, instead of pitying him, turned the very image of rage—screamed, swore, shook

A TRUCK.

his fist, walked round the prostrate slave, and yelled till a crowd gathered round him.

With a friend I went to the Consulado, a department of the Customs having charge over

exports. Gangs of slaves came in con[...] with coffee for shipment. Every bag is [...] and a sample withdrawn while on the [...] head, to determine the quality and dut[...] tariff, based on the market price, is re[...] every Saturday. At present the duty a[...] to eleven per cent. o[...] and seven on sugar[...] instrument used t[...] draw samples of c[...] a brass tube, cut p[...] like a pen. The [...] pushed in at the un[...] of the bag, and the [...] pass through the t[...] handful is abstract[...] withdrawing the [...] ment, its point is [...] over, and closes th[...] ing. The operatio[...] pies but a few seconds. The samples [...] to some tons in a year. They, with t[...] exported sugars, are given to the Lazar[...] Every gang of coffee-carriers has a [...] who commonly sh[...] rattle, to the music o[...] his associates behi[...] chant. The load, [...] ing 160 lbs., rests [...] head and shoulde[...] body is inclined f[...] and the pace is a [...] half run. Most ar[...] and athletic, but a f[...] so small and slightl[...] that one wonders ho[...] manage to keep u[...] the rest. The aver[...] of a coffee-carrier d[...] exceed ten years. [...] time the work ruptu[...] kills them. They [...]

BEARING AN OIL CASK.

FIGURE 5-3 The booming flour imports were handled by enslaved longshoremen and waggoners. The author of the accompanying article noted that these men had pushed the ten barrels of flour over a mile through the city.

From Thomas Ewbank, "A Visit to the Land of the Cocoa and Palm," *Harper's New Monthly Magazine* 7, no. 42 (Nov. 1853): 728.

less exploitative employment arrangements, as many as 40 or 45 percent of registered Portuguese male immigrants entered the country as self-described sales clerks (*caixeiros*).[82] Artisans were another important urban middle-income group whose numbers expanded in the period. They were quite aspirational in terms of consumption, and they would likely have bought warm white bread when possible.[83]

The continued inflow of captives from both northeastern Brazil and Africa kept slave ownership within the reach of non-wealthy people in Rio. Individuals who owned one or two slaves often secured their own livelihoods by hiring them out and keeping the proceeds. Slave renting helped bring imported goods increasingly within reach of middle-income groups. These social sectors were also helped by the unprecedented amounts of money circulating in Rio. The successes of Brazil's export economy allowed the government to keep printing currency without causing inflation.[84] Coffee sales abroad, in other words, did not only attract mass amounts of new wheat flour. but it also made that flour affordable to a wider swathe of the population.

In addition, a massive informal credit network helped middling- and even working-class urbanites gain access to wheat flour products. The wealthy lent money to middle-income and poor residents of the city, at interest rates as high as 15 percent per year.[85] Owners of retail establishments, bakeries included, offered store credit at interest.[86] José Ferreira Maia Sobrinho, a baker and flour merchant in the 1850s, had direct ties to flour dealers based in Baltimore and New Orleans, from whom he made purchases on credit. At the same time, he was selling bread and flour on credit to his customers.[87] When the bakery proprietor José Joaquim Duarte Mendes disappeared after being accused of killing a slave, the flour broker Francisco José da Costa Lima appealed to a commercial judge in the village of Estrella. He was concerned less about the fate of the slave, than he was for the large debt the suspect owed him.[88]

When we take these kinds of credit arrangements into account, it is easier to imagine that "bread had become part of the consumption habits of the people. It no longer played a secondary role," as historian Juliana Teixeira Souza contends, "constituting instead part of the daily diets of the free poor."[89] An 1859 Brazilian cookbook's observation that "country folk and the poor" made breads from other grains like rye and millet "for relief in times of scarcity" suggests that even these groups ate wheat flour under normal circumstances.[90] Consumption of wheat products may even have included slaves, since over one thousand bondspeople labored in the bakeries of Rio in 1860.[91] It is doubtful that people toiling day in and day out in a bakery, as well as working delivery routes away from the prying eyes of masters, did not find ways to market some bread affordably within their own social networks.

Brazilian government statistics also indicate that plenty of professionally manufactured bread was being consumed. In Brazil as a whole there were 439 registered bakeries (*padarias*) in 1857, at least a quarter of them in the city of Rio.[92] While in 1849, there were only fifty bakeries in the city, a decade later the number had risen to 137 (Figure 5-4).[93] Demand for high-end bakers was growing apace. For the year of 1840, bakery proprietors posted just eight want ads for master bakers in the *Jornal do Commercio*, but five times as

BOUTIQUE DE BOULANGER.

FIGURE 5-4 A small Rio bakery of the 1830s that was grinding some of its own local wheat, using a small number of enslaved operatives. Notice the sack of wheat (presumably Brazilian) in the foreground, the barrels of flour in the background, the boys heading out on delivery runs, the female food vendor, and the white proprietor. By the 1850s the average Rio bakery would have used imported flour and would have exploited a larger number of slaves.

From Jean Baptiste Debret, 3 vols, vol. 2, *Voyage pittoresque et historique au Brésil, ou Séjour d'un artiste français au Brésil, depuis 1816 jusqu'en 1831 inclusivement* (Paris, Firmin Didot frères, 1834-39), plate 44. Rare Book and Special Collections Division of the Library of Congress, Washington, DC.

many in 1859.[94] Bakeries had become so much a part of the urban landscape of southeastern Brazil that they were used as general points of rendezvous. People who wanted to take an omnibus ride to the Botanical Garden of Rio, for example, were instructed to meet at the bakery of Mr. João Rodrigues.[95]

The democratization of imported white flour made the region as a whole quite dependent on the economic fluctuations of the Atlantic system for its everyday needs—thus bread became a political issue. The half-dozen-or-so "flour brokers" who controlled the supplies of flour imported by firms like Maxwell, Wright were a magnet for resentments. Because wheat flour was the second-largest import business in the country, accusations that this small group maintained a "monstruous monopoly" may not have been far from the truth.[96] As prices for flour began to rise in the mid-1850s, Amedéo Carruette, José Joaquin de Barros, and two other broker-bakers named Mello and Guimarães were accused of shrinking the loaves "to homeopathic proportions," since city regulations prevented them from raising bread prices per loaf.[97] To make matters worse, these "foreigners" continued the practice as the price of flour began to level off, and in spite of the flour market "regurgitating with abundance." A spring editorial appealed to the government to "alleviate the hunger of the people by striking a mortal blow against the sordidness of these perverts."[98]

It is hard to reconcile the newspaper's characterization of Rio's flour brokers with their self-representation as conscientious craftsmen who used only the best of raw materials to better serve their customers. However, Carruette, like his fellow flour monopolists, was also a baker.[99] He grew his small empire throughout the 1850s and opened a third location in 1860. His firm also supplied English and French warships with bread.[100] Thus the sweetness and durability of the flour he purchased was reflected in the quality of products sold to fairly influential customers.

Moreover, the hundred-plus bakers whom the brokers sold to were willing to pay premium prices. In 1849, fifty bakers were identified in the city's business almanac, but only eleven of them owned real estate.[101] The baker-brokers like Carruette formed part of an elite stratum of bakers who owned their own buildings, along with a dozen or more slaves, and had financial backing. They promoted the consumption of imported white flour and professionally baked loaves. One unfortunate baker who was not able to meet his financial obligations had his belongings auctioned off in in 1856, including "seven slaves, all of whom work in the bakery." The auction also provides a snapshot of the raw materials a Rio baker might have on hand: Haxall, Gallego, New York, Trieste, Odesse, and "bulk flours."[102] This inventory was probably typical, in that most bakers did not buy just one type of flour. They used different kinds of flours for different kinds of products, creating flour blends to give their bread a unique flavor. As Maxwell reported, each shipment of flour "acquires a character from its own qualities."[103] The baker at Rua Conde 4 boasted that "certain speculators want to imitate" his bread, "but the esteemed public should not be fooled."[104]

Tapping into the "French craze" that swept Rio in the first half of the nineteenth century, some bakers emphasized the Frenchness of their concoctions. A new "French bakery" opened by the Estrue Bros. addressed "lovers of good bread" in the pages of the daily paper. They sold all types of loaves from Languedoc and Provence, as well as other types of bread never before available in the country, like "allure, the best there is," "*tresado*," and "true Parisian *navetos*."[105] The bakery at Carmo 37 specified their master baker be French.[106] Looking to contract "a master baker, who will without a doubt be paid well, as long as he is perfect in his craft," Padaria dos Amantes also sought "a perfect ovenman to operate a French oven."[107] Such bakeries were often located in and around Ouvidor Street, a district featuring shops full of French imports and fine consumer goods.[108]

While the quality of the baked goods clearly influenced brokers' preference for Richmond flour, their selectiveness may also have been driven by Barros and Carruette's speculations. Among other things, they allegedly sent away large shipments of flour during times of shortage in Rio.[109] Chasing price differentials and reducing supply, the flour brokers drew their "game" straight from the traditional merchant's playbook. However, the creole technologies of fine, dry, white flour in hermetically sealed barrels enabled this speculation, since the flour offered extended storage time, which was accentuated by rapid shipping from Richmond to Rio. The Richmond product was worth the premium brokers paid in part because it offered them a unique ability to maneuver in the market and manipulate price changes throughout the seasonal cycle.

Preservability may have even been more important with affordable dry baked goods like *bolachas* and *roscas*, forms of water cracker, or flat pies, made of wheat flour. Known for their durability and low bulk, they were ideal for long-term shipment. After being made with imported flours, *roscas* were frequently shipped to Luso-African outposts like Benguela and Loanda in the 1850s. Debret, a well-known French visitor to Rio in 1817, found Brazilian bakers to "excel in the fabrication of *biscoutos salgados, roscas*, and *bolachas*."[110] Some bakers sold batches already packed in barrels, "*para embarque*," most likely as provisions for crews.[111] Not only were baked products sent to faraway places, but in the 1840s somewhere between one-quarter and one-third of flour was reexported from Brazil to other destinations.[112] San Francisco was a major market for Gallego and Haxall brands, "receiving some 743,000 barrels of Atlantic flour in the 1850s."[113] Compared to that of southeastern Brazil, California settlers' demand for Richmond flour was not short-lived, as they soon had their own wheat farms and flour mills in operation. Nevertheless, Rio's status as a transshipment point for much of this California-bound product enabled Richmond flour to reach beyond just Rio consumers. The particular geographic and temporal horizons of Greater Caribbean trade in the era of the Second Slavery accentuated the value of Richmond brands' preservative characteristics.

Keeping a variety of flours on hand and selling an array of differently priced goods for local as well as international distribution, Rio bakers along with their inventories remind us that not all wheaten products were created equal. The distinction between customers who had *pão quente* on the table twice a day, and those families who made do with *roscas, bolachas*, and *biscoutos* had class and racial valences among the region's city dwellers. Big commercial bakers tried to produce wheat goods for a spectrum of social classes. In one 1850 ad, Pedro Brunet, owner of the "Padaria Franceza," bragged of making bread "of such superior quality, as until now no other baker has been able to make. French, Portuguese, English breads, *pão de café*," and more would be available at his establishment.[114]

At the same time, Brunet used his elite reputation to expand into a mass market for cheaper wheaten goods. In a separate ad, he informed the public of his new factory, which would produce *bolachas, roscas, biscouto doce*, and *bolachinhas americanas* by machine.[115] His middling- and working-class consumers did not have direct access to French-style bread. Nor did Brunet promise a taste of home for Portuguese newcomers. On the contrary, he highlighted the Americanness of the products.[116] Writing in 1841, Maxwell hoped bakers might in the future "purchase in moderate quantity, and at a fair difference of price, the western descriptions" of flour, and it is true that their preference for Richmond flour was never exclusive.[117] In conceding to the necessity of buying cheaper, lower-quality flours along with premium Richmond barrels, bakers like Brunet were not overcoming a prejudice. Instead they were in the process of widening their markets by offering more affordable products, and found it necessary to cut costs where they could.

Brunet advertised his new machinery for making bread that brought whiteness within reach of immigrants and free people. For these new mass market products, Brunet invested in the "Systema Rolland," with its mechanical mixer/kneader and an "aerothermal oven." Investment in such hardware, of course, presupposed a large consumer market. While he did emphasize the rapidity with which the mixer turned flour and water into thoroughly mixed dough, Brunet focused on its hygienic benefits. "The bread we eat every day," he reminded his readers, "is irrigated by the extremely copious sweat" of the bakery workers, while his goods were "fabricated entirely by mechanical processes."[118] Thus "all the contact and sweat of the workers, that in the old mode made the fabrication of a staple of primary necessity disgusting, is done away with."[119] In Brazil, racial identity and legal status were often expressed through sumptuary laws, such as regulations against slaves wearing shoes. Accentuating the racial aspect of white bread consumption, Brazilians called different varieties of bread "castas," with one type of loaf identified by the explicitly racial term *crioulo*.[120] Through white-flour-based goods, the promise of whiteness, freedom, and social ascent could be consumed by ex-slaves and new immigrants—but not if the white bread was "irrigated" by the sweat of the poor and dark skinned. Brunet's marketing tapped into anxieties about the porousness of the boundary between enjoying the products of enslaved people's labor, and consuming enslaved people's physical bodies by eating what they made. Thus the French machine offered something different in Rio from what it had offered in Paris. By 1860, at least two more Rio bakeries had adopted the Rolland System.[121] Yet the fantasy racial-hygienic of automation eluded Brunet. He was looking to hire a kneader in 1857.[122]

African-Descended Bakers Reshape the Greater Caribbean

As in all other aspects of daily life in Rio, slaves were central in bakeries. From small, general shops, to large, specialized ones, "African male slaves were the bakers of Rio," laboring in numbers of a dozen or more.[123] They toiled long hours, undertaking strenuous manual labor in hot conditions. As "master bakers," slaves could also be brokers of technological and quality control. One bakery placed an ad for a master oven handler or baker, "slave or free, being skilled in the service."[124] A slaveholder pursuing profits offered for rent a master baker and ovenman.[125] An indebted bakery proprietor by the name of Joaquim Manoel de Moraes Bandeira took to the pages of the *Jornal* to protest the repossession of his goods. He was particularly upset that authorities had taken "my master baker."[126] The goods of another impecunious baker named José da Rocha Leão were put up for auction, including several slaves "who are quite skilled in their craft, especially one of them who makes the bread called de Provença, to the highest degree of perfection."[127]

With those of less rarified craft skills, specialized labor and drudgery still made them key to bread quality: The bakery on Rua do Fogo 51 wanted to rent "a good black ovenman."[128] When Francisco dos Santos Freire died in 1851, his widow put up "a portion of the slave bakers, ovenmen, and kneaders."[129] Describing themselves as "true professional bakers," the Estrue Brothers sought "to employ blacks for kneading work." Because the kneading of the bread was as important for the newest styles of French breads as the rest of the preparation process, they needed masses of skilled slave labor to work the dough.[130]

In Brazil, master bakers numbered among those relatively autonomous slaves in the food trade who were permitted to hire out their services, although they had to give most of their earnings to their masters. Throughout the country, African-born former slaves engaged in craft occupations were often able to accumulate enough wealth to open a business and buy slaves of their own.[131] A large number of Rio's bakers may have been free people of color who had followed the painstaking trajectory of gaining skills in slavery, hiring themselves out to purchase freedom, and rising socially by using slaves of their own to deal in imported flours to make European or North American–style wheat products.

Other captive bakers followed a more direct road to freedom. Escapes could be especially damaging in time-sensitive bakeries, where flour was souring, and customers losing patience, while a master baker ran off to the newspaper offices to place an ad for a fugitive baker. In 1857, for example, an owner offered a reward for "two black ovenmen," who were "known fugitives." One, named Luiz, had already served time in prison for previous misconduct.[132] A Mozambican baker named José wore shoes when he departed. "Footwear might have formed part of his strategy to pose as a free man," but it also suggests that a certain amount of cultural capital accrued to enslaved bread makers.[133] As much as the marks of cultural capital, fugitive bakers also bore the marks of slavery, ticked off with unsettling casualness by their owners. José had "signs of significant punishment on his back."[134] A bakery fugitive named Januario had "the marks of fire on his back, regular weight and height, speaks a bit pedantically."[135] A slave named Felix who escaped from the bakery at Rua de Lapa do Desterro 13 A was distinguished by a "lack of hair caused by carrying loads."[136]

The conduct of free black bakers, as well as fugitive bakers, indicates they had developed a strong personal identification with their craft in spite of having had no choice in originally taking it up. Many fugitives in Rio were caught plying their trade in other parts of the city. A twenty-year-old African-born blacksmith named Joaquin took with him "an anvil and all his smithing tools" when he fled.[137] Tools of the trade, worn with use, could perhaps be used for self-defense in case of an encounter with slave patrollers who roamed the city in search of escapees. When the bakery slave Lorenzo struck out for freedom, he "carried a sack of clothing, and a worn-out table knife."[138]

The collective experience of laboring in bakeries sometimes led black bakers to seek immediate self-emancipation through the general strike. One such case involves a formerly enslaved baker from Santos, João de Mattos. He had learned through harsh experience that even free black bakers could be beaten by masters, forced to work nineteen-hour days, or dismissed from employment for any reason. Mattos used his unusual literacy to forge letters of manumission for his enslaved fellow bread makers. Then, amid abolitionist furor in the 1870s, Mattos gave the signal for what he called the "first general rising" of bakers in Santos. In a highly disciplined plan, they abandoned their posts on the designated day and fled town with falsified papers. The fugitives then split up, arriving at some other town where they were not well known, and presented themselves as free men. When authorities located Mattos, he was thrown in prison.

Finding himself unwelcome in the small baking community of Santos after his release, he moved to São Paulo and organized a similar plan among the eleven or twelve bakeries of that city. The group fled together into the hills, and many of the slaves found work as free people. However, Mattos and a small group headed for Rio, where they arrived just in time for the height of baking season in early September of 1878. By 1880, he had organized a new group of one hundred Rio bakers into "The Combat Bloc of Bakery Workers" (*Bloco de Combate dos Empregados de Padaria*), whose motto was "For Bread and Freedom." Radicalized by the presence of other working-class organizations in the city, yet still insisting on their special status as bakers, Mattos emphasized the Bloc was not yet another mutual aid society, but a "society of class conflict." Mattos thus distinguished his organization from the various manumission societies (*juntas da alforria*), within which enslaved and formerly enslaved people pooled money to buy freedom for members.[139] Mattos intended to expedite the eight-to-ten-year process of self-purchase. The enslaved among them fled for the country again with false papers, while Mattos and a few free comrades returned to Rio. He was imprisoned again, this time for three months, after which he was forced to go back to São Paulo, as he could no longer secure employment in any of the bakeries of Rio.

Among his extensive social networks, he had heard of bakeries opening in the countryside, and apparently worked in several of them, helping slaves achieve freedom until abolition in 1888.[140]

In spite of the conditions in which they learned how to run a bakery, bread making had become part of the identity of many of these individuals. They carried that remunerative know-how into freedom, whether through gradual and painstaking self-purchase, sudden but risky flight, or a collectively premeditated general strike of bakers. The skills and knowledge of the great majority of non-property-owning, non-white bakers, often built up during bondage, pivoted on the quality and durability of their most important raw material: wheat flour. As they paid higher prices for it and purchased more of it, they exerted influence on the milling and coopering technologies of Richmond millers. In the 1850s, not only did the black bakers of Rio share a common condition with one another, but their working lives also became enmeshed with those of slaves laboring on the wheat farms and in the flour mills of faraway Virginia. Brazilian bakers' know-how could not have been more different from the racial expertise Robert Harvey was looking for in his *Richmond Dispatch* ad for prospective railway managers schooled in slave driving, and yet they drew together the economic life of the Greater Caribbean.

6

Entangled Technologies

RICHMOND AND THE TRANSFORMATION
OF AMERICAN FLOUR MILLING

UNTIL THE 1860S, the transformation of flour-milling technology in the United States was led by Richmond millers overwhelmingly focused on the single market of Rio de Janeiro.[1] The quality control and brand recognition prized in the Brazilian market made major capital investments, as well as unprecedented horizontal integration, worthwhile for Richmond industrialists. At the height of the Civil War, the US Commissioner of Agriculture was forced to acknowledge that "the flouring mills of Richmond are probably equal to any in the world, both in perfection of their machinery and in the quantity and quality of the flour produced."[2] The present chapter explores how and why they achieved that position.

Richmond's rapid takeover of an expanding wheat flour market in southeastern Brazil was not an automatic or natural process. The product, and the modes of fabricating and transporting it, had to be reinvented to reach the predominance it achieved in Rio by the end of the 1850s. Richmond took over the leading role through three kinds of trade systemization. First, since wheat flour had a shelf life of around three months, timely delivery of perishable flour had to be ensured. Hoping to keep more of the profit to themselves, Richmond millers built a fleet of packet liners shuttling back and forth on a nonstop flour-coffee circuit between Rio and the Upper South. They also formed new mercantile partnerships with Baltimore and British commercial firms. Finally, Virginia's pro-slavery oceanographer, Matthew Fontaine Maury, halved travel times between Richmond and Rio through the invention of new navigational methods and charts.[3]

Richmond's major flour mills also underwent major technological transformations. The Oliver Evans design had emerged in the context of a history of low-grade meal and flour consumption on West Indian plantations. Richmond millers, increasingly specialized in the Brazil trade, re-creolized the milling complex for a different consumer market. The markup that recognized Richmond firms consistently enjoyed in Rio made consolidation worthwhile; the more flour made in the same mill by the same firm, the higher the price it seemed to bring. The extra capital that came with firm consolidation also allowed the millers to incorporate milling micro-inventions tailored for white flour's tropical survival. Mill proprietors could also afford specialized personnel, such as "wheat receivers" and "barrel receivers," dedicated entirely to quality control, which helped differentiate their product from that of the thousands of small mills scattered along the rivers and creeks of the Upper South.

By the 1850s, Richmond millers had used these investments to win the respect of Brazil's "fastidious" bakers. Much like the white-sugar machinery discussed in earlier chapters, these expensive machines and processes were preservative technologies that promised to freeze biological time in the barrel. Admirers of Richmond flour implied that no changes occurred on the trip to Rio inside the hermetically sealed containers filled with clean and pure white flour—a product that small-time country millers could not typically make. It was not technological magic alone that allowed Richmond brands to win the Rio market. Just as Brazil's illegal slave trade, along with planters' coercive power over slaves, ultimately stood behind the coffee boom, Virginia slaves were necessary to keep Brazilian coffee flowing into Yankee bellies.

Consolidated mills had the money to purchase or hire as many as eighty bondspeople for the constant processes of cleaning, maintenance, and repair that helped Richmond flour arrive in Rio "fresh" and "sweet." The "tropicality" of Richmond's vaunted flour was predicated on the mechanical stamping out of fungus and mold. Enslaved men, women, and children who climbed up into the flour-caked shaftwork of the mills with buckets and brushes were safeguarding the reputation of Richmond brands. In Rio, racialized consumption practices amplified the value accruing to flour's whiteness. In Richmond mills, that whiteness was produced by the combination of forced labor with targeted technological transformations.

Richmond millers benefitted from a "build-burn-build" pattern of innovation. Flour dust is quite flammable, and nineteenth-century mills were mostly of wooden construction, meaning fires were common. For this reason, new fire insurance companies often refused to cover them. Richmond millers, however, gained seats on the boards of directors of two of the city's newest and most important insurance companies. Once the millowners had access to insurance, frequent fires actually encouraged innovation and expansion by destroying existing structures. This was yet another advantage Richmond millers enjoyed over smaller competitors lacking in elite connections among Richmond men of capital.

With all the capital and labor dedicated to perfecting a particular type of white flour, packing it for export was no less important than the product itself. The growing export business encouraged the rise of a new steam-powered coopering factory in Richmond in the 1850s. Weed & Howe's factory accelerated production to keep up with Richmond millers' growing demand for barrels. The machinery also facilitated the standardization of staves, headers, and hoops for a more durable, watertight enclosure.[4] Thorough kilning of the staves killed pests in the wood and discouraged the growth of molds and fungus on the voyage south. The creolization of Richmond's coopering industry helps explain the success of the city's "tropical" flour, as well as the durability of that flour's fragile whiteness.

Given the daily expenses of large labor forces, as well as the capital sunk in extensive milling complexes, barrel factories, and insurance policies, the firms felt compelled to arrange the steady, predictable influx of wheat and barrels, along with the provision of sufficient water power. Thus the capital-intensive companies expanded into the city, creating a "spreading machine" of warehouses, railroads, and conveyor belts to facilitate throughput.[5] The power of millers over urban space was at times controversial, especially when the needs of firms conflicted with the priorities of other Richmonders. Moreover, the spreading machine also sent enslaved firm workers out into the city as teamsters and dockworkers, intensifying white anxieties about capital-sponsored black mobility and general lawlessness. In spite of such concerns, which were heightened by mounting northern abolitionism and consistent escapes by the enslaved, black workers continued to move around the city in service to the mills, but often in their own interests as well.

By the late 1850s, it had become clear to many observers that small country mills, lacking in capital, labor, brand recognition, and quality barrels, were losing out in their competition for Virginia's export markets. Some state politicians of a Jeffersonian bent sought to protect country millers, who had long been a public utility of sorts for the virtuous yeoman farmer. But changing technologies and changing market dynamics rendered futile most efforts to conserve the infrastructures of rural republicanism. Country millers no longer met with success when selling their "canal flour" through Richmond or

Georgetown commission merchants. Wheat planters often preferred sending their product by rail to Richmond, where they could get better prices as long as they delivered early. Increasingly, planters stopped milling locally, invested the extra capital in more slaves and plantation machinery, and reduced the time that slaves spent on subsistence activities, in order to accelerate the production of wheat and tobacco. As a result, hundreds of country mills shuttered their doors in the 1850s.[6] Gaining in size, productivity and specialization, Virginia's wheat hinterland became a propitious environment for new kinds of targeted technological shifts.

Richmond as Mill Seat and Port

Neutral shipping status and the agility of Baltimore's fast ships had helped the merchants of the Maryland city establish relations with Brazil in the late eighteenth century. As one North American visitor recalled, it was not "uncommon for American vessels, after disposing of their cargoes in Rio de Janeiro, to go down to Rio Grande do Sul, lay in a cargo of dried beef, carry it to Havana, and there dispose of it for goods suitable to the American market."[7] While a US South–Cuba–Brazil triangular trade existed before 1820, the transition to packet lines shuttling a Richmond-Rio circuit in the 1850s shows how much Brazilian planters' success in forcing slaves to cultivate coffee in the Paraíba Valley altered trade dynamics in the Greater Caribbean.

Virginia Governor Henry Wise, who served as Minister to Brazil in the 1840s, lamented that most of the profits from the coffee-flour trade went into the pockets of northern shippers and merchants. While he may have been right, Richmond flour manufacturers seemed less dependent upon New York and Baltimore transporters by the end of the 1850s, when they had established direct trade with Brazil.[8] Even though most of the vessels continued to be built and equipped in Baltimore, they were owned and operated by Richmond merchant millers and their associates. For example, in 1859 Baltimore shipbuilders Abrahams and Ashcraft completed the 250-ton flour brig *Virginia* for the Crenshaws. On its maiden voyage it carried a load of flour to Rio. Another new vessel of 400-ton capacity was already under construction for the same owners, presumably for the same purpose.[9] The size of Richmond-owned vessels seemed to be increasing as well. Leading local shipping agents Currie and Co. added a vessel of 1800 tons, and another of 850 to their holdings in the late 1850s.[10]

Richmond's geographic situation made the idea of the city ever becoming a major Atlantic port unlikely. One hundred miles upriver from the

Chesapeake Bay, Richmond could not be reached by any but the smallest of oceangoing ships.[11] Rocketts Landing, about two miles downriver from the mills, was the major loading point for tobacco, lumber, and other products. Even from there, some ships required multiple stages of loading and a tow over the bar at Harrison's Point, about twenty-five miles downriver.[12] But a poor harbor did not prevent Richmond from becoming a major exporter of flour. The water power available at the James River fall line, combined with the considerable costs already sunk into improving the river with power canals to supply the large mills, as well as a turning basin for visiting vessels, mitigated its topographical shortcomings. Virginians also actively promoted new efficiencies to offset the extra shipping costs associated with Richmond's location.

Specialized packet liners, plying back and forth along known routes with pre-fixed cargoes, reduced shipping costs substantially by shortening time at sea and in port. By the late 1850s, twenty-one Richmond-owned vessels belonged "to regular lines between this port and Rio, New York, and Boston."[13] Five of the twenty-one vessels specialized in the Richmond-Rio circuit. The total tonnage of Richmond's merchant fleet may have been small, but the merchant-millers' dedication to smoothing ties to Rio and to systematizing commodity exchanges through the expansion of packet lines suggests a significant transformation. In spite of New York's growing commercial hegemony, Richmond shipping news was replete with reports of the hometown flour brigs bringing coffee from Rio to either Richmond or Baltimore. For example, on January 21, 1859 "The Sallie McGee" returned "from Rio de Janeiro with 3664 bags of coffee on board, to be sold at auction by Edmund, Davenport and Company.... After discharging cargo, she will load with flour and sale again for Rio."[14] It is hard to tell what percentage of Richmond flour exports were being carried in Virginia vessels by 1860, but clearly the flour-coffee circuit was becoming more systematized and specialized. What was not carried by Richmond shippers was usually carried by Baltimore ones, who used their access to the product to accumulate cargoes of Brazilian coffee beans.

The larger commercial metropolises of New Orleans and New York, with quicker connections to masses of new coffee drinkers in the western states via the Mississippi River, the Erie Canal, and a burgeoning western rail system, imported slightly more Brazilian coffee than Baltimore. However, they had access only to midwestern flour, which sold for far less in Rio. Thus, while the merchants of New Orleans and New York had to scramble to assemble more diverse cargoes to exchange for Brazilian coffee, Baltimore and Richmond loaded uniform cargoes of Richmond and Baltimore flour bound for Rio. This specialization occurred because only Rio could furnish full cargoes of coffee, and import-export houses in Rio demanded Richmond flour in return.[15] Richmond flour thus played an important role in Baltimore's control of nearly a third of US coffee imports, reshaping the commercial networks of the antebellum United States in the Atlantic World.

With good connections to local shipping companies, Richmond millers also partnered with experienced English merchants in Brazil. The son of miller William Crenshaw recounted the antebellum arrangements of one of the major millers: "Haxall-Crenshaw Flour Mills furnished the cargo for export in Crenshaw & Co.'s ships, managed by Currie & Co., and J. L. Phipps & Co., of London, England, had a two-third interest in the return cargoes of Coffee to Richmond in which Crenshaw & Co., had the other one-third interest, and the ships of Crenshaw & Co., earned the carrying charges for the freight."[16] Phipps & Co. was one of the primary exporters of coffee in Rio, and it would have behooved the company to also deal in the only North American commodity that appeared to exchange advantageously with Brazilian coffee: Richmond-branded flour. Through such shipping and mercantile relationships, the millers were able to offset some of the transshipment costs imposed by Richmond's less than ideal port conditions. Shipping times added to the cost of flour, and the limited shelf life of flour shipments also motivated shippers to accelerate their transportation.

In 1859, Richmond's local paper republished a report from Rio's *Jornal do Commercio*, which boasted of "an instance of remarkable dispatch." *Dawn*, a Richmond vessel, "arrived at Rio on Dec 18, with 2650 barrels of flour and an assorted cargo. She was cleared for New York on the 21st, with 4000 bags coffee, thus remaining in port but three days to discharge one cargo and take in another."[17] Shortened port times both cut costs and prevented spoilage. The increasingly systematized circuit between Richmond and Rio smoothed transactions and allowed for labor costs on board to be reduced. In this case, reports of rapid loading and unloading silently acknowledged the hard labor of Rio's enslaved stevedores, longshoremen, and wagon drivers.

In the name of trade acceleration, Richmond's port infrastructure was considerably improved. Haxall had its own canal that borrowed water from the James, as well as docks and slips for rapid and traffic-free shipping. Gallego had a water basin three city blocks long to store up power supply and allow ships to turn after loading.[18] The state Board of Public Works completed the Tidewater connection canal in the 1850s, which linked the turning basin to the city docks by using a system of locks that raised and lowered vessels

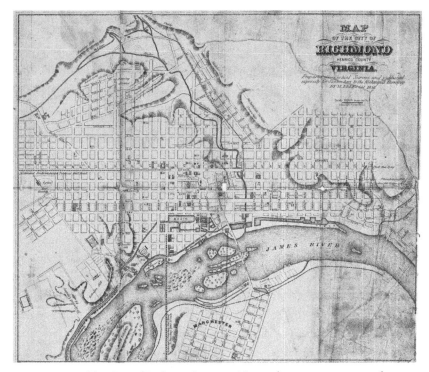

FIGURE 6-1A The City of Richmond in 1856. Notice the various provisions for water power and transport north of the river. These improvements included the new turning basin, the reservoirs and docks, and the James River and Kanawha Canal running along the river just below the basin and supplying power to Gallego Mills (32), Haxall's mill (35), and parts of the Tredegar iron-making complex (42–44).

From M. Ellyson, "Map of the City of Richmond Henrico County Virginia: Prepared from Actual Surveys, and Published Expressly for Subscribers to the Richmond Directory" (1856). Courtesy Library of Virginia.

between the river and the basin (Figure 6–1a and Figure 6-1b). Millers like R. B. Haxall and Abraham Warwick sat on the Board of Directors of the Richmond and York River Railroad, which sped Richmond exports out to sea via West Point on the York River. This railroad facilitated a boom of wharf construction and expanded ship tonnage in the previously minor tidewater port town of West Point.[19] Together, these costly improvements smoothed the transition between rail, wagon, and water transport for incoming shipments of wheat and outgoing cargoes of flour.

Faster times at sea also helped diminish Richmond's locational disadvantages. Oceanographer Matthew Fontaine Maury sought to use novel forms of collecting and analyzing maritime knowledge to quicken connections among the lands of the Second Slavery.[20] As Superintendent of the US

FIGURE 6.1B Detail of the City of Richmond in 1856.

Naval Observatory, Maury mapped the wind and water currents, as well as the weather patterns in the South Atlantic, with unprecedented detail. The Virginian was interested in Brazil primarily because he saw it as the future home of a US-controlled plantation kingdom that would siphon off excess slave population from North America, ensuring the racial order of the southern states.[21] Thus, the antebellum phase of Maury's career was marked by a preoccupation with Brazil, including travel times from Baltimore and Richmond.[22] One of his first detailed charts, titled "The Route to Rio and Back," signals the importance of southeastern Brazil in the minds of the leaders of the East Coast maritime community. A commercial vision of slavery-based "free trade" tying together Virginia and Brazil was clearly formulated in his writings and graphically embodied in his "to Rio and Back" chart. The chart was at once inspired by the circuits already flowing between the two locales and a projection of the future to be enjoyed by the Richmond-Rio circuit.[23] One maritime historian points out that "the type of chart he envisioned looked nothing like the ones then in use. He intended to depict the patterns of wind and currents as tracks in the sea," like railroads. Less concerned with increasing the safety of merchant voyages, his new charts were aimed at speeding up commodity shipments in the South Atlantic.[24]

The method of chart production that he pioneered was new. Unable to subsist on the quantity of data supplied by the small US Navy, Maury successfully tapped the information-gathering power of the world's growing merchant fleet. Once powerful mercantile and shipping magnates had seen the profit in his project, they started pressuring their captains to fill out the tables of Maury's "abstract log" and submit it to him. One group of Boston shippers went further: they offered to raise $50,000 to fund the construction of a research vessel that could be used by Maury's staff to test and improve the

Atlantic charts.[25] He ended up collecting the data from over a million voyages sailed by the leading maritime nations of the world, while his army of military clerks in Washington, DC analyzed the information on winds and currents on particular days in particular quadrants of the sea (Figure 6-2). Widespread participation from the merchant community soon paid off. Spotlighting the

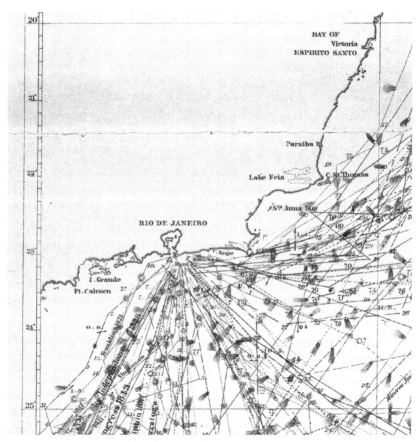

FIGURE 6.2 Maury's Wind and Current Chart of the South Atlantic. Maury used novel visualizations like this one to transform the sea into a calculable web of probabilities. These kinds of probabilistic guides accelerated travel times without any change in the architecture of sailing vessels, and also transformed how sea captains, insurers, and investors envisioned the Atlantic. Maury's staff processed data from hundreds of thousands of merchant voyages into reference maps like these, which offered to sea captains conditions coming into and out of the port of Rio de Janeiro—the strength, frequency, and direction of both winds and currents, as well as water temperature and magnetic variation.

Detail from Lieut. M. F. Maury, "Wind and Current Chart of the South Atlantic," United States Hydrographic Office, 1853. From the American Geographical Society Library, University of Wisconsin-Milwaukee Libraries.

centrality of the flour-coffee exchange, "the barque W. H. D. C. Wright," named after the founding partner of Maxwell, Wright & Co., was the first vessel to try the accelerated route between Baltimore and Rio, cutting ten to fifteen days off the trip. Thereafter, demand for the charts mounted.[26] Highly publicized clipper races ensued, and the vessels using Maury's charts between New York City and San Francisco finished in half the time of those using old charts.[27] Most shipmasters came to realize that Maury's routes to Rio and San Francisco were the quickest.[28]

Richmond millers' promotion of railroads to bring in clean wheat, their systemization of trade through packet liners, and the promotion of expedited shipping between the Upper South and Rio kept the larger system in constant, calibrated motion, serving the demands of perishable whiteness. In the mills themselves, an important overhaul was undertaken to better serve the demands of the flour market of southeastern Brazil.

Flour Milling

In the milling process, mill mechanisms dropped the grains between the spinning millstones after preliminary cleaning in a "smut machine." Despite their hardy appearance, millstones were not intended to crush the grain of wheat. Instead, the stones were set so as to pass very closely without touching. The shearing action of the spinning stone delicately peeled the hull of the grain away from the fruit without shattering the hull. Excessive pressure from the millstones would have made the product difficult to sift and resulted in a browner flour. The millers also had to take care that the friction of grinding wheat between the stones not overheat the flour and sour it. After cleaning and grinding, the physically separated constituents of the grain would be sifted, or "bolted," into different grades in another step of the automatic process. The flour then underwent cooling and drying before being machine packed into barrels, stamped with a grade, and readied for shipment.

The millers of Richmond took this Oliver Evans concept of automated milling to its highest development.[29] They began to expand the size of their mills in the 1830s, incorporating new inventions particularly effective for the South American trade. Haxall and Crenshaw's Columbia Mills were able to fill 160,000 barrels per year by 1860 [30] (Figure 6-3). Instead of the one or two pairs of stones of Evans's 1790s design, Columbia's two giant waterwheels spun as many as forty pairs of stones to grind grain. Meanwhile, in the years prior to the Civil War, Warwick and Barksdale of Richmond conducted business

FIGURE 6-3 The remains of just one of Warwick and Barksdale's six breast wheels. While "undershot" wheels, typical of small-scale colonial-era mills, were simply powered by the impact of flowing water in a river, "overshot" designs used a headrace arrangement to bring water to the top of the wheel and drop it on to the buckets, meaning that the weight of the water drove the wheel. Increasingly popular among large-scale mills of the nineteenth century, the "breast" wheel also received water from above, but the water fell on the near side of the wheel. When the buckets moved downwards, the "apron," a curved brick wall following the circumference of the wheel, held the water in the buckets longer, adding to the power drawn from the water. A breast wheel also moved in the same direction as the current, and could continue to operate in flood conditions if necessary. Drawing water from the James River and Kanawha Canal, Gallego's wheels powered thirty-one pairs of millstones along with the rest of the auxiliary machinery in the mill.

Interior view of Gallego Mills, April 1865. Library of Congress Prints and Photographs Division, LC-DIG-cwpb-03732.

in a twelve-story brick building, claimed to be the largest in the country. Adopting recent advances in water-power technology, its six "huge wheels designed to use water twice over" spun thirty-one pairs of millstones (Figure 6-4). This impressive structure was thought capable of putting out 190,000 to 200,000 barrels per year by 1860—nearly seven times the capacity of the Ellicott mills of early republican Baltimore.[31] In 1854 it was estimated that the Gallego and the Haxall mills turned out 2,000 barrels per day. The four other major firms in town produced an additional 1,000 barrels daily.[32]

FIGURE 6-4 Haxall & Crenshaw's Columbia Mills in 1859.
Detail of photo from Library of Congress Prints and Photographs Division LC-DIG-cwpb-00392.

The half-dozen major milling firms of Richmond geared to the Brazilian market by working within the "macro-technology" of the Evans system, increasing its productive capacity at least fivefold. With automated technology, economies of scale and skill, and a supply of labor, Richmond's flour mills produced in the same league as the leading flour cities of Philadelphia and Baltimore throughout the 1840s and 1850s.[33] In 1858, the seven mills of Richmond, plus some country mills whose flour was inspected in and shipped through Richmond, produced at least 650,000 barrels of flour, rivaling the output of Baltimore's approximately fifty flour mills in 1859 of over a million barrels.[34]

Given the three-month shelf life of flour, the window of time was narrow to move flour from American factories to the bakeries of southeastern Brazil. To keep "new wheat" flowing into the mill, as opposed to sitting in railroad depots, millers had to move what was already at the mill through the process as quickly as possible. Prices often declined in early autumn, as more and more flour was brought to coastal markets. In the Richmond-Rio circuit in particular, then, rapid movement of materials was sufficiently important to bear the cost of scale and mechanization. For mills with steep capital costs and a strict schedule, depending on daily market transactions to ensure supply was out of the question. Since the annual July-August wheat harvest coincided with low water on the rivers, millers promoted the construction of hinterland railroads. In addition to the four railroads bringing wheat from west of Richmond, the Richmond and York River Railroad allowed planters to float shipments of wheat down the Pamunkey and Mattaponi Rivers to West Point, where they could be put on the railroad and transported rapidly to Richmond mills.[35] City Point Railroad between Petersburg and City Point also brought wheat up to Richmond.

After ensuring a steady inflow of grain, millers built large structures to store it. At the Columbia Mills there was a wheat warehouse "connected to the mill by a conveyor that supplied wheat 'as wanted' to the mill and an inclined plane returned barreled flour to this same storehouse."[36] The eight-story warehouse also had four pairs of burr millstones. Not to be outdone, Warwick and Barksdale built a new complex that combined the functions of mill and warehouse.[37] Most likely, these auxiliary warehouse-mills smutted incoming grain to forestall spoilage before grinding and to prevent molds and fungi from entering the main mill buildings. Haxall also employed a "special carrier" whose six horse-drawn wagons shuttled grain continuously from railroad depot to warehouse.[38] Even the railroad depot had become part of the "spreading machine" of the Evans-model mill. With the centralization of wheat storage at the mill site, and the automation of raw materials transfer from warehouse to mill with conveyor belts, Haxall-Crenshaw had expanded upon Evans's smaller conception. To maintain the constant, calibrated flow of production, the firm spread its mechanical reach beyond the confines of the factory.

Some observers felt that the mills threatened to suck in the whole of Richmond. In 1853, a large city wall on 12th Street near the Gallego Mills collapsed for mysterious reasons. The local paper suggested that Warwick and Barksdale's new construction project was to blame. Workers digging a deep foundation for an additional mill undermined the foundation of the wall. When a heavy rain softened the ground, the wall sank further. When it finally collapsed, the wall took "with it about one third of that portion of 12th Street adjoining it, and the 6 inch gas pipe which led down to Haxall's mill and along to Byrd Street."[39] The newspaper warned that "the little small houses upon the bank will yet be precipitated into the foundation prepared for Warwick and Barksdale's new mill."[40]

Although the industrial complex of the Richmond mills and their specialized infrastructures produced commodities on an entirely different scale and pace than their Evans-model predecessors of the early nineteenth century, the Evans automatic mill remained the basic conceptual model. Although this persistence might suggest little innovation, incremental improvements had considerable cumulative impacts on productivity.[41] The Richmond mills' changes may have been incremental, but the thirty-one-fold increase in milling capacity threw up stiff engineering challenges requiring innovative solutions. Transmitting power from the waterwheel to the millstones was simple in the single-task gristmill, but when one power source was used to drive multiple operations, complex gearing, cams, shafts, and pulleys became necessary. The automation of cleaning, bolting, cooling, and packing also forced designers to take friction losses into account in more precise ways.[42] The larger the power requirements of the mill, the more complicated the infrastructural elements became. In the eighteenth century, not much attention was dedicated to dams, reservoirs, and canals, but "as hydraulic power increased in scale and sophistication to meet the needs of large, market-serving mills and factories ... the facilities required to supply the huge breast wheels of many large mills came to absorb much the greater part of the capital investment and engineering skills represented by the entire power installation."[43] In Richmond proper, the James River and Kanawha Canal was transformed for the provision of power.

The flow of materials through the factory and the transmission of power through the factory's various mechanisms had been revolutionized, as with the spreading machine of the flour mills. At the same time, the canal and railroad were speeding the flow of raw materials and finished goods into and out of factories, and steady improvements in agricultural production offered more wheat to the mill.[44]

In industrial economies, how the raw material was transferred through the various moments of transport and production was as important as how that raw material was transformed into a finished good. In other words, means of flow could be the secret weapon in low-cost mass production, which was exactly what Evans made possible for the Richmond millers, who adapted and transformed the original design to serve larger and choosier mid-nineteenth-century markets. The linked automations of barrel making, wheat harvesting, flour making, and shipping systemization froze biological processes for later release during baking. Richmond millers and coopers sank considerable capital into maintaining the appeal of Virginia wheat to discerning Brazilian bakers and their moneyed local consumers.

Labor and Quality Control

The unusually consolidated pattern of Richmond's milling industry emerged in response to the demands of the Rio market, whose bakers had dealt for years with imports of "wormy" or stale flour. In the early 1850s, Richmond's large mills consolidated their hold on this market by incorporating micro-inventions that would have been particularly important for firms exporting through the tropics. New bolting cloths made re-grinding unnecessary (the cloth, acting as a filter, separated the meal more cleanly into different grades of fineness and made for whiter white flour with less bran and less propensity to spoil); improved winnowing machines cleaned the grains before grinding; automatic packing machines enclosed export wheat flour more securely and cleanly; and improved grinding stones quarried in France and finished in Utica, New York yielded a superfine product. More recently invented smut machines, which scraped the grains clean of mold or fungus before grinding and forestalled spoilage, were also important.[45] One of the major Richmond mills ran twenty pairs of burr stones for grinding, and four additional pairs for "cleaning and smutting wheat."[46]

Ever alert to dirty or diseased grain entering the mill, Richmond firms invested in many of these technologies. Mechanization and scale in this case were driven by needs for stringent and cleanliness. Quality assurance also required specialized laborers to inspect and select incoming raw materials: Haxall employed two "wheat receivers" named G. W. Pendleton and G. W. Yeager. Gallego employed three wheat receivers. A father-son team named F. W. and Robert Redford split duties between Henrico County and Manchester, Virginia, handling wheat brought in from different parts of the state. Gallego's third wheat receiver was J. A. Chevallié, a civil engineer who came from a long line of elite Richmond millers. Gallego even had on its payroll a "wheat trimmer." Finally, Haxall (unlike Gallego, which had its own cooper's department) had a barrel receiver on the payroll.[47]

Factory maintenance was also crucial. After the nine-month grinding season ended in May, business operations were suspended for three months to allow for "the general renovation of the mills." As the *Richmond Dispatch* explained, "The renovation consists in cleaning the mills throughout—in brushing up the machinery, and strengthening and repairing that which is weakened or broken."[48] The paper emphasized that the renovation and maintenance, "conducted in the most systematic and complete manner" each year, explains "the high reputation enjoyed by the Richmond city mills in foreign markets."[49]

Removing flour dust minimized fire hazards, while "the proper cleaning and dressing up of machinery" made the mill "run more smoothly, more glibly, and with less injury to the parts subjected to friction."[50] Large millers' capacity for "manufacturing flour to keep so well," a later piece in the *Dispatch* reiterated, explains why the best of Richmond flour "stands so high in South America." To prove it, the local paper told the story of a shipment of Haxall-Crenshaw flour shipped to Rio de Janeiro. Since the hold was already full, twelve of Haxall-Crenshaw's barrels were stored in the cabin. During the rapid unloading process in Rio, these barrels were forgotten and taken home. Upon arrival in Richmond, the barrels sat around for a few more days. Although feared ruined, "a few days since, one of these barrels were opened, and the flour was found to be so sweet and nice, that the other eleven were thoroughly tested, and proved to be the best perfect order as on the day they were first shipped."[51] The tale implied that the excellence of manufacture had frozen biological time despite considerable changes in temperature and humidity. This sweetness and the overall tropicalization of Richmond flour was achieved through the combination of mechanized technology and the maintenance work of enslaved Richmonders.

Cleanliness was of utmost importance to the success of Richmond flour in Rio, and enslaved mill workers made it possible. In spite of the vaunted "automation" of the Richmond mills, frequent construction projects, constant maintenance, and handling large shipments of incoming wheat and outgoing flour called for a labor force of about eighty slaves per firm.[52] Chevallié, owner of the Gallego Mills before Warwick and Barksdale took it over, had a "Negro Account" in his business ledger, which details his purchases and sales of slaves and his renting of slaves from local owners.[53] The continuing importance of workers in the mills was made apparent in the fact that Haxall-Crenshaw had "buildings erected for laborers."[54] Enslaved workers remained the employees of choice in the integrated Richmond mills. "It was during these years," Midori Takagi finds in her study of slavery in Richmond, "that the small shop run by an owner and a slave assistant—a common working arrangement of the early nineteenth century—became a relic."[55] With increasing prices for slaves in the antebellum years, they also tended to be concentrated into larger urban firms. Millers' access to capital through local banking and insurance connections, urban real estate investment, and mercantile activities (which all would have been inseparable from Richmond's other major line of business in the antebellum period, selling enslaved people to the southwest) enabled them to cobble together the kind of workforce that small country millers could not.

In 1856, Gallego also employed a range of free workers, including sixteen millers, nine carpenters, two laborers, and one packer, along with a "machinery tender."[56] While this working staff of twenty-nine was quite considerable, they were outnumbered by the slaves whom Gallego exploited. The limited records of the antebellum mills make it difficult to tell precisely what different members of the workforce were doing, but firm managers very likely took advantage of the considerable milling, carpentry, and smithing skills possessed by enslaved Virginians. Hiring out, along with the general expansion of urban slavery in the state capital, was necessary to the expansion of Richmond mills.

The institution of slave hiring, whereby masters rented out their bondspeople to other whites, made it possible for many Virginia slaveholders to hold onto their captives through economic difficulties. The income garnered from a flexible system of hiring made more Virginia masters decide to keep slaves rather than sell them South; this practice partly explains why the state still had the most slaves in the nation in 1860, in spite of also being the epicenter of the domestic slave trade. Skilled bondspeople hired out to industry wielded considerable control over the own lives.[57] By earning "overwork" money and working for renters who lacked their skill set, enslaved artisans controlled their labor to an unusual degree. They could sometimes pay for their own housing in the city, and frequently carried out long-term plans to free themselves and their loved ones through "self-purchase."[58] Often choosing their own employer, this select group of hired slaves evaded masters' control and were likely to engage in rebellious acts when their autonomy was challenged.[59] In the 1850s, maritime escapes had been so frequent that Virginia's docks, as well as vessels visiting the state, were subjected to frequent searches—the General Assembly even entertained the possibility of stationing an armed steamship at the outlet of the James River to defend white citizens' enslaved property.[60]

Black Richmonders were using the prevalence of hiring arrangements, along with the emerging urban infrastructure, to change their fortunes. In 1854, for example, black dock workers and sailors helped an enslaved baker named William Gilliam flee north with other hired slaves in the hold of a steamship. Rocketts Landing was surrounded by an interracial working-class neighborhood, so fugitives waiting for the chance to escape northward by vessel could blend in.[61] Although growing panic about secret networks of abolitionists led Richmond authorities to pass new laws "designed to curtail hired slaves' activities, especially their moving about the city," the legislation was largely ignored, both by slaves themselves, and by those who benefitted from the mobility of hired slaves.[62]

In the city itself, the enslaved teamsters of Warwick and Barksdale seemed to pique the anxiety of local law enforcers. As a driver for the firm, Jordan was tasked with delivering various milled grains to local merchants, but he seemed to have combined it with doing some work for himself. On an unlucky day in 1854, Jordan was spotted while he was making an unscheduled stop at the Shockoe Hill residence of Joseph Mosby, to whom he allegedly delivered some stolen sacks of horse feed.[63] While automatically suspected of wrongdoing by virtue of being mobile in this case, Jordan was whipped four years later by order of the mayor "for driving his team along Broad Street, faster than a walk, after being cautioned against doing so."[64] It appears that the enslaved workers who actually made possible the acceleration of Warwick and Barksdale's business were also castigated for violating local ordinances.

Nevertheless, such forms of licit mobility allowed black Richmonders access to certain kinds of limited freedom and small trading opportunities, which they appear to have taken advantage of. In the case of Ned Smith, the spreading machine created mobility opportunities beyond city borders. While the newspaper does not make clear what Smith was doing when accused of carrying a forged pass on a fall day in 1853, the pass was supposed to have been written for him by a clerk at Gallego Mills. "From the appearance of the pass there is no doubt that it was written by a Negro or a badly taught school boy," the accuser said.[65] In spite of the writer's ridicule, this story suggests how African-American employees at the major mills could facilitate the illicit urban mobility of other enslaved Richmonders. The problem was common enough that anti-fugitive legislation passed by the General Assembly in 1856 singled out free blacks aiding in the escape of slaves by writing false passes and threatened sentences of five to ten years in prison, along with a whipping.[66] Increasingly finding themselves tasked with moving goods and animals throughout Richmond and its environs, slaves of the milling firms found ways to use the urban spatiality of the millers' spreading machine to their own ends, even within an increasingly fraught political environment where mobile black people were viewed with suspicion.

Build-Burn-Build: Fire Insurance, Access to Capital, and Firm Concentration

Sources are sparse for the Richmond mills, but the few extant ones give a general idea of how the big mills incorporated technological advances in the antebellum period. In the fall of 1830, for example, Chevallié rebuilt the Gallego Mills. He paid Campbell Blades $50.98 for elevator buckets that automatically transported the meal from one phase of the milling process to another, and also bought $48 worth of sheet iron from Thomas A. Rust for the making of screens to filter the flour. He paid M. Kuhn for making bolting cloths that were used to sift the flour into different grades, and in a separate transaction he gave J. Van Lew & Co. $144 for bolting cloth; he also bought carpentry and timber supplies from several individuals and paid David J. Burr & Co. $100 for castings. A blacksmith named John Hitchcock earned $275 for his services to the mill. Hitchcock probably did finishing work on castings, to get gearing and shafts to fit snugly. In addition to several small purchases of leather belting to connect machines to the power source, "mill lamps" for night-time operation, and timber haulage, Chevallié paid Richardson & Bragg (or Cragg) of Baltimore $62.50 for a packing machine to load the flour tightly and cleanly into barrels. Finally, the firm brought in three new millstones from Baltimore while the new cast-iron mill shaft was purchased from a local foundry.[67] The account book shows that a combination of metal-working, wood-working, and building know-how from local smiths were required for the renovation of mills. A mere three years after Chevallié's reconstruction, the Gallego mill complex suffered one of its several fires, leading to insurance claims of $100,000. The mill was immediately rebuilt, on an expanded scale. It was then rebuilt on an even larger scale following another devastating fire in 1848.

Like the rest of urban America, Virginia's nineteenth-century cities lived under the constant threat of conflagration, which promoted the growth of a non-maritime insurance industry. The Mutual Assurance Society, Richmond's largest insurance company, was able to profit from fire policies "by limiting the number of high-risk properties the Society insured." Because of the combined factors of the extreme flammability of flour dust, the rapidly spinning stones, which could give off sparks if they accidentally touched, and the grease lubricating the wood and iron machinery, which provided ample fuel once a blaze had ignited, mills were particularly fire prone. While the society typically refused to insure mills, the big flour companies like Warwick and Barksdale were able to get coverage.[68] This favoritism was likely due to a striking overlap between the heads of the Richmond flour mills and the leadership of the firm. John Rutherfoord was the Principal Agent of the insurance firm from 1837 to 1866, while other important antebellum flour millers and merchants or their relatives sat on its board of directors.[69] The board of another Richmond insurance firm was even more stacked with millers, including Abraham Warwick, G. A. Barksdale, Lewis Dabney Crenshaw, and others.[70] Together the insurance industry and the big flour interests of Richmond oversaw a consistent cycle of construction-conflagration-reconstruction throughout the antebellum period.

Fire insurance was another form of investment capital sunk into mill expansion. In the case of the flour industry, flammability seemed to encourage innovation, as it was a far easier decision to rebuild on a pile of ashes than it was to replace an existing factory with newer technologies. The build-burn-build pattern of urban flour milling, with its constantly renewing fixed capital for those with enough money or insurance coverage to survive, made merchant milling more capital-intensive and concentrated.[71] Even the earliest Evans mills required $8,000 to start up, which was "more than five times greater than the cost of building and outfitting a schooner for transatlantic commerce, and just slightly less than constructing a textile mill with the most up-to-date technology."[72] By the 1850s, entry into the Richmond milling business was even more costly: Warwick and Barksdale's brick flouring mill with a roof of tin, five stories above ground and two stories underground, was valued at $50,000, while the machinery alone was valued at $70,000.[73]

With unique access to capital, Richmond millers were highly conscious of the importance of scale and spoke eloquently of the novelty of the Richmond system of flour milling in its centralized, integrated, large-scale form. Oriented to long-distance markets, the flour millers' quality control efforts necessarily extended to packaging. Coopering was focused on the consistent achievement of a precise, hermetic seal; mechanically made barrels provided secure, dry, and pest-free enclosure for the journey south.

Barrels and Barrel Making at Richmond

Proper flour packing was just as important as the cleaning and frequent renewal of the mills in sustaining the famed freshness of Richmond flour.[74] In fact, an 1856 editorial in the *New York Weekly Herald* explained that barrels partly determined the price difference between New York flours (selling at $6.25 per barrel), and Gallego, Haxall, and Crenshaw brands (selling at around $10.50). The price gap, which had seldom "if ever" been so large, was partly due to the "roughly and badly" assembled New York barrels. By contrast, Richmond's clean and carefully milled southern flour was packed in "neat, strong, and well made and well secured barrels[, which] accounts for the wide difference in prices."[75]

Coopering in Richmond had not always been so superior. As an industry auxiliary to the export flour sector, barrel manufacturing was overhauled in service to the demands of Brazilian export market. Before the quality of Richmond's barrels could be improved, however, the city's coopering industry had to catch up with the scale and centralization of flour production. While new cooperages quickly opened their doors in the early 1850s, "the millers find it almost impossible to procure adequate amount of hoops, staves, and heading neatly done up, to answer their purposes."[76] In 1854, Warwick and Barksdale, apparently still seriously in need of quality barrels because Weed &

Howe was just getting started, built their own cooperage in Richmond. Their highly valued architect and manager, Joseph Hall, however, fell victim to the millers' inflated ambitions. "He was endeavoring to put in operation the machinery of the new coopering establishment," a local newspaper reported, "when his right hand was accidentally caught in a band, bringing it in contact with the pulley or drum over which it passed, crushing it so badly that the thumb had to be amputated at once, and it is greatly feared that he will also lose the next finger to it, if not the hand. . . ."[77] After this "serious accident," it seems that Warwick and Barksdale gave up maintaining their own expensive, mechanized, and dangerous cooperage.

They still employed fourteen free coopers as of 1856.[78] But five years later they put up their old cooperage building for rent, including "a large frame building 60 × 32′ with three good floors and a basement; and two good fireproof one-story brick buildings in the yard, which are well adapted for kiln drying all kinds of timber. There is under the Main building an overshot waterwheel of about 20 hp, by which the machinery through the house is driven."[79] By 1861, they had abandoned the business. Perhaps because Weed & Howe began to dedicate themselves to making high-quality barrels on a large scale, it became both unprofitable and unnecessary for Warwick and Barksdale to make their own. While seeming to have gladly given up coopering to concentrate more on flour making, the industrial millers insourced other operations once handled by commission merchants and so spread the machine more deeply into the city.

The *Richmond Daily Dispatch* estimated in 1854 that each year the seven mills of Richmond would spend $300,000 on their approximately 600,000 barrels.[80] Maybe Messrs. Weed and Howe took note. That year they commenced constructing a mechanized barrel-making establishment. Much like the Richmond millers whom it sought to supply, the coopering firm quickly outgrew its fellow barrel makers. The simple waterpower equipment of Gallego's cooperage contrasts starkly with the multiple steam engines powering the machinery of Weed & Howe. The firm was not only different in scale; it also manufactured barrels by using a very different method. At Weed & Howe, marveled the *Dispatch*, "the entire work of barrel making, except putting on the hoops, is completed by machinery. . . . From the time the tree is felled, until the barrels are prepared for use, every particle of the labor except hooping, is completed by machinery."[81] While the newspaper was quite taken with the idea of machinery replacing human labor, technology more often transformed labor, without dispensing with the need for human brain and muscle. The coopering machinery accelerated production without making workers any less necessary. In spite of the extent of mechanization, at least fifty free coopers were working for Weed & Howe by 1856. This number would presumably be increased by slaves in their employ, as well as carpenters, machinists, blacksmiths, loggers, and sawyers.[82]

To begin the process of making barrels, the firm's loggers and sawyers cut timber from a 400-acre tract of forest that Weed & Howe owned outside of town. At the wooded site, workers used a thirty-horsepower steam engine to mill the lumber, preparing it for railroad transport on the Richmond and Danville line. Once their business got off the ground, Weed & Howe quickly exhausted their considerable stretch of woodland. A mere three years after initiating operations, Weed & Howe found themselves in the market for 4000 cords of "good stave timber."[83]

Once their supplies of wood had arrived at the shops at 11th and Byrd (just a block from Gallego Mills), where all the machinery was driven by a twenty-horsepower engine, the blocks were cut into raw staves "as fast as a man can count" by a steam-powered circular saw. In the same room of the factory was a steam-powered jointer, which cut precise edges so the staves would fit tightly together when the barrels were assembled. This process, too, was carried out "as quick as thought, almost."[84]

At the same time, the tops and bottoms of the barrels, called headings, were made in three steam-powered steps. First, operatives passed the blocks of wood through a circular saw that cut them into boards. Then a planing machine flattened both faces of the staves to correct any warping caused by the pull of the wood grains. Finally, the boards were "taken to the 'rounding knife,' where three pieces of boards are put in and speedily come out handsomely rounded off and ready for use." The machinery thus created headings that would seal either end of each flour barrel. Coopers at Weed & Howe next stacked the raw staves on a rail car. The loaded car was drawn on rails into a room heated by surplus energy from the furnace that also fueled the steam engine driving all the aforementioned machinery.[85] Kiln drying would have killed bugs in the wood, but it was thought necessary for other reasons as well.

Barrel making in general was a bit easier for liquids: once poured into the container, the liquid (whiskey, molasses, wine, etc.) soaked into the wood, causing it to expand, and the joints to tighten, creating a watertight seal. With dry goods like flour, the staves had to seasoned, planed, and jointed accurately enough to ensure a seal. Moreover, white flour would have drawn remaining moisture out of the wood. Too much of that moisture would have spoiled the product. Thus the barrels had to come out completely dry from the factory, with a watertight seal, and remain that way through the journey from Richmond to Rio.[86] That is precisely how the paper explained the specifics of their manufacture: as Weed & Howe's barrels "appear to be unusually dry and well seasoned, we suppose they are mostly for the foreign trade." The considerable investments in new machines like rotary planers, as well as the painstaking steam softening and kiln drying of each stave, ideally suited Weed & Howe's barrels for the demands of the Rio market.[87] While the flour coming out of the mills was drier, finer, and whiter than that produced by mills in the rest of the country, the high-value product was also packed into machine-made barrels that helped sustain its value across time and space.

State Inspections and Changing Technologies

Given the painstaking manufacturing, selection, and packing of Weed & Howe barrels, it is no surprise that Richmond's export millers found state-mandated inspection practices vexing. To prevent fraud, government appointees inspected the flour after its being packed in barrels. Inspectors drilled a long, thin, hollow tube called the "tryer" into each barrel twice and "drafted" a specified amount of flour for inspection. Afterward, the inspector plugged the holes in the barrel with a wax seal.[88] City millers resented inspectors' auguring of barrels primarily because the barrels themselves were weakened for a strenuous trip on the sea, and the wax seal often melted away, leaving the product exposed. The auguring also compromised the tight packing of the flour itself. From time to time the Brazilian commercial papers advertised special auctions of Richmond flour, selling at reduced prices because of "damage by salt water."[89] Perhaps the inspectors' methods were responsible for the damage.

While inspectors claimed their actions were necessary to prevent millers and merchants from adulterating their product, major millers countered that technological change had made false packing irrational. Lewis Dabney Crenshaw informed his readers "that all the flour, now and for some time back, packed at Richmond, is put in the barrel by machinery, and is not, in truth, seen by the miller, except in its passage through the elevators, conveyors and spouts, until the barrel is full and the head ready to be put in." The millers went to great lengths to separate flour from organisms, including humans, as much as possible. Moreover, since the city flour was shipped with the name of the particular miller on the barrel, the damage that a fraudulently packed barrel would do to "the reputation of his brand, could not by possibility be made up by the extra profit upon a year's grinding." Finally, Crenshaw concluded, "the expense of false packing, which must be done by hand, is very much greater than that done by machinery."[90] Adulteration by manually mixing in foreign substances would have slowed the process of production, adding expenses that would never have been outweighed by selling a falsified good. Crenshaw ventured that machinery imposed capitalist virtue on the miller, while he portrayed the inspectors as relics who failed to understand that automation had depersonalized the industry.

The growth in flour milling and its changing technology encouraged Crenshaw and Frank Ruffin to spearhead a legal challenge to the inspection system.[91] In January 1859, Crenshaw sued Daniel S. Delaplaine, flour inspector of Richmond, for keeping millers' flour for his own profit. At the climactic moment of the case, "the Judge and jury went down to the mills and saw the flour inspected, and the 'draft flour' then drawn by the Inspector was weighed in their presence. . . ." It was found to remove between seven and ten ounces of flour per 170-lb. barrel. Then the half-inch tryer stipulated by the state's inspection statute was used and it drew out only one-and-a-half ounces![92] The Delaplaine case was a smart one for the millers to take on, because the inspector's actions would have conjured potent associations with corruption, waste, and concentrated power.[93] The plaintiffs used Delaplaine's abuses to challenge the overall prerogative of the inspector to keep the "draft flour." The presiding judge, seeing no legal basis for drafting, found for the plaintiffs in the amount of $2,361.08 in damages for lost flour.[94]

The court's decision recounted the recent history of Richmond milling in order to explain the fresh wave of protest against the inspections regime. In the first few decades of the nineteenth century, the appellate court wrote, when widely scattered country and city mills of various sizes produced small quantities of flour, "the quantity taken from any one owner was not sufficient to induce him to make any objection." However, the total amount of flour "gradually continued to increase until as it appears in one year alone, the quantity of the draft flour received by the inspector and appropriated to his own use must have amounted to upwards of fifteen hundred barrels; and when the large manufacturers of the article began to realize the large quantities of flour which they were thus made to contribute to the store of the inspector, their attention was drawn."[95] Crenshaw addressed this issue in an 1860 pamphlet, pushing for the cessation of all flour inspections. Focusing, as the court had done in the 1859 suit, on the issue of scale and increasing concentration as fewer firms produced more flour, he pointed out that the fiscal burden was most onerous upon makers of large quantities of high-end flour. For example, Haxall & Crenshaw's expenses for all activities relating to inspection averaged just under $6,000 per annum. Thus the takings from one miller in 1860 equaled the total income of the inspector's office in 1832. As the price per barrel and the number of barrels produced increased over time, while the size of the tryer also increased, the takings of the inspector augmented alarmingly.[96] The money that Delaplaine made by selling the draft flour, the Richmond paper concluded, "makes the Inspector's office the most profitable ever known in Virginia."[97]

Frank G. Ruffin, a Virginia planter and newspaper editor, had laid the groundwork for Crenshaw's damaging characterization of the inspector in an 1856 essay. In the piece, Ruffin associated inspectors with a mercantile past of intrusive regulations and oppressive taxation out of step with the times, but especially lamented the lack of precision or standard. "Uniformity [of inspections] is also unattainable as to time, place and duration," Ruffin complained. "The guides to judgment are the eye and the touch; the flour is seen and felt. It is on the fleeting memory of these evanescent sensations that an imaginary standard of quality is to be formed in the mind, and retained from year to year, to be transmitted unimpaired to each succeeding inspector."[98] Now that the process of production was increasingly insulated from manual labor, inspectors' greedy hands threatened to pollute the sweet, white flour. Conducting inspections with only the rule of thumb and the vagaries of memory as guides, entirely lacking reproducible standards, the inspectors practiced techniques that clashed noticeably with the changing shades of industrial flour production in Richmond. Country millers were spoken of in similar terms.

The inspections were supposed to protect small country millers by maintaining the reputation of the Virginia state brand, but big Richmond mills stood on the reputation of their firm brands, not the stamp of state inspectors. Besides, Crenshaw pointed out, the government's favor would not be sufficient to save country millers. Following the completion of the James River and Kanawha canal in 1840, the percentage of Richmond's flour inspections constituted by flour ground at hinterland mills decreased 75 percent from 1830 levels, while the flour ground in the city skyrocketed.[99] Of over 600,000 barrels of flour inspected at Richmond in 1860, only 28,000 had come down the canal.[100] Wheat, on the other hand, flooded in by multiple avenues, with railroads playing a dominant role (Table 6-1).

Crenshaw claimed that manufacture of flour at Richmond increased 500 percent between 1832 and 1856. This, he noted, "show[s] that the present law has entirely failed to enable the country miller to compete with the city miller."[101] He continued, "The truth is, they cannot grind to the city mill standard, and many of the most intelligent of the country mill owners have

Table 6-1 Bushels of Wheat and Barrels of Flour Received in Richmond, by Mode of Transport

	Wheat bushels by dock and river	Wheat bushels by canal	Wheat bushels by railroad	Barrels of flour by canal
1856		623,773	740,321	
1857	300,000	603,703	793,047	
1858	446,346	856,134	973,448	
1859	472,834	743,427	760,908	33,000
1860	496,530	812,844	1,038,938	28,000

From "Statistics of Trade and Commerce: Virginia Flour Trade," *Hunt's Merchant Magazine and Commercial Review* 43 (Aug 1860): 230.

made this discovery, and either abandoned the business altogether, or confined themselves to neighborhood operation."[102] Country millers' inability to match the durability and consistency of Richmond flour was revealed in the growing price spread between country and city products, price differentials that Virginia merchants often discussed in the antebellum years and that varied widely over time, reaching as much as one dollar per barrel.[103] The shrinking opportunities available to millers were also reflected in the census data. While in 1850, 2,173 free Virginians called themselves "millers," that figure dropped to 751 ten years later (a decrease of 65.4 percent).[104]

Crenshaw justified the new need to distinguish between city and country flour by remarking upon consumer preferences for city-milled products in "the markets of the world."[105] He implied that the increasing divergence of economic roles between Richmond and its wheat and tobacco hinterland was a creature of Brazil's unprecedented coffee boom. The coffee trade even reached its way into the hinterland of Virginia. In Piedmont and Shenandoah Valley, declining milling sectors and increasing specialization in export-quality wheat made the hinterland a propitious environment for new experiments in agricultural mechanization.

7

An International Harvest

THE DEVELOPMENT OF THE MCCORMICK REAPER

BY THE LATE 1850s, Central Piedmont wheat traveled down Virginia railroads, passed through the Richmond mills, was transported in at least two stages out to sea, and rode in Virginia or Baltimore clipper ships along an accelerated route to Rio.[1] Then, after warehousing, auctioning, and transshipment, it went to Rio bakeries, or up the railroad line to smaller bakeries in coffee towns of the Paraíba Valley. This circuit, dependent on the labor of slaves from start to finish, not only transformed large-scale flour mills in Richmond, but also pulled inland parts of Virginia into a new type of global entanglement, transforming lives and landscapes far from the coast.

In the Piedmont, planters responding to the demand of Richmond's export mills led efforts to revitalize Atlantic seaboard agriculture through frequent experimentation with new techniques, crop varieties, and machines, as well as new ways of organizing and coercing laborers.[2] In addition to homegrown agricultural technologies like steam-driven threshing machines, general improvements included the limitation of acreage, five-field rotation systems, marling, improved plows, intensive weeding, "improved" livestock breeds, and imported guano from South America. Such efforts paid off in increased yields of wheat per acre. These time-consuming and labor-intensive activities would have occupied slaves during the dead months between the harvest and preparations for the next crop. Coupled with animal care, subsistence cultivation, and all the tasks involved with tobacco production, increasingly widespread soil-mending practices throughout the wheat hinterland may help explain the increasing numbers of slaves in the antebellum Piedmont.[3] Such activities also played a key role in suppressing crop diseases, helping slaveholders increase crop yields and bring disease-free grains to market. Along with an increased investment in slaves, wheat-growing zones in contact with Richmond tended toward a concentration of landholdings and away from diversified agricultural production for local consumption.[4] As this chapter shows, a new depth of commitment to the Greater Caribbean flour-coffee circuit gave rise to a perceived need for faster harvesting. Various Virginia entrepreneurs, in particular Cyrus McCormick, sought to mechanize felling and gathering wheat. He hailed from a part of the state particularly suited to technological developments made in service to monocrop wheat plantations.

McCormick's farm straddled the border between Augusta and Rockbridge, neighboring counties that make up the Middle Shenandoah Valley. While country mills declined by large percentages in almost every Virginia county where plentiful wheat was grown, these two counties expanded their milling capacity in the antebellum period.[5] The continued expansion of the milling industry there can be explained by plentiful local iron- and wood-working know-how, and by partial isolation from Richmond.[6] The Shenandoah River gave millers in the northern half of Augusta county access to the flour markets of Alexandria, Baltimore, and Philadelphia. With unconcentrated milling industries turning out a low-quality product, these cities would have offered a more opportune market for country-milled flour.[7]

Mills at the southern end of Augusta County and much of Rockbridge, on the other hand, lay within reach of the Virginia Central Railroad by 1854 and were thus more directly tied to Richmond. Augusta and Rockbridge counties were different from deindustrializing wheat counties in the Piedmont— isolated enough from the pressures of the Brazilian connection to maintain mills and iron-making capacity, but still connected enough to respond to the pull of the Greater Caribbean by developing technologies for planters who sought to harvest wheat faster. This chapter focuses on this area (the Middle Shenandoah Valley), where agricultural improvement, a wheat boom, and iron-working skills cross fertilized (Figure 7-1). In this experimental milieu, residents understood the major challenges of extensive wheat planting and had the requisite machinist know-how to develop a workable solution to the problem of harvesting large fields of wheat faster and more thoroughly.

Scores of experiments, alterations, and an embarrassing failure or two stood between McCormick's original reaper model of 1831 and the wide sales it was to achieve by the mid-1840s.[8] The incremental character of the reaper's invention made Richmond's hinterland a laboratory for the intensified labor and management experience of the brief wheat harvest. In ways not always foreseen, the machine transformed the customary organization of the time-sensitive wheat harvest. Although some planters sought to use the new reaper

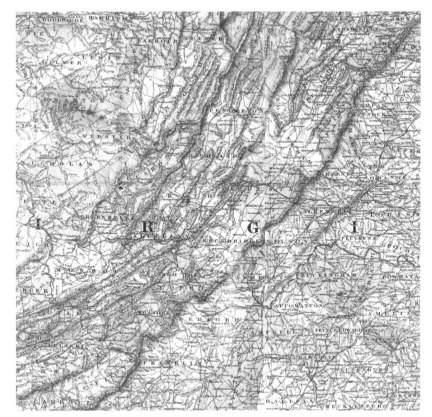

FIGURE 7-1 The Middle Shenandoah Valley. To the north of these counties lay the
lower Valley, which fed its products more frequently into Alexandria, Washington, DC,
and Baltimore. To the east just over the Blue Ridge, lay the central Piedmont, which, dominated by Richmond, lost most of its milling capacity in the antebellum decades.

Detail from Colton's New Topographical Map of the States of Virginia, Maryland & Delaware:
Showing also Eastern Tennessee & Parts of All the Fortifications, Military Stations, Railroads,
Common Roads, and Other Internal Improvements (1862). Library of Congress Geography and
Map Division, http://hdl.loc.gov/loc.gmd/g3790.ct001187.

to wrest power from skilled wheat cradlers, thereby amplifying their own
power, technological change forced them to recalibrate the tempos among
laborers, machines, and landscapes. In a context where every hour counted,
otherwise clear racial hierarchies of power and knowledge could become
blurred. Skilled slaves, especially plantation blacksmiths, cradlers, plantation carpenters, and field workers, appear to have played important roles in
the development of the automatic harvester. On the other hand, some field
workers successfully discouraged adoption of the reaper. Their craft skills, the
brevity of the harvest, and the need for pace and precision in the Brazilian-
focused milling industry provided openings for a wrought-iron politics to
become central in the making of the McCormick reaper.

The "invention" of the reaper was an extended stop-and-start, trial-and-error, piecemeal, and collaborative process that took place over several years within the wheat hinterland of Virginia. While Obed Hussey, McCormick's main competitor, traveled from Ohio to New York and beyond to publicize his machine, McCormick stayed right at home in Virginia.[9] Between the first trial run in 1831 and the beginning of large-scale marketing in 1843, all of the experiments, all of the sales, and most of the publicity took place within a seventy-mile radius around the McCormicks' Walnut Grove plantation.[10] When McCormick's machine achieved national and international fame, and was being mass produced with interchangeable parts in a Chicago factory during the Civil War, its inventor made sure it was known as the Virginia Reaper. The brand name of the product suggests that its point of origin was integral to its success. As the labor-saving device that enabled the settlement and cultivation of millions of acres, the McCormick reaper is typically associated with postbellum farmers in the Midwest. Yet this quintessentially American machine was a tropical technology, and a product of the reinvention of Atlantic slavery in the 1840s (Figure 7-2).

FIGURE 7-2 The automatic reaper had a main driving wheel supporting the platform, which ran the other parts of the machine by connecting belts or gears. As the team began to pull forward, putting the main wheel in motion, it caused the set of horizontal wooden bars (arranged like the paddles of a steamship wheel, over the raker's right shoulder) to start rotating. The paddles guided the wheat stalks against the saw-toothed blade (in the figure, just to the right of the platform where the cut wheat is lying), which was itself set in rapid back-and-forth motion by a crank attached to the driving wheel. The revolving paddles then pushed the cut stalks down onto the bed. The stalks were raked off the machine onto the ground, then picked up and bound into sheaves. Early accounts estimate a field workforce of ten people: two to drive the machine, and eight to pick up and bind as they followed in its train.

Detail from H. McCormick & Co., "McCormick's Patented Virginia Reaper Broadsheet," 1851. Wisconsin Historical Society, WHS-40419.

The state's railroad-facilitated entanglement with southeastern Brazil exerted widely disparate effects on black Virginians in different parts of the state. While the dynamic growth of industrial Richmond increased opportunities for urban slaves to hire themselves out and a wrought-iron politics emerged in the Middle Shenandoah Valley, the deindustrialization of the Piedmont threw many black millers, rivermen, teamsters, canal men, and coopers out of work. The disappearance of mobile, masterless, and often well-paid occupations limited the off-plantation mobility of enslaved men. While these new constraints do not appear to have been the primary motive of transportation changes, it certainly would have been welcomed by planters and state officials increasingly anxious about social stability. The divergence in fortune for enslaved people across these regions affirms the increasingly stark territorial divisions of labor within Virginia, largely caused by the state's incorporation within the flour-coffee circuit of the Second Slavery.

Commodity Intersections: Wheat, Iron, and Slaves in the Middle Shenandoah Valley

Cyrus McCormick embodied the synergy of wheat cultivation, ironworking, and slave ownership typical of other wealthy planters in the Middle Shenandoah Valley. William Weaver, a well-known ironmaster in Rockbridge County, managed a highly productive 800-acre wheat plantation by using six McCormick ploughs as well as other agricultural technologies. He also had two mills on his property: a grist mill, which ground corn into meal to feed his enslaved workforce, and a merchant mill, which manufactured flour bound for Richmond.[11] On the McCormicks' estate, the flour mill and the blacksmith shop, sharing power from a nearby stream, stood side by side, reflecting the intertwining of ironworking, wheat planting, and flour milling.[12]

Just on the other side of the Blue Ridge from McCormick's farm, Piedmont wheat planters like William Massie experienced the pressure of East Coast manufacturing differently. When the James River and Kanawha Canal (1840) and the Orange and Alexandria Railroad (early 1850s) entered his part of Nelson County, the resulting reduction in transport costs encouraged specialization and freed up capital for experimentation.[13] Massie and other wealthy Piedmont planters willingly sacrificed a locally grown Jeffersonian ideal of independence to pursue larger fortunes on the global market (Tables 7-1 and 7-2). Massie imported new crop varieties and improved livestock breeds from abroad, while enriching his soil with South American guano and using mechanized farm equipment to prepare and clear his fields. Abandoning his

Table 7-1 Animal Production on Central Piedmont Farms
(Caroline, Charlotte, Goochland, Halifax, Hanover, and
Henrico Counties)

Year	Horses and Mules	Cattle	Swine	Average Total Livestock per County	Average Tons of Hay per County
1840	21,803	52,848	109,005	30,609	13,125
1850	17,192	51,990	109,511	29,782	6,422
1860	19,567	52,465	60,360	22,065	9,749

Table 7-2 Crop Production on Central Piedmont Farms (Caroline, Charlotte, Goochland, Halifax, Hanover, and Henrico Counties)

Year	Acres of Improved Land	Bushels of Wheat	Average Bushels of Wheat per County	Pounds of Tobacco	Average Pounds of Tobacco per County	Bushels of Indian Corn	Average Bushels of Indian corn per County
1840	not reported	390,183	65,031	16,313,152	2,718,859	2,599,647	433,275
1850	904,670	818,176	136,363	12,346,115	2,057,686	2,572,722	428,787
1860	902,968	1,242,503	207,084	23,516,456	3,919,409	2,727,552	454,592

Table 7-1 and Table 7-2 show the changing patterns of farm production in the Central Piedmont. The six counties in this zone tributary to Richmond lost much of their milling capacity while increasing wheat yields by a factor of three between 1840 and 1860. A closer look at the numbers demonstrates that this growth did not happen due to a simple increase in improved acreage. Nor did it happen at the expense of tobacco or corn production, nor the keeping of horses, mules, and cattle. Farmers in these counties did make less hay; perhaps they transformed some meadowland into crop land and thus provided less winter fodder for their livestock. They also appear to have dedicated significantly fewer resources to the raising of hogs, perhaps because hogs were typically free range during this period, and thus a major nuisance to crops. This part of the rural economy fell victim to the same enclosure movement that claimed so many country mills and millponds as ambitious wheat farmers serving the Brazilian market used increasing numbers of slaves to cultivate land much more intensively through crop rotation, fallowing, weeding, and the application of manure and guano. New wheat varieties may also have played a role in the increased yields upon roughly similar areas of improved acreage. Figures from US Department of State, Census Office, Compendium of the Sixth Census: 1840, pt. II, Mines, Agriculture, Commerce, Manufacturing, etc. (Washington, 1841), 154–177; US Department of Interior, Census Office, Manufactures of the United States in 1860; compiled from the Original Returns of the Eighth Census, under the Direction of the Secretary of the Interior (Washington, DC, 1865), 638; U.S. Department of Interior, Census Office, Agriculture of the United States in 1860 (Washington, DC, 1864), 154–165.

flour and gristmills, Massie was typical of a large minority of improving, book reading, scientific agriculturists in the Valley who increasingly specialized their plantations and focused on supplying Richmond's mills with clean, dry grains.[14]

Such planters became preoccupied with the logistical complexities of the wheat harvest. It was imperative that slaves and other harvesters fell the crop at just the right moment so it did not become overripe. Once it had been downed by skilled cradlers, laborers had to work quickly to gather the crop into bundles of stalks known as sheaves; the sheaves were then propped against one another in groups of three or four, with one sheaf laid over the top. This operation, called "shocking," helped grains dry in the fields. Next, slaves took the sheaves to a horse- or steam-powered threshing machine that separated the grain from the rest of the plant; then a wheat fan separated the wheat from the chaff. While the norm in the south was to use livestock to thresh grain by walking over it on a threshing floor, this method tended to soil the grain. Cleanliness was very important to the high-end Richmond millers and quality-conscious Brazilian bakers, so planters increasingly invested in mechanized threshing.[15] After the grain was threshed, fanned, and packed in barrels, it was carted to the nearest railroad depot and sent on to Richmond. Because the entire process had to be completed within a week or so, mostly to avoid blight, rust, or other pests, the pace of daily life on the plantation accelerated considerably at reaping time.[16]

Agricultural and marketing factors associated with the new export-oriented enterprise further sped the pace. New varieties of wheat adopted in the mid-Atlantic region during the nineteenth century ripened early. Even though the price they brought was at times lower, the varieties were widely adopted, showing how important early harvesting had become.[17] Piedmont planter and nationally known agricultural improver Edmund Ruffin had long advocated early reaping. He was thus pleased to note that, since 1821, "a very general change has taken place, by somewhat advancing the time of reaping." He nevertheless urged farmers to gather their crops even earlier, observing that "there are but few farmers who will venture to reap as soon as the time we advocated."[18] More generally, planters hoping to minimize the impact of crop diseases and capitalize on seasonal price variations began gathering crops earlier in the summer.

An 1837 letter to the editor of the *Richmond Enquirer* helps explain why planters were adopting various means to achieve accelerated delivery of their goods. A self-professed advocate of the small farmer, "Agricola" accused the Richmond millers of forming a "combination" that conspired to push prices downward as the harvest season progressed and that favored those suppliers who could deliver early in the summer, when markets were bereft of fresh flour. Meanwhile, the wheat "which is sent in by that class of farmers who are obliged to carry their crops to market at a particular period, to wit, in August and September, is bought at a reduced price."[19] Richmond millers sought to capitalize on the trans-hemispheric peculiarities of the Brazil trade by shipping off new flour as early as possible to one of the few city millers. Big wheat suppliers who could meet millers' early summer demand had an advantage over smaller farmers who had formerly been in competition only with other farms in the neighborhood of a local country mill. While wheat planting had long been out of reach for poor farmers, Agricola pointed out that the exigencies of Greater Caribbean trade magnified the advantages of consolidating wheat plantations into larger, specialized units.[20] Those who could afford extra laborers or time-saving machinery to expand acreage thus had a double advantage over their competitors. Many planters sought to press this advantage by investing in the development of new farm machines.[21]

Wrought-Iron Politics in the Wheat Hinterland

In the summer of 1831, on a Shenandoah wheat farm, McCormick carried out the first experimental run of his mechanized reaper. The moment was famously memorialized in an 1883 painting, in which a slave from a nearby farm operates the reaper, while a mixed-race crowd looks on. Scenes like this one took place in the 1830s and 1840s throughout the wheat-growing areas of Virginia that supplied Richmond's millers (Figure 7-3).

As McCormick and his two or three competitors ran dozens of field tests on plantations, they followed in the footsteps of slaveholding Upper South experimenters such as George Washington, Thomas Jefferson, the Randolph family, John Taylor (author of an important 1813 farming manual), and Edmund Ruffin. However, the antebellum period witnessed a shift in the class makeup of implement vendors and users, as a colonial-era elite was joined by pragmatic, improving agriculturalists looking to spend a little money and increase profits with easy-to-use, dependable machines.[22]

Skeptical about the reaper at first, and unconvinced by the boosterism of farming journals and implement salesmen, Upper South wheat growers turned out in large numbers to watch "practical field tests."[23] At "A Public Exhibition" of Hussey's reaper in Maryland, for example, "several hundred persons principally farmers, assembled to witness it, and express themselves highly satisfied with the result."[24] Such well-attended performances

THE TESTING OF THE FIRST REAPING MACHINE NEAR STEELE'S TAVERN, VA. A.D. 1831.

FIGURE 7-3 A company-produced print to celebrate the fiftieth anniversary of the McCormick reaper's first run at Steele's Tavern, Virginia in 1831. The Jim Crow–era depiction tells a story of brute Uncle Toms liberated by the strange genius of white invention. The truth, however, was quite different. Far from passive witnesses, enslaved workers played various parts in the development of the new harvesting machinery. Moreover, its adoption rarely had the effect of freeing them, as the image implies.

McCormick Harvesting Machine Company, "Testing the First Reaping Machine," Advertising Lithograph, 1883. Wisconsin Historical Society, WHS-2497.

demonstrated new technologies to a broad spectrum of the population, enslaved and free, rich and poor. Once planters had become convinced of the potential of the invention, they often collaborated in its refinement by running field experiments and suggesting particular improvements. But they were not the only collaborators in the picture.

Enslaved workers played various parts in the development of the new harvesting machinery. Local historians in Augusta County even claim that "much of the credit [for the invention of McCormick's reaper] may belong to a farm slave" named Joe. A blacksmith on the plantation, Joe fashioned the first reciprocal cutting bars that were to distinguish McCormick's reaper from those of his competitors by allowing damp and thick stands of wheat to be felled cleanly.[25] Joe was one of many skilled slaves in the Valley who possessed a potent combination of iron-working expertise and a familiarity with the challenges of wheat harvesting.[26] When harvest time care around, many plantation blacksmiths laid down their aprons and picked up wheat cradles, eager to make some cash during the hectic weeks of harvest time. As a new technology like the reaper was incorporated into the flow of production on the plantation, and maintained in working order, planters and overseers submitted to the skills and the hard-won practical knowledge of the enslaved.

When it came to explaining the operation of the machine he had just delivered to William C. Peyton's Roanoke plantation in 1843, McCormick chose not to discuss technical matters with the machine's new owner. Instead, he sat down with "the negro mechanic, Edmund," to explain how the reaper worked and, presumably, how best to repair it. Edmund must have been a quick study, for Peyton was soon boasting of the harvester's efficient mode of clearing his wheat fields.[27] In the same year, McCormick asked the wealthy planter Corbin Braxton to help him break into the eastern Virginia sales market. Braxton "assured him that his plantation carpenter would add the raker's seat improvement [the machine's newest feature] to those reapers if their owners requested it."[28] As rival reaper entrepreneur Obed Hussey noted on one of his plantation visits, "the farmer, as is often the case, depends entirely on his laborers to manage the machine."[29]

While slaves like Joe, Edmund, or Braxton's unnamed plantation carpenter often helped promote, disseminate, and refine new farm technologies, sometimes field workers saw their interests threatened by mechanization. Hazard Knowles, chief machinist of the United States Patent Office, made a reaper in 1837 that attracted the eye of a Shenandoah Valley farmer. The farmer purchased the patent rights, but abandoned the project in 1841 "when laborers in his neighborhood threatened its destruction."[30] Another reaper inventor frustrated with a failed experiment complained darkly of "the *designed* awkwardness of a class of cradlers, whose interest it is that the machine should fail."[31] At times, skilled workers (who could well have been enslaved or free, white or black) warily defended the limited prerogatives they gained during harvest season. They accurately saw how their harvest-time access to money and mobility was endangered by the machine. They also occupied a strategic position that enabled them to foil its adoption in certain instances. Whether active participants in the reaper's improvement or its determined foes, agricultural laborers shaped the trajectories of farm mechanization.

The pools of expertise required for the development of the reaper design stretched beyond the fields and smithies of Shenandoah plantations. McCormick's corner of the South was a reservoir of experienced manufacturers and adroit iron mongers.[32] Increased demand for metal implements from improving wheat planters spurred growth in the agricultural tool manufacturing industry and the further multiplication of machine-shop skill. Local metals-industry competition in the Valley was magnified by the rise of larger urban firms like Richmond Plow Manufacturing, which built and marketed seed drills, harrows, and other farm machinery, in addition to the latest plow designs.[33] So when sales of his new reaper grew to over one hundred per year in Virginia after 1842, McCormick, along with his family and his enslaved workers, who had been pounding out the machines one by one at the family homestead, were able to job out some of the work to nearby machinists. These individuals continued to tweak the design. Thus, when developing his reaper, McCormick could enlist the help of local artisans like the well-known blacksmith John McCown, who used a water-powered tilt hammer to make important improvements to the cutting blade on McCormick's reaper during the 1830s.[34] J. M. Hite, a contractor in Clarke County, added a wheeled platform upon which the raker could stand while he gently swept the felled stalks from the platform.[35]

The McCormick Reaper, then, was clearly the product of a particular southern milieu. Ongoing field tests gradually transformed the machine from the clunky beginnings of a hopeful idea into an ever more useful harvesting aid that helped bring wheat harvesting up to speed with the accelerated pace of wheat flour marketing necessitated by the seasonal calendar of Atlantic trade. Masters saw potential in the machines for harvesting larger fields of wheat faster, and with less dependence on skilled manual laborers. However, skilled slaves charged with mastering and maintaining the machine wielded power and knowledge in the wheat-cultivating hierarchy. Early experiences with the machine made clear to planters and managers that they could not simply maintain the customary order of things out on the wheat plots. The field experiments, dependent as ever on the know-how of black workers, occasioned a moment of instability in the racialized power/knowledge hierarchies that had evolved over a century of wheat cultivation in Virginia.

Lords of Lash, Loom, and Landscape

The new reaper technology matured in step with the seasonal rhythms governing life on the farm. Experiments in the fields during harvest time were followed by a long winter of improvements based on those tests. As in the case of plantation experiments taking place at the same time on Cuban sugar estates, the short harvest time of winter wheat meant that experiments had to be conducted quickly on actual wheat crops from which farmers desperately needed to make money.[36] While grinding season in Cuba lasted around five months, however, wheat harvesting provided only a two-week window for experiments.

Inventor Obed Hussey noted the difficulty that the short harvests presented for the cycle of experimentation-improvement. That the question of his machine's usefulness "is not so settled in many sections of the country," Hussey remarked, "may be accounted for by the very short time it can be used in each year, and from the fact that, like all other machines, it must be tried, improved, and tried again. Hence the reaping machine requires more time to perfect it than those improvements which can be experimented with every day in the year."[37] Experimenters sometimes ran tests through rusted wheat or less valuable grains such as oats, but the knowledge gained was of limited use, since the physical properties of a harvest-ready wheat crop were unique.[38] As planter William B. Harrison acknowledged in 1841, "so much depends on the locality, the length of the rows and the heaviness of the crop."[39]

Because of the unique topographical, botanical, and climatic characteristics of each field of wheat, as well as the compressed time-frame of the harvest, McCormick and his contemporaries were forced to gather data from the uninterrupted flow of commodity production. Men like wheat estate manager A. Nicol, an early buyer of the Hussey reaper who published an account of the 1841 harvest, were forced to mesh a hybrid force of slaves, hirelings, machinery, and environment, as well as produce reliable data about how they all fit together. He constantly tweaked the ratios in response to changing and unpredictable conditions in the field.

Working without a machine on the first day of the 1841 harvest, Nicol transferred his "ploughing force of 15 hands" (who had been tilling other parts of the farm) to cradling. His concerns about overripening grain were exacerbated by rainfall. Just as quickly, he instructed some of the slaves to drop their cradles and help arrange the binds of wheat into shocks to avoid "passing showers." After three more days of frustrating rain delays, the weather finally turned favorable for reaping, but then it became so hot that "laborers suffered considerable inconvenience in consequence; four reapers became unwell and unable to work."[40] Under frustrating circumstances, Nicol's employer Robert Bolling had decided to give the automatic reaper a try.

On the morning of the fifth day of the harvest, an odd-looking contraption appeared at the end of the field. Obed Hussey's new reaper had arrived, "and after some little delay was got into operation." For the estate manager, incorporating the machine into a preexisting work routine was the paramount challenge. "After a short trial and some experience on the part of the laborers and teams employed," Nicol exclaimed, the reaper "performed its work beautifully." He acknowledged that slaves learning on the fly how to handle the machine were central to its success. "The awkwardness of the hands employed," Nicol noted, caused "several delays." Once the proper dexterity had been achieved and the machine brought up to speed, "all the operations connected with reaping it performed infinitely better than that done by the cradles."[41]

Yet July's urgency was barely mitigated by the arrival of the reaper. "Our harvest operations are now hastily drawing to a close," Nicol reported on the first of the month. "Hussey's reaping machine was again started this morning so soon as the dew had dried off, and after some little delay, caused by a bolt becoming loose and dropping out, performed admireably." In a business in which delays were not acceptable, Hussey's clunky reaper could add to the difficulties. On July 2, Nicol increased the number of cradlers to thirty-eight. His timing was fortunate, as the reaper's "large propelling wheel became loose and shifted its position, and before it could be again put to rights, caused the loss of a half day's work." Nicol, his enthusiasm somewhat tempered, opined that Hussey's machine performed well when not in need of repair.[42] Then, on the third of July, an expanded workforce of forty-two cradlers swept the remainder of the standing wheat into sheaves, while one acre (out of a few hundred on the plantation) seems to have been politely "left for reaping with Hussey's reaper."[43]

That evening, Nicol sat down to write in his journal. "Our harvest operations may now be considered as nearly completed. The laborers, including hirelings, have wrought well and cheerfully." In Nicol's experiment-derived estimation, Hussey's machine required three horses, one driver, one raker, and eight binders to harvest one acre per hour. Focusing again on the importance of labor discipline to the success of the machine, he thought that the reaper would be "capable of performing from one-third to one-half more, as the laborers become more efficient." Nicol added an unsettling afterthought about the laborers who had made up for the reaper's shortcomings: "As was to be expected, amongst so many negroes, frequent reproofs and admonitions were necessary; it is, however, a gratifying retrospect that in no instance was corporeal punishment deemed necessary, or inflicted." During the harvest, Nicol felt compelled to add explicit threats to remind bondspeople of his freedom to whip.[44]

While Nicol boasted of withholding physical violence, the press of heightened tensions at harvest time between overseers and slaves sometimes erupted into open conflict. In the Buckingham County harvest season of 1856, a slave named Peter was accused by his owner of "inefficiency." When the overseer attempted to whip him, the bondsman beat the man about the head and shoulders with a wheat fan. A specialized tool of the harvest used to separate wheat from chaff, the fan was an instrument Peter obviously knew how to wield for different purposes—a wrought-iron politics in the fields for which Peter paid dearly.[45]

On the large plantations of the Upper South, the automatic reaper had to be incorporated into a highly organized mode of production during the short harvest. Gears, wheels, saws, and belts sometimes complicated the tactics of incentive and threat more traditionally utilized on antebellum plantations. While enslaved blacksmiths like Joe or Edmund maintained and improved the machines, experts in the technologies of coercion like Nicol were in charge of incorporating them efficiently into the system of harvest labor. During harvest time, knowledge production was folded into and concealed within the uninterrupted flow of farm work by plantation experts like Nicol. Field experiments temporarily transformed the plantation into a laboratory for technical innovation as well as a source of empirical data.

However, incorporating the reaper also required experimental openings in the organization of labor. Field experiments featuring an expensive and unfamiliar machine increased the likelihood of a master deferring to the know-how of skilled bondsmen in the rush of a harvest. In spite of this vexing side effect of reaper adoption, hundreds of Virginia planters bought them in the 1840s. Given the likelihood that these costly reapers were shared by landowners throughout wheat districts, many more planters probably used them than the sales numbers indicate. While the majority of Virginia wheat was probably still harvested by cradle-wielding men in 1861, mechanical reapers had become the main event on a considerable number of plantations, permanently recasting racial divisions of labor and knowledge in unpredictable ways.

Contexts of Mechanization

Not designed for frequent turnarounds or changes in direction, McCormick's contraption was an economy of scale technology ineffective in small batches. The reaper was first designed for use in uninterrupted fields of grain amid a perceived surplus of workers. The traditional view is that the abundance of captive labor under a slave regime obviated the need to pursue labor-saving innovations.[46] However, this machine was not developed to save labor, but to save time. Thus early reaper adopter William Harrison focused on "timing these machines repeatedly" during harvest experiments. Making clear the priority of accelerated harvesting, he complained, "the time saved is constantly varying; and to approximate the truth, therefore, is as much as can be expected."[47] When later operated on the western prairies, the reaper became a labor-saving device. After McCormick departed for Chicago in 1846 and marketed his products to labor-poor midwestern farmers, a raker attachment and reaper-binder were added so that the farmer, and perhaps one assistant, could handle the harvest operations. On the Virginia slave plantation, however, the reaper was aimed at harvesting more acreage before the crop overripened in a humid summer marked by sudden thundershowers. Another strong selling point was the marketing advantage associated with early delivery to Rio de Janeiro. In fact, early experimenters noted that the automatic reaper, far from saving labor, brought increased drudgery upon enslaved field workers. The laborers working as "binders" and "pickers-up" found it nearly impossible to keep up with the horse-drawn apparatus and often had to be increased in number.

Planter William B. Harrison discovered that early models of the automatic reaper, as opposed to reducing the need for manual labor, altered the ratios between different harvest-time tasks. Like A. Nicol of neighboring Sandy Point Estate, Harrison found that using the automatic reaper did in fact reduce the number of laborers engaged directly in reaping. At the same time, the reaper created the need for more binders in order to keep up with it. These workers had to be drawn from the cradling force, giving the observer the false impression that the total number of cradlers had been reduced with the help of the machine. Harrison worried about the number of cradlers he might lose and about having to give up his best cradlers to tend the reaper. While "good policy . . . would always suggest the propriety of stopping the worst" of the workers, he also wanted his most trusted slaves to manage the expensive machine. Trying to translate the harvest operations to the simple language of an account book, Harrison found that the skill of individual workers had to be included in any accurate cost-benefit analysis. A maze of variables, like the variety and condition of the wheat, the topography of the fields, and amounts of recent rainfall, had to be factored into the equation "in order to determine precisely the time saved." Wringing dependable measurements out of an actual harvest represented a daunting transformation of plantation management and record keeping.[48]

Harrison learned by hard experience that when weather did not cooperate, and the wheat got damp, Hussey's reaper became ineffective. In such an unfortunate situation, he informed readers, "the hands that tend the machine have to be employed in some other way; and moving from one kind of work to another is always attended with more or less loss of time."[49]

Harrison's technocratic prose evoked both the capriciousness of nature and procedural concerns with the judicious expenditure of qualitatively uneven labor power across time and space. Burdened by the presence of too many workers, the planter pondered how the machine could transform the distributions of differently skilled operatives. Not simply a problem of industrial factories, how to fully utilize stocks of depreciating and expensive capital preoccupied antebellum Virginia planters like Harrison. This is what the machine may have promised: by excluding cradlers, the most skilled, powerful, and expensive workers in the fields, Harrison could hope to save money and extend his monopoly on power. While he quickly discovered that he needed precisely these dependable workers to drive the machine, he needed fewer of them, in combination with a greater number of lesser-paid rakers, binders, and pickers-up.

Harrison's constant reallocation of labor around the machine made time lost particularly vexing.[50] Since he always used "the same horses and hands" to run the machine in order to avoid training different shifts of workers, he was frustrated by the unavoidable refueling of this machine-tending workforce. Eventually, he planned to put together a relief team that could take over while the first group of "horses and hands" ate, "so as to lose no time in feeding."[51] Meals of the enslaved members of Harrison's "plantation family" were thus folded into a survey of management logistics. Indeed, he wrote of the enslaved as sources of friction that had to be smoothed over in order to achieve continuous operation of the automatic reaper. His plans, and the assumptions that underlay them, laid bare the functional equivalence of slave, animal, and machine in the minds of a plantation expert confronted with a harvest timetable.

Incorporating the machine into the flow of production on the plantation required management at different scales of removal from actual work. Harrison, the planter, was out in the fields, watching the system as a whole, while "my overseer, Mr. Adams, who superintended the machines," dealt with the technology up close.[52] From plantation level, the concentric circles of management continued to replicate. During the wheat harvest, for example, large planters in a given neighborhood pooled local slaves, tenants, and hirelings, and allocated the group estate by estate, depending on whose crop ripened first.[53] Wheat planters thus integrated management across properties and cobbled together a sequential geography of labor exchange.

Of course, the writings that planters and managers left behind provide reliable snapshots only of their ambitions, rather than the realities of power and efficiency on the plantation. With the actions of slaves like Joe and Edmund taken into account, Harrison's picture of an enslaved workforce eminently relocatable and responsive looks overly optimistic. For the early phases of the reaper's technical development, nonetheless, no other region of the country combined the requisite characteristics of accelerated grain harvesting, iron-working skill, and mass labor control. The lone-prairie farmer in the western territories could not share the Upper South's proto-Taylorist approach to farm management. While it is true that a general spirit of "improvement" helped rationalize this reinvention of the plantation, such a sentiment did not alone drive it. More directly responsible were the automated, industrial-scale Richmond mills and the demand for specific kinds of flour issuing from the slave society of Brazil.

An Unmanned Landscape: Gendered labor, Black Mobilities, and the Transformation of the Wheat Hinterland, 1840–1860

The age of country flour (approximately 1760–1840) had opened up new occupations for some laborers. The shift to a more diversified crop mix by colonial Virginia's tobacco planters had created opportunities for the enslaved to gain skills; most of these new tasks—such as plowing, harrowing, reaping, and carting—were given to men.[54] The equipment these new undertakings required created the need for skilled enslaved blacksmiths and black millers, both of whom became common in rural Virginia.[55] These individuals' mechanical know-how granted them an unusual amount of autonomy and authority, as they oversaw agro-industrial operations on behalf of white proprietors. The Chesterfield County mill of Anderson and Moody, for example, paid $1,875 to hire a local slave named Rubin. Contracting with the owner to keep Rubin for fifteen years, the proprietors clearly associated the long-term viability of their enterprise with the skills of the enslaved miller. By 1834, Rubin had run the mill and handled the books, with "no white man at the mill" for two years.[56] Tidewater planter Daniel Park Custis also trusted the skills of his enslaved miller. Having nine salaried overseers and a plantation manager to administer his sprawling estates, Custis could have employed a hireling, but left the processing of grain to his bondsman instead.[57] Even if they did not run the mill, enslaved millhands could earn cash. Country mills were a relative exception within a "cash poor" rural setting, even though many farmers paid for the miller's services with part of their wheat. On one day during the grinding season of 1838, a Lynchburg merchant mill "Paid Dancer 2.00 for overwork; Joe, 3.50, Peter 2.00, Daniel

2.50 and John .75." The same men were paid cash on at least two other occasions that summer.[58]

For enslaved men on plantations and in country mills, the wheat flour industry before widespread railroads also necessitated frequent travel beyond the boundaries of home.[59] Throughout Virginia, it had become customary for slaves to transport wagonloads of harvested grain to the neighborhood mill. Surviving account books record the seller of a batch of wheat, along with the name of the person who delivered it. If the owner brought the bushels, the book read "seven bushels, per Self." Often, however, it read, for example "per servant," "per boy," "per Stratton."[60] Among his other tasks, Rubin delivered corn and wheat on behalf of Anderson & Moody.

Enslaved men also transported barrels of flour from the mill to local distribution sites. Tucker Coles of Charlottesville was one of many white mill owners who employed slaves as waggoners to transport country flour from his mill to the James River and Kanawha Canal. In September 1834, a slave named Jesse went back and forth to Scottsville almost every other day, taking 260 barrels there for the month. Of 2,738 barrels carried to Scottsville between July 1833 and June 1834, Cole's enslaved waggoner took almost all of them.[61] After Jesse delivered the flour to Scottsville, the barrels were then consigned for shipment down the canal to Richmond. At the time, small merchant partnerships that plied the James River between inland cities and Richmond controlled the transport of country flour. Black and white watermen, with their own flat-bottomed "batteaux," each capable of carrying multiple hogsheads of tobacco and fifty or sixty barrels of flour, moved along the James, Appomatox, and York Rivers. These watermen were known as heroic, daring, and virile laborers with a willingness to navigate treacherous rapids, performing nimble-footed balancing acts on the narrow walkways of their crafts. However, unlike ocean sailors, they were closely connected to the world of the plantation, where they spent long stretches each year.[62]

Starting in the 1830s, higher-capacity canal boats replaced bateaux in transporting the flour of hinterland merchants. James River canal boat captains often accepted cargos of barrels from Lynchburg merchants who had purchased the flour from wagon men who had hauled them over the mountains. The watermen plying the canal then delivered the commodities to merchants at Richmond, in a trip that took four or five days.[63] The watermen had their own partnerships, often a simple arrangement of one partner on horseback pulling the boat down the canal, while the other rested on deck. Faster and safer, canal boats largely displaced the traditional batteaux, but offered similar opportunities for slave mobility. Even if owned by whites, the canal boats were often managed by free or enslaved blacks.[64] Moreover, the provisioning, waggoning, carting, and other off-plantation occupations were still conducted along the rivers and canals of the Piedmont.

This industry's geographic and economic mobility for African-American men is highlighted in a case from Richmond in 1847. A man recognized by the court only as "Smith . . . a free water-man plying on the James river and the canal thereof" was charged with having "embezzled thirty-six barrels of flour which had been put upon his boat in the county of Fluvanna to be carried to the city of Richmond."[65] Smith was accused of having "brought the flour to Richmond and . . . left it with a commission merchant to be sold as his own, and had obtained an advance thereon from the merchant." The defendant's counsel claimed that the prosecutor had to prove "that the boat was the boat of the prisoner, and not barely in charge of him as such captain or master." In convicting Smith, in other words, the Virginia court presumed he was not only "master" of the boat, but also its owner; in the end the court was confident that Smith was acting independently, using his own boat to conduct his own black market transaction.

Slaves' freedom of movement sometimes proved too much for certain whites. In the wake of Nat Turner's 1831 revolt, country mills increasingly became construed as a gathering place for the "dangerous classes" of rural society. "Once, when James Henry Hammond encountered a neighbor's bondsman 'at the mill without a pass,'" historian Stephanie Camp reports, "he took it upon himself to 'flog him' then and there."[66] While on the one hand, slaveholders could violently police the movements not only of their own slaves, but of other men's property as well, it is also noteworthy that the enslaved man whom Hammond attacked was working in broad daylight at a local mill, meaning that the man was there to do business. The rage provoked by his mere presence hints at how threatening slaves' economic activity, and the relatively open spatial politics upon which it was predicated, could be to an elite planter like Hammond, especially in the South's heightened state of racial fear.

In the 1852 Virginia plantation novel *Swallow Barn*, the narrator tells of a neglected Virginia millpond that "afforded a passage, though somewhat complicated, from one estate to another," and was considered by "the negroes . . . the finest place in the whole country to catch vermin" like raccoons, possums, and rabbits. In a sketch accompanying the passage, a group of Afro-Virginian men lounge and converse while exchanging game they had trapped on the banks of the millpond. The text thus characterizes the old Virginia millpond, which had provided power to a plantation gristmill in former

times, as an uncontrolled domain where the enslaved could secretly participate in a subterranean economy under the noses of whites.[67] Literally the
unclaimed boundary zone between two plantations, the old millpond was a
liminal space, an abode of idle daydreaming for whites and a hidden alcove
of freedom for blacks—an uncommon place where the fruits of slaves' labor
could be enjoyed by themselves. White, southern readers of *Swallow Barn*
would have immediately associated the millpond with the unsettling specter
of black freedom. [68]

Independent watermen like Smith or the lounging traders of *Swallow
Barn* operated in a gray area between legal and illegal commerce, and in
spaces where informal, illicit, and interracial practices could take place.[69] In
the wake of the bloody 1831 uprising led by Nat Turner, whose final con-
spiratorial gathering took place "by a remote mill pond" in Southampton
County, watery avenues of black mobility, autonomy, anonymity, and enterprise came increasingly under attack.[70] Fears of rowdy, prideful, and unsu-
pervised black boatmen were often expressed in terms that conflated wheat
transport, black autonomy, and the violation of property rights. One James
River planter complained that watermen "were sometimes so bold as to"
come ashore and "thrash shocks of wheat in [his] field during the night."[71]
The will of another wheat grower instructed executors to bury him by the
riverside so, even in death, he could stand sentinel against black boatmen
who supposedly stole his fence rails.[72] Edmund Ruffin used the image of
free black watermen poling cargoes along the Appomatox River to convince
readers that all blacks would naturally lapse into idleness without the guiding hand of white masters.[73] Finally, free black boatmen frequently aided
fugitive slaves.[74] Although many whites found blacks' mobility on rivers and
canals disconcerting, it was so indispensable to the functioning of a pre-rail-
road export economy that whites never banned the employment of slaves on
the waterways.

After 1840, however, links between the farms of the interior and coastal
entrepots, and the old chains of intermediaries between them, were reconfigured. An increasing use of warehouses, as well as commission merchants
to transport goods, replaced a system in which a small chain of intermediaries managed the passage to Richmond or other port towns. For example,
local elites from Augusta, Rockbridge, and Shenandoah Counties marshalled
major resources to make the Shenandoah River navigable in the 1820s. Twenty
years later the B&O and the Winchester and Potomac Railroads made that
system of riverine transport, with its networks of small-town intermediaries,
obsolete.[75]

The Southside Railroad, going west-east from Lynchburg through Farmville and Petersburg on the way to its terminus at City Point on the James, passed just north of the intensifying Piedmont wheat zone. The completion of these railroad projects had immediate effects on men like Ben White, a free black resident of Prince Edward County. A boat owner of local renown in 1850, White "ended the decade working as a depot hand on the new South Side Railroad."[76] Not only was transportation simplified and placed in different hands, but also hundreds of mills shut down once railroads and canals had begun pulling unprocessed wheat out of their reach. Piedmont deindustrialization worsened with the 1854 completion of the Appomatox High Bridge (Figure 7-4), which accelerated the shipment of wheat and made river and wagon transport a thing of the past for major wheat shippers. One of the highest and longest bridges in the world at the time of its completion, the High Bridge was built by a workforce including over 1,000 slaves. It provided a stark example of the transformed landscape of the wheat hinterland (Figure 7-4).[77]

FIGURE 7-4 The Appomatox High Bridge spanned the Appomatox River, which, as a main tributary of the James, had been a highway for free black bateauxmen and canal boat runners. The clear-cut landscape crossed by the narrow and regulated passageway of the railroad suggested a drastically altered landscape of mobility for workers in country flour transportation.

From Edward Beyer, *Album of Virginia; Illustrated by Ed. Beyer* (Richmond, VA, 1858). Rare Book and Special Collections Division of the Library of Congress, Washington, DC.

Also in 1854, the same pattern of railroads, wheat, slavery, and deindustrialization reached into parts of the Shenandoah Valley. That year, the Virginia Central Railroad finished a tunnel through the Blue Ridge Mountains. Built by a combination of enslaved labor and transportation engineering, the 4,200-foot tunnel was then the longest in the country. Along with a telegraph line, the rails reached the Augusta County seat of Staunton and linked it directly to Richmond.[78] Drastically reducing travel time, the railroad lowered the cost of shipping wheat to the state capital by cutting out the chains of waggoners and batteauxmen who had previously handled the goods. Years later, George Bagby's pro-slavery reminiscence of life on the James River recorded a similar transition with a poignant image. "Fleets of these batteaux used to be moored on the riverbank near where the depot of the Virginia and Tennessee railroad now stands."[79]

While opportunities for self-hire, overwork earnings, autonomy, control over daily life, and the chance for a competency may have increased in Richmond, in the wheat hinterland such aspects of slave life received a blow with the coming of the railroad. During the years of Rubin's custodianship of the mill, for example, the grain milling industry of Chesterfield County was in crisis, and Rubin's employers were no exception. They went out of business in 1836. While Rubin's fate may be unknown, *Swallow Barn* offers another enslaved man with knowledge of the milling arts. In the midst of a book whose black characters are mostly plantation stereotypes, an "arch looking negro" informs the puzzled planter that his new creek-side contraption is only a "two-hour-mill," doomed to failure by insufficient waterflow. While the furious planter was tempted to beat the man for offering his unsolicited opinion, the white hireling miller himself was forced to agree that the slave was right. The "arch looking negro," it seems, was a miller without a mill.[80] In the Piedmont, other skilled crafts declined, reducing opportunities for autonomy that had formerly existed for enslaved men in the countryside— coopering, riverboat making, plough making, shoemaking, waggoning, transport—because of the arrival of railroads, the concentration of manufacturing in Richmond, and the influence of the Brazilian consumer market, which bought large percentages of Virginia's flour.

Drastic landscape changes, noted by observers of contrasting political stripes, shrank the limited opportunities that enslaved men as well as free African-Americans had possessed in the age of country flour. In Prince Edward and the four counties abutting it (Charlotte, Cumberland, Buckingham and Appomatox) the number of grain mills declined by 82 percent between 1840 and 1860. Meanwhile, the 1860 census lists a single shoe manufacturer for all of Prince Edward County, with two people working there. The decline of these skilled jobs would have sharply narrowed the already limited avenues to independence available to Afro-Virginians. Ironically, booming harvests of wheat may even have made it more difficult for rural slaves to get sufficient food for their loved ones.

Post-1840 deindustrialization in the Virginia Piedmont suggests that master-sanctioned forms of mobility were highly constrained. Capital largely determined the topography of the possible for Afro-Virginians; even when they moved under cover of darkness, in secret, and against the will of an individual master, they still passed over a landscape made by and for masters as a class. This shifting landscape made new demands on the hard-won spatial knowledge of the enslaved, setting limits on their modes and moments of mobility.[81] Any benefits accrued by the enslaved were entirely incidental. The inherent vulnerability of licit mobility became apparent in the late antebellum years, when transformations of the techno-economic landscape accompanying the Atlantic grain trade sharply constricted opportunities for black mobility and destroyed the interracial male space of inland Virginia roads and waterways. Counterinsurgent priorities conveniently dovetailed with the transformation of commodity transport. Antebellum landscape changes were the product of a complicated conjuncture of factors not necessarily about policing black mobility but about economic growth outside the country.

It is perhaps a wild surmise to ask what would have happened had John Brown invaded Virginia in 1829, at the height of enslaved men's mobility, instead of 1859, the age of the unmanned landscape. Brown could not have chosen a more inopportune time. He hoped a militia of fugitive slaves would follow him into the Blue Ridge Mountains and initiate a long guerrilla war that would spread across the south. His strategy pivoted on the premise of a mobile population that W. E. B. DuBois dubbed "the black phalanx," but this Virginia geography filled with "out-and-about" male slaves on horseback, riding the rails, or leading wagon teams through the hills no longer existed in 1859.[82] However, with the arrival of Union troops in the Piedmont, the Shenandoah Valley, and the Tidewater, where some of the most sustained military and guerrilla conflict took place during the Civil War, use of the old highways and byways was to reemerge.

Epilogue

FUTURES OF RACIAL CAPITALISM

IN MOVING TO Chicago and siding with the Union during the Civil War, Cyrus McCormick was exceptional among Greater Caribbean experts. During the conflict, the sugar chemist Richard McCulloh plotted to burn down New York City with newly invented incendiary devices; iron-bridge builder Wendell Bollman went against the Unionist tide in Maryland and voted for secession; Tredegar director Joseph R. Anderson became a Confederate brigadier general but spent most of the war trying to keep the "Iron-maker to the Confederacy" in operation; railway engineer Isaac Ridgeway Trimble fought under Stonewall Jackson; and sugar planter Judah Benjamin became Secretary of State under Jefferson Davis. In Cuba's Ten Years War (1868–1878), the littoral merchant-planter elites who oversaw the creolization of the Derosne system as well as the reinvention of Cuba's transportation infrastructure fought for the continuation of Spanish colonial rule in Cuba, along with the perpetuation of slavery. The transnational bloc of masters and experts examined in this book took up arms to perpetuate the Greater Caribbean racial-technological networks they had built throughout the 1840s and 1850s and thus committed themselves to a particular vision for the future of racial capitalism. But even before the wars of the 1860s broke out, some intellectuals taking stock of recent developments in slavery's growing pan-American empire forecast the ways in which certain aspects of Greater Caribbean history would inform a post-abolition world.

When an antebellum Virginian with deep ties to the engineering arm of the US military, Matthew Fontaine Maury, announced his plan for forcefully expanding southern plantation slavery into Amazonian Brazil, he was not fantasizing loosely. Maury's imperial plans for a hemispheric cotton complex were rooted in the previous decades' intensifying exchanges of commodities, capital, and expertise among the southern United States, Cuba, and Brazil. Maury believed that the Amazon basin could field the expansion of the plantation system. As the South's slave population grew dangerously large, he thought, carrying "surplus" slaves to the southern hemisphere would avert racial conflict while maintaining white rule in the United States. By minimizing the likelihood of revolt, exporting African-Americans to Brazil would safeguard the millions of dollars in "industrial capital" that slaves represented. Maury informed his readers that, after the northern states passed laws abolishing bondage, most blacks "were sold to the South, and so the South may sell to the Amazon." Seemingly incapable of conceiving of a person of color who was not a slave, Maury embraced a historical narrative that ignored the existence of free black populations in northern states.[1]

In proposing to relocate masses of non-white laborers, Maury was far from a fringe figure. In fact, his plan fit seamlessly in a new age of racial allocation: the idea of moving large human agglomerations long distances to meet particular strategic or demographic goals, which was enabled by notions of racial difference.[2] Maury's plan existed alongside such proposals as Treasury Secretary Walker's demographic and racial justifications for annexing Texas, the Indian Removal Act of 1836, and popular colonization schemes to remove African-Americans to Africa or Central America. Moreover, ambitious schemes of population reorganization based on race encompassed a broad sweep of the political spectrum. British post-emancipation economist Herman Merivale proposed using the power of the British Empire to bring South Asians and Chinese to the West Indies. Programs for white emigration would further populate the Caribbean islands with artisans and farmers once slavery had been completely abolished. Increased population density, the economist noted, would restore a "natural equilibrium" in land-to-labor ratios, forcing ex-slaves back to work on plantations robbed of labor by emancipation. Ultimately, Merivale predicted that ex-slaves brutalized by generations of slavery and handicapped by innate racial inferiority would slink away into wretched mountain hollows and surrender themselves to extinction.[3] Merivale and those who thought like him implied that an invisible hand (racially determined fitness for survival), assisted by imperial population policies, would carry out a final solution for the post-emancipation "Negro problem."[4] The kinds of imperial thinkers who had counted on the fantasy of colonial black surplus for a century or more now drew up utopian schemes for the disappearance of Black Atlantic populations. Post-abolition leaders in the British Empire, Brazil, the United States, and Cuba who could not think of a better question to ask than *"what shall we do with the Negro?"* in the hand-wringing words of the *New York Times* in 1863 had fallen into the mindset of planters and experts throughout the history of the Greater Caribbean.[5] Tragically, the nineteenth and twentieth centuries were to see the fulfillment of grandiose schemes of racial allocation.[6] But these ideas were born in the Atlantic slave trade, which over four centuries transferred 12.5 million people from Africa to the Americas.[7]

Second Slavery experts' adaptation of nineteenth-century languages of physics, biology, and political economy led them to reimagine the racialized worker as an element of a mechanized productive apparatus. By instrumentalizing labor, and imprinting racial difference onto the spaces of a machine-based economy, they modernized practices of allocationism that began in the slave trade's unprecedented commodification of people.[8] The reinventions and perpetuations of the Second Slavery ensured that the legal end of chattel slavery would unfold within a longer Greater Caribbean philosophy that confused persons and things. The commodity fetish, the invisible hand of the market, and above all the historical fabrication of "the Negro" testify to this pervasive confusion, which had a long and surprising career in the Atlantic World: the Las Casas-Sepúlveda debates of 1543 on whether or not Indians had souls, slaveholders' self-assured proclamations on the insentience of Africans, debates on the insurability of black bodies in the Zong case, Justice Taney's decision in Dred Scott, and post-emancipation doubts throughout the Greater Caribbean about the properly acquisitive nature of African-descended former slaves.

Clearly, programs for abolition in Brazil and Cuba developed within the logic of the plantation complex. In both places, the gradual emancipation of slaves was carried out through the bodies of enslaved mothers: lawmakers determined that slavery would gradually be ended by still-captive women giving birth to free children.[9] On the one hand, the official gendering of freedom placed black women at the heart of the process of ending slavery. On the other hand, the very idea that slavery was abolished in part through powerful white men debating "what to do with" the wombs of African-descended women indicates their arrogation of the right to legislate and disaggregate racialized bodies, even in the process of revolutionizing their societies.

The US Civil War itself can be seen as a conflict that attempted to resolve the confusion between persons and things once and for all. Confederate leaders like J. R. Anderson and Judah Benjamin inherited a Second Slavery way of thinking of bondspeople "as part of the nation's natural resources, like the size of its territory or value of its cotton crop." Believing that southern slaves would cooperate with any work regime forced upon them, advocates of secession buttressed their case with the calming pieties of racial knowledge: under a proper system of management, the "negro character" was uniquely pliable.[10] Only under the sway of such assumptions could the southern political economist J. D. B. DeBow list "the negro" as one of the "Industrial Resources" of the South in 1854.[11]

Leaders on the Union side indulged in similar kinds of thinking. Defending his decision to arm black soldiers, Abraham Lincoln likened them to "steam-power," whose military contributions could be "measured and estimated" with precision.[12] This comforting notion closely echoed the sugar expert Ramón de la Sagra's comparison of Chinese workers to chugging pistons.[13] While Lincoln eventually came around to the idea of incorporating ex-slaves into the nation as citizens, many Union leaders during the Civil War thought "colonization" the only palatable answer to the question of "what to do with the Negro" after emancipation. While northern plans for mass deportation were often talked about as "voluntary emigration" schemes, they shared much with Maury's alternate plan for cleansing the nation of black people. As a historic offshoot of the Greater Caribbean, perhaps the United States government found allocation and cleansing the only conceptual tools for imagining a future without slavery.

Lincoln's insistence that the Emancipation Proclamation was primarily a military measure to rob secessionists of what DeBow called "Industrial Resources" shows how deep this logic went. Even many advocates of ending legal slavery during the Civil War could not help speaking of black Americans as property, or, as Union terminology went, "contraband" that could be "confiscated" for military purposes. Strategically, this formulation took slaveholders' logic and used it to weaken the institution. Yet, recasting acts of self-emancipation by slaves as "Confiscation Acts" of the State further ensconced the idea that natural liberty did not apply to African-descended people. Freedom could be bestowed upon them—but only to meet strategic ends.

Throughout the Black Atlantic, particularly in the Spanish Empire, military service had often been a path to freedom. During the American Revolution, British general Lord Dunmore promised to liberate American slaves in exchange for fighting against the patriots. Tens of thousands heeded his call, as cynical as it was. The mobilization of black soldiers in the US Civil War, the Ten Years War in Cuba, and the Paraguayan War in Brazil did lead to limited forms of black citizenship in the Greater Caribbean. However, no other group of people in the Atlantic World so consistently had to confront death in order to become free. The prominent role of soldiering in the end of legal slavery in the United States, Cuba, and Brazil suggests a tragic conclusion: emancipation itself was another chapter in the history of black surplus. Forced into overpaying for what was others' free birthright, former slaves were pushed into subprime citizenship from the beginnings of their enfranchisement.[14]

While rooted in the long history of the plantation complex, the allocationist ideal that underwrote both pro- and anti-slavery programs for the future of capitalism loomed large in the 1860s because of its reinvention during the Second Slavery. The decades after formal abolition in Brazil, Cuba, and the United States showed how deeply the idea of racialized labor as a pliant, moveable, and calculable commodity had set.[15] Indeed, an enduring logic of plantation vitalism continued to shape the migration patterns, labor conditions, and unequal access to the law of those whom W. E. B. DuBois called "the black, brown, and yellow workers of the world" in the twentieth and twenty-first centuries.[16]

Notes

INTRODUCTION

1. For recent analyses of African and Afro-Cuban roles in challenging mid-century slavery, see Michele Reid-Vazquez, *The Year of the Lash: Free People of Color in Cuba and the Nineteenth-Century Atlantic World* (Athens, GA: University of Georgia Press, 2011); Aisha K. Finch, *Rethinking Slave Rebellion in Cuba: La Escalera and the Insurgencies of 1841–1844* (Durham, NC: University of North Carolina Press, 2015); and Manuel Barcia, *The Great African Slave Revolt of 1825: Cuba and the Fight for Freedom in Matanzas* (Baton Rouge: Louisiana State University Press, 2012).

2. For helpful primers on the "Second Slavery," see Dale Tomich and Michael Zeuske, "Introduction, The Second Slavery: Mass Slavery, World-Economy and Comparative Microhistories," *Review of the Fernand Braudel Center* 31, no. 2 (2008): 91–100; and Anthony Kaye, "The Second Slavery: Modernity in the Nineteenth-Century South and the Atlantic World," *Journal of Southern History* 75 (August 2009): 627–650.

3. Mariana Muaze and Ricardo Salles, eds., *O Vale do Paraíba e o Império do Brasil nos quadros da Segunda Escravidão* (Rio de Janeiro: 7 Letras, 2015), 15.

4. For a masterful political account of how the Haitian Revolution shaped the rise of Cuba's Second Slavery, see Ada Ferrer, *Freedom's Mirror: Cuba and Haiti in the Age of Revolution* (New York: Cambridge University Press, 2014).

5. Edward Baptist, *The Half Has Never Been Told: Slavery and the Making of American Capitalism* (New York: Basic Books, 2014); Walter Johnson, *River of Dark Dreams: Slavery and Empire in the Cotton Kingdom* (Cambridge, MA: Harvard University Press, 2013); Joshua Rothman, *Flush Times and Fever Dreams: A Story of Capitalism and Slavery in the Age of Jackson* (Athens, GA: University of Georgia Press, 2012); Adam Rothman, *Slave Country: American Expansion and the Origins of the Deep South* (Cambridge, MA: Harvard University Press, 2005); Sven Beckert, *Empire of Cotton: A Global History* (New York: Knopf, 2014); Seth Rockman and Sven Beckert, eds., *Slavery's Capitalism: A New History of*

American Economic Development (Philadelphia: University of Pennsylvania Press, 2016); and Diane Barnes, Frank Towers, and Brian Schoen, eds., *The Old South's Modern Worlds: Slavery, Region, and Nation in the Age of Progress* (New York: Oxford University Press, 2011). See also Matthew Karp, *This Vast Southern Empire: Slaveholders at the Helm of American Foreign Policy* (Cambridge, MA: Harvard University Press, 2016); Robert E. May, *The Southern Dream of a Caribbean Empire, 1854–1861* (Baton Rouge: Louisiana State University Press, 1973); and Robert Bonner, *Mastering America: Southern Slaveholders and the Crisis of American Nationhood* (New York: Cambridge University Press, 2009).

6. On how ideas of the Spanish Empire's "off-whiteness" contributed to the construction of US racial ideology, see María DeGuzmán, *Spain's Long Shadow: The Black Legend, Off-Whiteness, and Anglo-American Empire* (Minneapolis: University of Minnesota Press, 2005).

7. For discussion of the term "Greater Caribbean," see Edward B. Rugemer, "The Development of Mastery and Race in the Comprehensive Slave Codes of the Greater Caribbean during the Seventeenth Century," *William and Mary Quarterly* 3d ser., 70, no. 3 (July 2013): 429–458. For some exciting, more recent work on the linkages among various parts of the nineteenth-century Atlantic World, see Rebecca Scott and Jean Hébrard, *Freedom Papers: An Atlantic Odyssey in the Age of Emancipation* (Cambridge, MA: Harvard University Press, 2014); Adam Rothman, *Beyond Freedom's Reach: A Kidnapping in the Twilight of Slavery* (Cambridge, MA: Harvard University Press, 2015); and Julia Gaffield, "Haiti and Jamaica in the Remaking of the Early Nineteenth-Century Atlantic World, *William and Mary Quarterly* 69, no. 3 (July 2012): 583–614.

8. Robin Blackburn pairs the end of European colonial rule with the end of slavery in the Americas. Robin Blackburn, *The Overthrow of Colonial Slavery: 1776–1848* (London: Verso Press, 1988).

9. Rafael Marquese and Dale Tomich, "O Vale do Paraíba escravista e a formação do mercado mundial do café no século XIX," in *O Vale do Paraíba e o Império do Brasil*; Jeffrey Needell, *The Party of Order: The Conservatives, the State, and Slavery in the Brazilian Monarchy, 1831–1871* (Stanford, CA: Stanford University Press, 2006); Ilmar Rohloff de Mattos, *O tempo saquarema* (São Paulo, Brazil: HUCITEC, 1987); Stanley Stein, *Vassouras: A Brazilian Coffee County, 1850–1900* (Princeton, NJ: Princeton University Press, 1957); and Ricardo Salles, *E o Vale Era o escravo: Vassouras, século XIX. Senhores e escravos no coração do Império* (Rio de Janeiro, Brazil: Editora Civilização, 2008).

10. In spite of this fact, US historians' foil for the ultramodern Second Slavery of the cotton states is often "moribund" Virginia, whose "surplus" slaves became the backbone of the Mississippi Valley cotton economy. Baptist, *The Half Has Never Been Told*, 30–35, 267.

11. For reevaluations of Upper South slavery in the antebellum years, see Calvin Schermerhorn, *Money over Mastery, Family over Freedom: Slavery in the Antebellum Upper South* (Baltimore: Johns Hopkins University Press, 2011); Midori Takagi, *"Rearing Wolves to Our Own Destruction": Slavery in Richmond, Virginia, 1782–1865* (Charlottesville: University Press of Virginia, 1999); Jessica Millward, *Finding Charity's Folk: Enslaved and Free Black Women in Maryland* (Athens, GA: University of Georgia Press, 2015); Frank Towers, *The Urban South and the Coming of the Civil War* (Charlottesville: University of Virginia Press, 2004); Diane Barnes, *Artisan Workers in the Upper South: Petersburg, Virginia, 1820–1865* (Baton Rouge: Louisiana State University Press, 2008); and Max Grivno, *Gleanings of Freedom: Free and Slave Labor along the Mason-Dixon Line, 1790–1860* (Urbana: University of Illinois Press, 2011).

12. The essential starting point for the study of sugar, slavery, and capitalism in Cuba is Manuel Moreno Fraginals, *El Ingenio: Complejo económico social cubano de azúcar.* 3 vols. (Havana, Cuba: Editorial Ciencias Sociales, 1978). Cubanist scholarship has focused on the changes of 1760–1810 that prepared the island for its transformation into an industrialized plantation colony fully integrated into the world market. Mercedes García Rodríguez, "Azúcar y Modernidad: La experimentación tecnológica de la oligarquía habanera: 1700–1820," *Revista de Indias* 72, no. 256 (2012): 743–769; María Dolores González-Ripoll Navarro, *Cuba, La Isla de los Ensayos: Cultura y Sociedad (1790–1815)* (Madrid: Consejo Superior de Investigaciones Científicas, 1999); and Dale Tomich, "The Wealth of Empire: Francisco Arango y Parreño, Political Economy, and the Second Slavery in Cuba," *Comparative Studies in Society and History* 45, no. 1 (2003), 4–28. Rebecca Scott and Laird Bergad set the precedent for a reevaluation of Cuban slavery and capitalism after Moreno. Rebecca Scott, "Explaining Abolition: Contradiction, Adaptation, and Challenge in Cuban Slave Society, 1860–66," in *Between Slavery and Free Labor: The Spanish-Speaking Caribbean in the Nineteenth-Century,* Manuel Moreno Fraginals, Frank Moya Pons, and Stanley Engerman, eds. (Baltimore: Johns Hopkins University Press, 1985), 25–53; Laird Bergad, "The Economic Viability of Sugar Production Based on Slave Labor in Cuba, 1859–1878," *Latin American Research Review* 24, no. 1 (1989): 95–113. Among the few recent works to concentrate on mid-century developments are Antonio Santamaria García and Alejandro García Alvarez, *Economia y colonia: La economia cubana y la relacion con españa, 1765–1902* (Madrid: Consejo Superior de Investigaciones Científicas, 2004), 187–207; Dale Tomich, "World Slavery and Caribbean Capitalism: The Cuban Sugar Industry, 1760–1868," *Theory and Society* 20, no. 3 (1991): 297–319; José Guadalupe Ortega, "Machines, Modernity, and Sugar: The Greater Caribbean in a Global Context, 1812–50," *Journal of Global History* 9, no. 1 (2014): 1–25; and Leida Fernández Prieto, "Islands of Knowledge: Science and Agriculture in the History of Latin America and the Caribbean," *Isis* 104, no. 4 (December 2013): 788–797.

13. On the importance of warehouse construction materials, see Dara Orenstein, "Offshore/Onshore: A History of the Free Zone on US Soil" (Ph.D. diss., Yale University, 2012), 103.

14. *Richmond Daily Dispatch,* August 31, 1858.

15. World system theorists emphasize that "the semiperiphery is fertile ground for social, organizational, and technical innovation and has an advantageous location for the establishment of new centers of power." Semiperipheries were marked by their likelihood to change position within capitalism's global division of labor. They were fluid, dynamic, indeterminate spaces struggling for position, often "generating new institutional forms that transform system structures and modes of accumulation." Christopher Chase-Dunn and Thomas Hall, *Rise and Demise: Comparing World-Systems* (Boulder, CO: Westview Press, 1997), 79. Various historians have attempted to place the US South within the framework of dependency theory or world systems by labeling it a "colonial" economy. This categorization might work for the cotton states, but does not seem to apply to antebellum Virginia. See Susanna Delfino, "The Idea of Southern Economic Backwardness: A Comparative View of the United States and Italy," in Susanna Delfino and Michele Gillespie, eds., *Global Perspectives on Industrial Transformation in the American South* (Columbia: University of Missouri Press, 2006); Elizabeth Fox-Genovese and Eugene Genovese, *Fruits of Merchant Capital: Slavery and Bourgeois Property in the Rise and Expansion of Capitalism* (New York: Oxford University Press, 1982).

16. Jason Moore, "Sugar and the Expansion of the Early Modern World-Economy: Commodity Frontiers, Ecological Transformation, and Industrialization," *Review (Fernand Braudel Center)* 23, no. 3 (2000): 427. For a useful early version of this argument, see Ralph Davis, *The Rise of the Atlantic Economies* (Ithaca, NY: Cornell University Press, 1973).

17. Dale Tomich, "Rethinking the Plantation: Concepts and Histories," *Review (Fernand Braudel Center)* 34, nos. 1–2 (2011): 32. Eric Williams, *Capitalism and Slavery* (Chapel Hill and London: University of North Carolina Press, 1994). See also Barbara Solow, ed., *Slavery and the Rise of the Atlantic System* (New York: Cambridge University Press, 1991); For a comprehensive review of the debate over slavery's role in European economic growth, one that strongly favors externalist explanations, see Joseph Inikori, *Africans and the Industrial Revolution in England: A Study in International Trade and Economic Development* (New York: Cambridge University Press, 2002), 89–149. For other broad surveys, see Gavin Wright, *Slavery and American Economic Development* (Baton Rouge: Louisiana State University Press, 2006); Mark M. Smith, *Debating Slavery: Economy and Society in the Antebellum American South* (New York: Cambridge University Press, 1998); and Kenneth Morgan, *Slavery, Atlantic Trade and the British Economy, 1660–1800* (New York: Cambridge University Press, 2000). For a classic internalist account, see the Introduction to Joel Mokyr, ed. *The British Industrial Revolution* (Boulder, CO: Westview Press, 1993).

18. C. L. R. James, *Black Jacobins: Toussaint L'Ouverture and the San Domingo Revolution* (New York: Vintage Books, 1963); and Sidney Mintz, *Sweetness and Power: The Place of Sugar in Modern History* (New York: Penguin Books, 1985). See also Sylvia Wynter, "1492: A New World View," in *Race, Discourse, and the Origin of the Americas: A New World View*, Vera Lawrence Hyatt and Rex Nettleford, eds. (Washington, DC: Smithsonian Institution Press, 1995); Antonio Benitez-Rojo, *The Repeating Island: The Caribbean and the Postmodern Perspective* (Durham, NC: Duke University Press, 1992); and Michel-Rolph Trouillot, *Silencing the Past: Power and the Production of History* (Boston: Beacon Press, 1995).

19. Paul Gilroy, *The Black Atlantic: Modernity and Double Consciousness* (Cambridge, MA: Harvard University Press, 1993). Sidney Mintz and Richard Price, *The Birth of African-American Culture: An Anthropological Perspective* (Boston: Beacon Press, 1992). For some critical reflections on the concept of creolization, see Bill Maurer, "Fact and Fetish in Creolization Studies: Herskovits and the Problem of Induction, or, Guinea Coast, 1593," *New West Indian Guide/Nieuwe West-Indische Gids* 76, nos. 1–2 (2002): 5–22; Stephan Palmié, "Creolization and its Discontents," *Annual Review of Anthropology* 35 (2006): 433–456; Aisha Khan, "Journey to the Center of the Earth: The Caribbean as Master Symbol," *Cultural Anthropology* 16 (2001): 271–302; Ira Berlin, "From Creole to African: Atlantic Creoles and the Origins of African-American Society in Mainland North America," *William and Mary Quarterly* 53, no. 2 (April 1996): 251–288; and James Sidbury, "Globalization, Creolization, and the Not-So-Peculiar Institution," *Journal of Southern History* (2007): 617–630.

20. "Calculate and improvise" paraphrases Ferrer, *Freedom's Mirror*, 327.

21. Some scholars propose that the colony be understood as a kind of political space where more intrusive forms of government action have been possible, as a "laboratory" enabling ambitious experimentation in new technologies of governance. C. A. Bayly, *Imperial Meridian: The British Empire and the World, 1780–1830* (London: Longman, 1989); Richard H. Grove, *Green Imperialism: Colonial Expansion, Tropical Island Edens and the Origins of Environmentalism, 1600–1860* (New York: Cambridge University Press, 1995); William Beinart, "Politics of Colonial Conservation," *Journal of South African Studies* 15 (1989); and Irene Silverblatt, *Modern Inquisitions: Peru and the Colonial Origins of the Civilized World* (Durham, NC: Duke University Press, 2004).

22. Sidney Mintz, "Enduring Substances, Trying Theories: The Caribbean Region as Oikumene," *Journal of the Royal Anthropological Institute* 2 (1996): 297.

23. For more on ideas of "tropicalism," see K. Sivaramakrishnan, "Environment and Empire History: Comparative Perspectives from Forests in Colonial India," *Environment and History* 14, no. 1 (Feb 2008): 46–47; David Arnold, *The Problem of Nature: Environment, Culture and European Expansion* (Oxford: Blackwell

Publishers, 1996); Nancy Stepan, *Picturing Tropical Nature* (Ithaca, NY: Cornell University Press, 2001); Fredrik Albritton Jonsson, "Rival Ecologies of Global Commerce: Adam Smith and the Natural Historians," *American Historical Review* 115 (December 2010): 1342–1363; and Felix Driver and Luciana Martins, "Views and Visions of the Tropical World," in *Tropical Visions in an Age of Empire*, Felix Driver and Luciana Martins, eds. (Chicago: Chicago University Press, 2005), 10. For the links between consumption of "civilized" foods and the maintenance of European identity, see Rebecca Earle, *The Body of the Conquistador: Food, Race, and the Colonial Experience in Spanish America, 1492–1700* (New York: Cambridge University Press, 2012).

24. Susan Scott Parrish, *American Curiosity: Cultures of Natural History in the Colonial British Atlantic World* (Chapel Hill: University of North Carolina Press, 2006); Jorge Cañizares-Esguerra, *Nature, Empire, and Nation: Explorations of the History of Science in the Iberian World* (Stanford, CA: Stanford University Press, 2006); James Delbourgo and Nicholas Dew, eds., *Science and Empire in the Atlantic World* (New York: Routledge, 2007); Londa Schiebinger and Claudia Swan, eds., *Colonial Botany: Science, Commerce, and Politics in the Early Modern World* (Philadelphia: University of Pennsylvania Press, 2005); Harold Cook, *Matters of Exchange: Commerce, Medicine, and Science in the Dutch Golden Age* (New Haven: Yale University Press, 2007); Londa Schiebinger, *Plants and Empire: Colonial Bioprospecting in the Atlantic World* (Cambridge, MA: Harvard University Press, 2004); and Anthony Lewis, "A Democracy of Facts, An Empire of Reason: Swallow Submersion and Natural History in the Early American Republic," *William and Mary Quarterly* 62, no. 4 (October 2005): 663–696.

25. Recent scholars have shown how indigenous and enslaved people's hard-earned botanical, geographical, and pharmacological expertise of the New World was central to knowledge making in various European empires. Neil Safier, *Measuring the New World: Enlightenment Science and South America* (Chicago: Chicago University Press, 2008); Harold Cook, "Global Economies and Local Knowledge in the East Indies: Jacobus Bontius Learns the Facts of Nature," in *Colonial Botany*, 100–118; Susan Scott Parrish, "Diasporic African Sources of Enlightenment Knowledge," in *Science and Empire in the Atlantic World*, 281–310; Neil Safier, "Global Knowledge on the Move: Itineraries, Amerindian Narratives, and Deep Histories of Science," *Isis* 101 (March 2010): 133–145; Helen Tilley, "Global Histories, Vernacular Science, and African Genealogies; or, Is the History of Science Ready for the World?" *Isis* 101 (March 2010): 110–119; Kathleen Murphy, "Translating the Vernacular: Indigenous and African Knowledge in the Eighteenth-Century British Atlantic," *Atlantic Studies* 8 (March 2011): 29–48; and Cameron Strang, "Indian Storytelling, Scientific Knowledge, and Power in the Florida Borderlands," *William and Mary Quarterly* 70, no. 4 (October 2013): 671–700.

26. Christopher Iannini, *Fatal Revolutions: Natural History, West Indian Slavery, and the Routes of American Literature* (Chapel Hill: University of North Carolina Press, 2012), and Parrish, *American Curiosity*.

27. As Kevin Dawson shows in his compelling work on enslaved harbor pilots in the Black Atlantic, skilled navigators assumed control over merchant vessels as they guided anxious sailors through the most dangerous part of their long journey (as most shipwrecks occurred near shore). Kevin Dawson, "The Cultural Geography of Enslaved Ship Pilots," in *The Black Urban Atlantic in the Age of the Slave Trade*, Jorge Cañizares-Esguerra, Matt Childs, and James Sidbury, eds. (Philadelphia: University of Pennsylvania Press, 2013), 163, 167.

28. For links between labor and power see Anthony Kaye, *Joining Places: Slave Neighborhoods in the Old South* (Chapel Hill: University of North Carolina Press, 2010); and Joseph Reidy, "Obligation and Right: Patterns of Labor, Subsistence, and Exchange in the Cotton Belt of Georgia, 1790–1860," in *Cultivation and Culture: Labor and the Shaping of Slave Life in the Americas*, Ira Berlin and Philip D. Morgan, eds. (Charlottesville: University Press of Virginia, 1993). See also Mary Turner, ed., *From Chattel Slaves to Wage Slaves: The Dynamics of Labor Bargaining in the Americas* (Bloomington: Indiana University Press, 1995).

29. A relatively recent and prominent article locates "the rise of racial theory . . . in Western Europe in the early decades of the nineteenth century": Jan E. Goldstein, "Toward an Empirical History of Moral Thinking: The Case of Racial Theory in Mid-Nineteenth-Century France," *American Historical Review* 120, no. 1 (February 2015): 1. For a brief review of the history of racial theory that traces it back to the early modern Atlantic, see Joyce Chaplin, "Race," in David Armitage and Michael Braddick, eds., *The British Atlantic World, 1500–1800*, (New York: Palgrave, 2002), 173. For a fascinating Atlantic genealogy of racial science, as well as a look at the ways in which Black Atlantic writers "vibrantly engaged" the nostrums of racial sciences, see Britt Rusert, "Delany's Comet: Fugitive Science and the Speculative Imaginary of Emancipation," *American Quarterly* 65, no. 4 (December 2013): 799–829. For the rise of the idea of "the Negro," see Linda M. Heywood and John K. Thornton, *Central Africans, Atlantic Creoles, and the Foundation of the Americas, 1585–1660* (New York: Cambridge University Press, 2007), 312; Vincent Brown, *The Reaper's Garden: Death and Power in the World of Atlantic Slavery* (Cambridge, MA: Harvard University Press, 2008), 28; Andrew Curran, *The Anatomy of Blackness: Science and Slavery in an Age of Enlightenment* (Baltimore: Johns Hopkins University Press, 2011), 10; Suman Seth, "Materialism, Slavery, and The History of Jamaica," *Isis* 105, no. 4 (December 2014): 771–772; Cedric Robinson, *Black Marxism: The Making of the Black Radical Tradition* (Chapel Hill: University of North Carolina Press, 2000), 81; and Karen E. Fields and Barbara J. Fields, *Racecraft: The Soul of Inequality in American Life* (New York: Verso Books, 2012), 98, n8. On the material process whereby individuals were transformed into commodities on slave ships, see Stephanie Smallwood, *Saltwater Slavery: A Middle*

Passage from Africa to American Diaspora (Cambridge, MA: Harvard University Press, 2008).

30. Curran, *Anatomy of Blackness*, 116.

31. Economistic critics of slavery, in both the antebellum period and our own time, likewise assumed underconsumption in slave societies. John Majewski and Viken Tchakerian, "Markets and Manufacturing: Industry and Agriculture in the Antebellum South and Midwest," in *Global Perspectives*.

32. "The 'Peculiar Institution' Illustrated," *Liberator*, June 12, 1863, 3; "The Scourged Back" (reprinted from *The Independent*), *Liberator*, 19 Jun 1863, 1. Quoted in Joseph Reidy, "Emancipation Time: The Rocky Road to Freedom in the Midst of Social Revolution (unpublished paper, 2015), 20, n2.

33. Elizabeth Maddock Dillon, *New World Drama: The Performative Commons in the Atlantic World, 1649–1849* (Durham, NC: Duke University Press Books, 2014), 31.

34. Ian Baucom, *Specters of the Atlantic: Finance Capital, Slavery and the Philosophy of History* (Durham, NC: Duke University Press, 2005); and Smallwood, *Saltwater Slavery*.

35. Louis Pérez, *Cuba: Between Reform and Revolution* (New York: Oxford University Press, 1995), 98.

36. On the ecological devastation wrought by the plantation complex, see Reinaldo Funes Monzote, *De Bosque a La Sabana: Azúcar, deforestación y medioambiente en Cuba (1492–1926)* (Mexico City: Siglo XXI, 2004), and John Richards, *The Unending Frontier: An Environmental History of the Early Modern World* (Berkeley: University of California Press, 2003), 412–460.

37. For a Cuban example of the pushing system, see *Cartilla Práctica del manejo de ingenios ó fincas destinadas a producir azúcar, escrito por un montuno* (Irun, Spain: Imprenta de la Elegancia, 1862).

38. Sidney Chalhoub, "The Politics of Silence: Race and Citizenship in Nineteenth-Century Brazil," *Slavery and Abolition* 27, no. 1 (April 2006): 73–87; Sidney Chalhoub, "The Politics of Disease Control: Yellow Fever and Race in Nineteenth Century Rio de Janeiro," *Journal of Latin American Studies* 25, no. 3 (1993): 453; Julyan Peard, *Race, Place, and Medicine: The Idea of the Tropics in Nineteenth Century Brazilian Medicine* (Durham, NC: Duke University Press, 1999).

39. Saco quoted in David Sartorius, *Ever Faithful: Race, Loyalty, and the Ends of Empire in Spanish Cuba* (Durham, NC: Duke University Press, 2013), 48–49. The useful category "pan-American master class" comes from Matthew Pratt Guterl, *American Mediterranean: Southern Slaveholders in the Age of Emancipation* (Cambridge, MA: Harvard University Press, 2008).

40. Jason Moore, "Nature in the Limits to Capital (and vice versa)," *Radical Philosophy* 193 (September–October 2015): 16. See also Elizabeth Dillon's idea of "the colonial relation," in Dillon, *New World Drama*, 32.

CHAPTER I

1. This phrase is the subtitle of Manuel Moreno Fraginals, *El Ingenio: Complejo económico social cubano de azúcar,* 3 vols., vol. 1 (Havana, Cuba: Editorial Ciencias Sociales, 1978).

2. Laird Bergad, "Slavery in Cuba and Puerto Rico, 1804 to Abolition," in *World Encyclopedia of Slavery,* vol. 4, Stanley Eltis and Seymour Drescher, eds. (New York: Cambridge University Press, forthcoming).

3. Antonio Santamaria García and Alejandro García Alvarez, *Economía y colonia: La economía cubana y la relacion con España, 1765–1902* (Madrid: Consejo Superior de Investigaciones Científicas, 2004), 102–103. For statistics that show this rapid transformation between 1830 and 1868, see Leví Marrero, *Cuba: Economía y sociedad,* 14 vols., vol. 12 (Madrid: Editorial Playor, 1984), 212–213.

4. Bergad, "Slavery in Cuba and Puerto Rico, 1804 to Abolition."

5. Robert Paquette, *Sugar Is Made with Blood: The Conspiracy of La Escalera and the Conflict between Empires over Slavery in Cuba* (Middletown, CT: Wesleyan University Press, 1988), 234–235.

6. Laird Bergad, *Cuban Rural Society in the Nineteenth Century: The Social and Economic History of Monoculture in Matanzas* (Princeton, NJ: Princeton University Press, 1990), 235.

7. Quotation from Rafael Marquese and Dale Tomich, "Naturaleza, tecnología y esclavitud en Cuba. Frontera azucarera y revolución industrial, 1815–1870." Unpublished paper, 2008. See also Santamaria y García, *Economía y colonia,* 188.

8. Gloria García, *Conspiraciones y revueltas: La actividad política de los Negros en Cuba, 1790–1845* (Santiago de Cuba: Editorial Oriente, 2003), 127. "Ingenio" refers to both field and factory on the plantation.

9. Aisha Finch, "Insurgency at the Crossroads: Cuban Slaves and the Conspiracy of La Escalera, 1841–1844" (PhD diss., New York University [ProQuest, 2007]), 192.

10. Paquette, *Sugar Is Made With Blood,* 210; García, *Conspiraciones y revueltas,* 127.

11. Finch, "Insurgency at the Crossroads," 194.

12. Paquette, *Sugar Is Made With Blood,* 179.

13. García, *Conspiraciones y revueltas,* 130–132.

14. Marrero, *Cuba,* vol. 10, 52. For a succinct summary of these changes, see Dale Tomich, "World Slavery and Caribbean Capitalism: The Cuban Sugar Industry, 1760–1868," *Theory and Society* 20, no. 3 (1991): 297–319; and Noel Deerr, *The History of Sugar,* 2 vols., vol. 2 (London: Chapman and Hall, 1949), 527–533. See also the price series table in Alan Dye, *Cuban Sugar in the Age of Mass Production: Technology and the Economics of the Sugar Central, 1899–1929* (Stanford, CA: Stanford University Press, 1998), 30.

15. Oddly, the Jamaicans whom Cubans credited with development of the technology in the 1780s called it the "French method." Moreno surmises that this type of

boiling train had its origins in the French Caribbean, but that Cubans learned it from Anglophone planters. For once, no one seems interested in taking credit for methods of sugar processing.

16. For mentions of the hatchet near the mill, see Elizabeth Maddock Dillon, "The Cost of Sugar: Narratives of Loss of Life and Limb," plenary talk, Beyond Sweetness: New Histories of Sugar in the Early Atlantic World, John Carter Brown Library, Brown University, Providence, RI, October 2013.

17. As we will see in Chapter 2, "*El Principio Sacarino,*" the nomenclature of grades was variable, and the boundaries between them unclear. Nevertheless, a useful guide is the United States tariff classifications of 1861, which recognized four grades of purged sugar (excluding liquids or syrups, but again, the dividing line between liquid and solid commodities was itself debated): (1) raw sugar, also called *mascabado* or *muscovado,* brown, or *cucurucho;* (2), *quebrado,* a yellowish grade; (3), white and clayed, but unrefined; and (4) refined. Deborah Jean Warner, "How Sweet It Is: Sugar, Science, and the State," *Annals of Science* 64, no. 2 (2007): 151–152.

18. Ramón de la Sagra, *Cuba en 1860, ó sea cuadro de sus adelantos en la poblacion, la agricultura, el comercio y las rentas publicas: Suplemento a la primera parte de La Historia Politica y Natural de la Isla de Cuba por D. Ramon de la Sagra* (Paris: Hachette y Cía, 1862), 81. Sucrose, or $C_{12}H_{22}O_{11}$, is a fructose and glucose molecule bonded together. This bond makes it behave in very particular ways both in the barrel and on the tongue, factors that will be discussed in more detail in Chapter 2, "*El Principio Sacarino.*"

19. José Luis Casaseca, "*Expediente sobre comision conferida al Sr. Dn. José Luis Casaseca para examinar en lo paises estrangeros los progresos en los procederes de elaborar azúcar,*" 1842, Archivo Nacional de Cuba (ANC), Fondo de Real Consulado y Junta de Fomento (JF), Legajo (Leg) 95, expediente (exp) 3996.

20. Justo Germán Cantero, *Los ingenios: Colección de vistas de los principales ingenios de azúcar de la Isla de Cuba* (Havana, Cuba: 1857), Luis Miguel García Mora and Antonio Santamaría García, eds. (Madrid: Editorial CSIC, 2005), author's 1857 introduction. Translations are my own.

21. Sagra, *Cuba en 1860,* 109.

22. Judah Benjamin, "Article III: Louisiana Sugar," *The Commercial Review of the South and West: A Monthly Journal of Trade, Commerce, Commercial Polity, Agriculture. Manufacturers, Internal Improvements, and General Literature* 2 (January 1847): 334.

23. Benjamin, "Louisiana Sugar," 331–332.

24. Luis Martínez-Fernández, *Torn between Empires: Economy, Society, and Patterns of Political Thought in the Hispanic Caribbean, 1840–1878* (Athens, GA: University of Georgia Press, 1994). The relative proportion of slaves in Cuba's overall population actually peaked at 40 percent in 1827. Louis Pérez, Jr., *Cuba: Between Reform and Revolution,* 2nd ed. (New York: Oxford University Press, 1995), 86–87, 110–112.

25. Cantero, *Ingenios,* 191. Of course, the boilers competed with large populations of livestock, as well as cane plants, for this water.

26. Cantero, *Ingenios,* 190.

27. Cantero, *Ingenios*, 136.

28. Cantero, *Ingenios*, 171.

29. Cantero, *Ingenios*, 165.

30. Marrero, *Cuba*, vol. 10, 176–178.

31. Cantero, *Ingenios*, 177.

32. Cantero, *Ingenios*, 148.

33. Sagra, *Cuba en 1860*, 95.

34. Casaseca, *"Expediente."*

35. Sagra, *Cuba en 1860*, 95.

36. Casaseca, *"Expediente."*

37. M. Norton Wise and Crosbie Smith, "Work and Waste: Political Economy and Natural Philosophy in Nineteenth Century Britain (II)," *Journal of the History of Medicine and Allied Sciences* 27 (1989): 392.

38. Philip Mirowski, *More Heat Than Light: Economics as Social Physics, Physics as Nature's Economics* (New York: Cambridge University Press, 1989), 25.

39. Wise and Smith, "Work and Waste: Political Economy and Natural Philosophy in Nineteenth Century Britain (I)," *Journal of the History of Medicine and Allied Sciences* 27 (1989): 272.

40. Chemists thought the filters so effective because, as the English sugar chemist John Scoffern put it in 1848, "all the coloring matter, of whatever kind, to which brown or yellow sugar owes its peculiarities, is not deposited within the [sugar] crystals, but on their outer surface." John Scoffern, *The Manufacture of Sugar, in the Colonies and at Home, Chemically Considered* (London: Longman, Brown, Green, and Longmans, 1849), 19. Some of the bone char was manufactured domestically. Cuba had a long-standing cattle industry in the center of the island, and there is a "fábrica de carbón animal" along the Río la Chorrera in a Havana map from 1881.

41. Benjamin, "Louisiana Sugar," 338.

42. Casaseca, *"Expediente."* Filtration's purpose is to make unrefined white sugar. In the nineteenth century, the term "refining" often seemed to refer not to any consistent difference in the final product, but to the act of redissolving raw sugar in a mix of water and phosphoric acid (a whitening agent) in the metropole. In the United States, however, "the authoritative understanding has been that all factories that make white sugar count as refineries, whether they are merely boiling houses on plantations or Boston refineries." Deerr, *History of Sugar*, vol. 2, 449.

43. Wenceslao de Villa Urrutia, *Informe presentado a la Real Junta de Fomento de Agricultura y Comercio de esta isla, por el Sr. Dn. Wenceslao de Villa Urrutia sobre los resultados de la zafra que este año ha hecho su ingenio en un tren de Derosne* (Havana, Cuba: Oficina del Faro Industrial, 1843).

44. Carlos Moissant, "Memoria sobre la conservacion y depuracion del guarapo ó zumo de caña," in *Anales y Memorias de la Real Junta de Fomento y de la Real Sociedad Economica*, serie 4, vol. 6 (1861).

45. Cantero, *Ingenios*, 137. My reading differs from that of the 2005 editors of Cantero's atlas, n149, p. 138. Merrick and Son of Philadelphia, the same firm that sold steamships to Pedro Lacoste and manufactured some of Rillieux's system (under the name Merrick and Towne), also built the revivification ovens.

46. Sagra, *Cuba en 1860*, 98.

47. Cantero, *Ingenios*, 160.

48. Cantero, *Ingenios*, 148.

49. Sagra, *Cuba en 1860*, 94.

50. Cantero, *Ingenios*, 190.

51. Cantero, *Ingenios*, 159.

52. On colonial islands as early sites of resource preservation, see Richard H. Grove, *Green Imperialism: Colonial Expansion, Tropical Island Edens, and the Origins of Environmentalism, 1600–1860* (New York: Cambridge University Press, 1995). Even in the epicenter of Britain's Industrial Revolution, fuel savings could override notions of "efficiency." In striving toward a "perfect" steam engine, for example, James Watt was not trying "to maximize 'energy' output or conversion; he was seeking to minimize waste." David Phillip Miller, "Seeing the Chemical Steam through the Historical Fog: Watt's Steam Engine as Chemistry," *Annals of Science* 65, no. 1 (January 2008): 60.

53. *Memoria del Ferrocarril del Oeste* (1865), quoted in Oscar Zanetti and Alejandro García, *Sugar and Railroads: A Cuban History, 1837–1959*, trans. Franklin Knight and Mary Todd (Chapel Hill: University of North Carolina Press, 1998), 112.

54. Cantero, *Ingenios*, 142.

55. Benjamin, "Louisiana Sugar," 339–340. Pneumatics (the study of air pressure, and the manipulation of vacuums), hold an important place in the history of European science. See especially Steven Shapin and Simon Schaffer, *Leviathan and the Air-Pump: Hobbes, Boyle, and the Experimental Life* (Princeton, NJ: Princeton University Press, orig. 1985, 2011). As of 1846, "vacuum pan technology was in use throughout the sugar industry as well as in the manufacture of condensed milk, soap, gelatine and glue. . . ." George P. Meade, "A Negro Scientist of Slavery Days [Rillieux]," *Scientific Monthly* 62 (1946): 317. See also Deerr, *History of Sugar*, vol. 2, 562–563.

56. Casaseca, "*Expediente.*"

57. Villa Urrutia also competed with Casaseca in terms of diffusing the latest knowledge. One thousand copies of Villa Urrutia's "*Informe*" were printed and distributed free of charge to planters. Significantly, the private representatives of Derosne were denied patent protection for similar reasons: that other parties had already experimented with Derosne systems in Cuba. "*Dn Joaquin de Arrieta, com agente de los Sres Derosne y Cail, solicitando cédula de privilegio para un nuevo sistema de fabricar azúcar,*" 1842, ANC, Fondo Gobierno Superior Civil (GSC), Leg 1476, exp 58365. A booster of Cuba's technical advancement like Villa Urrutia, Justo Cantero spoke of the "satisfaction" he felt when, being told that "in the Universal

Exposition of Paris, intellectuals were admiring the ingenious system of using escape heat for great fuel economy," he could point out that "such a system had already been in use on the Island for three years." Cantero, *Ingenios*, author's 1857 introduction.

58. On these travels, see Daniel Rood, "Plantation Technocrats: A Social History of Knowledge in the Slaveholding Atlantic World" (PhD diss., University of California, Irvine, 2010), chapter 1.

59. Sagra, *Cuba en 1860*, 113.

60. Villa Urrutia, *Informe;* Casaseca, *Expediente.*

61. Leida Fernández Prieto coined this phrase in "Islands of Knowledge: Science and Agriculture in the History of Latin America and the Caribbean," *Isis* 104, no. 4 (December 2013): 788–797.

62. Casaseca, "*Expediente.*"

63. Charles Derosne and Jean-François Cail, "De la elaboración del azúcar en las colonias y de los nuevos aparatos destinados a mejorarla" (Madrid: Imprenta del Gobernio por S.M., 1844), 15. Translated into Spanish by José Luis Casaseca. His translation is included in Casaseca, "Expediente," 1844, ANC, JF, Leg 95, exp 3996.

64. Sagra, *Cuba en 1860*, 57.

65. Sagra, *Cuba en 1860*, 57, 61. Sagra's was one of a range of opinions on the relative merits of African and Chinese workers. The discursive eclecticism is probably a faithful reflection of the messiness of racial divisions of labor being assayed on different estates at the time. Consuelo Naranjo Orovio and Armando García Gonzalez, *Racismo e inmigracion en Cuba en el siglo XIX* (Madrid: Ediciones Doce Calles, 1996).

66. Lisa Yun and Ricardo Rene Laremont, "Chinese Coolies and African Slaves in Cuba, 1847–74," *Journal of Asian American Studies* 4, no. 2 (2001): 99–122.

67. J. G. Macintosh, *The Technology of Sugar* (London: Scott, Greenwood, and Co., 1903) credits Rillieux with inventing "the sight glass, or lunette." See also Meade, "Negro Scientist," 325.

68. Observers had been linking the purity of race and sugar in the wider Atlantic World for at least a half-century. A 1791 British cartoon shows an overseer forcefully dunking a slave into a pan of boiling sugar as punishment for claiming to be too sick to work. In the background, a severed arm hangs on the wall. The enslaved man was said to have "steeped" in the scalding liquid, a word that tapped into English anxieties about consuming the death and filth affiliated with West Indian slavery. Vincent Brown, *The Reaper's Garden: Death and Power in Atlantic Slavery* (Cambridge. MA: Harvard University Press, 2008), 195. For an analogous "deep discomfort . . . about the ties of blood, sex, and maternal milk that via enslaved women's bodies bound slaveholders to their slaves" in Cuba and Brazil, see Camillia Cowling, *Conceiving Freedom: Women of Color, Gender, and the Abolition of Slavery in*

Havana and Rio de Janeiro (Chapel Hill: University of North Carolina Press, 2013), 83.

69. Casaseca, "*Expediente.*"

70. Cantero, *Ingenios*, 195–196.

71. Casaseca, "*Expediente.*"

72. Sagra, *Cuba en 1860*, 57, 61.

73. Sagra, *Cuba en 1860*, 56.

74. Sagra often contradicted himself as well, pointing out that slaves adopted the newest plows and harrows better than did small farmers who were white. Sagra, *Cuba en 1860*, 61.

75. Wise and Smith, "Work and Waste," 411.

76. Benjamin, "Louisiana Sugar," 344–345.

77. On changes in worldwide racial categories that rationalized racial divisions of labor, see Andrew Zimmerman, "Three Logics of Race: Theory and Exception in the Transnational History of Empire," *New Global Studies* 4, no. 1 (2010): 3–9; Michael Adas, *Machines as the Measure of Men: Science, Technology, and Ideologies of Western Dominance* (Ithaca, NY: Cornell University Press, 1989); James Delbourgo, "The Newtonian Slave Body: Racial Enlightenment in the Atlantic World," *Atlantic Studies* 9. no. 2 (June 2012): 197–198; and Michael J. Barany, "Savage Numbers and the Evolution of Civilization in Victorian Prehistory," *British Journal for the History of Science* 47, no. 2 (2014): 1–2. On the increasing biologization and hardening of racial categories in the first half of the nineteenth century, see Ann Fabian, *The Skull Collectors: Race, Science, and America's Unburied Dead* (Chicago: Chicago University Press, 2010), 102, 105–111.

78. Benjamin, "Louisiana Sugar," 339–340.

79. Mirowski, *More Heat Than Light*, 25.

80. Comparing the Derosne system to the cotton textile mills of England or New England is instructive: while the spinning and weaving machines of North America's Industrial Revolution were ingenious and quite complex, the transfer of materials from point to point in the production process was rudimentary. Powered by falling water until at least the 1870s, the textile mills of North America had nothing that approached the sophistication in throughput technology, and the ingenuity in fuel economy, that was starting to become common practice in the global archipelago of sugar knowledge in the 1840s. For a revealing comparison of New England textile mills to cotton-carrying Lower Mississippi steamboats, see Walter Johnson, *River of Dark Dreams: Slavery and Empire in the Cotton Kingdom* (Cambridge, MA: Harvard University Press, 2014), 6.

81. Sagra, *Cuba en 1860*, 97.

82. Benjamin, "Louisiana Sugar," 341. See also John Heitman, *The Modernization of the Louisiana Sugar Industry, 1830–1910* (Baton Rouge: Louisiana State University Press, 1987), 34–37.

83. The Junta de Fomento gave 1,500 pesos per year to Torre. The Junta (renamed the Direccion de Obras Públicas after the effective dismantling of the Junta in 1854) was the main official agency responsible for the disbursal of funds allocated for innovations to benefit the Cuban economy. See Marrero, *Cuba*, vol. 10, 41–42, and Moreno, *Ingenio*, vol. 1, 106–112.

84. Marrero, *Cuba*, vol 10, 40; Jorge Macle Cruz, "José María de la Torre: A Reference Obliged in the History of the Cuban Cartography" (paper presented at the 21st International Conference on the History of Cartography, Budapest, Hungary, 2005).

85. Cantero, *Ingenios*, 159.

86. Benjamin, "Louisiana Sugar," 341.

87. Deerr, *History of Sugar*, vol. 2, 569.

88. On this readaptation, see Deerr, *History of Sugar*, vol. 2, 569-570.

89. Meade, "Negro Scientist," 321–322.

90. Sagra, *Cuba en 1860*, 83; Moreno, *Ingenio*, vol. 3, 204.

91. Cantero, *Ingenios*, 148.

92. Cantero, *Ingenios*, 159.

93. Cantero, *Ingenios*, 148.

94. By 1861, sugar and its derivatives made up almost 97 percent of Cuban exports, and 64.5 percent of total agricultural production measured in pesos. Another historian estimates that the average production per mill went from twenty-seven to 406 tons per year between 1792 and 1860 (the 5 percent completely mechanized "ingenios gigantes" were responsible for pushing this average so). Total sugar production in Cuba increased 1,450 percent between 1819 and 1868, an average of 29 percent per year. The quantity of production rose steadily from 55,000 metric tons in 1820 to 720,000 in 1868. Marrero, *Cuba*, vol. 10, 31, 135, 198; Santamaria and García, *Economía y colonia*, 198; and Marrero, *Cuba*, vol. 10, 32.

95. Moreno, *Ingenio*, vol. 3, 35–36.

96. Sagra, *Cuba en 1860*, 83. Some planters with modern trains still did not work the syrups, but many did. Casaseca shared Sagra's interest in how this reuse of syrups transformed ratios of sugar to molasses. Sagra, *Cuba en 1860*, 89–92. Working the syrups ratcheted these ratios higher, as in another modern *ingenio*, the colored sugars obtained from reworked syrups constituted 20 percent of total boxed sugar. Working the syrups also reduced the share of white sugar to total purged sugar. Sagra, *Cuba en 1860*, 98.

97. Bergad, *Cuban Rural Society*, 154.

98. In western Cuba, 55 percent of sugar exported was white in 1860. Marrero, *Cuba*, vol. 10, 215–216. But Marrero does not say if this percentage is measured by weight, or by monetary value. White sugar production would begin decreasing soon after. My calculations are based on statistics recorded in Sagra, *Cuba en 1860*, 99, 105–106.

99. Moissant, "Memoria," 119.

CHAPTER 2

1. Bruno Latour has shown how scientists like Anselme Payen and Louis Pasteur, armed with notions of a hyperactive but invisible enemy, sought to control microbes in order to restore transparency to socioeconomic interactions. Bruno Latour, *The Pasteurization of France* (Cambridge, MA: Harvard University Press, 1988). For a more recent analysis of the modern notion of microorganisms as interlopers impeding knowable two-way relationships in political economy, medicine, and other disciplines, see Jeremy Brice, "Killing in More-Than-Human Spaces: Pasteurization, Fungi, and the Metabolic Lives of Wine," *Environmental Humanities* 4 (2014): 174.

2. R. S. McCulloh, *Reports from the Secretary of the Treasury of Scientific Investigations in Relation to Sugar and Hydrometers, under the Superintendence of Professor A. D. Bache* (Washington: Wendell and Van Benthuysen, 1848), 19.

3. Judah Benjamin, "Article III: Louisiana Sugar," *Commercial Review of the South and West: A Monthly Journal of Trade, Commerce, Commercial Polity, Agriculture. Manufacturers, Internal Improvements, and General Literature* 2 (January 1847): 331–332.

4. John Scoffern, *The Manufacture of Sugar, in the Colonies and at Home, Chemically Considered* (London: Longman, Brown, Green, and Longmans, 1849), 9.

5. New awareness of the organic sources of sugar losses during manufacturing should be viewed within early biology's reconceptualization of the origins and particularity of "life." Lynn Margulis, *What Is Life?* (Berkeley: University of California Press, 1995); and Timothy Lenoir, *The Strategy of Life: Teleology and Mechanics in 19th-Century German Biology* (London: D. Reidel, 1982), 197–199.

6. On this approach to nature, see Philip Mirowski, *More Heat than Light: Economics as Social Physics, Physics as Nature's Economics* (New York: Cambridge University Press, 1989).

7. M. Norton Wise and Crosbie Smith, "Work and Waste: Political Economy and Natural Philosophy in Nineteenth Century Britain (I)," *Journal of the History of Medicine and Allied Sciences* 27 (1989): 263.

8. Contrast to Britt Rusert, "Delany's Comet: Fugitive Science and the Speculative Imaginary of Emancipation," *American Quarterly* 65, no. 4 (December 2013): 800, where she shows how African-American newspapers cultivated a counter-narrative to the association of whiteness with purity, successfully "wresting human skin from the domain of pro-slavery science."

9. Carlos Moissant, "Memoria sobre la conservacion y depuracion del guarapo ó zumo de caña," *Anales y Memorias de la Real Junta de Fomento y de la Real Sociedad Economica,* serie 4, vol 6 (1861), 133.

10. Benjamin, "Louisiana Sugar," 333.

11. Scoffern, *Manufacture of Sugar,* 81–83.

12. Archibald Clow and Nan Clow, *The Chemical Revolution: A Contribution to Social Technology* (London: Batchworth Press, 1952), 474–475, 517; Noel Deerr, *The History of Sugar,* vol. 2 (London: Chapman and Hall, 1949), 578–579.

13. See Scoffern, *Manufacture of Sugar*, 61–64.

14. H. C. Prinsen Geerligs, *On Cane Sugar and the Process of Its Manufacture in Java* (Altrincham: Office of The "Sugar Cane," 1902), 28–31.

15. Arthur Hill Hassall, *Food and Its Adulterations: Comprising the Reports of the Analytical Sanitary Commission of "The Lancet" for the Years 1851 to 1854 Inclusive, Revised and Extended: Being Records of the Results of Some Thousands of Original Microscopical and Chemical Analyses of the Solids and Fluids Consumed by All Classes of the Public* (London: Longman, Brown, Green, and Longmans, 1855), 16.

16. Moissant, "Memoria," 124.

17. Hassall, *Food and Its Adulterations*, 16.

18. Scoffern, *Manufacture of Sugar*, 9.

19. Richard Feynman, *Six Easy Pieces* (New York: Basic Books, 1995), 53. See also Joseph Stewart Fruton, *Proteins, Enzymes, Genes: The Interplay of Chemistry and Biology* (New Haven: Yale University Press, 1999), especially Chapter Four.

20. McCulloh, *Reports*, 208; Manuel Moreno Fraginals, *El Ingenio: Complejo económico social cubano de azúcar*, 3 vols, vol. 3 (Havana: Editorial Ciencias Sociales, 1978), 246.

21. *"Expediente sobre el Arcanum del Doctor Stolle [of Berlin] para la clarificacion del guarapo de la caña de azucar,"* 1853, ANC, JF, Leg 97, exp 4067. On the basics of quicklime clarification, see Moreno, *Ingenio*, vol. 1, 92–94.

22. *"Arcanum del Doctor Stolle."*

23. *"Arcanum del Doctor Stolle."*

24. Casaseca dipped litmus paper in the cane juice to measure its acidity, adopting a convention practiced by many planters and sugar masters.

25. *"Arcanum del Doctor Stolle."* The reassertion of the primacy of the artisan's "touch" over the instruments of the scientist cuts against the literature on nineteenth-century chemistry, which posits a transition to dependence on measuring implements. Lissa Roberts, "The Death of the Sensuous Chemist: The 'New' Chemistry and the Transformation of Sensuous Technology," *Studies in History and Philosophy of Science* 26 (1995): 503–529. Other historians of chemistry, however, emphasize the continuing importance of the empirically minded tinkerer's unmediated physical access to the materials under investigation. Simon Schaffer, "Experimenters' Techniques, Dyers' Hands, and the Electric Planetarium," *Isis* 88, no. 3 (1997): 456–483. For more on contests of knowledge between artisan sugar masters and enlightened sugar professionals, see María Portuondo, "Plantation Factories: Science and Technology in Late-Eighteenth-Century Cuba," *Technology and Culture* 44, no. 2 (2003): 231–257.

26. Moissant, "Memoria." Dr. Stolle's alchemically inspired branding of his product with the mysterious name "Arcanum" was actually a mixture of aluminum sulfate and ammonia, according to Ramón de la Sagra, *Cuba en 1860, ó sea cuadro de sus adelantos en la poblacion, la agricultura, el comercio y las rentas publicas: Suplemento a la primera parte de La Historia Politica y Natural de la Isla de Cuba*

por D. Ramon de la Sagra (Paris: Hachette y Cía, 1862), 87. For a more skeptical reading of Casaseca's Arcanum experiments, see Manuel Moreno Fraginals, *El
Ingenio: Complejo económico social cubano de azúcar*, 3 vols., vol. 1, 223–226. For a
history of efforts to use aluminum sulfite clarifiers in the early nineteenth century,
see Scoffern, *Manufacture of Sugar*, 114.

27. Casaseca wanted to assist average planters—not only the wealthiest minority. At
the same time, he did encourage planters to modernize their equipment.

28. *"Arcanum del Doctor Stolle."*

29. *"Arcanum del Doctor Stolle."*

30. The first pages of Casaseca's report, written in Paris, are spent comparing and contrasting his findings with those of a renowned French chemist who used cane juice
sent to him from Martinique. Eugène-Melchior Péligot was known for his isolation
of uranium; he also identified methylene. *Expediente sobre comision conferida al
Sr. Dn. José Luis Casaseca para examinar en lo paises estrangeros los progresos en los
procederes de elaborar azúcar*, 1842, ANC, JF, *Leg* 95, 3996.

31. Susan Scott Parrish, *American Curiosity: Cultures of Natural History in the
Colonial British Atlantic World* (Chapel Hill: University of North Carolina Press,
2006); Jorge Cañizares-Esguerra, *Nature, Empire, and Nation: Explorations of
the History of Science in the Iberian World* (Stanford, CA: Stanford University
Press, 2006); and Antonio Barrera-Osorio, *Experiencing Nature: The Spanish
American Empire and the Early Scientific Revolution* (Austin: University of Texas
Press, 2010).

32. Joaquin Aenlle, *Química Industrial: Algunas ideas acerca del empleo del acido sulfu-
roso y del bi-sulfito de cal en la elaboracion del azúcar* (Havana, Cuba: Imprenta de la
Viuda de Barcina y Cia, 1867), 8. This work was originally published as a *Memoria*
in 1861.

33. Benjamin, "Louisiana Sugar," 331. The trace minerals and proteins of beet sugar
and cane sugar behave differently during processing. Miriam Morgan, "Sugar,
Sugar: Cane and Beet Share the Same Chemistry but Act Differently in the
Kitchen," *SFGATE* March 31, 1999.

34. *"Expediente promovido por el Sr D José Luis Casaseca, en solicitud de alguna recom-
pensa por el proceder que ha inventado para quitar a los aguardientes el olor a mosto,"*
1841, ANC, JF, Leg 95, 3995.

35. Aenlle, *Química Industrial*, 35, 28. In spite of their disagreement over the subject
of sulfide precipitants, Aenlle thanked the great chemist for "first introducing
him to the work of Berthollet and Lavoisier." On the influence of these late-eighteenth-century French chemists, see Wilma Anderson, *Between the Library and the
Laboratory: The Language of Chemistry in 18th Century France* (Baltimore: John's
Hopkins University Press, 1984).

36. For more on Casaseca's biography and career, see Roland Misas Jimenez, "Un
Químico Español del reinado de Fernando VII: José Luis Casasea y Silván," *Llull* 19
(1996): 131–160.

37. Aenlle, *Química Industrial*, 30.
38. Aenlle, *Química Industrial*, 30.
39. Scoffern, *Manufacture of Sugar*, 76.
40. Casaseca, *"Expediente."*
41. Moissant, *"Memoria,"* 130–131. Benjamin, "Louisiana Sugar," 335. In the presence of lime, sulfurous acid, instead of evolving into H_2SO_4 (the sulfuric acid so noxious to sucrose), becomes calcium bisulfite, or $Ca(HSO_3)_2$, which has a neutral pH of 7, and would not negatively effect the sucrose. Moissant, *"Memoria,"* 128–129. Calcium bisulfite's decoloring power is also rooted in its affinity for oxygen. Because colorizing is basically oxidation, like an apple slice turning brown in the open air of your kitchen, colorization can be prevented by isolating the fruit from oxygen. Because of its anti-microbial properties, as well as its characteristic of protecting food from oxidation-related deterioration, calcium bisulfite is still used as a food preservative today.
42. Notable critics of a mechanical philosophy in chemistry like Joseph Black and Joseph Priestley were also cited by sugar chemists. Peter Hanns Reill, "The Legacy of the 'Scientific Revolution': Science and the Enlightenment," *The Cambridge History of Science*, vol. 4, *18th Century Science*, Roy Porter, ed. (Cambridge, UK: Cambridge University Press, 2003); David Knight, *The Age of Science* (Oxford: Basil Blackwell, 1986), 55.
43. For bell hooks's formulation of "deathly representations of whiteness," see Katherine McKittrick, *Demonic Grounds: Black Women and the Cartographies of Struggle* (Minneapolis, University of Minnesota Press, 2006), 13. While the standard take on vitalism has been that it was a progressive countermove to a mechanistic and life-denying Enlightenment rationalization of nature, critical scholars have shown how the putative evils of modernity do not necessarily come from a mechanized worldview, but precisely from an embrace of "living forces." Nazi ideologists, for example, adapted vitalist philosophy to justify the conquest of "less vital" races. Georges Canguilhem, *Knowledge of Life* (New York: Fordham University Press, 2008), 72. Jane Bennett, *Vibrant Matter: A Political Ecology of Things* (Durham, NC: Duke University Press, 2010), 83. In the case of plantation vitalism, there is not so much an embrace of living forces as an effort to neutralize them.
44. Moissant, *"Memoria,"* 129.
45. Ideas of "the vulnerable purity of white blood" have been central to American racial discourse since at least the early eighteenth century. Patrick Wolfe, "Land, Labor, and Difference: Elementary Structures of Race," *American Historical Review* 106, no. 3 (June 2001): 882, 884.
46. Orlando Patterson, *Slavery and Social Death: A Comparative Study* (Cambridge, MA: Harvard University Press, 1982). While the concept of "social death" has come under sustained criticism over the years, it is clear that one intent of the slave trade was to impose a pastless, networkless abjection on captives. The

enslaved understood this tendency clearly. Vincent Brown, "Social Death and Political Life in the Study of Slavery," *American Historical Review* (December 2009): 1231–1249.

47. Rafael Marquese and Dale Tomich, "Naturaleza, tecnología y esclavitud en Cuba. Frontera azucarera y revolución industrial, 1815–1870." Unpublished paper, 2008.

48. McCulloh, *Reports*, 132. "Sugar in disguise" was the wording used by Treasury Department contact William F. Wilkins in McCulloh, *Reports*, 147.

49. McCulloh, *Reports*, 135.

50. "Report of the Secretary of the Treasury, in Compliance with a Resolution of the Senate, Relative to Frauds in Recent Importations of Sirups and Molasses from the West India Islands, and the Measures Necessary to Be Adopted to Prevent Their Recurrence" (1846), in *Tariff Proceedings and Documents 1839–1857 Accompanied by Messages of the President, Treasury Reports, Bills, and Laws of 1857* (Washington, DC: Government Printing Office, 1911), 2048.

51. Included in McCulloh, *Reports*, 120.

52. McCulloh, *Reports*, 135.

53. Included in McCulloh, *Reports*, 153–154.

54. McCulloh, *Reports*, 139.

55. Noel Deerr, *Sugar and the Sugar Cane: An Elementary Treatise on the Agriculture of the Sugar Cane and on the Manufacture of Cane Sugar* (Manchester, UK: Norman Rodger, 1905), 300–313.

56. McCulloh, *Reports*, 161.

57. Casaseca, "*Expediente.*"

58. Benjamin, "Louisiana Sugar," 332.

59. A merchant and the patriarch of the Drake family, Santiago (James), Senior, had emigrated from England, arriving in Havana in the 1790s. After marrying into a family of elite planters, he diversified his economic interests by purchasing sugar plantations. The family soon expanded their mercantile and planting interests into Matanzas and Sagua la Grande, remaining an important conduit between Cuban creole planters and Anglophone merchants and financiers. Roland Ely, *Comerciantes cubanos del siglo XIX* (Havana, Cuba: Editorial Liberia Martí, 1960), 55–85.

60. Sven Beckert, *The Monied Metropolis: New York City and the Consolidation of the American Bourgeoisie, 1850–1896* (New York: Cambridge University Press, 2001), 26; Ely, *Comerciantes cubanos*, 39–42, 45, 73, 99.

61. McCulloh, *Reports*, 167.

62. McCulloh, *Reports*, 129.

63. McCulloh, *Reports*, 129.

64. McCulloh, *Reports*, 130. For more on McCulloh, saccharimeters, and the state, see Deborah Jean Warner, "How Sweet It Is: Sugar, Science, and the State," *Annals of Science* 64, no. 2 (2007), 150.

65. "Report of the Secretary of the Treasury," 2042–2043.

66. Personal conversation with Scott Nelson. Ironically, Walker had been one of the major proponents of debt repudiation by slaveholders in 1839. For more important details on Walker's financial politics, see Edward Baptist, *The Half Has Never Been Told: Slavery and the Making of American Capitalism* (New York: Basic Books, 2014), 289, 302. In the 1850s, Walker changed tack: he became an opponent of slavery and secession.

67. Daniel Walker Howe, *What Hath God Wrought: The Transformation of America, 1815–1848* (New York: Oxford University Press, 2007), 685. For the 90 percent claim, see R. J. Walker, "The Sugar Culture of Louisiana in 1845 and 1853," *Hunt's Merchant Magazine* 30 (1854): 499. Walker also used the occasion to justify his tariff with statistics showing growth in Louisiana's "plantation white" sugar industry.

68. The idea of black people's level of civilization as a carefully maintained balancing act, hovering tenuously between savagery and civilization (freedom leading to a quick collapse back to savagery, and civilization only maintained by constant tutelage under the guiding hands of whites) informed racial policies across the Atlantic World. Consuelo Naranjo Orovio and Armando García Gonzalez, *Racismo e inmigracion en Cuba en el siglo XIX* (Madrid: Ediciones Doce Calles, 1996), 39; Daniel Rood, "Herman Merivale's Black Legend: Rethinking the Intellectual History of Free Trade Imperialism," *New West Indian Guide/Nieuwe West-Indische Gids* 80, nos. 3– 4 (2006): 181–182; and Thomas Hietala, *Manifest Design: American Exceptionalism and Empire* (Ithaca, NY: Cornell University Press, 2002), 26–27, 167. Walker's staunchly free-trade, anti-protectionist tariff plan was approved by the narrowest of margins: the votes of two newest members of Congress from Texas, newly admitted to the Union, thanks to Walker's exertions on their behalf. Howe, *What God Hath Wrought*, 765.

69. Moissant, "*Memoria*," 129.

70. Walter Johnson, *River of Dark Dreams: Slavery and Empire in the Cotton Kingdom* (Cambridge, MA: Harvard University Press, 2014), 361–365.

71. A preoccupation with whitening the island did not necessarily represent antislavery dreams. Black rural labor, in the whiteners' way of thinking, could safely and effectively be combined with skilled, white labor in the cities. Miscegenation in the Cuban case held the promise of breeding blackness out of the population over several generations—this solution was acceptable as long as interracial sex meant white men's access to women of color, and not white women partnering with men of color. Luís Martinez Fernandez, *Fighting Slavery in the Caribbean: The Life and Times of a British Family in Nineteenth-Century Havana* (Armonk, NY: M. E. Sharpe, 1998), 68.

72. In the 1790s the *Sociedad Economica de Amigos del País* created a "*Comisión de Población Blanca*." Even though the promise of racial equilibrium in Cuban policy circles dates to the period of the Haitian Revolution, earlier debates around alternatives to slave labor were driven more by security concerns than by technological change, two priorities that by the 1840s had become inseparable. María Dolores González-Ripoll Navarro, *Cuba, La Isla de los Ensayos: Cultura y Sociedad*

(1790–1815) (Madrid: Consejo Superior de Investigaciones Científicas, 1999), 114–121; José Gomaríz, "Francisco de Arango y Parreño: El discurso esclavista de la Illustración Cubana," *Cuban Studies* 35 (2004): 48–52. On post-Escalera whitening projects, see Michele Reid-Vazquez, *The Year of the Lash: Free People of Color in Cuba and the Nineteenth-Century Atlantic World* (Athens, GA: University of Georgia Press, 2011), 150–151.

73. David Sartorius, *Ever Faithful: Race, Loyalty, and the Ends of Empire in Spanish Cuba* (Durham, NC: Duke University Press, 2013), 41.

74. Michael J. Barany, "Savage Numbers and the Evolution of Civilization in Victorian Prehistory," *British Journal for the History of Science* 47, no. 2 (2014): 14.

75. On the "inchoate" character of eighteenth century ideas about the intellectual capacity of different races, which solidified partly in response to the Haitian Revolution, see Christopher Iannini, *Fatal Revolutions: Natural History, West Indian Slavery, and the Routes of American Literature* (Chapel Hill: University of North Carolina Press, 2012), 37.

76. María Portuondo shows that sugar planters were often more concerned with artisan sugar masters' jealous protection of their craft knowledge than they were with slaves as barriers to technological change. Portuondo, "Plantation Factories," 231–257.

77. "*Expediente promovido por Dn Pascasio Ruiz de Cordova a nombre y como apoderado de Dn Juan Ramos, vecino de Pto Rico, proponiendo vender a la Junta un proceder inventado por este para la elaboracion del azúcar,*" 1853, ANC, JF, Leg 97, exp 4066.

78. Not looking into the matter of Cuban sugar factories, Joel Mokyr singles out British civil engineer John Smeaton (for Mokyr the personification of the Industrial Enlightenment) as "the first to realize that improvements in technological systems can be tested only by varying components one at a time holding all others constant." Quoted in Robert Allen, *The British Industrial Revolution in Global Perspective* (New York: Cambridge University Press, 2009), 242.

79. For an example of his use of "los brazos" as a generic label, see Sagra, *Cuba en 1860*, 88.

80. Sagra, *Cuba en 1860*, 126.

81. *Cartilla Práctica del manejo de ingenios ó fincas destinadas a producir azúcar, escrito por un montuno* (Irun, Spain: Imprenta de la Elegancia, 1862), 7.

82. McCulloh, *Reports*, 195–196.

83. McCulloh, *Reports*, 205.

84. McCulloh, *Reports*, 205.

85. McCulloh, *Reports*, 205.

86. The related but distinct genre of plantation manuals, which talked at length about the agricultural phases of production, in other words focusing on the spaces of coercion, also tended to talk much more explicitly about labor. See, for example, *Cartilla Práctica*.

87. For an eloquent exploration of slaves' experience of this new form of racial management, see Stephan Palmié, *Wizards and Scientists: Explorations in Afro-Cuban Modernity and Tradition* (Durham, NC: Duke University Press, 2002), 65–67.

88. Guy R. Hasegawa, *Villainous Compounds: Chemical Weapons and the American Civil War* (Carbondale, IL: Southern Illinois University Press, 2015), 30–31.

CHAPTER 3

1. *El Diario de la Marina,* December 2, 1844. For similar projects in New York City, see Dara Orenstein, "Offshore/Onshore: A History of the Free Zone on US Soil" (Ph.D. diss., Yale University, 2012), 47.

2. On the tendency of modern societies to "turn large swaths of ocean space into places more closely resembling land than ever before, especially with the installation of permanent and semipermanent structures," see Helen Rozwadowski, "The Promise of Ocean History for Environmental History," *Journal of American History* 100, no. 1 (June 2013): 136–138.

3. Roland Ely, *Comerciantes cubanos del siglo XIX* (Havana, Cuba: Editorial Liberia Martí, 1960), 10–11.

4. *El Diario de la Marina,* December 2, 1844.

5. At least for a time. A very similar system reemerged in the 1880s and 1890s, after emancipation. Personal conversation with Reinaldo Román.

6. Havana was uniquely convenient for the marketing of imports, since only it had bonded warehouses where imports could temporarily be stored without duties being levied. At ports like Matanzas, importers had to pay duties immediately upon disembarkation of goods. For statistics on Matanzas imports, see *Letter of the Secretary of State Transmitting a Report on the Commercial Relations of the United States with Foreign Countries, for the Year Ended September 30, 1863.* Part One (Washington, DC: Government Printing Office, 1865), 232.

7. Allan J. Kuethe, "Havana in the Eighteenth Century," in *Atlantic Port Cities: Economy, Culture, and Society in the Atlantic World, 1650–1850*, Peggy Liss and Franklin Knight, eds. (Knoxville: University of Tennessee Press, 1991), 14.

8. Leví Marrero, *Cuba: Economía y sociedad*, 14 vols., vol. 12 (Madrid: Editorial Playor, 1984), 194. See also Carlos Venegas Fornias, *La urbanización de las murallas: Dependencia y modernidad* (Havana, Cuba: Editorial Letras Cubanas, 1990), 65.

9. Marrero, *Cuba*, vol. 12, 194.

10. In May 1839, the mean tonnage of vessels entering the port of Havana was 163.57. In May 1861 it was 342.54. Calculations based on Entrada de buques, libro 1158 (1839), ANC, Aduana de la Habana; and Entrada de buques, libro 1159 (1861), ANC, Aduana de la Habana. May was the height of sugar export season, near the end of the harvest.

11. Albear left Havana for Madrid as a teenager and enrolled at the Academia de Real Cuerpo de Ingenieros. He then embarked on a military career. In 1845 he was

called back to Cuba, where he quickly earned an appointment as the Directing Engineer of Public Works for the Junta de Fomento. He therefore was absent from the island during the debates over the Regla Warehouses, and the Escalera counterinsurgency. Rolando García Blanco, *Francisco de Albear: Un genio cubano universal* (Havana, Cuba: Editorial Científico-Técnica, 2007), 206–219, 261.

12. Francisco de Albear, "Reforma de los muelles de la habana," *Anales de las Reales Junta de Fomento* I, Jul-Dic 1849." Reproduced in García, *Francisco de Albear,* 253–260.

13. "*Reglas adicionales al Reglamento de policía de muelles . . . ,*" 1821, ANC, GSC (Gobierno Superior Civil), Leg 700, exp 23079.

14. Albear, "Reforma," 255. A visitor voiced strikingly similar complaints regarding the busy wharves of New York in 1823. Robert Albion, *The Rise of New York Port, 1815–1860* (New York: Charles Scribner's Sons, 1939), 221.

15. "*D. Pedro Lopez en solicitud de privilegio por la maquina para la traslacion sobre el muelle de grandes pesos desde los buques,*" ANC, GSC, Leg 1476, exp 58276, 1837.

16. This idea was not new. See "*Sobre construcción del muelle de San Francisco hasta unirlo con el de Caballería,*" 1817, ANC, JF, Leg 81, exp 3291; and "*Exp sobre ensanchar el muelle frente a los almacenes de la Aduana nueva,*" 1828, ANC, JF, leg 81, no. 3318.

17. "*A los autos que sigue D. Juan Giraud contra D. Juis Bourdaut y Timeolon Bartemeli sobre acreditar que es socio des estos en unos almacenes . . . contra D. Pedro Lacoste,*" 1847, ANC, Escribanías de Pontón, Leg 119, exp 1.

18. *Memoria sobre el progreso de las obras publicas en la isla de Cuba desde 1 de enero de 1859 a fin de junio de 1865* (Havana, Cuba: Imprenta del Gobierno, 1866).

19. *Memoria sobre el progreso.*

20. Albeit on a smaller scale, landfill projects were being completed all over the bay, much to the consternation of naval officials, who had final say over embankment approvals.

21. José María de la Torre, *Lo que fuimos y lo que somos, o la Habana antigua y moderna* (Havana, Cuba: Imprenta de Spencer y Compañía, 1857), 14.

22. Carlos Venegas, "La habana, puerto colonial: Reflexiones sobre su historia urbana," in *La Habana, Puerto Colonial (Siglos XVIII–XIX)*, Agustín Guimerá and Fernando Monge, eds. (Madrid: Fundación Portuaria, 2000), 60–61.

23. Bales of cotton were handled in much the same way in antebellum New Orleans. Walter Johnson, *River of Dark Dreams: Slavery and Empire in the Cotton Kingdom* (Cambridge, MA: Harvard University Press, 2013), 256.

24. "*Expediente promovido por D Eduardo Fesser solicitando permiso para establecer muelles y almacenes de deposito en la parte oriental de esta bahia,*" 1842, ANC, JF, Leg 76, exp 2973.

25. "Owing to high dock charges or Spanish laws," a later observer noted, "foreign boats seldom make a landing at Havana," using lighters instead. Elliott Durand, *A Week*

in Cuba (Chicago: Belford-Clarke Co., 1891), 20. Visiting ships were subject to other charges as well. "Tonnage Dues on Coal-Laden Vessels at Havana," *Hunt's Merchant Magazine* 30 (1854): 495.

26. Justo Germán Cantero, *Los ingenios: Colección de vistas de los principales ingenios de azúcar de la Isla de Cuba* (1857); Luis Miguel García Mora and Antonio Santamaría García, eds. (Madrid: Editorial CSIC, 2005), 124.

27. Cantero, *Ingenios*, 123.

28. Cantero, *Ingenios*, 123–124.

29. Marrero, *Cuba*, vol. 12, 188.

30. *Architects' and Mechanics' Journal* (October 1859): 23. Quoted in Margot Gayle and Carol Gayle, *Cast-Iron Architecture in America: The Significance of James Bogardus*, (New York: W. W. Norton, 1998), 197.

31. *Diario de la Marina*, December 6, 1844.

32. *Diario de la Marina*, December 6, 1844.

33. "*Sobre aumento del capital de la empresa de los Almacenes de Regla*," 1857, ANC, GSC, Leg 1571, exp 81322.

34. "*Informe presentado por la Administracion y Direccion de la Empresa, a la Junta General Ordinaria celebrada en 16 de Juio de 1862*," 1862, ANC, GSC, Leg 1581.

35. No title, 1858, ANC, Obras Públicas (OP), Leg 2, exp 48. See also "*Expediente sobre la construccion de un barracón en Marianao para los trabajadores de las obras*," 1838, ANC, JF, Leg 37, exp 1623.

36. "*Sobre fusion entre Companía de Vapores de la Bahía y la Companía ferrocarrilera de Havana-Matanzas*," 1861, ANC, Intendencia General de Hacienda, Leg 747, exp 71.

37. Jacobo de la Pezuela, *Diccionario geográfico, estadístico, histórico de la Isla de Cuba*. 4 vols., vol. 3 (Madrid, 1863), 316.

38. *Diario de la Marina*, December 6, 1844

39. "*Expediente promovido por D Eduardo Fesser*."

40. *Diario de la Marina*, December 6, 1844

41. "*Expediente promovido por D Eduardo Fesser*."

42. José Ortega, "The Cuban Sugar Complex in the Age of Revolution, 1789–1844" (PhD diss., University of California, Los Angeles, 2008), n.p.

43. "*Expediente promovido por D Eduardo Fesser*."

44. On illegal slave traders at the center of elite society, see Martín Rodrigo y Alharilla, "Spanish Merchants and the Slave Trade: From Legality to Illegality, 1814–1870," in *Slavery and Antislavery in Spain's Atlantic Empire*, Josep M. Fradera and Christopher Schmidt-Nowara, eds. (London: Berghahn Books, 2013), 192–196; Inés Roldán de Montaud, *La Restauración en Cuba: El fracaso de un proceso reformista* (Madrid: Editorial CSIC, 2001), 33; Hugh Thomas, *The Slave Trade: The Story of the Atlantic Slave Trade: 1440–1870* (New York: Simon & Schuster, 1999), 642.

45. Laird Bergad, *Cuban Rural Society in the Nineteenth Century: The Social and Economic History of Monoculture in Matanzas* (Princeton, NJ: Princeton University Press, 1990), 49.

46. This group of littoral powerholders also formed what one scholar has called "the axis of the pro-slavery Spanish party," anti-independence reactionaries during the post-1868 wars. Roldán, *Restauración en Cuba*, 33.

47. Perhaps to extend the shelf life of syrups, some wealthier merchants had large syrup tanks built on their property. *"A los autos que sigue D. Juan Giraud contra D. Juis Bourdaut y Timeolon Bartemeli sobre acreditar que es socio des estos en unos almacenes . . . contra D. Pedro Lacoste,"* 1847, ANC, Escribanías de Pontón, Leg 119, exp 17. Extreme heat and humidity, temperature fluctuation, and the lack of completely airtight containers shortened the shelf life of molasses, which can last for years under the right conditions.

48. Manuel Moreno Fraginals, *El Ingenio: Complejo económico social cubano de azúcar,* 3 vols, vol. 3, 12–13.

49. John Scoffern, *The Manufacture of Sugar, in the Colonies and at Home, Chemically Considered* (London: Longman, Brown, Green, and Longmans, 1849), 79.

50. Moreno, *Ingenio*, vol. 3, 12–13, 17, and 143. While a box of sugar was 400–500 lbs., a hogshead loaded with molasses could weigh as much as 1,265 lbs. José María de la Torre, *El libro indispensable en la Isla de Cuba: Colección de noticias sobre pesas, medidas y monedas* (Havana, Cuba: Imprenta y Librería Militar, 1862). Escribanías de Pontón, Leg 119, 1, 1847.

51. On the better prices obtained for the whiter grades, see *"Informe presentado a la Real Junta de Fomento de Agricultura y Comercio de esta isla, por el Sr. Dn. Wenceslao de Villa Urrutia sobre los resultados de la zafra que este año ha hecho su ingenio en un tren de Derosne"* (Havana, Cuba: Oficina del Faro Industrial, 1843). Nevertheless, the largest Matanzas warehouse, which "serves the same function for Matanzas that the Warehouses of Regla fulfill for Havana," were constructed so as to hold 80,000 boxes of sugar and 20,000 hogsheads of molasses, so at least some unpurged sugar was warehoused, probably because molasses played such an important role in Matanzas's export fortunes. Pezuela, *Diccionario*, vol. 4, 40, quoted in Bergad, *Cuban Rural Society*, 170.

52. *"Expediente sobre aumento del capital de la empresa de Almacenes de Regla,"* 1857, ANC, GSC, Leg 1571, exp 81322.

53. Fernando Charadan Lopez, *La industria azucarera en Cuba* (Havana, Cuba: Editorial Ciencias Sociales, 1982), 43.

54. In 1851 the district of Cárdenas produced almost one-quarter of the island's total, while 28.7 percent of the lower-cost byproduct went directly out of Cárdenas. Jose Maria de la Torre, *The Spanish West Indies: Cuba and Porto Rico; Geographical, Political, and Industrial* (New York: Colton, 1855), 122–123; and Marrero, *Cuba*, vol. 12, 126.

55. "Cuba," *Hunt's Merchant Magazine* 28 (1852): 153; "Commerce of Havana," *Hunt's Merchant Magazine* 28 (1852), 480.

56. US vessels were charged $1.50 per ton for merely entering the port. "Of Navigation between the United States, Cuba, Etc. Etc.: Circular Instructions to the Collectors and Other Officers of the Customs," *Hunt's Merchant Magazine* 27 (1852): 238.

57. David Murray, *Odious Commerce: Britain, Spain, and the Abolition of the Cuban Slave Trade* (Cambridge, UK: Cambridge University Press, 1980), 208–210.

58. Murray, *Odious Commerce*, 243. One cwt ("hundredweight") equals approximately 112 US pounds: http://www.convertunits.com/from/cwt/to/pounds. For more detail on the takeoff in sugar consumption among non-elites in Britain in the 1850s, see Sidney Mintz, *Sweetness and Power: The Place of Sugar in Modern History* (New York: Penguin Books, 1985), 133, 143, and 161.

59. "Exports of Produce from Havana and Matanzas," *Hunt's Merchant Magazine* 22 (1850): 662.

60. Matanzas also exported 16,261 hogsheads of mascabado, 13,204 of which went to the United States, 2,958 to Europe (81 percent to the United States). When it came to molasses, the United States took 17,640 of a 32,147-hogshead total. Europe took the remainder. *Letter of the Secretary of State, Transmitting a Report of the Commercial Relations of the United States with Foreign Nations, for the Year Ending September 30, 1861* (Washington, DC: Government Printing Office, 1862), 167–168.

61. On the US Treasury Department limiting the number of ports of entry so as to better surveil international transactions, see Orenstein, "Offshore/Onshore," 118.

62. *"Informe que pide el Escmo Sor Gobr Capn Gral sobre el espediente relativo a la Empresa de Almacenes de Depósito en esta plaza formada por una sociedad anónima,"* 1854, ANC, JF, Leg 76, exp 3006.

63. *"Expediente promovido por D Eduardo Fesser."*

64. *"Expediente promovido por D Eduardo Fesser."*

65. Moreno, *Cuba/España, España/Cuba, historia común* (Barcelona, Spain: Critica, 2002), 90.

66. Robert Paquette, *Sugar Is Made with Blood: The Conspiracy of La Escalera and the Conflict between Empires over Slavery in Cuba* (Middletown, CT: Wesleyan University Press, 1988), 107–108. Militia service had long been a source of power and respect for free people of color. Matt Childs, *The 1812 Aponte Rebellion in Cuba and the Struggle against Atlantic Slavery* (Chapel Hill: University of North Carolina Press, 2006), 157. See also David Sartorius, *Ever Faithful: Race, Loyalty, and the Ends of Empire in Spanish Cuba* (Durham, NC: Duke University Press, 2013).

67. Paquette, *Sugar Is Made with Blood*, 109.

68. F. Wurdeman, *Notes on Cuba: Containing an Account of Its Discovery and Early History ; A Description of the Face of the Country, Its Population, Resources, and Wealth; Its Institutions, and the Manners and Customs of Its Inhabitants; with Directions to Travellers Visiting the Island* (Boston: J. Munroe and Company, 1844), 24.

69. James Alexander, *Transatlantic Sketches* (London, 1833), quoted in Marrero, *Cuba*, vol. 12, 192.

70. Wurdemann, *Notes on Cuba*, 40.

71. Dale T. Graden, *Disease, Resistance, and Lies: The Demise of the Transatlantic Slave Trade to Brazil and Cuba* (Baton Rouge: Louisiana State University Press, 2014), 59.

72. Paquette, *Sugar Is Made with Blood*, 139.

73. Aisha Finch, "Insurgency at the Crossroads: Cuban Slaves and the Conspiracy of La Escalera, 1841–1844" (PhD diss., New York University [ProQuest, 2007]), 114.

74. Finch, "Insurgency at the Crossroads," 117.

75. Michele Reid-Vazquez, *The Year of the Lash: Free People of Color in Cuba and the Nineteenth-Century Atlantic World* (Athens, GA: University of Georgia Press, 2011), 130.

76. Reid-Vazquez, *Year of the Lash*, 110.

77. Paquette, *Sugar Is Made with Blood*, 242.

78. Carlos Hellberg, *Historia Estadística de Cárdenas* (Cárdenas: 1893), 44; Paquette, *Sugar Is Made with Blood*, 228.

79. Paquette, *Sugar Is Made with Blood*, 239. On Carabalí and Abakuá dockworkers in the Escalera uprising, see Reid-Vazquez, *Year of the Lash,* 110.

80. Reid-Vazquez, *Year of the Lash,* 76.

81. *Standard Guide to Cuba: A New and Complete Guide to the Island of Cuba, With Maps, Illustrations, Routes of Travel, History, and and English-Spanish Phrase Book* (New York: Foster and Reynolds, 1905), 98.

82. Cantero, *Ingenios*, 123.

83. Paquette, *Sugar Is Made with Blood*, 151.

84. Gayle and Gayle, *Cast-Iron Architecture*, 83.

85. On the increasingly tenuous position of Cuban-born craftsmen in the building trades, see Venegas, *Urbanización*, 39–41.

86. Gayle and Gayle, *Cast-Iron Architecture*, 83.

87. Gayle and Gayle, *Cast-Iron Architecture*, 102.

88. Gayle and Gayle, *Cast-Iron Architecture*, 102.

89. Marrero, *Cuba*, vol. 12, 171.

90. Reid-Vazquez, *Year of the Lash*, 104.

91. "*Expediente promovido por la Empresa de Almacenes de Marimelena para que se les permita introducir libres de derechos los efectos de hierro colado necesarios para la construccion de los mismos,*" 1858, ANC, GSC, Leg 1180, exp 46106.

92. "*Documentos relacionados con la Sociedad Almacenes de Marimelena,*" 1856, GSC, Leg 1582, exp 81459. It is likely that a drop in molasses prices in 1825 encouraged planters to move into rum production: they could no longer profit from shipping it off, because of all the disadvantages of moving hogsheads of molasses. Moreno, *Ingenio*, vol. 1, 244.

93. "*Sobre formacion de la sociedad anónima titulada Almacenes de Marimelena,*" 1857, ANC, GSC, Leg 1582, exp 81437.

94. "*Espediente instruido en averiguacion del estado de esta Sociedad,*" 1862, ANC, GSC, Leg 1582, exp 81438.

95. Marimelena's board of directors declined this offer because they thought the building in question was their last hope for an influx of business. The Ayuntamiento (city council) finally located a merchant who would rent its existing cast-iron warehouse to store inflammable goods. With this lifeline, the directors could liquidate the corporation and start paying off their debts. *"Almacenes de Marimelena,"* 1865, ANC, GSC, Leg 1582, exp 81439.

96. *"Espediente sobre aumento del capital."*

97. *"Informe presentado por la Administracion y Direccion de la Empresa, a la Junta General Ordinaria celebrada en 16 de Junio de 1862,"* 1862, ANC, GSC, Leg 1581, exp 81432.

98. *"Informe presentado por la Administracion."*

99. The WRC began construction in 1858 and built lines westward in order to compete with the HRC around Guanajay and beyond. Eduardo L. Moyano Bazzani, *La nueva frontera del azúcar: El ferrocarril y la economía cubana del siglo XIX* (Madrid: CSIC, 1991), 308.

100. *"Informe presentado por la Administracion."*

101. *"Informe presentado por la Administracion."* Moyano Bazzani, *La nueva frontera*, 308. Mariel, Bahia Honda, and Guanajay, all to the west of Havana, were still making a great deal of sugar at this time. See Jose María de la Torre, *The Spanish West Indies: Cuba and Porto Rico; Geographical, Political, and Industrial* (New York: Colton, 1855), 122–123.

102. For another wealthy planter's tribulations with infrastructure for sugar byproducts, see *"Expediente promovido por D. Juan Poey sobre construccion de un muelle en Ensenada de Atares,"* 1856, ANC, OP, Leg 42.

103. Other big warehouse promoters further complicate the story that merchant-loathing planters pioneered the Warehouse Revolution. Manuel Pastor was a planter with noble status, as well as an Andalucian military engineer who worked on Tacón's Cárcel Nueva and Mercado de Cristina urban renewal projects. Along with Antonio Parejo, he was intimately involved in the Regla and San José Warehouses. Venegas, *Urbanizacion*, 28, and Marrero, *Cuba*, vol. 12, 221–222.

104. Bergad, *Cuban Rural Society*, 63. See also *Standard Guide to Cuba*, 98, for some fascinating Regla origin stories.

105. Bergad, *Cuban Rural Society*, 177.

106. Marrero, *Cuba*, vol. 12, 188; Ely, *Comerciantes cubanos*, 10–11.

107. *"Conde de Fernandina, Presidente de la Primera Compañía de Almacenes de deposito de Regla, para construir un camino de hierro desde estos hasta entroncar con el de Güines,"* 1850, ANC, JF, Leg 137, exp 6680.

108. Jose Antonio Echeverría, *"Manifestando la conveniencia trasladar a otro parage mas oportuno el actual paradero de Villanueva . . . ,"* 1852, ANC, JF, Leg 137, exp 6682.

109. Pezuela, *Diccionario*, vol. 3, 67.

110. Pezuela, *Diccionario*, vol. 3, 67.

111. Echeverria, "*Manifestando la conveniencia.*" They had also tried and failed to form a concord with Regla Warehouses, whose owners obviously saw much greater potential profit in having their own railroad access to the sugar heartland. *Informe presentado pr la junta directiva de la Compañía de Caminos de Hierro de la Habana a la general de accionistas. . . .* (Havana, Cuba: Imprenta del Tiempo, 1858), 27 (held in ANC, JF, Leg 164, exp 7908).

112. "*Sobre embarque de bocoyes de azúcar por el muelle de Luz,*" 1856, ANC, OP, Leg 10, exp 226.

113. "*Extracto del expediente pro por el Administrador Gral de la Cía de Caminos de Hierro de la Habana, D. José A. Echeverria sobre la trasladacion del paradero principal de cargas – Villanueva – a orillas de la Bahía,*" 1858, ANC, OP, Leg 60, exp 779; and Moyano, *La nueva frontera*, 238–247.

CHAPTER 4

1. Alfred Chandler, *The Visible Hand: The Managerial Revolution in American Business* (Cambridge, MA: Harvard University Press, 1993).

2. For the contract hiring manufacturer and engineer Edmund Ivens as the firm's New Orleans agent, see Contract Book (1859 July–1865 April), January 4, 1860, Series V, Box 176, Tredegar Records.

3. "*Ferro-Carril de la Bahía de la Habana a Matanzas: Informe Presentado por su Administrador General para demostrar el estado de los fondos y de los trabajos ejecutados hasta fin del mes de Diciembre del año de 1858*" (Havana, Cuba: Establecimiento tipográfico La Cubana, 1858), ANC, JF, Leg 164, exp 7909.

4. James Dilts, *The Great Road: The Building of the Baltimore and Ohio, the Nation's First Railroad, 1828–1853* (Stanford, CA: Stanford University Press, 1993), 49–50.

5. Charles Dew, *Ironmaker to the Confederacy: Joseph R. Anderson and the Tredegar Ironworks* (New Haven, CT: Yale University Press, 1966), 29; Midori Takagi, "*Rearing Wolves to Our Own Destruction*": *Slavery in Richmond, Virginia, 1782–1865* (Charlottesville: University Press of Virginia, 1999), 92. Dew gives evidence of iron masters prioritizing the skilling of slaves, who would find it more difficult to depart after receiving training than white workers did. Charles Dew, *Bond of Iron: Master and Slave at Buffalo Forge* (New York: W. W. Norton, 1994). For other valuable studies of enslaved ironworkers, see James Sidbury, "Slave Artisans in Richmond, Virginia, 1780–1810," in *American Artisans: Crafting Social Identity, 1750–1850,* Howard Rock, Paul Gilje and Robert Asher, eds. (Baltimore: Johns Hopkins University Press, 1995); Ronald L. Lewis, *Coal, Iron, and Slaves: Industrial Slavery in Maryland and Virginia, 1715–1865* (Westport, CT: Praeger, 1979); Robert Starobin, *Industrial Slavery in the Old South* (New York: Oxford University Press, 1971); and John Bezis-Selfa, "A Tale of Two Ironworks: Slavery, Free Labor, Work, and Resistance in the Early Republic," *William and Mary Quarterly* 56, 4 (1999): 677–700.

6. Dew, *Bond of Iron* looks at a much different place. No puddling or rolling was going on in even the largest rural ironworks. Skilled slaves in Richmond worked at a strategic wrought-iron node, which by the 1850s had differentiated itself from struggling Shenandoah Valley iron producers.

7. Tredegar built at least forty-one locomotives between 1850 and 1855, mostly for southern railroads. Gregg Kimball, *American City, Southern Place: A Cultural History of Antebellum Richmond* (Athens, GA: University of Georgia Press, 2000), 21.

8. Dew, *Ironmaker to the Confederacy*, 12–13. For a sense of the southwesterly orientation of Tredegar's business in the 1850s, see especially Box 176, Series V, Contract Books, Tredegar Business Records, Manuscripts Collection (Library of Virginia Archives, Richmond) (henceforth Tredegar Records). See also Dew, *Ironmaker to the Confederacy*, 34–36.

9. Matthew J. Karp, "Slavery and American Sea Power: The Navalist Impulse in the Antebellum South," *Journal of Southern History* 77, no. 2 (2011), 286, 305.

10. From building the furnaces with quarried limestone blocks, to digging the ore out of the hillsides of the Shenandoah Valley, to maintaining the large dams and waterworks necessary to power the bellows, enslaved people were central to every aspect of rural iron production in antebellum Virginia.

11. Cast iron products were made directly from pig iron, An alloy with 2 to 4 percent carbon and silicon, cast iron could be melted down and worked at much lower temperatures than wrought iron. Robert Gordon, *American Iron, 1607–1900* (Baltimore: Johns Hopkins University Press, 1996), 10.

12. They supplemented their supplies with pig iron from Boston and England. Ser V, box 176, Contrct Bks, pp. 50–90).

13. Minute Book, 1837–1850, Series I: Administrative Records, Misc. Reel 2642, Tredegar Records. For a similar set of racialized labor experiments in a major Virginia infrastructural project, see Linda Upham-Bornstein, "'Men of Families': The Intersection of Labor Conflict and Race in the Norfolk Dry Dock Affair, 1829–1831," *Labor: Studies in Working-Class History of the Americas* 4, no. 1 (2007): 65–97.

14. Minute Book, 1837–1850.

15. Minute Book, 1837–1850.

16. David Montgomery, *The Fall of the House of Labor: The Workplace, the State, and American Labor Activism, 1865–1925* (New York: Cambridge University Press, 1989), 15.

17. Minute Book, 1837–1850.

18. Minute Book, 1837–1850.

19. Even among the white artisans, ethno-national divisions guided the administration of tasks. An ethnically and racially differentiated workforce sprawled across the five-acre Tredegar complex, with "Irish puddlers, Welsh heaters, and English

rollers" supported by "a large force of Irish and German workers" who constituted "the bulk of Tredegar's ordinary working population" of 800 people by 1860. Dew, *Ironmaker to the Confederacy*, 28.

20. For an account of how notions of racial difference shaped the development of the working class in America, see David Roediger, *Wages of Whiteness: Race and the Making of the American Working Class* (New York: Verso, 1991).

21. For other accounts of the strike, see Patricia A. Schechter, "Free and Slave Labor in the Old South: The Tredegar Ironworkers' Strike of 1847," *Labor History* 35 (1994), 165–186; and Kimball, *American City, Southern Place*, 167–171.

22. "Joseph R. Anderson to My Late Workmen . . . 26 May 1847," Tredegar Scrapbook, Tredegar Records.

23. It was also one of the most physically taxing of jobs. As David Landes writes, puddling "calls for exceptional strength and endurance. There was simply a limit to what the flesh could stand. . . ." David Landes, *The Unbound Prometheus: Technological Change and Industrial Development in Western Europe from 1750 to the Present* (New York: Cambridge University Press, 1969), 92. For an explanation of casting, see Louis Hunter, *A History of Industrial Power in the United States*, 3 vols., vol. 2 (Charlottesville: University Press of Virginia, 1985), 187–193.

24. This explanation, and that in the previous paragraph, is drawn from Frederick Overman, *The Manufacture of Iron, in All Its Various Branches: Including a Description of Wood-Cutting, Coal-Digging, and the Burning of Charcoal and Coke; the Digging and Roasting of Iron Ore; the Building and Management of Blast Furnaces, Working by Charcoal, Coke, or Anthracite; the Refining of Iron, and the Conversion of the Crude into Wrought Iron by Charcoal Forges and Puddling Furnaces* (Philadelphia: Henry Baird, 1854), 267–270.

25. Gordon, *American Iron*, 7.

26. Chris Evans and Goran Ryden, eds., *The Industrial Revolution in Iron: The Impact of British Coal Technology in Nineteenth-Century Europe* (London: Ashgate, 2005), 11, 103.

27. Evans and Ryden, *Industrial Revolution in Iron*, 30–31.

28. Most antebellum machine shop and ironworks "were not large, impersonal factories where workers performed rote tasks; instead they were experimental shops or even laboratories where innovation in relatively new arts and sciences was taking place." Monte Calvert, *The Mechanical Engineer in America, 1830–1910: Professional Cultures in Conflict* (Baltimore: Johns Hopkins University Press, 1967), 12.

29. Antebellum ironworks, for the most part, "undertook to build almost any kind of industrial equipment and machinery," since there was not enough of a market in any one product to underwrite the costs of specialization. Hunter, *Steam Power*, 178.

30. Oscar Zanetti and Alejandro García, *Sugar and Railroads: A Cuban History, 1837–1959* (Chapel Hill: University of North Carolina Press, 1998), 58, 125.

31. John Zabourney, *Slaves for Hire: Renting Enslaved Laborers in Antebellum Virginia* (Baton Rouge: Louisiana State University Press, 2012), 126.

32. Quoted in Aaron Marrs, *Railroads in the Old South: Pursuing Progress in a Slave Society* (Baltimore: Johns Hopkins University Press, 2009), 58.

33. Quoted in Zabourney, *Slaves for Hire*, 130.

34. On railroads' preference for hiring slaves, see Marrs, *Railroads in the Old South*, 62–66.

35. "*Reconocimiento de los ferrocarriles,*" Inspector de Ferrocarriles de la isla Juan Campuzano, to Presidente of La Compañía de Caminos de Hierro de la Habana, Gonzalo Alfonso, November 2, 1855, ANC, JF, Leg 136, exp 6664.

36. "*Resultado del reconocimiento practicado en 1° de Ago pasado en la estension de la linea comprendida entre el deposito de Villanueva y la estacion del Rincon. . . ,*" 1855, ANC, JF, Leg 136, exp 6664.

37. Londa Schiebinger, *Plants and Empire: Colonial Bioprospecting in the Atlantic World* (Cambridge, MA: Harvard University Press, 2004).

38. Gloria García, *Conspiraciones y revueltas: La actividad política de los negros en Cuba, 1790–1845* (Santiago de Cuba: Editorial Oriente, 2003), 127; Aisha Finch, "Insurgency at the Crossroads: Cuban Slaves and the Conspiracy of La Escalera, 1841–1844" (PhD diss., New York University [ProQuest, 2007]), 192.

39. Robert Paquette, *Sugar Is Made with Blood: The Conspiracy of La Escalera and the Conflict between Empires over Slavery in Cuba* (Middletown, CT: Wesleyan University Press, 1988), 210.

40. Zanetti and García, *Sugar and Railroads*, 117–118.

41. Zanetti and García, *Sugar and Railroads*, 119–124.

42. For a survey of the laws, see Eduardo Moyano Bazzani, *La nueva frontera del azúcar: El ferrocarril y la economía cubana del siglo XIX* (Madrid: CSIC, 1991), 207–235.

43. "*Expediente relativo al reconocimiento de las Ferro-Carriles de esta isla por varios oficiales del Real Cuerpo de Ingenerios,*" September 9, 1853, ANC, JF, Leg 137, exp 6693.

44. "*Expediente relativo al reconocimiento.*" An important distinction must be made between the *guardiero* and the *celador*. The latter had quite considerable police powers along the line, and was normally a white man. "*Reconocimiento de los ferrocarriles.*"

45. The authors of the report emphasized that this project involved "topography of the country under different principles," suggesting that the Spanish military surveyors were quite aware of the undertaking's discontinuity with their traditional responsibilities. "*Expediente relativo al reconocimiento.*" For more details on the inspections regime, see "*Sobre la formacion de un reglamento para los celadores del camino de hierro de Güines,*" 1844, ANC, JF, Leg 133, 6526.

46. Manuel Bosque, *Caminos de hierro de la habana: Itinerarios e instrucciones para los maquinistas,* 1862, University of Miami Cuban Heritage Collection. For an earlier enunciation of similar policies, see "*Reglamento de los celadores del ferro-carril*

de la Habana" (Havana, Cuba: Imprenta del Gobierno por S. M., 1844), ANC, JF, Leg 133, exp 6526.

47. *"Reconocimiento de los ferrocarriles."*

48. *"Reconocimiento de los ferrocarriles."*

49. *"Resultado del reconocimiento."* Starting out cheaply and then improving the quality of lines after freight had been assured was widely practiced in the United States, unlike the extravagant up-front costs paid out by English railways. Upgrading to higher-quality infrastructure was not overwhelmingly difficult in logistical terms. Also, delaying investment in state-of-the-art equipment meant that a firm did not have to leverage itself until it was on more sure financial footing. George Vose, *Manual for Railroad Engineers and Engineering Students* (Boston: Lee and Shepard, 1872), 8–9.

50. *An Illustrated and Descriptive Catalogue of Manufactures of Tredegar Iron Works: Joseph R. Anderson & Co., Richmond, Va., Edmond M. Ivens, General Agent*, (Richmond, 1860), 17; Zanetti and García, *Sugar and Railroads*, 86.

51. J. R. Anderson & Co. to Sr. Dn. C. Cadalzo, August 1, 1860, Box 883, Subseries 1, Series VII, Tredegar Records.

52. Cruger went on to have an illustrious career on Cuban railroads until his death in 1846. Zanetti and García, *Sugar and Railroads*, 25, 114–115.

53. Moyano, *La nueva frontera*, 156.

54. J. Thomas Sharf, *History of Westchester County, New York, Including Morrisania, Kings Bridge, and West Farms*, 2 vols, vol. 1 (Philadelphia: L. E. Preson, 1886), 835.

55. *"Informe presentado pr la junta directiva de la Compañia de Caminos de Hierro de la Habana a la general de accionistas…."* (Havana, Cuba: Imprenta del Tiempo, 1858), ANC, JF, Leg 164, 7908.

56. Joseph Anderson to J. R. Trimble, October 12, 1858, Book One, Box 882, subseries 1, Series VII, Tredegar Records.

57. David C Trimble, *Furious, Insatiable Fighter: A Biography of Major General Isaac Ridgeway Trimble, C.S.A.* (Lanham, MD: University Press of America, 2005), 17, 20. They shared a future as officers of the Confederacy as well. Trimble graduated in 1822 and Anderson in 1836. Trimble, *Furious, Insatiable Fighter*, 10; Dew, *Ironmaker to the Confederacy*, 6. They both failed to reach the highest echelon of their class and ended up in Artillery divisions, but were promoted to the Corps of Engineers soon after. For military engineering as an avenue to middle-class status in the antebellum South, see Jennifer Green, "Networks of Military Educators: Middle Class Stability and Professionalization in the Late Antebellum South," *Journal of Southern History* 73, no. 1 (February 2007): 39–74

58. Dew, *Ironmaker to the Confederacy*, 8.

59. Bollman served as a delegate in the pro-secessionist "Peace Party" in Maryland's secession convention of 1861. *Baltimore Sun*, August 30 1861. Thanks to Frank Towers for locating this information. While Bollman does not appear to have joined the Confederacy after "Peace Party" efforts failed to convince the majority

of white Marylanders to secede, his politics did align closely with those of Trimble and Anderson. Bollman has been identified as "the first successful iron bridge builder in the world." Mike Hugh, *The C&O Canal Companion* (Baltimore: Johns Hopkins University Press, 2001), 196. See also Robert Vogel, "The Engineering Contributions of Wendel Bollman," in *Contributions from the Museum of History and Technology, Papers 34–44 on Science and Technology* (Washington DC: Smithsonian Institution, 1966), 82–83.

60. For example, Morris Tanner & Co. to Wendell Bollman, October 20, 1858, Book One, Box 882, Subseries 1, Series VII, Tredegar Records. The firm boasted to Bollman of "making 15 tons of each spikes & chairs per day so that we can always receive the largest orders with dispatch."

61. Calvert, *Mechanical Engineer*, 6.

62. Morris Tanner & Co, to M.O. Davidson, October 19, 1858, Book One, Box 882, Subseries 1, Series VII, Tredegar Records.

63. Morris Tanner & Co. to Wendell Bollman, October 20, 1858, Book One, Box 882, Subseries 1, Series VII, Tredegar Records.

64. Tredegar Co. to M.O. Davidson, 6 January 1859. Book One. Box 882, Subseries 1, Series VII, Tredegar Records.

65. One way to think about Tredegar's internationalization would be to say that it was the firm's way of resolving the "limited extent of market" plaguing southern regional economies, the small size of its urban population in particular. For long-distance trade as a practical response to limited local consumer markets in the South, see Brian Schoen, "Alternatives to Dependence: The Lower South's Antebellum Pursuit of Sectional Development through Global Interdependence," in *Global Perspectives on Industrial Transformation in the American South,* S. Delfino and M. Gillespie, eds. (Columbia: University of Missouri Press, 2006).

66. Contract Books, 1858–1865, September 21, 1859, Box 176, Series V, Tredegar Records.

67. Contract Books, 1858–1865, September 26, 1859, Box 176, Series V, Tredegar Records.

68. See Mark Aldrich, "Earnings of American Civil Engineers, 1820–1859," *Journal of Economic History* 31 (June 1971): 407–419.

69. Archer Co. Cash Book 1858, September 24, 1859, Box 82, Series II, Tredegar Records.

70. Archer Co. Cash Book 1858, September 26, 1859, Box 82, Series II, Tredegar Records. For the diversity of rail and fastening designs prevalent on mid-nineteenth-century railroads, and for a few specifics on how "piles" of rolled iron were finished into usable rails in the rolling mill, see Anthony J. Bianculli, *Trains and Technology: The American Railroad in the Nineteenth Century, Vol. 3, Track and Structures* (Newark: University of Delaware Press, 2003), 85–113.

71. In his study of changing relations of power between engineers and workers, John Brown writes that the new engineering drawings "gave the business firm new

power to direct production workers, a reflection of the political character of plans." John K. Brown, "Design Plans, Working Drawings, National Styles: Engineering Practice in Great Britain and the United States, 1775–1945," *Technology and Culture* 41 (April 2000): 199. For an interesting account of the often messy relationships between engineers' drawing offices and workers on the shop floor, see Boel Berner, "Rationalizing Technical Work: Visions and Realities of the 'Systematic Drawing Office' in Sweden, 1890–1940," *Technology and Culture* 48, no. 1 (2007): 20–42.

72. J. R. Anderson & Co. to M. O. Davidson, March 31, 1860, Box 882, Subseries 1, Series VII, Tredegar Records.

73. J. R. Anderson & Co. to M. O. Davidson, March 31, 1860, Box 882, Subseries 1, Series VII, Tredegar Records.

74. J.R. Anderson & Co. to M. O. Davidson, March 31, 1860.

75. J. R. Anderson & Co. to Manuel Bosque, May 17, 1860, Box 883, Subseries 1, Series VII, Tredegar Records. "Fastenings" referred to the chairs and spikes that fasten the rails to the crossties, and to the splices that join rails to one another and keep them in alignment.

76. For a useful description of the organization of labor later in the nineteenth-century, see Michael Nuwer, "From Batch to Flow: Production Technology and Workforce Skills in the Steel Industry, 1880–1920," *Technology and Culture* 29 (1988): 812–815. David Montgomery describes the "roller himself as a figure of great authority." Montgomery, *Fall of the House of Labor*, 11–12.

77. *Illustrated and Descriptive Catalogue,* Tredegar, 19.

78. Dew, *Ironmaker*, 49, 52.

79. Dew, *Bond of Iron*, 174–175.

80. J. R. Anderson & Co. to Manuel Bosque, June 23, 1860, Box 883, Subseries 1, Series VII, Tredegar Records.

81. On the rise of notions of precision as a cardinal value of machine making and measurement in eighteenth- and nineteenth-century Europe, see Norton Wise, ed., *The Values of Precision* (Princeton, NJ: Princeton University Press, 1995).

82. M. O. Davidson, Engineer's Office, Havana R .R. Co. to J. R. Anderson & Co., August 5, 1860, Box 883, Subseries 1, Series VII, Tredegar Records. It seems that Anderson took Davidson's complaints seriously, since the company's office clerk copied out his letter—it is one of the few incoming letters that appear in the archived copybooks of outgoing correspondence.

83. M. O. Davidson, Engineer's Office, Havana R. R. Co. to J. R. Anderson & Co., August 5, 1860, Box 883, Subseries 1, Series VII, Tredegar Records.

84. M. O. Davidson, Engineer's Office, Havana R. R . Co. to J. R. Anderson & Co., August 5, 1860.

85. David Meyer finds that "non-hub firms" cut costs by depending on a single regional hub firm for long-distance connections. Tredegar seemed to prefer hedging against the failure or unscrupulousness of any of these individuals by disintermediating and diversifying its links to Cuba. David Meyer, *Networked*

Machinists: High-Technology Industries in Antebellum America (Baltimore: Johns Hopkins University Press, 2006).

86. Zanetti and García, *Sugar and Railroads*, 116.

87. J. R. Anderson to Tegmeyer, November 23, 1859, Box 882, Book One, Subseries 1, Series VII, Tredegar Records.

88. J. R. Anderson & Co. to Sr. Dn. C. Cadalzo, August 1, 1860, Box 883, Subseries 1, Series VII, Tredegar Records.

89. J. R. Anderson & Co. to Sr. Dn. C. Cadalzo, August 1, 1860, Box 883, Subseries 1, Series VII, Tredegar Records, and J. R. Anderson & Co. to Eduardo Echarte, March 5, 1861, Box 885, Subseries 1, Series VII, Tredegar Records.

90. *Illustrated and Descriptive Catalogue*, Tredegar, 102.

91. *"Ferro-Carril de la Bahía de la Habana a Matanzas: Informe Presentado por su Administrador General para demostrar el estado de los fondos y de los trabajos ejecutados hasta fin del mes de Diciembre del año de 1858"* (Havana, Cuba: Establecimiento tipográfico La Cubana, Calle de la Lamparilla, No 2., 1859). This pamphlet can be found in ANC, JF, Leg 164, exp 7909.

92. Hugh, *The C&O Canal Companion*, 196.

93. J. R. Anderson & Co. to John F. Tanner, April 1861, Box 886, Subseries 1, Series VII, Tredegar Records.

94. Archer journal. In "Letters, etc." Box 4a, Series I, Tredegar Records.

95. "Letters, etc." Box 4a, Series I, Tredegar Records; T. C. DeLeon, *Four Years in Rebel Capitals: An Inside View of Life in the Southern Confederacy, from Birth to Death; from Original Notes, Collated in the Years 1861 to 1865* (Mobile: The Gossip Printing Company, 1892), 92. Also included in the Tredegar scrapbook was a clipping from *Richmond Magazine*, August 1931: "And not least of all are memories of that delightful picture T. C. DeLeon paints of the self-importance acquired by some of the swarthy operatives at the mill during the War between the States. One negro from the Tredegar, seated nonchalantly on the back of a train. . . ," and it goes on.

CHAPTER 5

1. The Richmond firm assured its prospective customers that "our Cuba friends purchase large quantities" of spikes. J.R. Anderson and Co. to Messr. Roberto Harvey and Co, Dom Pedro II Railway Co., Rio de Janeiro. March 23, 1860, Box 882, Subseries 1, Series VII, Tredegar Business Records, Manuscripts Collection (Library of Virginia Archives, Richmond, VA) (henceforth Tredegar Records).

2. John W. Jordan, *Encyclopedia of Pennsylvania Biography*, vol. 13 (New York: Lewis Historical Publishing Company, 1921), 104–105.

3. John Thomas Scharf and Thompson Wescott, *History of Philadelphia, 1609–1884*, vol. 3 (Philadelphia: Lippincott, 1884), 2204.

4. John and Margaret Peters, *Virginia's Historic Courthouses* (Charlottesville: University of Virginia Press, 1995), 123.

5. Aaron Marrs, *Railroads in the Old South: Pursuing Progress in a Slave Society* (Baltimore: Johns Hopkins University Press, 2009), 81.

6. Secondarily, Harvey offered employment to "men who have been accustomed to work white labor." *Richmond Daily Dispatch,* August 31, 1858.

7. "The Bark Parthian," *Richmond Daily Dispatch,* December 8, 1858.

8. Regina Moreno Kirchoff Mandrell, William S. Coker, and Hazel P. Coker, *Our Family, Facts and Fancies: The Moreno and Related Families* (Pensacola, FL: Perdido Bay Press, 1988), 101, 338.

9. New York merchants also exported massive quantities of cheap western flour to Great Britain in particular years. Between 1847 and 1851, the United States shipped an annual average of 776,125 barrels to England. Brazil was a distant second with 317,182 barrels per year, but as we will see these are different kinds of flour. J. D. B. DeBow, *The Industrial Resources, Statistics, &c. of the United States and More Particularly of the Southern and Western States,* 3d ed., vol. 1 (New York: Augustus Kelley, 1966, orig. 1854), 97.

10. "Commerce of Rio Janeiro," *Hunt's Merchant Magazine and Commercial Review* 24 (May 1851): 621. Import figures varied, depending on the source. The *Diário de Rio de Janeiro,* February 4, 1852 (Suplemento ao Diário do Rio de Janeiro) reported that Rio imported 363,294 barrels of flour in 1851. DeBow reported 374,711 barrels of US flour went to Brazil in 1851, a figure that represented 17 percent of total US flour exports. The difference in the two figures might be accounted for by reexports out of Brazil. DeBow, *Industrial Resources,* 97.

11. On the perils of reenslavement for free blacks, see Sidney Chalhoub, "Illegal Enslavement and the Precariousness of Freedom in Nineteenth-Century Brazil," in *Assumed Identities: The Meanings of Race in the Atlantic World,* John Garrigus and Christopher Morris, eds. (College Station, TX: Texas A&M University Press, 2010).

12. For some suggestive comments in this direction, see Rafael Marquese and Dale Tomich, "O Vale do Paraíba escravista e a formação do mercado mundial do café no século XIX," in *O Vale do Paraíba e o Império do Brasil nos quadros da Segunda Escravidão,* Mariana Muaze and Ricardo Salles, eds. (Rio de Janeiro, Brazil: 7Letras, 2015), 33, 43.

13. Brooke Hunter, "Wheat, War, and the American Economy during the Age of Revolution," *William and Mary Quarterly* 62, no. 3 (2005): 516.

14. Linda K. Salvucci, "Supply, Demand, and the Making of a Market: Philadelphia and Havana at the Beginning of the 19th Century," in *Atlantic Port Cities: Economy, Culture, and Society in the Atlantic World, 1650–1850,* Peggy Liss and Franklin Knight, eds. (Knoxville: University of Tennessee Press, 1991), 33–34.

15. Sherry Johnson, *Climate and Catastrophe in Cuba and the Atlantic World in the Age of Revolution* (Chapel Hill: University of North Carolina Press, 2011), 29–30. As the trade in foreign flour was gradually liberalized, the Ministry of the Indies did away with the flour-to-slave ratio.

16. Salvucci, "Supply, Demand, and the Making of a Market," 41.

17. Johnson, *Climate and Catastrophe*, 80, 105, 114, 171. See also Salvucci, "Supply, Demand, and the Making of a Market," 55, n27.

18. Leví Marrero, *Cuba: Economía y Sociedad. Azúcar, Ilustración y Conciencia (1763–1868)*, 14 vols., vol. 10 (Madrid: Editorial Playor, 1984), 85–86; and Rolando Misas, "El pensamiento con lucro en los orígenes de la ciencia agrícola: La Expedicion de Mopox (1796-1802)," in *Voces de la sociedad Cubana: Economía, política e ideología*, Mildred de la Torre Molina, ed. (Habana, Cuba: Editorial Ciencias Sociales, 2007), 106.

19. On the importance of distinguishing between custom mills and merchant mills, see Louis Hunter, *A History of Industrial Power in the United States, 1780–1930*, 3 vols., vol. 2 (Charlottesville: University Press of Virginia, 1979), 112–113; and Larry Hasse, "Watermills in the South: Rural Institutions Working against Modernization," *Agricultural History* 58, no. 3 (1984): 280–295. For a caution against overstating the distinction, at least in the late eighteenth century, see Hunter, "Wheat, War," 509n6.

20. George Terry Sharrer, "The Merchant-Millers: Baltimore's Flour Milling Industry, 1783–1860," *Agricultural History* 56, no. 1 (1982): 148–150.

21. Charles Byron Kuhlman, *The Development of the Flour-Milling Industry in the United States* (Boston: Houghton Mifflin, 1929), 39.

22. Steven Kaplan, *Provisioning Paris: Merchants and Millers in the Grain and Flour Trade during the Eighteenth Century* (Ithaca, NY: Cornell University Press, 1984), 245.

23. Hunter, "Wheat, War," 519.

24. Eugene Ferguson, *Oliver Evans: Inventive Genius of the Industrial Revolution* (Greenville, DE: Hagley Museum, 1980), 14.

25. Ferguson, *Oliver Evans*, 19.

26. Hunter, "Wheat, War," 520.

27. Christopher Schmidt-Nowara, "La España Ultramarina: Colonialism and Nation-Building in Nineteenth-Century Spain," *European History Quarterly* 34, no. 2 (2004): 191–214; Antonio Santamaría García and Alejandro García Alvarez, *Economía y colonia: La economía cubana y la relación con España, 1765–1902* (Madrid: Consejo Superior de Investigaciones Científicas, 2004), 128.

28. Louis A Pérez, Jr., *Cuba and the United States: Ties of Singular Intimacy* (Athens, GA: University of Georgia Press, 1990), 16–17. For the place of flour exports to Cuba in the worldview of US expansionists of the era, see Cora Montgomery, "Cuba: The Key of the Mexican Gulf: With Reference to the Coast Trade of the United States," *Hunt's Merchant Magazine* 21 (1849): 520–521. Montgomery condemned the "flour exclusion" with which the Spanish government ensured a market for its own "inferior" flour, often spoiled by its 4,000-mile journey. Spain's monopolistic policy, Montgomery lamented, limited "the luxury of good bread to the wealthier classes" in Cuba.

29. Geoffrey N. Gilbert, "Baltimore's Flour Trade to the Caribbean, 1750–1815," *Journal of Economic History* 37, no. 1 (1977): 251.

30. Hunter, "Wheat, War," 526; and F. R. Rutter, *South American Trade of Baltimore*, Johns Hopkins University Studies, vol. 15, no. 9 (Baltimore: Johns Hopkins University Press, 1897), 17. Some middle income and elite consumption existed in the British West Indies as well, but the class character of flour use was still quite different in Brazil.

31. Allan T. Comp, "Grain and Flour in Eastern Virginia, 1800–1860" (Ph.D. diss. University of Delaware, 1978), 167; "Commerce of Rio Janeiro," *Hunt's Merchant Magazine* 24 (1851): 621.

32. The two-thirds figure is extrapolated from 1858 figures. See "Exports of Flour to South America," *Hunt's Merchant Magazine* 40 (1859): 351; and "United States and Brazil," *Hunt's Merchant Magazine* 41 (July–December 1859): 556.

33. Michelle McDonald and Steven Topik, "Americanizing Coffee: The Refashioning of a Consumer Culture," in *Food and Globalization: Consumption, Markets and Politics in the Nineteenth and Twentieth Centuries*, Alexander Nutzenadel and Frank Trentmann, eds. (London: Berg, 2008), 121.

34. Alan dos Santos Ribeiro, "The Leading Commission-House of Rio de Janeiro": A firma Maxwell Wright & Co. no comércio do império do Brasil (c. 1827– c. 1850)" (Phd diss., Universidade Federal Fluminense, Niterói, Brazil, 2014), 41.

35. Sidney Mintz, "Food, Culture and Energy," in *Food and Globalization*, 25.

36. "United States and Brazil," *Hunt's Merchant Magazine* 40 (1859): 553–560.

37. Steven Topik, "The World Coffee Market in the Eighteenth and Nineteenth Centuries, from Colonial to National Regimes," Working Paper NO. 04/04 (May 2004), 19.

38. *O Vale do Paraíba e o Império do Brasil nos quadros da Segunda Escravidão*, 14. See especially Jeffrey Needell, *The Party of Order: Conservatives, the State, and Slavery in the Brazilian Monarchy, 1831–1871* (Stanford, CA: Stanford University Press, 2006).

39. Marquese and Tomich, "O Vale do Paraíba escravista," 25, 56. Vessels built in the United States accounted for 58 percent of all slaving voyages to the African coasts. Many of these voyages were also captained by US citizens. Leonardo Marquese, "The Contraband Slave Trade to Brazil and the Dynamics of US Participation, 1831-1856," *Journal of Latin American Studies* 47, no. 4 (November 2015), 663, 664. Even after the successful suppression of the African slave trade in 1850, "domestic" slaves continued to be taken from declining sugar plantations in the northern parts of Brazil. Between 1852 and 1862, 3,370 such captives arrived in the port of Rio per year. Camillia Cowling, *Conceiving Freedom: Women of Color, Gender, and the Abolition of Slavery in Havana and Rio de Janeiro* (Chapel Hill: University of North Carolina Press, 2013), 35.

40. Needell, *Party of Order*, 160–161.

41. Santos Ribeiro, "Leading Commission-House of Rio de Janeiro," 19, 43. On the new tariff rates for flour, see Daniel Kidder, *Brazil and the Brazilians, Portrayed in Historical and Geographic Sketches* (Philadelphia: Childs & Peterson, 1857), 579. Revenues from import tariffs on wheat flour dropped by around two-thirds between 1844 and 1858. *A Patria: Jornal da Provincia do Rio de Janeiro*, 16 October 1858.

42. Rafael de Bivar Marquese, "As desventuras de um conceito: Capitalismo histórico e a historiografia sobre a escravidão Brasileira," *Revista de Historia São Paulo*, no. 169, (Julho–Dez. 2013): 236, 241.

43. See the graph in Marquese and Tomich, "O Vale do Paraíba escravista," 42.

44. Topik, "World Coffee Market," 20.

45. Gregory Brown, "The Impact of American Flour Imports on Brazilian Wheat Production: 1808–1822," *Americas* 47, no. 3 (1991): 322.

46. Eugene Ridings, "The Merchant Elite and the Development of Brazil: The Case of Bahia during the Empire," *Journal of Interamerican Studies and World Affairs* 15, no. 3 (1973): 335–353. See also Eugene Ridings, "Class Sector Unity in an Export Economy: The Case of Nineteenth-Century Brazil," *Hispanic American Historical Review* 58, no. 3 (1978): 433, 437. However, Steven Topik cautions against giving too much agency to planters and merchants alone in shaping the trade policies of the Brazilian government. Steven Topik, "The State's Contribution to the Development of Brazil's Internal Economy, 1850–1930," *Hispanic American Historical Review* 65, no. 2 (1985): 203–228.

47. Although Wise did not explicitly say so, it seems likely that US merchants used bills of exchange on London because bills of exchange on US banks traded at a steep discount abroad, thanks to the state bond repudiations in the wake of the 1837 Panic, as well as the overall proliferation of bad paper in the "free banking era." See my discussion of Robert J. Walker and the tariff in Chapter 2, "*El Principio Sacarino*."

48. "The Foreign Trade of Virginia: Letter from Gov. Wise," *Richmond Daily Dispatch*, October 9, 1858.

49. Kidder, *Brazil and the Brazilians*, 238–239.

50. Of these 389 voyages, two hundred seven originated in Baltimore, one hundred twenty-three came from Richmond, and fifty-nine came from New York. Santos Ribeiro, "Leading Commission-House of Rio de Janeiro," 50, 58.

51. "United States and Brazil," *Hunt's Merchant Magazine* 41 (July–December 1859): 556.

52. Santos Ribeiro, "Leading Commission-House of Rio de Janeiro," 130.

53. Juliana Teixeira Souza, "A autoridade municipal na Corte imperial: Enfretamentos e negociações na regulação do comércio de gêneros (1840–1889)" (PhD diss., Universidade Estadual de Campinas, 2007), 89. Baltimore-based Maxwell Wright & Co. was the most important of an elite "group of eleven" foreign merchant houses that controlled the sale of about three-fifths of total Brazilian coffee production in 1849. Like other Anglo-American merchant firms, it got its start in

Brazil by providing Luso-Brazilian slave traders with vessels, but it appears to have jettisoned that business for coffee and flour produced by slaves. Santos Ribeiro, "Leading Commission-House of Rio de Janeiro," 50, 73.

54. For the number of flour brokers, see *Almanack Laemmert* (1857), 538; "Extract of a Letter Dated Rio de Janeiro," *Richmond Enquirer,* February 10, 1823.

55. Maxwell, Wright, *Commercial Formalities of Rio de Janeiro* (Baltimore: Sherwood and Co. Printers, 1841), 26.

56. *Commercial Formalities*, 26.

57. *Commercial Formalities*, 26.

58. *Jornal do Commercio*, September 18, 1859. Bakery located at Rua da Imperatriz 153.

59. *Jornal do Commercio*, May 23, 1859.

60. *Jornal do Commercio*, January 12, 1851.

61. "Bom Pão," *Diário do Rio de Janeiro*, November 26, 1839.

62. Calculated from *Diário de Rio de Janeiro*, February 4, 1852 (Suplemento ao Diário do Rio de Janeiro). Flour from Trieste and Belgium could sell as high as 18$500, but arrivals were occasional. The mil-réis, denoted 1$000, was worth 0.58 of a US Dollar in 1850. The *conto de réis*, written 1:000$000, was worth 1,000 *mil-réis*. It was worth $580 US. Zephyr Frank, *Dutra's World: Wealth and Family in Nineteenth-Century Rio de Janeiro* (Albuquerque: University of New Mexico Press, 2004), xv.

63. Carlos Valencia Villa finds that, in 1860, Baltimore accounted for 11 percent, New Orleans for 7 percent, Trieste for 11 percent, and "other" for 13 percent of wheat flour in the port of Rio. Carlos Eduardo Valencia Villa, "Fluxos de mercadorias entre o Rio de Janeiro e a Virgínia em meados do século xix," *História Econômica & História de Empresas* 17, no. 2 (2014): 20. However, Villa's estimates are based on newspaper reports of the "stocks available" on the Rio market at the end of every month. Thus his figures are not directly indicative of import totals. They are in fact an indication of which barrels of flour had yet to sell, and Richmond flour appears to have moved out of the warehouses fastest. For this reason, perhaps, Villa's estimates are much smaller than estimates coming from the United States. He found 190,000 imported barrels of flour in 1860, which seems very low, considering Rio imported 350,000 barrels in 1858 (see Table 5-4).

64. "Art. III: Commercial and Industrial Cities of the United States: Richmond, Virginia," *Hunt's Merchant Magazine* 41 (July–December 1859): 61.

65. J. D. B. DeBow, *The Industrial Resources, Statistics, &c. of the United States and More Particularly of the Southern and Western States*, 3d ed., vol. 1 (New York: Augustus Kelley, 1966, orig. 1854), 98; and William Carter Hughes, *The American Miller and Millwright's Assistant* (Philadelphia: Henry Cary Baird, 1855), 152.

66. For an extended comparison of New York to Virginia wheat, favoring the latter, see John C. Brush, *A Small Tract Entitled, A Candid and Impartial Exposition of the Various Opinions on the Subject of the Comparative Quality of the Wheat and Flour*

in the Northern and Southern Sections of the United States, with a View to Develope the True Cause of the Difference (Washington, DC: Jacob Gideon, 1820).

67. [Lewis D. Crenshaw], *Flour Inspection Laws* (Richmond, VA: 1860), 23.

68. Alcir Lenharo, *As tropas da moderação: O abastecimento da Corte na formação política do Brasil, 1808–1842* (São Paulo: Símbolo, 1979), 49. See also Vladimir Honorato de Paula, "Terra, comércio e comerciantes na vila cafeeira de Piraí," in *O Vale do Paraíba e o Império do Brasil*, 431.

69. Stuart Schwartz, *Slaves, Peasants, and Rebels: Reconsidering Brazilian Slavery* (Urbana: University of Illinois Press, 1996), 72.

70. On the continuation of diversified agriculture and food production in some parts of Rio de Janeiro province, see Rômulo Andrade, "African and Creole Slaves: From the Diversified Agriculture of Southern Rio de Janeiro to the Coffee Cultivation of Minas Gerais, 1802–1885," *Review (Fernand Braudel Center)* 34, nos. 1 and 2 (2011): 41–78.

71. Eulalia Maria Lahmeyer Lobo, *História do Rio de Janeiro: do capital comercial ao capital industrial e financeiro*. 2 vols. Vol. 1. (Rio de Janeiro: Instituto Brasilerio de Mercado de Capitais, 1978), 164–165.

72. Stanley Stein, *Vassouras: A Brazilian Coffee County, 1850–1900: The Roles of Planter and Slave in a Plantation Society* (Princeton, NJ: Princeton University Press, 1985, orig. 1958), 178. Manioc flour still "stood in for bread" in late-eighteenth-century Rio. Leila Mezan Algranti, "Alimentação e cultura material no Rio de Janeiro dos vice-reis," *Varia História* 32, no. 58 (2016): 30. One of manioc's major shortcomings as a staple was that "the crude root cannot be preserved three days by any possible care, and the slightest moisture spoils the flour." Kidder, *Brazil and the Brazilians*, 190.

73. Cotton textiles (mostly from Great Britain) accounted for just over one-third of total value, and wheat flour about 8 percent (6.977:849$). Ministerial Reports (1821–1960): Ministerio da Fazenda, 1861, Table 89. Reports available through the Center for Research Libraries Global Resources Network. By value, imports of wheat flour doubled between 1844, when imports were worth 3.112:031$, and 1860, but this number is not inflation-adjusted. "Commercial Statistics: Commerce and Navigation of Brazil," *Hunt's Merchant Magazine and Commercial Review* 19 (1848): 321.

74. *A Pátria: Jornal da província do Rio de Janeiro,* October 16, 1858. That total excludes all the reexports and shipments from Rio to other Brazilian ports, giving a conservative (it also excluded all unrecorded and smuggled entries) estimate of wheat flour consumption in the province of Rio.

75. A barrel of flour typically held 196 lbs. of flour, which yielded 273 1-lb. loaves of bread. "Manufacture and Cost of Bread in Lynchburg, Virginia," *Hunt's Merchant Magazine and Commercial Review* 38 (1858): 504. That would have been 238,356 loaves of bread per day consumed in Rio, leaving more loaves than people. If we take a much larger number (say, the free population of the city and province of Rio

de Janeiro in 1872), that still works out to 87 lbs. of imported flour per free person, per year, or 121 1-lb. loaves of bread. The 1872 population figures (716,000 free people in city and province of Rio) from Stein, *Vassouras*, 296.

76. Richard Morton, Diary, March 30, 1857–May 11, 1858, and August 15, 1857, Mss5:1 M8465:1, Virginia Historical Society, Richmond, VA. Wholesale merchants in Rio warned visiting traders that "bread is seldom or never in demand here," only flour. *Commercial Formalities*, 29. Stanley Stein also found that "bread was rarely baked on *fazendas* [farms or plantations]." Stein, *Vassouras*, 178.

77. On these rural social networks, see Marquese and Tomich, "O Vale do Paraíba escravista," 50.

78. Mariana Muaze, "Novas considerações sobre o Vale do Paraíba e a dinâmica imperial," in *O Vale do Paraíba e o Império do Brasil*, 95; Emilia Viotti da Costa, *The Brazilian Empire: Myths and Histories* (Chapel Hill: University of North Carolina Press, 2000), 190; and Bryan Daniel McCann, "The Whip and the Watch: Overseers in the Paraíba Valley, Brazil," *Slavery and Abolition* 18, no. 2 (1997): 30–47.

79. Honorato de Paula, "Terra, comércio e comerciantes," 422.

80. Rosana Barbosa Nunes, "Portuguese Migration to Rio de Janeiro, 1822–1850," *Americas* 57, no. 1 (July 2000): 41.

81. Thanks to Daryle Williams for insights on this topic.

82. Nunes, "Portuguese Migration to Rio de Janeiro," 48–49. For more on the influx of skilled Portuguese craftsman beginning in the 1840s, see Zephyr Frank, "Layers, Flows and Intersections: Jeronymo José de Mello and Artisan Life in Rio de Janeiro, 1840s–1880s," *Journal of Social History* 41, no. 2 (Winter 2007): 307–328.

83. Frank, *Dutra's World*, 114.

84. Frank, "Layers, Flows and Intersections," 308; Frank, *Dutra's World*, 71. It is important to distinguish between middle-income groups and an actual "middle-class" of "literate, white-collar employees, and professionals," which most Brazilianists agree did not exist until much later in the nineteenth century. Frank, *Dutra's World*, 8.

85. Frank, *Dutra's World*, 97, 104.

86. Frank, *Dutra's World*, 104, 107.

87. When he died in 1856, seventy people owed Sobrinho debts of under 100 *mil-reis*. Frank, *Dutra's World*, 106.

88. *Jornal do Commercio*, March 10, 1853.

89. Teixeira Souza, "A autoridade municipal," 87.

90. *Cozinheiro Imperial ou, nova arte do conzinheiro e do copeiro em godos os seus ramos . . . precedido do methodo para trinchar e servir bem á mesa, com uma estampa explicativa e seguida de um diccionario dos termos technicos da cozinha por R.C.M.* (Rio de Janeiro: E.&H. Laemmert, 1859), 311.

91. Number of workers based on the low end of Karasch's broad range of four to eighteen slaves working in each bakery in the 1830s. Mary Karasch, *Slave Life in Rio, 1808–1850* (Princeton, NJ: Princeton University Press, 1987), 195–196.

92. Lobo, *Rio de Janeiro*, 279.

93. For the 1849 count, see Frank, "Layers, Flows and Intersections," 316. For 1860, see the list of bakers in *Almanack Laemmert* (1860), 729–732.

94. *Jornal do Commercio*, various, 1840 and 1859, author's tabulation.

95. *Jornal do Commercio*, 11 Jan 1851.

96. For "monstrous monopoly," see *A Patria: Jornal da Provincia do Rio de Janeiro*, February 14, 1857.

97. *A Pátria: Jornal da província do Rio de Janeiro*, February 14, 1857.

98. *A Pátria: Jornal da província do Rio de Janeiro*, May 9, 1857.

99. In 1860, five of the nine brokerage houses sought a "*mestre padeiro*" (master baker) at some point. *Jornal do Commercio*, various.

100. *Almanack Laemmert* (1860), 729, 588.

101. Frank, "Layers, Flows and Intersections," 320.

102. *Diário do Rio*, July 21, 1856.

103. *Commercial Formalities*, 26.

104. "Pão Quente," *Jornal do Commercio*, October 5, 1851.

105. "Cattete," *Jornal do Commercio*, January 1, 1850.

106. *Jornal do Commercio*, May 22, 1859. The bakery at Assemblea, no. 12 also sought a French baker (*Jornal do Commercio*, June 1, 1859).

107. *Jornal do Commercio*, January 19, 1859.

108. Kari Zimmerman, "'As Pertaining to the Female Sex': The Legal and Social Norms of Female Entrepreneurship in Nineteenth-Century Rio de Janeiro, Brazil," *Hispanic American Historical Review* 96, no. 1 (2016): 45.

109. For a hostile description of their speculative stratagems, see *A Pátria: Jornal da província do Rio de Janeiro*, May 10, 1857.

110. Quoted in Augusto Cezar de Almeida Neto, *A História da Panificação Brasileira: A fantastica história do pão e da evolução das padarias no Brasil* (São Paulo, Maxxifoods, 2008), 68, 77, 90.

111. *Jornal do Commercio*, various.

112. "Commerce of Rio Janeiro," *Hunt's Merchant Magazine and Commercial Review* 24 (1850): 621.

113. Thomas S. Berry, "The Rise of Flour Milling in Richmond," *The Virginia Magazine of History and Biography* 78, no. 4 (1970): 385.

114. *Jornal do Commercio*, January 30. 1850.

115. *Jornal do Commercio*, October 13, 1850.

116. For other bakeries highlighting North American–style dry baked goods, see "Padaria Comercial Fama da Gloria," *Jornal do Commercio*, May 9, 1859; and *Jornal do Commercio*, October 13, 1850.

117. *Commercial Formalities*, 26.

118. "Sociedade dos Apparelhos de Panificação," *Jornal do Commercio*, January 15, 1854.

119. "Padaria Aperfeiçoada," *Jornal do Commercio*, August 3, 1853.

120. *Cozinheiro Imperial*, 311. Whereas elsewhere in the Atlantic world, "creole" referred to place of birth, and could thus be applied to America-born whites, in Brazil it was used as a label for locally born, dark-skinned people. João José Reis, "African Nations in Nineteenth-Century Salvador, Bahia," in *The Black Urban Atlantic in the Age of the Slave Trade*, Jorge Cañizares-Esguerra, Matt Childs, and James Sidbury, eds. (Philadelphia: University of Pennsylvania Press, 2013), 81.

121. *Almanack Laemmert* (1860), 729–732.

122. *Jornal do Commercio*, January 30. 1857.

123. Karasch, *Slave Life in Rio*, 195–196. Karasch found fifty-five bakers in Rio in 1833. There were at least 137 in Rio by 1860. *Almanack Laemmert* (1860), 729–732. Many lines of business in the service sector, like barbershops, followed fairly strict rules of segregation by gender. Bakeries appeared to be male spaces behind the counter. Frank, *Dutra's World*, 118.

124. "Mestre forneiro," *Jornal do Commercio*, January 7, 1850.

125. *Jornal do Commercio*, January 22, 1859.

126. "Ao Publico," *Jornal do Commercio*, March 20, 1859.

127. *Jornal do Commercio*, January 22, 1850.

128. *Jornal do Commercio*, February 18, 1851.

129. *Jornal do Commercio*, February 21, 1851.

130. "69 Rua de Cattete, Padaria Franceza," *Jornal do Commercio*, January 9, 1850.

131. Richard Graham, *Feeding the City: From Street Market to Liberal Reform in Salvador, Brazil, 1780–1860* (Austin: University of Texas Press, 2010), 20.

132. "Aos Srs. Pedestres de Botafogo e Nitherohy," *Jornal do Commercio*, August 24, 1857.

133. *Jornal do Commercio*, November 21, 1850; Flávio Gomes discusses the widespread existence of *ajuntamentos*, "small, mobile bands of fugitives" who formed Maroon communities in forests and hills on the borders of Rio. Gomes, "Africans and Petit Marronage in Rio de Janeiro, ca. 1800–1840," *Luso-Brazilian Review* 47, no. 2 (2010), 74. For another master baker advertising fugitive bread sellers, see Ian Read, *The Hierarchies of Slavery in Santos, Brazil, 1822–1888* (Stanford, CA: Stanford University Press, 2012), 73.

134. *Jornal do Commercio*, November 21, 1850.

135. *Jornal do Commercio*, November 29, 1850.

136. *Jornal do Commercio*, Febrary 10, 1851.

137. Gomes, "Africans and Petit Marronage," 77.

138. *Jornal do Commercio*, December 7, 1850.

139. These events were recounted in Mattos's handwritten memoir, which he penned near the end of his life in 1934. It appears in facsimile in Leila Duarte, *Pão e Liberdade: Uma história de padeiros escravos e livres na virada do século XIX* (Rio de Janeiro: FAPERJ, 2002). By 1900 Mattos and his fellow bread makers had formed a Baker's Union (a worker's cooperative to escape the control of the proprietors and brokers) and even had their own newspaper, *O Panificador*. On

juntas da alforria, see Reis, "African Nations in Nineteenth-Century Salvador, Bahia," 70.

140. Mattos memoir.

CHAPTER 6

1. In the last three years before seceding, Richmond sent 87 percent of its exported flour directly to Brazil. Daniel Rood, "Bogs of Death: Slavery, the Brazilian Flour Trade, and the Mystery of the Vanishing Millpond in Antebellum Virginia," *Journal of American History* 101, no. 1 (2014): 22.

2. "Report of the United States Commissioner of Agriculture for 1864," 18, quoted in Arthur G. Peterson, "Flour and Grist Milling in Virginia: A Brief History," *Virginia Magazine of History and Biography,* 43 no. 2, (1935): 105–106.

3. Maury's odd and fascinating career has been well covered in Matthew J. Karp, "Slavery and American Sea Power: The Navalist Impulse in the Antebellum South," *Journal of Southern History* 77, no. 2 (2011), 292–305; and Walter Johnson, *River of Dark Dreams: Slavery and Empire in the Cotton Kingdom* (Cambridge, MA: Harvard University Press, 2013), 296–302.

4. For more on how machine tools aided standardization of parts, see Merritt Roe Smith, *Harper's Ferry Armory and the New Technology: the Challenge of Change* (Ithaca, NY: Cornell University Press, 1980).

5. Michael Nuwer explains the economic import of "throughputs." In the early US steel industry, "increasing productivity and decreasing unit cost resulted not from growth in the size of the factory or plant but rather from increases in the volume and velocity of throughput. Economies of speed, according to Chandler, 'came more from the ability to integrate and coordinate the flow of materials through the plant than from greater specialization and subdivision of the work within the plant.'" Michael Nuwer, "From Batch to Flow: Production Technology and Workforce Skills in the Steel Industry, 1880–1920," *Technology and Culture* 29 (1988): 810.

6. For a more detailed examination of this process, see Rood, "Bogs of Death."

7. Henry Breckenridge, *Voyage to South American Performed by Order of the American Government in the Years 1817 and 1818 in the Frigate Congress* vol. 1 (London, 1820): 129. Quoted in Gregory Brown, "The Impact of American Flour Imports on Brazilian Wheat Production: 1808–1822," *Americas* 47, no. 3 (1991): 328.

8. "The Foreign Trade of Virginia. Letter from Gov. Wise," *Richmond Daily Dispatch*, October 9, 1858. On Richmond's establishment of direct trade, see F. R. Rutter, South American Trade of Baltimore," Johns Hopkins University Studies, vol. 15, no. 9 (Baltimore: Johns Hopkins University Press, 1897), 21.

9. *Richmond Daily Dispatch*, July 13, 1859.

10. "Commercial and Industrial Histories of the United States. Number LX. Richmond, Virginia," *Hunt's Merchant Magazine and Commercial Review* 40, no. 1, (January 1859): 62.

11. "Commercial Cities and Towns of the United States: Richmond, Virginia," *Hunt's Merchant Magazine and Commercial Review* 20 (1849): 54.

12. See, for example, the Schooner *Virginia* in "Marine News," *Richmond Daily Dispatch*, September 30, 1853.

13. "Commercial and Industrial Histories of the United States," 62.

14. *Richmond Daily Dispatch,* January 21, 1859.

15. Ships returning from Venezuela entered Baltimore's port at an average of half-capacity. Rutter, *South American Trade,* 28, 33.

16. Biographical memoir, 1938, of William Graves Crenshaw, Jr. (1848–1918), written by Thomas Armstrong (unpublished, 1938), Crenshaw Family Papers, C8635a 114, Section 7, Virginia Historical Society, Richmond, VA.

17. "From Rio," *Richmond Daily Dispatch*, January 31, 1859.

18. Gregg Kimball, *American City, Southern Place: A Cultural History of Antebellum Richmond* (Athens, GA: University of Georgia Press, 2000), 40.

19. Information on the Richmond and York River Railroad from Jack Temple Kirby, *Mockingbird Song: Ecological Landscapes of the South* (Chapel Hill: University of North Carolina Press, 2006), 260; and Library of Virginia online catalogue record for Richmond and York River Railroad Company, Records, 1854–1877.

20. Maury's charts were later used to patrol Confederate coastlines; in combination with several British steamships that the Confederates used as "commerce raiders" to destroy Union commercial shipping, the charts helped wreak serious havoc on Federal shipping. Hearn claims that American shipping never recovered from this destruction, and that in 1872 the British agreed to compensate the United States for the damage the British had helped incur by having provided naval destroyers to the Confederacy. Chester Hearn, *Tracks in the Sea: Matthew Fontaine Maury and the Mapping of the Oceans* (New York: International Marine, 2002), 224, 233–234.

21. For a cogent survey of Maury's views on Brazil, see Gerald Horne, *The Deepest South: The United States, Brazil, and the African Slave Trade* (New York: New York University Press, 2007), 113–127.

22. Starting with Maury's first 1834 work "On the Navigation of Cape Horn," *American Journal of Science and Arts* 26 (July 1834): 54–63; Hearn, *Tracks in the Sea*, 67.

23. Matthew Fontaine Maury, "Our Commerce with Brazil and the Amazon," *Hunt's Merchant Magazine* 27 (1852): 265.

24. Hearn, *Tracks in the Sea*, 94.

25. Hearn, *Tracks in the Sea*, 127.

26. It took the barque seventy-five days, excluding time spent in port. "Maury's New Route to Rio and Back," *Hunt's Merchant Magazine and Commercial Review* 29 (1848): 104. Hearn, *Tracks in the Sea*, 130.

27. Hearn, *Tracks in the Sea*, 138.

28. Hearn, *Tracks in the Sea*, 134.

29. Allan T. Comp, "Grain and Flour in Eastern Virginia, 1800–1860" (Ph.D. diss. University of Delaware, 1978), 131.

30. Peterson, "Flour and Grist Milling," 106.

31. Thomas S. Berry, "The Rise of Flour Milling in Richmond," *Virginia Magazine of History and Biography* 78, no. 4 (1970): 406.

32. "The Richmond Flour Mills," *Richmond Daily Dispatch*, March 23, 1854. Other major mills mentioned were Taliaferro & Co. in Manchester (with eight pairs of five-foot three-inch stones), Crenshaw and Fisher's new mill (with seven pairs of five-foot three-inch stones), G. B. Bragg, and Mr. Layne & Co.

33. Brown, "The Impact of American Flour," 329.

34. Comp, "Grain and Flour," 131–133.

35. Kirby, *Mockingbird Song*, 260.

36. Comp, "Grain and Flour," 128–130.

37. " Richmond Flour Mills," *Richmond Daily Dispatch*, March 23, 1854.

38. Court of Appeals of Virginia, Richmond, 1859 October term, 434–454, Haxall Brothers & Co. v. Nelly Willis (absent Moncure, J.).

39. "The Burning Gas," *Richmond Daily Dispatch*, October 29, 1853.

40. "Burning Gas."

41. On the role of "macro-inventions" as well as the importance of "micro-inventions" that tweaked and improved upon, without overthrowing that macro-invention within which they functioned, see Joel Mokyr, *The Lever of Riches: Technological Creativity and Economic Progress* (New York: Oxford University Press, 1990).

42. Louis Hunter, *A History of Industrial Power in the United States, 1780–1930*, 3 vols., vol. 1 (Charlottesville: University Press of Virginia, 1979), 110–111.

43. Hunter, *History of Industrial Power*, vol. 1, 60.

44. John Storck, *Flour for Man's Bread: A History of Milling* (Minneapolis: University of Minnesota Press, 1952), 176.

45. On these improvements see William Carter Hughes, *The American Miller and Millwright's Assistant* (Philadelphia: Henry Cary Baird, 1855), 156.

46. *Richmond Daily Dispatch*, July 14, 1853.

47. Moses Ellyson, *Richmond Business Directory and Advertiser* (Richmond, VA: H. K. Ellyson, printer, 1856). Biographical information on Chevallié from Louise Catterall, *Richmond Portraits in an Exhibition of Makers of Richmond, 1737–1860* (Richmond, VA: Valentine Museum, 1949).

48. "Richmond Flour Mills," *Richmond Daily Dispatch*, March 23, 1854.

49. "Richmond Flour Mills."

50. "Richmond Flour Mills."

51. "A Thorough Test," *Richmond Daily Dispatch*, July 22, 1859.

52. Berry, "Rise of Flour Milling in Richmond," 406.

53. Peter Joseph Chevallié, Journal, 1825–1831, 1858–1859, misc reel 993, Library of Virginia Archives, Richmond, VA.

54. Haxall-Crenshaw to General M. R. Patrick, April 29, 1865, Crenshaw Family Papers, Correspondence, Section 3, Virginia Historical Society, Richmond, VA.

55. Midori Takagi, *"Rearing Wolves to Our Own Destruction": Slavery in Richmond, Virginia, 1782–1865* (Charlottesville: University Press of Virginia, 1999), 85.

56. Ellyson, *Richmond Business Directory.*

57. John Zabourney, *Slaves for Hire: Renting Enslaved Laborers in Antebellum Virginia* (Baton Rouge: Louisiana State University Press, 2012); Jonathan Martin, *Divided Mastery: Slave Hiring in the Antebellum South* (Cambridge, MA: Harvard University Press, 2004).

58. Kimball, *American City, Southern Place,* 131.

59. William Link, *Roots of Secession: Slavery and Politics in Antebellum Virginia* (Chapel Hill: University of North Carolina Press, 2003).

60. Link, *Roots of Secession,* 103.

61. Kimball, *American City, Southern Place,* 74, 152.

62. Zabourney, *Slaves for Hire,* 140.

63. "Receiving Stolen Goods," *Richmond Daily Dispatch,* September 22, 1854.

64. "Rapid Driving," *Richmond Daily Dispatch,* September 10, 1858.

65. "Caught It," *Richmond Daily Dispatch,* October 8, 1853.

66. Link, *Roots of Secession,* 104–105.

67. Chevallié, journal.

68. Richard Love, *Founded upon Benevolence: A Bicentennial History of the Mutual Assurance Society of Virginia* (Richmond, VA: Valentine Museum, 1994), 14.

69. They included Henry Moncure, James Dunlop, William Henry Haxall, Clement Barksdale, and Thomas Rutherfoord. The last three men did not actually sit on the board until the postbellum era. Love, *Founded upon Benevolence,* 30.

70. William G. Crenshaw, John Currie, Junior, ship owner; William B. Warwick of Warwick and Barksdale; Frank Ruffin, a wealthy and well-connected wheat planter; and flour merchant James Dunlop of Dunlop, Moncure & Co. Bolling W. Haxall was company president. "Insurance Company of the State of Virginia," *Richmond Daily Dispatch,* July 21, 1860.

71. Kuhlmann suggests that the new technologies "made possible production on a larger scale, which was only possible to men of large capital. This, in turn, led to a greater degree of concentration and localization in the industry." Charles Byron Kuhlmann, *Development of the Flour-Milling Industry* in the United States (New York: Houghton Mifflin, 1929), 100–101.

72. Brooke Hunter, "Wheat, War, and the American Economy during the Age of Revolution," *William and Mary Quarterly* 62, no. 3 (2005): 520.

73. Barksdale, William Jones, October 20, 1854, Mutual Assurance Society of Virginia. Declarations, Policy 628, Vol. 60, microfilm reel no. 7, Library of Virgina Archives, Richmond, VA.

74. Thanks to Scott Nelson for the tip on barrel production in Richmond.

75. "The Price of Flour: The Flour Trade," *New York Weekly Herald,* April 26, 1856.

76. "Barrel Manufactory," *Richmond Daily Dispatch*, February 22, 1854.

77. "Serious Accident," *Richmond Daily Dispatch*, March 9, 1854.

78. Author compilation made from list of individual occupations in Ellyson, *Richmond Business Directory*. Some of their enslaved workers may have made and repaired barrels as well.

79. "Water-Power for Rent," *Richmond Daily Dispatch*, January 31, 1861.

80. "Richmond Flour Mills," *Richmond Daily Dispatch*, March 23, 1854.

81. "Barrel Machine," *Richmond Daily Dispatch*, November 30 1854.

82. Author compilation made from list of individual occupations in Ellyson, *Richmond Business Directory*.

83. *Richmond Daily Dispatch*, August 26, 1857.

84. "Barrel Manufactory," *Richmond Daily Dispatch*, February 22, 1854.

85. "Barrel Manufactory," *Richmond Daily Dispatch*, February 22, 1854.

86. Personal conversation with Chris Shannon, East County Oak Timber Frames, Watkinsville, Georgia. Thanks to Mr. Shannon for more general expertise on the historical development of power-driven carpentry tools.

87. Finally, the firm's large staff of coopers and assistants assembled the barrels by hand, hooped them securely, and readied them for delivery to nearby flour mills. They were sold for fifty cents apiece.

88. In addition to the loss of the draft flour, the miller was charged two cents per barrel for the inspection. Comp, "Grain and Flour," 21.

89. See, for example, *Diário do Rio de Janeiro*, March 13, 1861.

90. [Lewis D. Crenshaw], *Flour Inspection Laws* (Richmond, 1860), 12.

91. Berry, "The Rise of Flour Milling in Richmond," 389n6.

92. *Richmond Daily Dispatch*, January 20, 1859.

93. For a similar controversy over the sale of draft tobacco by inspectors in the 1820s, see Joseph Clarke Robert, *The Tobacco Kingdom: Plantation, Market, and Factory in Virginia and North Carolina, 1800–1860* (Durham, NC: Duke University Press, 1938), 87–88.

94. These protests succeeded in changing the law. The following year, one commercial journal reported that flour meant for export was now exempt from mandatory inspections at Richmond. "Virginia Flour Trade," *Hunt's Merchant Magazine and Commercial Review* 43 (Aug. 1860), 231.

95. *Flour Inspection Laws*, 16–17.

96. *Flour Inspection Laws*, 16–17.

97. *Richmond Dispatch*, 20 January 1859.

98. Frank G. Ruffin, "An Essay on the Inspection Laws," *Southern Planter* 16, no. 3 (March 1856): 7. Yet, there are definitely interesting links between flour inspection and industrial chemistry in the nineteenth century. See "On the Adulteration of Wheat Flour," *Hunt's Merchant Magazine and Commercial Review* 18 (1848): 233.

99. Wheat shipments to Richmond increased over 400 percent during the same span of time. Comp, "Grain and Flour," 147.

100. "Canal Commerce," *Hunt's Merchant Magazine and Commercial Review* 43 (1860): 762.

101. *Flour Inspection Laws*, 36.

102. *Flour Inspection Laws*, 36. Crenshaw also claimed that the grade of flour stamped on each barrel by the inspector mattered little in foreign markets. By 1860, the grades (from best to worst) were "Family," "Extra," "Superfine," "Fine," "Middlings," and "Condemned." "Virginia Flour Trade," 231.

103. Berry, "The Rise of Flour Milling in Richmond," 390.

104. *The Seventh Census of the United States: 1850; Embracing a Statistical View of Each of the States and Territories, Arranged by Counties, Towns, etc.* (Washington, DC: R. Armstrong, 1853), 272; *Population of the United States in 1860: Compiled from the Original Returns of the 8th Census* (Washington, DC: Government Printing Office, 1864), 524–525.

105. *Flour Inspection Laws*, 6.

CHAPTER 7

1. For an earlier version of this chapter, see Daniel Rood, "An International Harvest: The Second Slavery, the Virginia-Brazil Connection, and the Development of the McCormick Reaper," in *Slavery's Capitalism: A New History of American Economic Development*, Sven Beckert and Seth Rockman, eds. (Philadelphia: University of Pennsylvania Press, 2016).

2. Steven Stoll, *Larding the Lean Earth: Soil and Society in Nineteenth-Century America* (New York: Hill and Wang, 2002), esp. 13–67.

3. On the time-consuming off-season tasks related to soil maintenance in the period before synthetic pesticides and herbicides, see E. A. Wrigley, *Continuity, Chance, and Change: The Character of the Industrial Revolution in England* (New York: Cambridge University Press, 1988), 44; and Alan Olmstead and Paul Rhode, *Creating Abundance: Biological Innovation and American Agricultural Development* (Cambridge, UK: Cambridge University Press, 2008).

4. Lynn Nelson, *Pharsalia: An Environmental Biography of a Southern Plantation, 1780–1880* (Athens, GA: University of Georgia Press, 2007). James Irwin, "Exploring the Affinity of Wheat and Slavery in the Virginia Piedmont," *Explorations in Economic History* 25 (July 1988): 295–322. Even hog raising, a traditional Virginian occupation, failed to grow alongside wheat and tobacco cultivation in the 1850s. William B. Blair, *Virginia's Private War: Feeding Body and Soul in the Confederacy, 1861–1865* (New York: Oxford University Press, 2000), 15. See also William M. Mathew, *Edmund Ruffin and the Crisis of Slavery in the Old South: The Failure of Agricultural Reform* (Athens, GA: University of Georgia Press, 1988).

5. For more detailed statistics, see Daniel Rood, "Bogs of Death: Slavery, the Brazilian Flour Trade, and the Mystery of the Vanishing Millpond in Antebellum Virginia," *Journal of American History* 101, no. 1 (2014): 19–43.

6. Augusta and Rockbridge Counties were top-ranked iron producers in the Valley, and in the top handful of counties at state level. US Department of Interior, Census Office, *Manufactures of the United States in 1860; Compiled from the Original Returns of the Eighth Census, under the Direction of the Secretary of the Interior* (Washington, DC: Government Printing Office, 1865), 604–637.

7. On parts of the Valley tributary to Baltimore and Philadelphia, which experienced the antebellum economic geography quite differently, see Kenneth Keller, "The Wheat Trade on the Upper Potomac, 1800–1860," in *After the Backcountry: Rural Life in the Great Valley of Virginia, 1800–1900*, Kenneth Koons and Warren Hofstra, eds. (Knoxville: University of Tennessee Press, 2000), 21–33. For internal differentiation within this part of the Shenandoah Valley, see Blair, *Virginia's Private War*, 17–18.

8. William Hutchinson, *Cyrus Hall McCormick: Seed-Time, 1809–1856* (New York: Century Company, 1930), 27.

9. Hutchinson, *Seed-Time*, 165.

10. Hutchinson, *Seed-Time*, 188.

11. "Farming of Mr. William Weaver, Rockbridge County, Virginia," *Farmer's Register* 10 (1843): 411–412. For a book-length analysis of Weaver's slave-centered agro-industrial complex, see Charles Dew, *Bond of Iron: Master and Slave at Buffalo Forge* (New York: Norton, 1994). McCormick's father also owned eighteen people.

12. Ironically, the McCormick plantation has been refurbished as part of the Agricultural Experiment Station of Virginia Tech.

13. Nelson, *Pharsalia*, 154.

14. Lynn Nelson, "The Pilot and the Storm: William Massie and the Agrarian Economy of the Tye River Valley, 1830-1860." In *After the Backcountry*, 270.

15. By the 1830s there were hundreds of different kinds of affordable threshers available on the market nationwide. Peter McClelland, *Sowing Modernity: America's First Agricultural Revolution* (Ithaca, NY: Cornell University Press, 1997), 167–170, 177.

16. Olmstead and Rhode, *Creating Abundance*, 43–45.

17. William Carmichael, "The Adaptation of Particular Wheats to Particular Localities: Patent Machines," *Farmer's Register* 10 (1842): 89.

18. Edmund Ruffin, "Experiments to Show the Proper State of Wheat for Reaping," *Farmer's Register* 9 (1841): 470.

19. Agricola [pseud.], "For the Enquirer: The Wheat Market of Richmond," *Richmond Enquirer,* August 4, 1837.

20. For wheat cultivation out of reach of poor farmers, see Blair, *Virginia's Private War*, 15.

21. Many wheat farms also grew tobacco for market. Tobacco was mostly grown in small patches, and its seasonal labor requirements lined up conveniently with those of wheat. New philosophies of crop rotation advocated the cultivation of tobacco-wheat-cover crops in consecutive seasons on particular fields. Robert Joseph, *The*

Tobacco Kingdom: Plantation, Market and Factory in Virginia and North Carolina, 1800–1860 (Durham, NC: Duke University Press, 1938), 30, 55.

22. McClelland, *Sowing Modernity*, 62.

23. Hutchinson, *Seed-Time*, 90–91.

24. "Hussey's Grain Cutter: Report of the Board of Trustees of the Maryland Agricultural Society for the Eastern Shore of Maryland," *Farmer's Register* 4 (1836): 413.

25. Gerald Judd of Virginia Tech's Agricultural Experiment Station writes that McCormick "had an excellent blacksmith, a slave named Joe. . . . His ingenuity, and the skills of the blacksmith, led to the reciprocal cutting bar demonstrated so successfully first in 1831." Janet Baugher Downs, Earl J. Downs, and Nancy T. Sorrells, eds., *Mills of Augusta County* (Staunton, VA: Augusta County Historical Society, 2004), 155. Joe Anderson, a slave of McCormick's interviewed in the 1880s, often worked as the raker for the early experiments and even assisted during the original 1831 trial at Steele's Tavern. Hutchinson, *Seed-Time*, 89.

26. Slaves in Virginia built and operated gristmills, worked as plantation blacksmiths, cobbled shoes, and otherwise took charge of rural manufacturing and handicrafts. Diane Barnes, *Artisan Workers in the Upper South: Petersburg, Virginia, 1820–1865* (Baton Rouge: Louisiana State University Press, 2008); Melvin Ely, *Israel on the Appomatox: a Southern Experiment in Black Freedom from the 1790s through the Civil War* (New York: Knopf, 2004); Dew, *Bond of Iron*; John Bezis-Selfa, *Forging America: Ironworkers, Adventurers, and the Industrious Revolution* (Ithaca, NY: Cornell University Press, 2004); and James Sidbury, "Slave Artisans in Richmond, Virginia, 1780–1810," in *American Artisans: Crafting Social Identity*, Howard Rock, Paul Gilje, and Robert Asher, eds. (Baltimore: Johns Hopkins University Press, 1995), 48–62.

27. Hutchinson, *Seed-Time*, 185.

28. Hutchinson, *Seed-Time*, 225; Corbin Braxton, "Account of the Operation of M'Cormick's Virginia Reaper," *Farmer's Register* 10 (1843): 503–504.

29. Obed Hussey, "Proposal to Try Hussey's Reaping Machine," *Farmer's Register* 9 (1841): 302.

30. Hutchinson, *Seed-Time*, 157. The laborers mentioned by Hutchinson were probably skilled cradlers, slaves or free workers who were well paid by wheat farmers in the rush time of harvest to apply their rare manual skill to the fields of the Valley. The cradle was an improvement over the scythe because it could mow the wheat and drop it into sheaves, which other slaves could more rapidly bind with twine. Arthur G. Peterson, "Flour and Grist Milling in Virginia: A Brief History," *Virginia Magazine of History and Biography* 43 (April 1935): 103.

31. Hussey, "Proposal," 302.

32. For more on skilled labor in southern cities, see Barnes, *Artisan Workers;* and Angela Lakwete, *Inventing the Cotton Gin: Machine and Myth in Antebellum America* (Baltimore: Johns Hopkins University Press, 2005).

33. Allan T. Comp, "Grain and Flour in Eastern Virginia, 1800–1860" (Ph.D. diss. University of Delaware, 1978), 112, 116.

34. Hutchinson, *Seed-Time*, 83.

35. Hutchinson, *Seed-Time*, 216.

36. Hutchinson, *Seed-Time*, 87–88. While sugar had to be pushed through the entire process quite hastily, once wheat had been reaped and protected from the rain, it "could be threshed when time permitted." Marketing factors more than chemical necessity pushed planters to gather wheat faster. Paul Gates, *The Farmer's Age: Agriculture, 1815–1860* (New York: Holt, Rinehart, and Winston, 1960), 35.

37. Hussey, "Proposal," 302.

38. "Hussey's Grain Cutter," 413–414.

39. William B. Harrison, "Hussey's Reaper," *Farmer's Register* 9 (1841): 434.

40. A. Nicol, "Notes on Sandy Point Estate, No. IV," *Farmer's Register* 9 (1841): 586.

41. A. Nicol, "Notes," 586.

42. A. Nicol, "Notes," 586.

43. A. Nicol, "Notes," 586.

44. A. Nicol, "Notes," 588. For a lengthy analysis of "the whipping machine" that may have helped drive productivity increases on antebellum cotton plantations, see Edward Baptist, *The Half Has Never Been Told: Slavery and the Making of American Capitalism* (New York: Basic Books, 2014).

45. The master took Peter to court, where he was convicted and sold out of state. William Link, *Roots of Secession: Slavery and Politics in Antebellum Virginia* (Chapel Hill: University of North Carolina Press, 2003), 50.

46. For the classic statement of this influential view, see H. J. Habbakuk, *American and British Technology in the Nineteenth Century: The Search for Labour-Saving Inventions* (New York: Cambridge University Press, 1962). For a recent criticism of the "induced innovation hypothesis" (the idea that the high cost of labor spurred the development of machines that would reduce work hours), see Olmstead and Rhode, *Creating Abundance*, 6–10.

47. Harrison, "Hussey's Reaper," 434.

48. Harrison, "Hussey's Reaper," 434. For an exploration of time consciousness and time discipline in a slave society, see Mark Smith, *Mastered by the Clock: Time, Slavery, and Freedom in the American South* (Chapel Hill: University of North Carolina Press, 1997).

49. Harrison, "Hussey's Reaper," 434.

50. For this aspect of Frederick Winslow Taylor's reform of the labor process, see Harry Braverman, *Labor and Monopoly Capital: The Degradation of Work in the Twentieth Century* (New York: Monthly Review Press, 1975).

51. Harrison, "Hussey's Reaper," 434.

52. Harrison, "Hussey's Reaper," 434.

53. Wilma Dunaway, *The First American Frontier: Transition to Capitalism in Southern Appalachia, 1700–1860* (Chapel Hill: University of North Carolina Press, 1996),

115–116. For evocative accounts of Maryland's polyglot crews of wandering cradlers, a characterization that emphasizes egalitarianism and disorder, see Max Grivno, *Gleanings of Freedom: Free and Slave Labor along the Mason-Dixon Line, 1790–1860* (Urbana: University of Illinois Press, 2011).

54. Lorena Walsh, *Motives of Honor, Pleasure, and Profit: Plantation Management in the Colonial Chesapeake, 1607–1763* (Chapel Hill: University of North Carolina Press, 2010), 622.

55. Melvin Ely suggests that black millers were commonplace in in the Piedmont counties. Melvin Ely, *Israel on the Appomatox: A Southern Experiment in Black Freedom from the 1790s through the Civil War* (New York: Vintage, 2004), 130.

56. Anderson and Moody Mill Accounts, 1831–1834, local government records collection, Chesterfield County Court Records (Library of Virginia, State Records Center, Richmond, VA). "Hire of my slave Rubin . . . for 15 years at $125 pr . . ." in 1825.

57. Walsh, *Motives of Honor, Pleasure, and Profit*, 446.

58. Unidentified Flour Mill Journal, 1838–1839 (Library of Virginia, State Records Center).

59. For an excellent account of the networks of kinship and friendship tying together enslaved Afro-Virginians in the early national period, a broad diasporic community that "extended east to west along the state's rivers," see James Sidbury, *Ploughshares Into Swords: Race, Rebellion, and Identity in Gabriel's Virginia, 1730–1810* (Cambridge: Cambridge University Press, 1997), 32. Sidbury and other scholars have emphasized how enslaved women cultivated a particular "geography of resistance" in the interstices of plantation society. Stephanie Camp, *Closer to Freedom: Enslaved Women and Everyday Resistance in the Plantation South* (Chapel Hill, 2004); Susan Eva O'Donovan, *Becoming Free in the Cotton South* (Cambridge, MA: Harvard University Press, 2007); and Rebecca Scott, *Degrees of Freedom: Louisiana and Cuba after Slavery* (Cambridge, MA: Harvard University Press, 2005).

60. Unidentified Flour Mill Journal, 1838–1839 (Library of Virginia, State Records Center).

61. Account Book of Tucker Coles, 1833–1834, Folder 1 (Small Special Collections Library, Charlottesville, VA).

62. The world of the Appomatox River, which differed from the Piedmont plantation society that surrounded it, sent enterprising whites and blacks to the river for opportunities and autonomy. In the Valley, on the other hand, the river world had more in common with dry-land occupations in the rough equality that could prevail across racial and class lines. Slavery flourished, but at a smaller scale, with a good deal of hiring, diverse job descriptions, and non-agricultural slavery. Because there was less river transportation, and more opportunities in other fields, there were fewer black boatmen in the Valley. Seth Bruggeman, "The Shenandoah River Gundalow: Reusable Boats in Virginia's Nineteenth-Century River Trade," *Virginia*

Magazine of History and Biography 118, no. 4 (2010): 314–349. Scholars of slavery in the Atlantic World have foregrounded how the spatial politics of the enslaved, especially on waterways, shaped and facilitated their struggles toward freedom. David Cecelski, *The Waterman's Song: Slavery and Freedom in Maritime North Carolina* (Chapel Hill: University of North Carolina Press, 2001); Douglas R. Egerton, "'Fly across the River': The Easter Slave Conspiracy of 1802," *North Carolina Historical Review* 68, no. 2 (1991): 87–110; Jeffrey Bolster, *Black Jacks: African American Seamen in the Age of Sail* (Cambridge. MA: Harvard University Press, 1997); and Peter Linebaugh and Marcus Rediker, *The Many-Headed Hydra: Sailors, Slaves, Commoners, and the Hidden History of the Revolutionary Atlantic* (Boston: Beacon Press, 2000).

63. Two bills of lading from "Lee & Johnson, wholesale and retail grocers and commission merchants, Main Street, Lynchburg, VA," 1856, Mss4L5164b, Virginia Historical Society, Richmond, VA.

64. Luther P. Jackson, *Free Negro Labor and Property Holding in Virginia, 1830–1860* (1942), quoted in Bruggeman, "The Shenandoah River Gundalow," 347, n45.

65. "Smith v. the Commonwealth," *Grattan's Reports of Cases Decided in the Supreme Court of Appeals of Virginia*, vol. 4 (June 1847). Smith was sentenced to three years in the penitentiary.

66. Camp, *Closer to Freedom*, 26. On the extent to which slaves' economic activities, as well as their use of cash and participation in a burgeoning consumer culture, constituted "resistance," see the interesting exchange between Douglas Egerton and Walter Johnson. Douglas Egerton, "Slaves to the Marketplace: Economic Liberty and Black Rebelliousness in the Atlantic World," and Walter Johnson, "Clerks All! Or, Slaves with Cash," *Journal of the Early Republic* 26 (Winter 2006).

67. John Pendleton Kennedy, *Swallow Barn; or a Sojourn in the Old Dominion* (Baton Rouge, 1986, orig. 1851), 145.

68. For the role of swamps in slave resistance, see Camp, *Closer to Freedom*, 6, 41, 69, and 73.

69. Philip Morgan, *Slave Counterpoint: Black Culture in the Eighteenth-Century Chesapeake and Lowcountry* (Chapel Hill: University of North Carolina Press, 1998), 239.

70. Jack Temple Kirby, *Poquosin: A Study of Rural Landscape and Society* (Chapel Hill: University of North Carolina Press, 1995), 174. The connection between country mills and insurgency preceded Turner's rebellion. "'Mill Dick (a man that kept stewarts mill),'" was implicated in an 1802 slave conspiracy along the Staunton River. Thomas Parramore, "Aborted Takeoff: A Critique of 'Fly Across the River,'" *North Carolina Historical Review* 68, no. 2 (1991): 114, n7.

71. Bruce Terrell, "The James River Bateau: Nautical Commerce in Piedmont Virginia," *Virginia Cavalcade* 38 (1989): 189–190.

72. Terrell, "The James River Bateau," 189–190

73. Ely, *Israel on the Appomatox*, 10.

74. Link, *Roots of Secession*, 105.

75. Bruggeman, "The Shenandoah River Gundalow," 320.

76. Ely, *Israel on the Appomatox*, 353–354.

77. Talk given by William G. Thomas, March 29, 2012 for "1862–2012: Making of the Great Plains Symposium at the Sheldon Museum of Art."

78. Aaron Marrs, *Railroads in the Old South: Pursuing Progress in a Slave Society* (Baltimore: Johns Hopkins University Press, 2009), 159.

79. George William Bagby, "Canal Reminiscences: Recollections of Travel in the Old Days on the James River and Kanawha Canal," in *Selections from the Miscellaneous Writings of Dr. George W. Bagby,* by George William Bagby, vol. 1 (Richmond, VA: Whittet and Shepperson, 1884), 123.

80. Kennedy, *Swallow Barn*, 135.

81. For a caution against the overly optimistic view of black mobility, see O'Donovan, *Becoming Free in the Cotton South.*

82. W. E. B. DuBois, *John Brown* (New York: Modern Library Classics, 2001, orig 1909), 44.

EPILOGUE

1. Maury quoted in Chester Hearn, *Tracks in the Sea: Matthew Fontaine Maury and the Mapping of the Oceans* (Camden, ME: International Marine Press, 2003), 162, 164.

2. My thinking on allocationism has been shaped by Madhavi Kale, *Fragments of Empire: Capital, Slavery, and Indian Indentured Labor in the British Caribbean* (Philadelphia: University of Pennsylvania Press, 1998).

3. Herman Merivale, *Lectures on Colonization and Colonies Delivered before the University of Oxford in 1839, 1840, and 1841 and Reprinted in 1861* (New York: Augustus M. Kelley Publishers, 1967). See Daniel Rood, "Herman Merivale's Black Legend: Rethinking the Intellectual History of Free Trade Imperialism," *New West Indian Guide/Nieuwe West-Indische Gids* 80, nos. 3–4 (2006): 163–190.

4. Another political economist, Edward Gibbon Wakefield, had a similar plan to end American slavery through "systematic colonization" of the English poor. With more whites competing over a limited amount of land, populations would be more concentrated, and whites forced to seek wage work would replace slave labor. Bernard Semmel, *The Rise of Free Trade Imperialism: Classical Political Economy and the Empire of Free Trade and Imperialism, 1750–1850* (New York: Cambridge University Press, 1970), 89. Would it be hyperbolic to point out the latent genocidal desires implicit in both schemes?

5. Eric Foner, *The Fiery Trial: Abraham Lincoln and American Slavery* (New York: W. W. Norton, 2010), 290, 322.

6. Highlighting the colonial origins of the classic racial allocations of Nazi Europe, Hannah Arendt called the Holocaust "a demographic ideology." Quoted in Corey Robin, "The Trials of Hannah Arendt," *Nation*, 1 Jun 2015. Similarly, Aimé Césaire explained World War II as racist colonial practices come home to roost. Aimé Césaire, *Discourse on Colonialism* (New York: Monthly Review Press, 2000, orig. 1955). Recent specialists affirm the connection. In the words of historian Donald Bloxham, Nazi Germany "imported to Eastern Europe the settler-colonialist practices and racial arrogance that marked white rule in non-white places." Donald Bloxham, "The Great Unweaving: The Removal of Peoples in Europe, 1875–1949," in *Removing Peoples: Forced Removal in the Modern World*, Richard Bessel and Claudia Hanke, eds. (New York: Oxford University Press, 2009), 186.

7. Marcus Rediker, *The Slave Ship: A Human History* (New York: Penguin Books, 2007), 5.

8. Stephan Palmié, *Wizards and Scientists: Explorations in Afro-Cuban Modernity and Tradition* (Durham, NC: Duke University Press, 2002), 65–67.

9. Camillia Cowling, *Conceiving Freedom: Women of Color, Gender, and the Abolition of Slavery in Havana and Rio de Janeiro* (Chapel Hill: University of North Carolina Press, 2013), 55.

10. Stephanie McCurry, *Confederate Reckoning: Power and Politics in the Civil War South* (Cambridge, MA: Harvard University Press, 2012), 223, 224.

11. J. D. B. DeBow, *The Industrial Resources, Statistics &c. of the United States and More Particularly of the Southern and Western States* (New Orleans: The Office of *DeBow's Review*, 1854), vol 2.

12. Quoted in Foner, *Fiery Trial*, 255.

13. Ramón de la Sagra, *Cuba en 1860, ó sea cuadro de sus adelantos en la poblacion, la agricultura, el comercio y las rentas publicas: Suplemento a la primera parte de La Historia Politica y Natural de la Isla de Cuba por D. Ramon de la Sagra* (Paris: Hachette and Co., 1862), 57, 61.

14. For contemporary manifestations of race, empire, and the subprime, see Paula Chakravartty and Denise Ferreira da Silva, "Accumulation, Dispossession, and Debt: The Racial Logic of Global Capitalism: An Introduction," *American Quarterly* 64, no. 3 (2012): 361–385.

15. Thomas Holt, *The Problem of Freedom: Race, Labor, and Politics in Jamaica and Britain, 1832–1938* (Baltimore: Johns Hopkins University Press, 1992); Saidiya Hartman, *Scenes of Subjections: Terror, Slavery, and Self-Making in the Nineteenth Century* (New York: Oxford University Press, 1997); and Rebecca Scott, Thomas Holt, and Fred Cooper, *Beyond Slavery: Explorations of Race, Labor, and Citizenship in Postemancipation Societies* (Chapel Hill: University of North Carolina Press, 2000).

16. W. E. B DuBois, "The African Roots of War," *Atlantic Monthly* 115 (May 1915): 707–714.

Index

Made in the USA
Las Vegas, NV
07 January 2023

65201987R00162